MW01480877

PRESSING ON
Two Family-Owned Newspapers in the 21st Century

John C. Hughes

Secretary of State
Kim Wyman

First Edition
Copyright © 2015
Washington State Legacy Project
Office of the Secretary of State
All rights reserved.
ISBN 978-1-889320-36-6
Front cover photo: Laura Mott
Back cover photos: Mike Bonnicksen/The Wenatchee World
Erika Schultz/The Seattle Times
Book Design by Lori Larson
Cover Design by Laura Mott

This is one in a series of biographies and oral histories published by the Washington State Legacy Project. Other history-makers profiled by the project include Northwest Indian Fisheries leader Billy Frank Jr; former Senate Majority Leader Sid Snyder; Congresswoman Jennifer Dunn; former first lady Nancy Evans; astronaut Bonnie Dunbar; Bremerton civil rights activist Lillian Walker; former chief justice Robert F. Utter; former justice Charles Z. Smith; trailblazing political reporter Adele Ferguson; Federal Judge Carolyn Dimmick; and Nirvana co-founder Krist Novoselic. For more information on the Legacy Project go to www.sos.wa.gov/legacyproject/

Also by John C. Hughes
Nancy Evans, First-Rate First Lady
The Inimitable Adele Ferguson
Lillian Walker, Washington State Civil Rights Pioneer
Booth Who? A Biography of Booth Gardner
Slade Gorton, a Half Century in Politics
John Spellman: Politics Never Broke His Heart
On the Harbor, From Black Friday to Nirvana
with Ryan Teague Beckwith

For Murray Morgan, a mentor and friend
and Carleen Jackson, the best teammate ever

Contents

The Seattle Times

1. A Complicated Legacy	1
2. The Colonel	8
3. Seeds of Discontent	21
4. Shared Burdens	29
5. The General Surrenders	40
6. Pulitzer Pride	48
7. The Third Edition	56
8. Changing Times	64
9. Growing Pains	70
10. An Irrational Decision	82
11. Bylaws and Bygones	89
12. The Golden Carrot of Togetherness	98
13. The Margin of Excellence and a Shocking Loss	110
14. Core Values	118
15. Fiduciary Duties	130
16. The Stare-Down	139
17. Roots and Branches	150
18. The Battle for Seattle	160
19. Momentum Meltdown	168
20. Joint Operating Angst	182
21. A Surprising Call	193
22. A Brief Reprieve	197
23. Swift, Surgical & Sad	205
24. The Brand Evolves	212
25. Here to Stay?	225

The Wenatchee World

1. Community	237
2. Two Million Wild Horses	248
3. "What a heritage!"	257
4. Wilf's World	266
5. The Second Rufus	276

6. "Now what the hell?"	285
7. Community Glue	293
8. Connecting	302
9. Hoping for a Few Nuggets	308
Source Citations	315
Bibliography	346
Afterthoughts & Acknowledgements	352
Index	356
About the author	370

Part One: The Seattle Times

"I think it would be fun to run a newspaper!"
—Charles Foster Kane in *Citizen Kane*

1 | A Complicated Legacy

In the lobby of The Seattle Times building there's a life-size bronze newsboy hawking a paper with a one-word banner headline: "TRUTH!" The slingshot in the back pocket of his knee pants is an apt metaphor for the personality of Colonel Alden J. Blethen, the mercurial genius who bought the newspaper in 1896. Unlike Pulitzer and Hearst, the colonel had a soft spot for the ragamuffin kids who sold his papers. At Thanksgiving, he'd invite them to a white-tablecloth dinner. Faces scrubbed, hair combed, bellies full, they'd pose for a photographer and get their picture in the paper. To anyone who had encountered the colonel brandishing his cane over the outrage of the week it was a surprising tableau.

On the wall behind the statue, the colonel is memorialized in bas-relief, with his mane of wavy silver hair, piercing eyes, pinched mouth and Welsh jaw. The inscription says: "Col. Alden J. Blethen, born Knox, Maine, 12/27/1846; schoolmaster, lawyer, journalist; owner, editor and publisher The Seattle Times from its establishment August 10, 1896, until his death July 12, 1915. Erected by his family as a tribute to his memory."

If the plaque was vetted by the copy desk, it missed two errors: Alden J. Blethen was born a year earlier, in 1845, and he did not establish The Seattle Times. The paper he purchased in 1896 descended from the Seattle Press-Times, founded five years earlier. Like many bigger-than-life characters, the colonel had a habit of making "revisions."

The sleek lobby features another memento from the salad days of newspapering: an ornate waist-high bin with a slot to receive classified ads for the next day's paper. Once in a while, people actually still drop things in the bin, usually subscription payments, according to a security guard behind a long counter. On the wall, a large-screen Samsung TV is tuned to CNN.

"The road to success in journalism," Colonel Blethen famously observed, "is to raise hell and sell newspapers." He did a lot of both. In *Skid Road*, by consensus the best book ever written about squirrely old Seattle, Murray Morgan wrote:

> Old newspapermen say that after a telephone conversation in which Blethen learned of a successful maneuver on the part of his greatest rival [the Seattle Post-Intelligencer], he ripped the phone from the wall and hurled it toward the P-I building, half a mile away. He had a remarkable memory and a considerable talent for invective. He concealed an almost unlimited vulgarity behind a façade of formal education. He loved children and soldiers and animals; he sometimes wept when he watched the flag being lowered; he never seemed to doubt that he was a hundred percent right.

The Times became Seattle's leading newspaper with the best presses, biggest newsroom and virtuoso bombast. On election eve 1928 its front page declared: TIMES SIGNALS TO FLASH ELECTION NEWS. "In streaming rockets, cutting an arc across the night sky; in brilliant flares illuminating the downtown section; in the echoing sound of a siren borne to the furthermost corners of the city; on a huge map and two stereopticon screens in front of the Times Building and in extra editions of this newspaper and radio reports, the answer to the question, 'How is the election going?' will be given tomorrow evening." Thousands of Seattleites learned Herbert Hoover was their new president when they heard two long siren blasts

Times Publisher Frank Blethen with the newsboy statue in the background. *Seattle Times photo*

and saw Elliott Bay ashimmer from red flares and rockets.

Marvel at what your iPhone can do now.

One of the often-quoted artifacts from the early history of The Times is a birthday telegram from the colonel to his son Clarance in 1913: "Congratulations on your part in the upbuilding of this great newspaper. Hope you echo my desire that one hundred years hence The Times may be a more powerful newspaper than today and be published among five million people, and in control of your great-grandsons."

At this writing 102 years hence, The Times is more, or less, powerful; it all depends on your point of view. It is published among 3.5 million people and in control of the colonel's great-grandson, Francis Alden Blethen Jr. You can call him "Frank," which certainly fits. Once described as "the last of the buckaroo publishers," Frank Blethen has raised a lot of hell of his own during his three decades as publisher. During a costly 49-day strike in 2000, he fired off an F-bomb email to a perceived traitor, cc'ing every publisher in the state. Somewhere the colonel was smiling. When the chairman of Nordstrom, the paper's second-largest advertiser, demanded that The Times stop reporting on the retailer's purported unfair labor practices, Blethen backed his newsroom. When Boeing pressured The Times to yank the reporter probing safety problems with its 737, Blethen urged his editors to expedite the story. The exposé led to emergency alterations on 3,000 jetliners, and won the Pulitzer Prize. Nominating Blethen for a national award in 2011, Executive Editor David Boardman described his boss as "a brave, idealistic, outspoken, iconoclastic man who loves journalists and journalism."

Offered $750 million in 2000 for his family's controlling interest in The Seattle Times Company, Blethen walked away. "It's a legacy," he says. "Our core value is to remain family-owned, private and independent." Critics, and there are many, say Blethen has jeopardized the legacy by being petulant and impetuous—"congenitally incapable of suppressing what he really thinks." He's a "legend in his own mind," wrote Knute Berger, a widely read columnist and Seattle historian. Blethen says he enjoys reading what people say about him—adding with a puckish smile, "for the most part."

By accounts that qualify as objective, The Seattle Times, survives as one of the best newspapers in America. Yet its owners are so steeped in a hundred years of controversy that discerning the "TRUTH!" about their stewardship is tricky. Most people, however, just want the news. When the Seattle Seahawks won the 2014 Super Bowl, 16 Times writers and photographers were there. Then, six weeks later as tragedy followed triumph, the newspaper mobilized all its resources to cover the deadliest landslide in U.S. history. The 43 people entombed under mounds of muck in Snohomish County north of Seattle were more than just names. They became your neighbors. The Times comforted the afflicted while exploring what caused the catastrophe. Cutting-edge technology and classic legwork produced a cautionary tale that may save more lives. The Times won its tenth Pulitzer Prize—the coveted award for breaking news—for its coverage of the disaster.

The colonel's competitors, with whom he fought so fiercely, are all gone. The Seattle Sun came up in 1913 and set two years later. The Gazette and Bulletin are also long forgotten footnotes. The Seattle Star, a blue-collar daily with a robust readership at the turn of the century, folded in 1947. Hearst's Post-Intelligencer, the pioneer Seattle daily known to all as the "P-I," fell behind The Times in the modern era even though its morning-delivery niche should have been an important advantage as sclerosis of King County's arterials set in. The P-I was judged to be in danger of failing, and in 1983 Hearst entered into a rocky marriage with The Times under the federal Newspaper Preservation Act. The pre-nup seemed stacked in favor of The Times. But 20 years later, after the costly strike, the dot.com crash and 9/11, it was Blethen who sued for divorce, asserting that The Times was losing money under the Joint Operating Agreement. Some believe it was Hearst who blinked, despite having far deeper pockets. The Post-Intelligencer ceased print publication in 2009 and exists only as an online news source and nostalgic recent memory of the days when Seattle was a two-newspaper town. Make that three if you count the short-lived King County Journal, an amalgamation of the Bellevue Journal-American and the Valley Daily News of Kent. When the Journal died in 2007, many pointed a finger at the Blethen braintrust. "In the glory years of the 1980s and '90s, The Times was thuggish to competitors—meaning everyone other than The Times who printed words on paper in the greater Seattle market," Berger charged.

The Stranger, a sassy free-distribution paper that won a Pulitzer of its own in 2012 and loves to tweak The Times, now cheekily bills itself as "Seattle's Only Newspaper." In edginess and ad lineage it is winning the war with Seattle Weekly, once the dominant voice of the alternative/politics-and-arts market. Besides TV, pi.com, Crosscut, publicola at SeattleMet, NPR and commercial drive-time radio, there are a host of other sources for local news and commentary, including a dizzying array of blogs, vlogs and the twittersphere. Many people say they have no time to read a newspaper.

In one sense—albeit the old one—The Times is the only game in town, the sole surviving general-circulation daily newspaper in greater Seattle. The McClatchy Company, which owns Tacoma's News Tribune and a hand-me-down, 49.5 percent share of The Times, may object to that characterization. The U.S Census Bureau counts Tacoma as part of Metropolitan Seattle. Duly noted. To the north, the competition is The Daily

Herald at Everett. After 35 years of ownership by the Washington Post Company, it was acquired in 2013 by Black Press, a Canadian newspaper group with a growing subsidiary in Washington State. Critics of Seattle Weekly under Black Press ownership worry about the Herald's future. What's indisputable in the Internet age is that the news cycle runs around the clock and competition is boundless. You don't need to buy ink at all, let alone by the barrel. The bronze newsboy in the lobby is a fossil. School kids on a tour might see him as a backdrop for a selfie.

"The rise of the Internet has been the biggest leap forward in communications since Gutenberg," Todd S. Purdum, a *Vanity Fair* columnist, wrote in 2013. The writer Susan Cheever observes, "We are all inundated with information and given no time to wonder what it means or where it came from. Access without understanding and facts without context have become our daily diet."

Still, with its strong investigative journalism, an array of columnists and one of the best sports sections in America, The Times in 2014 was advancing online and holding its own in print, especially compared to the once mighty Oregonian, which hemorrhaged more than 100,000 copies between 2004 and 2013.* The venerable Portland daily has cut its home delivery to four days a week and switched from broadsheet to tabloid, with color on every page. That may prove to be a shrewd decision. N. Christian "Chris" Anderson III, The Oregonian's publisher from 2009 to 2015 when he left to become editor and publisher of The Register-Guard in Eugene, is regarded as an idea man. He was Frank Blethen's managing editor at Walla Walla early in their careers and later an associate editor of The Seattle Times.

The colonel's great-great-grandson, Ryan Blethen, the

---

* As of March 31, 2015, The Times' circulation was 220,479 daily and 300,418 Sundays. The comparable-period audit 10 years earlier pegged daily circulation at 233,268 and Sunday circulation at 457,010. However, the 2005 Sunday circulation figure includes Post-Intelligencer subscribers, who received a jointly branded Sunday edition. Circulation audits are now a frequently changing hodge-podge of data as the industry debates how to measure readership accurately in the Internet era.

heir apparent among the family's self-described "fifth edition," is now tasked with figuring out how to sell news without paper in "a mobile-first and cloud-first world," as Microsoft's new CEO put it in the summer of 2014. "Integrated platforms" and portability are crucial. The Times has intuitive smartphone and tablet apps; it's your Facebook friend. Given what he describes as the "profound shift from fiber to cyber," David Boardman, now dean of the media school at Temple University, believes it's futile for metropolitan papers in particular to try to sustain their old model of a seven-day-a-week printed newspaper. Ryan Blethen agrees. At 42, he's young enough to embrace the cloud-first world yet old enough to still relish turning real pages, especially on Sunday. Yet some see a day—sooner rather than later—when printed newspapers will have only a cult-following by the same sort of people who still use typewriters and miss Kodachrome. "Majority of Newspapers Now Purchased by Kidnappers to Prove Date," The Onion reported recently, its snarky satire echoing popular belief. At the rate the times are changing, will there be news*papers* 25 years hence, let alone a hundred?

2 | The Colonel

In the beginning there was the colonel, who bounced into Seattle with desperate chutzpah after a series of devastating setbacks in Minneapolis. Alden J. Blethen inspired strong opinions from the day he hit town in 1896, flat broke at 50, until the day he died, certifiably rich, 19 years later.

"[W]hen he bought into The Times with $3,000 in borrowed capital" it "was a drab little eight-page paper, losing money," Sharon A. Boswell and Lorraine McConaghy write in *Raise Hell and Sell Newspapers*, a masterful biography of Colonel Blethen and the formative years of his newspaper. They tell us that ...

> During the two decades that he ran the paper, Alden Blethen infused The Seattle Times with his unmistakable personality—belligerent, decisive and obstinate. He was a man of deep and enduring contradictions. He combined rank opportunism with deeply held principles; no one was more patriotic or more generous. ... He seldom sheathed his own weapons, though he was easily wounded. Possessed of a long memory for favors and for insults, he could forgive with childlike eagerness or punish with vindictive energy.
>
> A Times employee during the glory days of Seattle journalism said the colonel couldn't write, couldn't spell and "never had any original ideas." Moreover, "he was coarse and intemperate and harsh and hasty and unreliable," but a great newspaperman nevertheless.

George F. Vanderveer, a young deputy prosecutor who prowled Seattle's seamy Skid Road district in the early 1900s, agreed with all of that except the conclusion. Excoriated by The Times as a reckless do-gooder, Vanderveer was more appalled by police graft than pimps and pickpockets. He quickly ran afoul of Blethen's favorite police chief, Charles W. "Wappy" Wappenstein, a Damon Runyon character with a walrus mustache. Wappy was accused of accepting protection money from gamblers, many of them in high places. When Vanderveer was elected prosecutor in 1908, Blethen declared he would run him out of town. "You frizzle-headed old bastard," Vanderveer shot back, "I'll still be here when you're dead and gone—and I'll go out and puke on your grave!" If this had been a telegram, it might have ended with "Stronger message to follow."

Colonel Alden J. Blethen around 1910. *Seattle Times photo*

Alden J. Blethen's life story reads like one of Horatio Alger's anything-is-possible-with-pluck yarns for 19th-century boys. He was born in the bleak winter of 1845 in wind-whipped Maine. When his father died, leaving his mother with six young children and a hard-luck farm, Alden was a month shy of 3. He ended up with an aunt and uncle. When he was 10, he was auctioned off like chattel to a callous farmer, whipped when he talked back and deprived of schooling. He ran away when he entered his teens. After a succession of odd jobs, he trudged back, "homesick, hungry and out of luck."

Books were Blethen's escape hatch. He appears to have been a remarkable autodidact. At a small college, he excelled at forensics and was elected editor of a literary journal. "Against tremendous odds," Boswell and McConaghy wrote, Blethen graduated as "a young man of great promise, possessed of a network of influential mentors" and industrious friends. He began to study law. Soon, however, he had a wife and infant son, so he took a job as teacher and principal at a boarding school for boys. By 27, he had become a prominent Maine educator.

Blethen went back to his law books and became a tenacious trial lawyer and spellbinding political orator. He was barrel-chested but not tall—about 5-6. His large head was accentuated by dark, wavy hair and muttonchop side-whiskers that sprouted like steel wool from his stony face and seemed to vibrate when he was fizzing with indignation.

"Go West, young man," Horace Greeley, the famous New York editor, admonished a restless generation. Blethen was 35 when he moved his growing family to Missouri in 1880. Kansas City, reminiscent of Carl Sandburg's Chicago, was the cattle- and hog-shipper of the West, a husky, brawling frontier metropolis of 60,000, crisscrossed by railroads, lined with saloons and replete with painted women servicing cowboys and brakemen. The prevailing legal code was not much elevated from that being adjudicated by Judge Roy Bean in a saloon along the Pecos some 800 miles farther west. Blethen abandoned lawyering, bought a share in The Kansas City Journal and signed on as its business manager. Everything wasn't up-to-date up in Kansas City, but it was on its way.

When Blethen joined The Journal, it was poised to capitalize on telegraph-transmitted news, lively design and the latest roll-fed presses. There were two other dailies in town, so he had a crash course in the newspaper business. He was a fast learner. Blethen sold ads, ordered the ink, inventoried the newsprint and negotiated wire-service and union contracts. The paper's labor troubles predated him but worsened when he went nose to nose with the International Typographical Union, which he viewed as a coven of radicals. Soon there was open warfare between the union and the newspaper. Blethen's partners had promoted him to vice president. Now they were distressed over the standoff and apparently counseled moderation. Blethen would have none of it. They bought him out for $100,000, the equivalent of $2.4 million today. At 39, he seemed set for life, having also shrewdly invested in real estate. He couldn't shake the newspaper bug.

Blethen moved to Minneapolis in 1884, became half-owner of the morning Tribune and also acquired an interest in the city's afternoon daily, the Minneapolis Journal. Before long, he was the most discussed and cussed man Minneapolis had ever seen. When he was burned in effigy the straw man even had side whiskers. He sold his shares in both newspapers, pocketing a cool $250,000, and decided he'd like to be mayor. In 1889, after losing a bid for the Republican nomination, he began sniffing around for other opportunities. Offered a chance to gain a free hand with The Tribune, he was exultant.

The bottom fell out of his world that winter. Seven people perished in a fire at the Tribune Building. The under-insured, supposedly fireproof structure was a total loss. Blethen's fortune was ravaged. He negotiated a loan to stay afloat, built a fine new plant and drank heavily to ease the stress. When the note came due, he lost his newspaper. The story might have ended there in boozy despair. Instead, with all his stubborn resilience, Blethen dusted himself off and plunged into banking. Before long, his political wick was flickering again. Another campaign for mayor of Minneapolis was thwarted by backroom machinations. For his loyal support of the Republican Party, Minnesota's governor bestowed on Blethen a consolation prize he coveted—the honorary title of "colonel."

When Blethen's bank folded in the national depression known as The Panic of 1893, he set out to launch a new newspaper—The Penny Press. It was a paper for the proletariat: "Independent, Aggressive, Enterprising, Honest, Fearless, Progressive" and affordable. "What more do you want in a newspaper?" Blethen asked Minneapolis. "Profitability?" he might have asked himself before plowing ahead with all he had left. Absent the economic doldrums, it might have found a winning niche. In the spring of 1896, Alden J. Blethen was practically penniless. Seattle, about as far west as one could go, seemed to offer the best chance for a fresh start.

Journalism on Puget Sound was barely 33 years old when Blethen arrived. The Seattle Daily Times was six. When you held a mirror to its mouth it fogged. At four pages, it was "a pale evening imitation of the big morning Republican daily, The Seattle Post-Intelligencer, whose circulation nearly equaled all the other state papers combined." However, the P-I, like the city itself, was slow to recover from the ruinous national depression.

Charles Fishback, Blethen's backer, was an attorney who also liked to be called "colonel." As to money, he appeared genuinely rich, having invested in silver mines. Now he was championing William Jennings Bryan's crusade to put silver on an equal basis with gold as legal tender. Blethen had the newspaper experience, Fishback the money and a cause. They reportedly paid $30,000 for The Times, the equivalent of about $800,000 today. "They" belongs in quotes. Fishback owned 514 shares, Blethen two. Fishback gave his partner free rein at the paper. Both stumped unctuously for Bryan during the 1896 presidential campaign. Blethen was now a Bryan doppelganger. The side-whiskers disappeared and his curly hair became a senatorial ducktail. The Times henceforth would be the voice of "the common people," Blethen declared, and the sworn enemy of the Post-Intelligencer, that "captive organ" of the Republican Party bosses. The Argus, an independent Republican weekly with a sharp tongue, ridiculed both dailies and characterized Blethen as a carpet-bagging opportunist who would have made The Times a Republican paper if only the P-I "had not preempted that role."

Blethen quickly doubled The Times' circulation to 7,000. Advertising took a similar jump. Come November, however, Bryan lost to McKinley, Fishback's fortune proved illusory, and Blethen's stay in Seattle looked to be brief. Though he would always deny it with indignant doubletalk, Blethen leveraged The Times' editorial influence to keep the presses running. Not that that was unusual. Those were the days of fully acknowledged "Republican" papers, and "Democrat" papers. Many had deep-pocketed backers, and few had compunctions about rabid partisanship.

Blethen's new benefactors were U.S. Senator Watson

Squire, a Seattleite who blew with the political winds, and James J. Hill, president of the Great Northern Railway. Hill had pushed across the plains from St. Paul to the shores of Elliott Bay three years earlier, encouraged by his next-door neighbor, Frederick Weyerhaeuser, a lumberman poised to go west. Seattle's delight at becoming the western terminus of a transcontinental railroad was dampened by the onset of the panic. Critics called the new rail line Hill's Folly, but it was significantly shorter and better engineered than his competitors'. The depression concentrated Hill's power. He cultivated editorial allies to ensure his rivals stayed sidetracked. Hill was in debt to Blethen for journalistic favors in Minneapolis and now for his fulsome support in Seattle. Hill happily loaned the publisher $23,000.* The transaction with Senator Squire, busy running for re-election, was an outright sale of editorial support for $3,000. This infusion of cash in February of 1897 allowed Blethen to gain control of The Seattle Daily Times. He immediately invested in new typesetters and hired more reporters. By spring, though circulation was growing again, the paper was still losing money.

Seattle's ship—Blethen's as well—came in on July 17, 1897. The previous day, Times newsboys shouted a tantalizing headline: "FAIRY TALE OF THE FABULOUS WEALTH OF THE CLONDYKE!" [sic] Whether it was "fact or fancy" remained to be seen, readers were told. Prospectors had been roaming the Yukon for three years, with increasing success. The word from San Francisco was that the steamer *Excelsior* had arrived from Alaska with a dozen miners who claimed to be filthy rich. Among them was Tom Lippy, the mild-mannered former secretary of the Seattle YMCA. He'd gone north the year before. Now he was clutching a sailcloth sack bulging with gold dust. Lippy said it was worth at least $65,000. Some of his ship-

---

* In 1899, the railroad tycoon covered all his newspaper bases by loaning former U.S. Senator John L. Wilson, a Republican from Spokane, $400,000 to buy the Post-Intelligencer. Weyerhaeuser, meantime, became a director of the Great Northern and in 1900 acquired from Hill nearly a million acres of timberland in Washington state.

mates reportedly had twice that. Another steamer, rumored to be bearing "an even more fabulous cargo," was due in Seattle.

The Post-Intelligencer chartered a tugboat to intercept the *S.S. Portland* off Port Angeles. Reporter Beriah Brown Jr. shinnied aboard at 2 a.m. and interviewed several miners who were too excited to sleep. He saw nuggets as big as crab apples. Brown leapt back onto the deck of the tug and told the captain to let 'er rip. They arrived two hours ahead of the steamship.

When the *Portland* docked at Schwabacher's Wharf, many in the crowd of 5,000 were clutching copies of the P-I. Its headline said it all four times: "GOLD! GOLD! GOLD! GOLD!" It wasn't the rumored ton of gold, "only" half a ton, but the newspapers and Chamber of Commerce played it for all it was worth. "When the first miner lifted a fat leather satchel to his shoulder and stepped onto the gangplank," the onlookers let out a cheer. The Times was too busy producing its own special edition to let being scooped fester. Soon everyone knew how to spell Klondike.

The Times had worried early on that a gold rush would cause a mass exodus to the Yukon. Instead, it transformed Seattle. San Francisco, Portland, Tacoma and Victoria pulled out all the stops to stake their own claims—Tacoma alleging that most ships headed north left from its docks. It cited "barons and dukes from Europe who said they planned to go to Tacoma to outfit rather than Seattle because they would get cheated in Seattle." Reading this, Colonel Blethen probably roared "sonsofbitches!" and yanked yet another telephone off the wall before dispatching this note to the Chamber of Commerce:

> Let me not only have the names of the steamboats that are owned and operated and have their principal offices and starting points at Seattle, but also the names of the steamers which operate from Tacoma, if any, and all of the sailings for the Yukon Territory …and I will give it to Mr. Cowles (the AP bureau chief in San Francisco), and we will pound the life out of those whelps in Tacoma.

He did just that, of course.

Within days of the steamer's arrival, merchants were doing a land-office business equipping gold prospectors. "There wasn't enough room in the stores for the merchandise. ...Up came stacks of merchandise as high as a man's head—and on both sides of the streets." The city gained "a virtual monopoly of the northern trade" when the federal government established an assay office in Seattle to test the purity of gold arriving from the Klondike. Seattle became not only the gateway to the gold fields but the preferred place for returning miners to dispose of their disposable income. The depression of 1893-1896 had stunted Seattle's growth. Now the hotels and boarding houses were sleeping six to a room. Some 20,000 newcomers—mostly single men—arrived in what seemed like overnight. Law and order was a tenuous proposition, especially south of the "Deadline" at Yesler Way, the legendary Skid Road of pioneer days. In the Restricted District—a misnomer if there ever was one—libations and lust flowed freely around the clock. Card sharks, crap-shooters and hookers were everywhere. Colonel Blethen and many others in high and low places shared the conviction that vice was best controlled by confinement and hefty license fees. Since a thousand-dollar investment could be recouped in one rowdy weekend, there was no shortage of entrepreneurs—or graft.

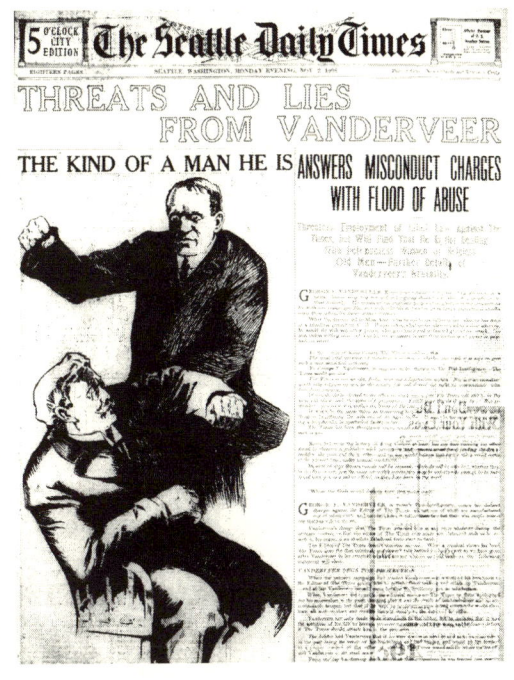

Colonel Blethen's front page diatribe against George Vanderveer, the reformer running for prosecuting attorney. *Washington State Library*

The colonel's elder son, Alden Joseph Blethen Jr., who went by "Joe," became his partner in the paper. Joe had acted in and written several theatricals while attending the University of Minnesota. When his father launched The Penny Press, he became its drama critic. Now, at the age of 27, he took up that post at The Times. Tall and slender, Joe had an engaging smile, an appetite for whimsy and genuine talent as a writer. In looks and temperament he was nothing like his father. The genuine junior edition was Joe's thickset, military-minded brother, Clarance Brettun Blethen—grandfather to The Times' present publisher. "C.B." was nearly nine years younger than Joe. While Joe gravitated to the business office, C.B. became managing editor at the age of 24 in 1903. He shared their father's growing fears about anarchists and fellow travelers. With each passing year, C.B. also grew to look more like the colonel. By his late thirties they were nearly carbon copies: same piercing eyes, same pursed lips, same 50-inch chests. C.B.'s mien was Blethen, from the cut of his suits to the brim of his hats. He was also steadily advancing as an officer in the National Guard. The colonel's teenage daughters, Florence and Marion, were "pampered and protected" and, like their mother, Rose Ann, always dressed to the nines. The Blethens were on a roll.

The 1900 Census found Seattle with 80,671 souls. A decade later there were 237,194. "The city grew so fast," someone said, "that its socks didn't fit anymore." With so much hell to raise, newspaper wars opened on multiple fronts. The Post-Intelligencer was stand-pat Republican, The Seattle Star pro-labor and The Times anti anything that wasn't "genuinely American." A debate between Rush Limbaugh and Don Imus would be patty-cake compared to Colonel Blethen's feud with the new editor of the Post-Intelligencer, Erastus Brainerd. Given later events in the hundred-year battle between the city's two big dailies, the irony is that their first run-in found Blethen defending William Randolph Hearst, whom the colonel admired and emulated. Indeed, The Seattle Daily Times featured such a distinctly "yellow" shade of scandal-mongering that the P-I suggested Hearst was Blethen's silent partner. (In 1903, it did not go unnoticed that Hearst appointed C.B. Blethen to the executive committee of the National Association of Democratic

Seattle Times carrier boys and other circulation workers, spiffied up for the occasion, pose outside the paper's offices at Second and Union streets around 1900. *Seattle Times photo*

Clubs.) When the P-I ran an unflattering photo of Hearst and mocked his candidacy for the 1904 Democratic presidential nomination, the colonel retaliated by printing a caricature of Brainerd that made him look like a jug-eared, weak-chinned creep with a wax mustache. When Blethen called the P-I's publisher a "political guttersnipe," Brainerd shot back with an editorial denouncing the colonel as a "debauched, half-insane and mouthing savage, who is almost nightly to be seen staggering, crazy drunk, in public resorts among decent people, who fear the foul tongue and are disgusted by the conduct of this journalistic strumpet." This was too much for even Harry Chadwick, editor and publisher of the Argus. He called it "the vilest attack on a human being which has ever been made in the press of the state of Washington." Chadwick and many others privately observed, however, that the feud was exaggerated by both sides to sell newspapers. Libel suits, grand jury indictments and lewd doctored photos ensued.

Blethen's checkered past, flamboyance and pugnacious duplicity made for an easy target. He kept one big toe over the line while prescribing piety and reform. The colonel could be

Colonel Alden J. Blethen, holding his ever-present cane, attends the groundbreaking for the new Seattle Times Building at Times Square in downtown Seattle in 1914, together with his sons. C.B. Blethen, an avid photographer, holds a camera. His brother Joe is at right. *Seattle Times Archives*

warm and compassionate one second—tousling a newsboy's hair, helping a hard-luck employee—and frothing with invective the next. That he had a genius for journalism is undeniable. He hired first-rate editors and reporters, bought the best presses and introduced a fat Sunday edition of his own to go head to head with the Post-Intelligencer. He opened a bureau in Washington, D.C., and won new readers with splashy color pages, big photos and graphics that are striking even today. It was titillation with a middle-class cast. Many stories and features in The Times shrewdly targeted a growing female readership. It became one of the most dynamic, frequently quoted newspapers in America. Everyone seemed to have an opinion about Alden J. Blethen, especially his fellow publishers. Rufus Woods, the exuberant editor and publisher of The Wenatchee Daily World, believed in "splash, color [and] action," but he decried Blethen's corrosive partisanship. He called the colonel "a journalistic prostitute." Woods' own widely circulated editorials were sprinkled with capitalized sentences and exclamation points; Blethen "speckled" his with boldface type. The Times' relentless, virulent criticism of city engineer Reginald Heber Thomson, a visionary who literally shaped modern Seattle, prompted four libel suits. The colonel claimed the taxpayers had been "skinned" by Thomson and contractors he favored, notably during the regrade of Denny Hill.

Colonel Blethen was an enterprising straddler—a lot like schizophrenic Seattle as it settled into the 20th century. Whether the city should be "open" or "closed" became "the moral yeast that served as leaven for much subsequent political action," Richard C. Berner wrote in his encyclopedic three-volume history of Seattle. Blethen's biographers, Boswell and McConaghy, cut to the chase: "Between 1897 and 1910, more ink and less sincerity were lavished on vice in Seattle than on any other issue." A "tolerance" policy was still being hotly debated in Seattle a half century later.

Chief Wappenstein reportedly provided police protection for pimps and their "girls" at $10 per month per prostitute. There were at least 500. The P-I said Wappy resembled "a somewhat disreputable walrus" as he made his rounds, collecting the boodle. Some even referred to the Restricted District as Wappyville. The muckrakers at *McClure's Magazine*, who had seen a lot of muck, were stunned at how much there was to rake in Seattle. Wappy was fired and rehired a couple of times, then convicted of bribery and extortion.

There were pitched debates about municipal ownership of utilities (largely opposed by the Blethens) and fear and loathing over the arrival of the Industrial Workers of the World agitating for One Big Union and the end of capitalism. Alden and C.B. Blethen came down with a raging case of what was called "The Wobbly Horrors" and saw reds on every street corner. They ginned up a riot targeting Wobblies and Socialists during the city's 1913 Potlatch celebration. The Times lit the fuse with what Seattle historian Roger Sale describes as possibly "the longest lead sentence, and the most loaded," in the history of American journalism:

> Practically at the very moment a gang of red flag worshippers and anarchists were brutally beating two bluejackets and three soldiers who had dared protest against the insults heaped on the American flag at a soap box meeting on Washington Street last night, Secretary of the Navy Daniels, in the great banqueting hall of the Rainier Club, cheered on by the wildly enthusiastic and patriotic Americans present, flayed as a type the mayor of any city

who permits red flag demonstrations in the community of which he is the head.

You may exhale.

Mayor George F. Cotterill, fearing more violence in the unruly community of which he was the head, had the Times Building cordoned off by police. He vowed to suppress publication of the paper unless page proofs were submitted for his review, surely the most dramatic attempt at prior restraint in the colorful history of Seattle journalism. Apoplectic, the colonel called his attorney. Afterward, he probably ripped yet another telephone off the wall. "The irony of Blethen's paper being suppressed on the grounds that it was creating anarchy in its advocacy of suppressing anarchy" was lost on the judge who promptly sided with the colonel. Many papers were sold that weekend.

Alden J. Blethen was in the thick of everything on Puget Sound for the rest of his days. "Few Seattle citizens found it possible to be non-partisan about him," Murray Morgan wrote. "He himself was one of the least non-partisan men who ever lived. ...But they bought more copies of his paper than they did of any other"—64,000 copies daily by 1912 and almost 84,000 on Sunday.

When Colonel Blethen died at 69 on July 12, 1915, it was front-page news in papers around the Northwest, and in Minneapolis and Kansas City, too. The consensus was that while "tranquility was not for him," he had actually mellowed a bit, "softening with age, making himself better understood and giving much time to upbuilding constructive efforts for Seattle." Scott Bone, the editor of the Post-Intelligencer, said the colonel was "a unique figure without counterpart in the history of newspaper-making." If brevity is the soul of wit, Harry Chadwick's eulogy in the Argus was the best: "Col. Alden J. Blethen is dead. And I am sorry. And I would not have said so a few years ago because it would not have been true."

3 | Seeds of Discontent

If "turmoil was his lot and portion," as one eulogist wrote, Alden J. Blethen's financial house was debt free and well insulated when he died. As the newspaper's profits steadily grew, the colonel attempted to ensure neither he nor his heirs would ever again face the financial abyss that once drove him to drink and despair. He created a closely held trust with nearly $2 million in assets—$47 million today—including the newspaper, prime holdings in Seattle real estate and a diversified portfolio of stocks. At his death, the colonel's share was split between his two sons. They now had 30 percent apiece. Their mother and two sisters shared the remainder. It was prescient of the colonel to worry that the crowning achievement of his newspaper career could be jeopardized by imprudent spending, family feuds or the sale of shares to outsiders.

C.B. and Joe Blethen became co-publishers, C.B. overseeing the newsroom, Joe the business office. The genial, artsy Joe proved to be a capable general manager. Like his father before him, Joe was out and about and soon immersed in Chamber of Commerce committees. He had imaginative ideas about marketing. Electric bulletin boards—high-tech in their day—were installed in The Times' street-side windows to provide coverage of University of Washington football games and the World Series. Thousands gathered to watch the play-by-play updates.

C.B. Blethen was a talented, hard-driving editor, much respected by his staff. He saluted scoops and other big stories with an award that became coveted: The Times T-Mat Honor Medal, a solid gold replica of the capital T matrix on a Linotype machine, "suitably engraved and presented by the boss himself before the assembled staff." C.B.'s zeal for photography—The Times was a wirephoto pioneer and color-printing innovator—brought modern verve to the paper. C.B. instituted more objectivity in the news columns, appropriating the slogan "All the News That's Fit to Print" from The New York Times. He imported aggressive East Coast reporters and hard-nosed editors, beefed up the sports section and pruned the snake oil and fortune-teller ads from the classifieds. C.B. also established an Information Bureau that was the Google of its day. Readers with questions could call "Main 300," The Times switchboard. Operators supplied ball scores and headlines around the clock. From 8 a.m. to midnight, editors, reporters and librarians would attempt to answer any question, from ancient-history homework assignments to how to contact the mayor. The service was a huge hit, averaging 15,000 calls per day in 1920. Unfortunately, C.B. was also profligate and arrogant. (The Star had a field day when he was ticketed for parking in front of a fire hydrant.) For all his faults, it seemed that Alden J. Blethen had more bedrock common sense than the son who succeeded him as editor in chief.

There were signs of friction between the Blethen brothers early on. When C.B. took a new wife in 1909, after only a year as a widower, more seeds of discontent were sown in the Blethen clan. Rachael Kingsley Blethen, a beautiful brunette who preferred to be called "Rae," was the daughter of a well-to-do architect and accustomed to luxury. At 21, she was 10 years younger than C.B. They were married by the Roman Catholic bishop of Seattle and toured Europe during a leisurely wedding trip. They returned with oriental rugs and a crate of other fine furnishings for a mansion on Queen Anne Hill. It was staffed by three servants.

The sons from C.B.'s first marriage, Francis Alden Blethen and Clarance B. II, had been 4 and 1½ when their mother died of pneumonia. Over the next nine years they acquired three new half-brothers—Alden Joseph III, William Kingsley Blethen and John Alden Blethen. The second Mrs. Blethen was devoted to philanthropy, especially Catholic charities, but by all accounts not the least bit charitable toward her stepsons.

In 1916, when Francis Alden Blethen was 12, he got in trouble at school for "various offenses ... against discipline." The principal instructed the boy to inform his father. The three of them were to meet the next day to discuss his deportment. Father was either unamused or never got the news. The boy disappeared after a dental appointment downtown and apparently hopped the 6:30 interurban train to Everett. The next day's editions of The Times featured a front-page photo of the missing boy and the promise of a "liberal" reward for any fruitful tips. Police scoured the state for the blond-haired, freckle-faced lad last seen wearing a gray Knickerbocker suit with "F.A.B." in the lining. He'd been missing for 29 hours when members of The Times' staff traced him to "an obscure hotel" in Tacoma. The paper couched the incident as a youthful adventure. The truth was that home was not a happy place.

"In the big mansion they had on Queen Anne, there'd be a birthday party for one of her sons," says the present-day publisher of The Times, Francis Alden Blethen Jr.—always called Frank, as was his father. "My dad and Clarance had to stay up in their rooms. They couldn't even come down to the party. They could only watch from upstairs. I have to be careful because she's the great-grandmother of my cousins, but she was truly evil." Frank Blethen Jr. says the first schism in the family and the insecurity and alcohol abuse that beset his

Son of Editor Goes in Search Of Adventure

FRANCIS A. BLETHEN.

REQUIRED by the principal of the Queen Anne School to ask his father, C. B. Blethen, to come to her office to discuss various offenses the boy had committed against school discipline, Francis Blethen, 12-year-old son of the editor, decided yesterday afternoon to go traveling instead.

Leaving the Cobb Building, where he had kept a dental appointment, shortly before 5 o'clock, and saying that he was going directly home, Francis completely disappeared and up to 1 o'clock today has not been located. Search commenced shortly after 6 o'clock was continued throughout the night and efforts were redoubled today.

A boy answering his description went to Everett on the 6:30 interurban train last night and was seen during the evening in the Strand Hotel.

The police departments of every city in the state have been furnished with the following description:

Light, rather stiff hair; blue eyes; light complexion; slightly freckled; bad teeth undergoing extensive dental work; probably wore checked gray hat; dark overcoat; gray knickerbocker suit with initials "F. A. B." inside inner breast pocket.

Information leading to the restoration of the boy to his parents will be liberally rewarded.

Washington State Library

father and uncle stem from her aloofness. Rae Blethen was also uppity with her sisters-in-law, flaunting her jewelry and sophistication. The Blethen girls had married well—Marion to a prosperous dentist, Florence to a leading engineer. They were active in the city's cultural affairs and didn't countenance disrespect. When C.B. bought a yacht, then commissioned one bigger yet, they were miffed and worried. More so when their brother acquired a splendid "summer" home in the tony enclave of Medina on the east side of Lake Washington. During winters when Seattle's hilly streets were treacherous, the publisher and his family often stayed downtown, occupying the entire top floor of the Olympic Hotel. They called it their "bungalow." C.B.'s excesses nearly sank The Times.

Jealousies and intrigue simmered for half a century. From the day he became publisher in 1985, Frank Blethen Jr. says his bedrock goal has been to build family harmony to protect their legacy and train the "fifth edition" to take over stewardship of the newspaper.

The division of labor between C.B. and Joe Blethen worked well for a while. They pushed ahead with a splendid new building on a triangle between Fourth and Fifth Avenues and dubbed it Times Square. Joe's influence at the paper waned steadily, however, as his brother's grew. Joe was charming and literary. C.B. was dogmatic and autocratic, striding chest first through the newsroom like the real colonel he now was. He had risen through the ranks to command the Coast Artillery of the National Guard. In 1925, as a reward for The Times' endorsement, C.B. was promoted to brigadier general by the state's new governor, Roland H. Hartley. There are several versions of what happened next. The most delicious has it that the grateful publisher—in a handsome new uniform and spit-shined shoes—presented himself at the governor's office. "General Blethen reporting for duty, sir!" he declared with a crisp salute. "Jesus Christ, Clarance," said the startled governor, "have we been attacked?"

The biggest battle of C.B. Blethen's career was fully joined on Dec. 27, 1921. The Post-Intelligencer for several months had been growing more Hearstian under a new owner. Ostensibly it was John H. Perry, a flamboyant Seattle attorney who declared that on his watch the P-I would "bend its knee to no one save God." Many suspected the majority owner was William Randolph Hearst. Now it was revealed that Seattle's morning daily was one of eight new links in his chain. Fifteen million people from coast to coast read Hearst newspapers. The P-I acquired a panoply of new attractions, including Hearst's International News Service and King Features syndicate, which provided influential columns, color comics and the American Weekly Sunday supplement. The P-I pulled out all the stops on circulation promotions.

  C.B. Blethen conceded that The Times lost $64,000 in 1921, "and we found ourselves fighting for our business lives." It was no longer "we." Joe Blethen, weary of his brother's ego, had cashed out, divorced, remarried and moved to San Francisco. (His only child died in infancy.) In the years to come, C.B. gave his brother scant credit for his significant role in establishing The Seattle Times as a successful newspaper. He also fired some of their father's most loyal longtime employees. Contrary to the colonel's legacy of "Advice and Recommendations," C.B. also dismissed the newspaper's longtime law firm. In the midst of much personal foolishness, that decision at least would prove to be a smart move. C.B.'s new lawyer, Elmer Ely Todd, a sagacious former United States attorney and Republican lawmaker, saved The Times for the Blethen family.

Seattleites had five dailies fighting for their allegiance in the booming postwar economy: the conservative Times and P-I; the business-oriented Bulletin; the blue-collar Star and the Union Record. Labor's strength in Seattle had been growing in fits and starts for seven years. When the Union Record went daily in 1918, it became the first trade-union daily in America. At its peak in the mid-1920s, it claimed to have 80,000 readers. The Star, owned by the Scripps Newspapers group, styled itself as a paper for the "100-percent-American" working man. It joined in the red-baiting during the Seattle General Strike of 1919. In 1920, the Star boasted a statewide daily circulation of 61,600 vs. 55,700 for The Times and 54,700 for the P-I. The Times enjoyed a 30,000 lead over the Post-Intelligencer on Sundays.

When the P-I became a Hearst paper it was quickly back on top. Within two years, its lead over The Times was 6,000 daily and, in a stunning reversal of fortunes, 40,000 on Sunday thanks to a wider reach than its rival. The Times countered that it still had the greater circulation in Seattle and its suburbs. It pointed defensively to "misrepresentations" and "garbled figures" from its competitors, and noted that its numbers reflected papers returned from vendors, while the P-I made newsstand operators eat unsold papers. The Star fell far behind as the P-I and Times co-opted the mainstream market.

The daily newspaper was a smorgasbord of world and local news, politics, sports and entertainment. There were chic, full-page department store ads and page upon page of classifieds. Dad consumed the editorial page and sports section; Mom turned first to Society, then the grocery ads; Junior got Krazy Kat and Buck Rogers, and Sis the cinema section. Sports were big everywhere but huge in Seattle. Royal Brougham, a sports writer with a great byline name and a "your-old-neighbor" persona, became a marquee attraction for the Post-Intelligencer. The dueling Sunday newspapers hit the porch with an impressive plop and, at 10 cents apiece, offered a moveable feast. Blethen countered the P-I's fat package of features with an 86-page Sunday edition of his own, including a classy Rotogravure pictorial section and eight pages of color comics.

As the Twenties began to roar, everyone seemed to own a Ford, a Victrola phonograph and a radio. People were crazy about movie stars, crooners and sports heroes. Women could smoke in public and vote in private. In Seattle, they helped elect the first female mayor of a major American city, Bertha K. Landes, although that experiment in reform was ephemeral. "Tolerance" was in Seattle's chromosomes. Prohibition was a joke on Puget Sound.

What historian Richard C. Berner describes as "the economic ebullience" of Seattle in the mid-Twenties saw the city acquire six new national chain stores and 70 new factories. "Office and store building surpassed all previous records." Pacific Rim trade was the dynamic backbone of Seattle's economy.

Manufacturing, however, was in steady decline, particularly shipbuilding, which had boomed during the First World War. The city had grown by 78,000 between 1910 and 1920. Many of those newcomers, and 50,000 more who arrived over the next decade, were unemployed single men. Seattle remained a hub of the radical labor movement, much to C.B. Blethen's distress. He headed a drive to raise $250,000 for a memorial to the four "brave patriots" who died in the sensational clash with Wobblies in Centralia on Armistice Day in 1919.

Politics was a contact sport in Seattle. For simplicity's sake, it was labor vs. industry and progressives vs. the mossbacks. You picked your paper by your political persuasion, though there were shades of gray—and red—in those black and white pages. Blethen's opinion-page masthead declared that his paper was "Absolutely Independent in Business and Religion and Independent Republican in Politics." In the Twenties, Blethen's Times and Hearst's Post-Intelligencer were for lower taxes and smaller municipal government and against union agitators. C.B. Blethen, however, was more strident about anything "alien," especially "Bolsheviks." "The big difference between the P-I, under its new ownership, and The Times lay in their respective attitudes toward public ownership of utilities," Berner wrote. The Post-Intelligencer, pre-Hearst, opposed public ownership as strenuously as The Times. Now it switched sides. The Times was adamantly opposed to City Light Superintendent J.D. Ross's "socialistic" hydropower project on the Upper Skagit River, as well as the Municipal League's 1925 city-manager charter amendment. "Council Clique, Not Superman, Would Run Affairs of Seattle" was the headline over one in a series of incendiary front-page editorials in The Times. The amendment was defeated. In 1930 as the Depression took hold, the State Grange pushed ahead with its initiative to allow formation of Public Utility Districts, which Blethen and other hardcore conservatives viewed as "communistic and confiscatory." The P-I and Star supported the initiative. The rural vote carried the day for public power.

Well before the Stock Market crash in 1929, the circulation battle was sapping the Blethens' profits, yet C.B. Blethen was publicly sanguine. In a signed front-page editorial the Sunday before Wall Street's "Black Monday," the editor and publisher declared, "There will be no real depression. What little disturbance there will be will pass off in a very few weeks." The Sunday Times' financial and business review section heralded 1930 with uplifting reports. Business leaders were said to be "particularly enthusiastic" over Puget Sound's prospects for the new year. They were all whistling past a graveyard. By 1931, Frederick & Nelson department store was selling golf clubs at fire sale prices and the city's leading purveyor of fancy lighting fixtures was offering "superb examples of the craft" at 30 cents on the dollar because "We Need the Money!"

C.B. Blethen had "disregarded expense in the pursuit of newsgathering." He kept living lavishly and brought The Seattle Times to the brink of bankruptcy. When the day of reckoning arrived he was forced to sell his 96-foot motor yacht, the *Canim*—Chinook for "Big chief canoe." The elegant vessel cost Blethen $150,000 in 1930, $2.1 million in today's dollars. Just two years later, when the big chief was up a creek, "the toast of the Seattle Yacht Club," fetched only $47,500 from the stone-faced comedian, Buster Keaton. He was "one of the few people in the United States who could still afford to pay even that much."

4 | Shared Burdens

A maudlin announcement that masked all manner of intrigue appeared at top center on the front page of The Sunday Seattle Times on January 5, 1930:

> The complex duties and responsibilities involved in publishing a newspaper the size and importance of The Seattle Times have become so great that no man can possibly face the task alone and approximate a truly high standard of efficiency. Therefore, I have determined to share my burdens with other experienced publishers and have taken into partnership with me, and have sold a minority interest in The Seattle Times to Ridder Brothers of New York and St. Paul. In thus uniting two of the oldest newspaper families in the United States, I feel satisfied that The Seattle Times will be the gainer. I have retained absolute control and management, and after me, it will remain with my family. I am honored that the Messrs. Ridder have agreed to this association. They own many newspapers and have ambitious plans for the future—plans which inevitably will benefit Seattle. – C.B. BLETHEN

He was sugar-coating a desperate act. Facing financial ruin and, worse, the shame of a general surrendering his family's legacy, Blethen needed an infusion of cash. Bernard H. Ridder and his twin brothers, Joseph and Victor, owned nine dailies—four in the East, two in Minnesota and three in the Dakotas. Their late father had published the largest German-language daily in America and helped organize the Associated Press. The brothers were canny, ambitious newspapermen. They smelled blood in Seattle. For approximately $1.5 million, they acquired 49.5 percent of the common-stock voting shares in The Seattle Times Company and 65 percent of its dividend-paying shares. C.B. was named company president and publisher "for a period of five years" at the munificent salary of $114,000 per year. This clearly was a short-term investment designed to ease Blethen out the door. "Because of C.B.'s faltering leadership, the Ridders believed they would eventually gain full control and ownership of the newspaper," a Harvard Business School study concluded. In the years to come, the Ridders worked behind the scenes "to create contention and distrust among the family, board of directors and bankers." If not for Elmer Todd they might have succeeded. C.B.'s mannerly yet astute lawyer had brokered an important side deal with the city's pioneer banking and investment firm, First Seattle Dexter Horton Securities Company, on whose board he had served. That news was announced on the Tuesday following C.B.'s "share-my-burdens" statement. Two-million dollars in Seattle Times Company bonds were sold by week's end, the "first major newspaper financing in Pacific Northwest history." Thanks to the Ridder bailout and the bond sale, C.B. was able to consolidate his control of The Times by acquiring additional shares of voting stock from his mother and sisters.

Elmer Todd, one of the most admired attorneys in the Northwest. *Seattle Times photo*

If C.B.'s ego had clouded his judgment—the yachts and over-spending to counter Hearst—his heirs say his heart was in the right place. Sixteen years later, when he was dead and buried and the Ridders were suing for control of the company, the Washington Supreme Court concluded: "If there is anything clear from these contracts and the circumstances surrounding their execution, it is that Blethen's unswerving purpose was to maintain his own and (after his death) his family's control of The Seattle Times."

When the deal was done, Elmer Todd became a Times stockholder and ex-officio publisher. At 56, he was one of the most admired and best connected attorneys in the Northwest. Donworth, Todd & Higgins represented Boeing, Union National Bank, railroads, shipbuilders and lumber companies. "Elmer saved the day for the Blethen family," Frank Blethen Jr. says, nodding in admiration 84 years later. "Todd told the bankers, 'Look, we're going to do this deal with the Ridders. We'll have a minor shareholder. Give us an infusion of cash and I'll get C.B. out of here for a year. Let me run the business and I'll get us out of debt.' The bankers really trusted him. So they sent C.B. Blethen to Hawaii for a year."*

It wasn't a whole year. That fall, the Blethens added heartbreak to their anxiety over the future of The Times—and the newspaper lost a promising member of the family's third generation. Alden Joseph Blethen III, the firstborn of C.B. and Rae Blethen's three sons, was killed in a motorcycle accident in Virginia three weeks after his 20th birthday. He and a prep school friend were visiting the University of North Carolina, where Blethen was enrolled as a freshman. His pal lost control of the motorcycle and "Buster" Blethen was thrown into the path of an oncoming car. Blethen, handsome and charismatic, had been a cadet captain during his senior year at a military academy. He showed "considerable aptitude" both as a cub reporter and ad salesman during two summers at The Times and was excited about a career in newspapering. C.B. Blethen made a sad journey east to bring home his boy's body. The presses at The Times were halted during the Requiem Mass.

---

* After listening to his father relate this story about his great-grandfather, Ryan Blethen quipped, "I think the most interesting thing I heard today is that if you're a publisher here and you do a crappy job you're going to get sent to Hawaii for a year!"

Rose Ann Blethen, Colonel Blethen's widow, poses with her grandchildren around 1925. Back row, from left: William K. "Bill" Blethen, Francis A. "Frank" Blethen, Clarance B. "Judge" Blethen II, Mrs. Blethen and Alden J. "Buster" Blethen III. Front row, from left, Mary Jane Mesdag, John A. "Jack" Blethen, Joseph B. Mesdag and Gilbert L. Duffy II. *Seattle Times photo*

The Post-Intelligencer offered its condolences in an elegiac editorial, saying Seattle had lost a youth of "great promise."

C.B. Blethen retreated to his editorial writing and military interests, relying increasingly on Elmer Todd's steady hand. With his bald head, tidy mustache and impeccable three-piece suits, Todd exuded gravitas—but kindliness, too. Before long he knew the names of copy editors, pressmen and delivery truck drivers. On Todd's watch, despite the Depression, The Times got out of debt and moved into an imposing new headquarters, an Art Deco armory along Fairview Avenue. The Times capitalized on Hearst's own self-inflicted wounds to whittle away at the Post-Intelligencer's circulation lead. Harry Cahill, the circulation manager, undercut the P-I by reducing the price of the daily edition to two cents as unemployment on Puget Sound neared 30 percent. Hearst management beefed up special promotions in an attempt to wring more profits from the underperforming P-I. Todd parried and The Times captured the lion's share of the meager pie of advertising revenue during the 1930s. (Hearst's ad revenues chain-wide declined "by 15 percent in 1930, 24 percent in 1931 and 40 percent in 1933.") The Star was hit hardest by the Depression. Its blue-collar readership had little disposable income, and advertisers knew it.

Time and again, Todd would keep the Ridders at bay while ensuring Blethen's sons learned the ropes. He was unable to suppress C.B.'s tendency to go off the rails editorially. When it came to political rancor, however, not to mention impetuous spending, Clarance Brettun Blethen was a piker compared to William Randolph Hearst. The newspaper tycoon owned a castle in Wales, gave his movie-star mistress a mammoth beach house at Santa Monica and plundered Europe to furnish a 165-room Mediterranean castle overlooking the Pacific at San Simeon, California. Hearst had over-expanded his media empire by borrowing recklessly in the giddy 1920s. Now, as the Depression decimated profits, his hubris caught up with him. He would squander his political power, too.

Hearst played a key role in role in securing the 1932 Democratic presidential nomination for Franklin D. Roosevelt and thumped relentlessly for the New York governor. C.B. Blethen backed hapless Herbert Hoover. Hearst early on was more progressive than his candidate, advocating a $5 billion public-works program to jumpstart the economy. Blethen was appalled. He maintained that "foolish fears" about the underlying health of the economy would soon evaporate if Hoover's steady, conservative hand remained on the tiller for a second term.

Roosevelt won 42 states and 57 percent of the popular vote. The Times printed a front-page editorial wishing the new president well, emphasizing that it was Seattle's "truly independent newspaper." And for a while at least, to the astonishment of the diehard downtown establishment, the New Deal got a square deal in The Times.

Hearst's shrill opposition to the 1934 San Francisco general strike won him the enduring enmity of the bloodied but unbowed longshoremen who lit the fuse. They distributed "I Don't Read Hearst" buttons and stickers up down the coast. By 1936, Hearst had broken noisily with the New Deal over reforms targeting tax loopholes and its "sympathy and encouragement for the fomenters of revolution." The Chief, as Hearst liked to be called, was on a red-baiting rampage. The American Federation of Teachers urged a boycott of his papers, calling him a "constant enemy of academic freedom" and the "chief exponent of Fascism in the United States." C.B. Blethen was no less worried by the renewed Red Menace. He filled a whole page in his paper with the text of Al Smith's broadside denouncing FDR for "tilling the soil" for the seeds of Communism by promoting class hatred.

When the New Deal's National Labor Relations Act codified collective bargaining, millions of Americans joined trade unions. On what truly was the left coast, Seattle was a hotbed of labor unrest. If you were lucky enough to still have a job, your hours or wages—often both—were being slashed. A "Hooverville" of destitute squatters in tarpaper shacks arose near the rail yards south of Seattle's Pioneer Square. University intellectuals, young Communists and militant CIO unionists, as well as old Wobblies and Socialists, formed a potent Popular Front coalition. FDR's campaign manager, Postmaster General James A. Farley, famously proposed a droll toast in 1936 "to the American Union—47 states and the Soviet of Washington."

Seattle's Central Labor Council, ironically, had morphed into craft-union conservatism. It was dominated by Dave Beck, who had muscled his way from a laundry truck to the presidency of the Puget Sound local of the Teamsters. His cherubic face and middle-class paunch belied an iron will. As a kid, he peddled the P-I in the morning and The Times after school—sometimes the Star, too. "You had to be a hustler," Beck liked to remember. When he was eight, bigger kids tried to displace him from a prime street corner. They learned not to mess with Dave.

Along the waterfront in 1935, Beck's Teamsters faced a threat from the left. The longshoremen's union, led by Harry Bridges, a scrawny Australian immigrant, had designs on controlling Seattle's dockside warehouses. Besides being an "alien," Bridges was a former Wobbly and transparently a communist agitating for industrial unionism. He was also a force of nature and a businessman's worst nightmare. Beck didn't like him either. They first clashed the year before when Seattle longshoremen joined the coast-wide strike. Beck waded in as an arbitrator at the behest of the governor. Forty years later, the old Teamster could be found most Sundays ensconced in a high-back chair at the counter of the 13 Coins restaurant across from The Seattle Times, watching the chefs flame up his favorite dishes. If asked about the 1930s he would happily regale anyone with what happened when he showed both Hearst and Blethen who was boss and outflanked Harry Bridges.

In 1936, half of the some 70 workers in the Post-Intelligencer's newsroom had the temerity to join the fledgling American Newspaper Guild. Hearst was not amused. He maintained they were "professionals," not time-clock laborers. This struck many of his reporters as the height of hypocrisy, given his arbitrary and capricious conduct. Those who talked back or otherwise seemed subversive were yanked off prime beats or fired. In their book, *Unionism or Hearst,* William E. Ames and Roger A. Simpson, University of Washington communications professors with wide-ranging newspaper experience, analyzed the conditions that led to a landmark American strike:

> The newspaper's writers, unprotected by union contracts, knew what it meant to take unnegotiated pay cuts. More fear was created among the higher paid employees by the Hearst policy of replacing high-salaried "stars" on a newspaper staff with inexperienced youngsters who could be hired for a pittance. ... To many it was the insecurity of the situation which bothered them most. Should they be fired without warning, as many were, there was no severance pay; ...should they have complaints about working hours, assignments, and conditions, there was no guarantee that anyone would heed

them. Many of the staff felt trapped at the same time they were grateful for having a job.

When the trouble started in Seattle, Hearst and an entourage of 16 were touring Europe. In Rome, the 74-year-old mogul paused from the purchase of $70,000 worth of paintings and a crate-load of 17-century furniture to meet with reporters. "It has cost me over $1,000,000 to conduct my paper in Seattle all through the Depression and up to date," he said. "If the Communists want to relieve me of that cost and of the duty of supplying jobs to labor, it is not an unmixed evil. I would save money. However, there is a greater issue at stake than saving money. There is the issue of a free press and free country ...whether anybody else makes the fight against Communism and mob rule or not, I am going to make it; and I am enlisted for the duration of the war."

General Blethen, likewise, would report for duty.

On August 12, 1936, the Seattle Central Labor Council voted 347-3 to condemn Hearst as unfair to labor. The next day, the handful of neophyte Newspaper Guild strikers parading outside the P-I soon "found themselves being elbowed aside as the more powerful and experienced labor elements of Seattle moved down from the hills, up from the waterfront, and out of the Labor Temple." There were loggers, mill hands, metal workers and a platoon of longshoremen. Some wondered whether Beck's Teamsters would keep the faith. Around noon a cheer went up as broad-shouldered Teamsters arrived in force. "The enemies of the Guild—Hearst and the Post-Intelligencer—had become the enemies of all Seattle labor." When the pickets heard Hearst planned an end-around by having the P-I printed by brother publishers, "swarms of pickets were crowded into Teamster-driven cabs, and within minutes new picket lines were formed around the Times and the Seattle Star plants."

C.B. Blethen went ballistic. Thirty-five Guild members had shut down a newspaper with more than 600 employees. In a front-page editorial, the editor and publisher of The Times declared:

> Yesterday was written the most shameful page in Seattle's history.

By order of a labor leader, the Post-Intelligencer, Seattle's oldest newspaper, was compelled to suspend publication.

Out of the quiescent fingers of a complacent mayor and chief of police, slipped the government of this once great city. Today it rests in the firm hands of Dave Beck and his brawny crew of teamsters, loggers and longshoremen.

Gone is constitutional government. Gone is majority rule and freedom of speech.

Seattle is now the plaything of a dictator. Practically without an hour's warning a newspaper has been put out of business. ...If a newspaper—why not a department store? Or a bank? ...

Seattle definitely has been on the downgrade for some years, just because of our labor situation. Our city for a long time has been on industry's blacklist. Our progress has been stopped.

The suspension of the Post-Intelligencer is more likely than not to mark the place where Seattle lies—dead.

Dave Beck and his following comprise a very small fraction of the city's population. But one bandit can hold up a whole roomful of people.

How do you like the look of Dave Beck's gun?

Beck sued The Times for $250,000. He demanded a half million more from the P-I and two Seattle radio stations that had aired Hearst's own defamatory editorials naming the Teamster boss as the villain in the strike.

After 15 weeks of lost revenues, a relentless flogging by unionists and an FDR landslide, Hearst knew he was licked. The American Newspaper Guild's first victory reverberated nationwide for white-collar workers. Beck settled the libel cases out of court for $10,000 from Blethen and $15,000 from the others. What he had really won—power—was priceless. Seattle's business/industrial establishment understood power. Dave Beck's three-piece suits were well tailored. He disliked "reds" as much as they did. They came to see that this was a guy—rough around the edges, granted—they could do business with.

Interior Secretary Harold Ickes gloated that Hearst "slobbered all over" the re-elected president in a congratulatory editorial. The Depression and boycotts "had had a devastating effect on the Hearst empire," David Nasaw wrote in his award-winning biography of Hearst. "The only part … that was thriving was the Sunday papers, nearly all of which held their circulation—in large part because of the popularity of their comic supplements." This was particularly so in Seattle.

Hearst made a strategic peace offering to Seattle: The appointment of the president's son-in-law, John Boettiger, as publisher of the Post-Intelligencer. The former Chicago Tribune reporter had met Anna Roosevelt during the 1932 presidential campaign. The dashing young couple "arrived triumphantly" in Seattle and were feted by Beck and his favorite mayor, John "Irish Johnny" Dore. Anna's job was to oversee the society pages. Hearst said they had carte blanche to "make it the best paper in Seattle." They didn't. The Hearst empire was $126,000,000 in debt and on the precipice of bankruptcy. Boettiger's salary—only $37,500 a year—testified to the Post-Intelligencer's puny profits. Seattle liberals nevertheless thrilled to visits by Anna's mother. The Times took particular delight in noting that the First Lady's nationally syndicated "My Day" column was a fixture on its editorial page, not the P-I's.

As for C.B. Blethen, every time he saw a Guild member walk past his plant, he boosted newsroom salaries. Times reporters were "now getting much higher than the Guild scale provides," the weekly Argus observed in 1937.

The reverse was true at the P-I and Hearst's other newspapers. Painful cuts were being made. The Chief had finally faced reality, relinquishing financial control to a trusted adviser who assembled a "Conservation Committee." A major portion of Hearst's art collection was sold off at bargain-basement prices; construction work halted at his San Simeon castle;

money-losing newspapers were liquidated. The presence of the president's daughter and son-in-law probably ensured that the Post-Intelligencer remained a Hearst newspaper.

Boettiger's tenuous tenure as publisher of the P-I was underscored by the Hearst newspapers' strong opposition to FDR's 1940 bid for a third term. Boettiger left for Army duty in 1943. Anna moved back to the White House to become her father's confidant. Hearst's new acting publisher in Seattle, P-I advertising director Charles B. "Charlie" Lindeman, was not of the liberal persuasion. A photo of Eleanor Roosevelt shaking hands with Harry Bridges was almost more than he could bear. Boettiger resigned as the P-I's publisher after his discharge from the military at war's end, citing "irreconcilable differences" with William Randolph Hearst. Lindeman, a decisive old-school manager, was no longer "acting." Seattle's morning daily tacked hard right in the crusade against Communism, built a new plant and set out to beat The Times.

Both papers gave Dave Beck a wide berth for the next 20 years, especially The Times. There was praise for his appointment as a University of Washington regent, and hometown pride in 1952 when he was elected Teamsters international president. Eisenhower wanted him to be his secretary of labor. Beck appeared on the cover of *Time* magazine. It wasn't until 1957 that he met someone even tougher and craftier than he was—Robert F. Kennedy, a young labor-corruption investigator for the U.S. Senate—and ended up serving two years in prison for income-tax evasion.

5 | The General Surrenders

By 1940, two of C.B. Blethen's sons were moving through the ranks at The Times. Another was a summer intern. Conspicuously absent was the publisher's namesake, disinherited for besmirching the family name.

Clarance Brettun Blethen II was a spindly young man who wore thick glasses. He looked somber when deep in thought, and in boyhood received a nickname that would prove incongruous—"Judge." He became a first-rate copy editor, admired by his peers, but also a thoroughly injudicious alcoholic. Even when sober, young Blethen had had the temerity to stand up to his imperious father. He was demoted from assistant managing editor in the early 1930s. Accounts vary as to whether he was subsequently fired or just decided he'd had enough of his father's censure. He landed for a while at The Seattle Star where everything he wrote was prominently labeled "By Clarance B. Blethen 2d." That needling byline was but a pin prick compared to how "Judge," on the rebound from a year at McNeil Island Penitentiary for forgery, attempted to get even.

The general's sons began their newspaper careers in the newsroom. Carl Brazier, the no-nonsense editor-in-chief, and the chain-smoking guys around the "rim" of the copy desk cut them no slack. The Blethen boys remembered—mostly fondly—being barked at for reporting errors or failing to follow the newspaper's voluminous, exacting stylebook. They were diligent, unfailingly polite and, with the exception of "Judge," a bit distant, shying away from the joshing and camaraderie of the newsroom.

Francis A. "Frank" Blethen had been coxswain of the

national champion junior varsity crew at the University of Washington, graduating in 1927. He received a commission as a second lieutenant in the Marine Corps Reserve, which pleased his father, but thereafter seems to have lost his stroke. Frank gravitated toward the relative anonymity of the production side of the family business. Married five times, he was a negligent father to four children and drank heavily, though not nearly so much as his star-crossed kid brother. Their stepmother's chilliness had pockmarked their childhood. Frank and "Judge" resented the deference accorded their half-brothers. Frank Blethen Jr., who became publisher in 1985, surmises that his uncle was referred to as C.B. Blethen II rather than "Jr." because of the stepmother's petulance.

Bill Blethen, a Yale graduate, was being schooled in advertising as well as newswriting. John Alden "Jack" Blethen, the youngest son, attended Dartmouth and started his apprenticeship in the newsroom during summer break. Family lore has it that he was flunking out of college when he enlisted as a buck private in the National Guard in 1940 as fascism was swallowing Europe. By war's end Jack was a major.

It was around this time that General Blethen and his red-faced, efficient aide-de-camp, business manager Harry Cahill, resolved that The Times' moral and competitive niche should be that of "a family newspaper." Banner headlines like "AX SLAYER FOUND INSANE!" would no longer do. They devised a "clean-editing" policy to position The Times as "a down-to-earth" yet respectable newspaper "welcome in every home and of interest to each member of the family." Words like "nude," "gun" and "blood" were banished. The copy desk rolled its eyes and set about doing what all good copy desks do—"follow style."

The general, his health failing, lost his last editorial battle and surrendered gracefully.

C.B. now spent much of the year at the Blethen summer home on the east side of Lake Washington and didn't mind the drive around the lake. He was adamantly opposed to the proposed $9 million "floating" bridge championed by Miller and Kemper Freeman and other East Side businessmen. They believed growth on all fronts—industrial, commercial and residential—was sure to follow if a span linked Seattle and Mercer Island to the East Side. Though the Romans had sent legions over pontoon bridges, C.B. Blethen maintained the scheme was an extravagant boondoggle. When the Post-Intelligencer and Bellevue American noted that 40 percent of the cost would be financed by New Deal programs, Blethen called it pork-barrel spending. Cartoons on his editorial page showed "broken chunks of concrete on a desolate shore as the only remains of an ill-conceived venture." And even if it didn't sink like a stone, it was ugly, the general said. By the time the bridge opened in the summer of 1940, however, Blethen realized it was an amazing feat of engineering, "a new great wonder of the world"—and "the durned thing really does float!" Moreover, its beauty "was utterly amazing," he wrote in a statesman-like editorial that borrowed a line from *Alice in Wonderland*: "There are two reasons for eating crow. One is because you have to and the other is because you feel you should."

C.B. Blethen, just 62, died in the fall of 1941. "He was one of only a few publishers familiar with every process that had transformed the newspaper business into a complex industry," the front-page obituary said with the flowery obeisance accorded all departed publishers. "He had breathed the air of editorial rooms almost since he could walk, and the idea of spending his life in any other atmosphere never had occurred to him."

Frank, Bill and Jack inherited their father's stock, with the codicil that Elmer Todd would oversee their shares for the next 10 years. Neither Frank nor Bill was ready to succeed their father as publisher. Jack was a 23-year-old Army lieutenant on active duty with the Coast Artillery. Todd became the first non-family publisher of The Seattle Times as well as company president. Frank and Bill were elected vice presidents and named associate publishers. Frank would continue as production manager. With the outbreak of World War II, Bill went on active duty as a Navy lieutenant.

In 1943, Frank Blethen married for the third time. The bride was Kathleen Mary Ryan, a sprightly young woman who worked on The Times switchboard. The Ryans were a big Irish Catholic family several rungs below the Blethens on the Seattle social ladder. If they'd never been inside the posh Rainier Club, with its dark-paneled walls and overstuffed club chairs, they were also happily devoid of pretension. Kathleen's father, a Seattle policeman, died of a brain tumor in 1940 after being conked from behind while breaking up a barroom brawl.

Elmer Todd inspects a new press. *Seattle Times photo*

Her widowed mother, who became a police matron, was a down-to-earth character. She adored her grandchildren and they her. The Blethens' daughter Diane was born in 1944; Frank Jr. the next year. The couple divorced in 1951. Kathleen moved to Arizona with her kids. Frank Jr. rarely saw his father. He remembers his itinerant "Uncle Judge" inviting himself to dinner to try and cadge some cash from his mom. By then, Clarance Brettun Blethen II had burned all his bridges.

The Ridders, with the disowned C.B. II as their ally, filed a series of lawsuits against the Blethens, beginning in 1942. The first objected to a resolution adopted by the new board of directors authorizing The Seattle Times Company's purchase of the Times Building from the Blethen Corporation for $400,000. (This move was Todd at his canniest, protecting the family's holdings. He had 10 shares of voting stock.) The purchase should be voided, the Ridders asserted, arguing that the directors should be removed from office.

The second suit got to the heart of the matter: The Ridders charged that by disinheriting C.B. II, General Blethen's will breached the requirements of the 1930 contracts between the two families. All four surviving sons were entitled to divide their father's shares, the Ridders said.

All the et als, therefores and thereafters boiled down to this: If C.B. II won back his inheritance—and the right to vote at board meetings—he would side with the Ridders and they could gain control of The Seattle Times. It was "just another Ridder suit," Todd said with a confident shrug.

A U.S. District Court judge dismissed the complaint, but the Ninth Circuit Court of Appeals reversed the judgment. The case bounced back to King County Superior Court. The judge there sided with the Blethens after hearing evidence that C.B. II had assigned to one of the Ridders any voting-stock rights he might obtain through the litigation. The Ridders took their case to the Washington Supreme Court. On February 28, 1946, they lost. That C.B. Blethen "had good and sufficient reason" to disinherit his son "is not only demonstrated by the evidence, but also in the very inception of this suit," the justices wrote. "What he greatly feared has come to pass: The control of the Times by the Blethen family is threatened by the action of an irresponsible son."

The responsibility for advancing the family's responsible sons rested with Elmer Todd. With Bill and Jack Blethen away for most of the war, he concentrated on Frank, who was emerging as an earnest yet curiously colorless fellow—especially for a Blethen.

Puget Sound during the war years epitomized FDR's "arsenal of democracy." In war contracts per capita, Seattle was among the top three cities. B-17 bombers bristling with machine-gun turrets streamed out of Boeing's factories. Seattle Times reporter Richard Williams gave the sleek warplane its name—the "flying fortress." The shipyards clanked around the clock. In all, a quarter million people in King County owed their employment to defense contracts.

Among the newcomers were 25,000 African-Americans, many of whom wrongly assumed they were leaving Jim

Crow behind. The local of the Aeronautical Mechanics Union, aided by Boeing management, stonewalled the hiring of blacks despite the growing need for war workers. If all you had to go by was microfilmed newspapers from the war years, you'd think Seattle was the whitest place on Earth.

As Negroes were arriving, some 7,000 Seattle-area residents of Japanese descent were being hauled away to desolate camps. Though many were U.S. citizens, the three dailies branded them all enemy aliens, a view shared by most of their readers. In a letter to the editor of the "fiercely pro-internment" Post-Intelligencer, a man from suburban Auburn summed up the hatred and fear that gripped America after Pearl Harbor: "The way I look at it, the average tame American Jap is hard to tell from the wild Jap. The Japs in Tokyo, no doubt, intended to use the Japs already here as a screen to filter into our midst, then stab us in the back." An analysis of wartime editorials in seven major West Coast newspapers found that The Seattle Times featured "the second highest number of pro-internment editorials. The Times recommended that "able-bodied Japanese men be employed building a new highway through Canadian territory to Alaska." The Seattle Star, anti-Japanese since the 1920s, became more strident after it was sold to local interests in 1942. On Bainbridge Island, home to a considerable number of Japanese Americans, mostly farmers, the weekly Bainbridge Review was one of a handful of West Coast newspapers to oppose incarceration.

With the energized economy and demand for the latest news, The Times and Post-Intelligencer thrived during the war years. "Hearst astounded observers, both friend and foe, by shedding his spendthrift ways and focusing on the superior production of his newspapers." He also bought several newsprint mills, an investment that would prove shrewd.

The transition to peace brought open warfare on the labor front. Factories slashed their payrolls and the unions fought wage cuts. Seattleites had no daily newspapers for 56 days during a strike by the printers' union.

As Dave Beck and Harry Bridges resumed their battle for control of the waterfront, Beck was also busy branching out. Ever the opportunist, the Teamster boss played both ends against the middle when the Aero Mechanics Union struck Boeing. William Allen, the plane-maker's new president, came hat in hand asking Beck for help. In labor unrest, Seattle was a microcosm of postwar America. It became the epicenter of red-baiting at the dawn of the Cold War.

Seattle became a two-newspaper town on August 13, 1947, when The Seattle Star ceased publication. Disruptive strikes and the cutthroat competition for Depression-era ad revenues had reduced the Star to an also-ran. In 1941, it switched briefly to a tabloid format. The Scripps chain sold the paper to a group of Seattle businessmen the following year. For war coverage, the Star couldn't compete with The Times and P-I. Then, as advertising exploded to capitalize on pent-up postwar demand for autos, appliances and clothing, the industry was hit with a newsprint shortage that sent prices soaring.

The printers' strike was one of the last straws for the Star. The Star's stockholders accepted Elmer Todd's offer of $360,000 for the newspaper's circulation lists, goodwill and newsprint supply contracts, the real prize. "Seattle Times Buys Out Star, Then Closes It," the Post-Intelligencer's headline said. What closed the Star was a changing firmament.

The Times had already acquired one of the Star's budding stars. Emmett Watson was a young sports writer with a nose for news and an ear for dialogue. He didn't hesitate when Alex Shults, the new sports editor at The Times, offered him a job. Compared to the ragtag Star "the stately Times was like entering a lint-free news laboratory," Watson recalled.

The editor was Russell McGrath, a tall, thin, tweedy man who wore a green eyeshade and the last sleeve garters seen in a Seattle newsroom. No one dared to call him by his first name. "McGrath ruled with an iron hand, doing so through short memos that came out of his office like shrapnel," Watson wrote years later. Those who couldn't get past his exacting exterior missed a man who relished painstaking attention to detail and fine writing. Shown a headline that declared "Blue Skies for Seafair!" McGrath grunted, "There's only one sky." To the surprise of many in the newsroom, McGrath admired Watson's stylistic experiments and gave his sports column front-page plugs.

Watson also worked with, and sometimes for, a wiry newsman with an extraordinary memory. Henry MacLeod had been elevated to sports editor at 27. Now, eight years on, he was city editor—one of the best in the country, in Watson's view.* MacLeod asked Watson about another refugee from the Star, Ed Guthman. "Hire him," Watson said. Guthman had compiled box scores for the Star's tiny sports department as a student at the University of Washington before the war. As an Army captain he'd led reconnaissance platoons in Italy and North Africa. He was wounded in combat and received the Silver Star for his valor. Guthman easily passed muster with MacLeod and McGrath. Watson was a first-rate talent scout.

The Times would rue the day in 1950 when it allowed the Post-Intelligencer to woo away Watson with the promise of a bit more money and a lot more freedom. He became Seattle's favorite columnist, with a breezy blend of names, news and gossip—the "three-dot" style Herb Caen had elevated to an art form in San Francisco. But more than that, Watson could spot hypocrisy at a hundred paces. He championed civil rights, helped save the historic Pike Place Market and railed against gentrification by launching a "Lesser Seattle" movement. It would be 33 years before The Times got him back.

Guthman stayed with The Times for a decade and became one of the greatest reporters in Seattle history.

---

* A city editor oversees the reporters and photographers who cover local news. Seattle Weekly's Rick Anderson, who began his long career in journalism as a copy boy at the Post-Intelligencer in the 1960s, recalls that Ray Collins, a P-I artist and cartoonist, used to greet groups of kids touring the paper with a wry tutorial on how newsrooms really work: "Those people over there, they can write but they can't spell. They're reporters. Those people over there, they can spell but they can't write. They're copy editors. The guy in the middle? He can't do either. He's the managing editor."

6 | Pulitzer Pride

"Have you no sense of decency, sir? At long last, have you left no sense of decency?" In 1954, an outraged Boston attorney uttered the legendary words that helped end Wisconsin Senator Joseph McCarthy's witch hunt for Communists. Six years earlier, Albert F. Canwell, a freshman state legislator from Spokane, met his own match in Elmer Todd and Ed Guthman.

Canwell's heroes were two noisy proto-McCarthyites, Congressmen Martin Dies and J. Parnell Thomas. Their House Un-American Activities investigations were front-page news during the 1940s. Dies' committee suggested that Shirley Temple, 10 at the time, was a Commie dupe. Thomas subpoenaed almost everyone in Hollywood except Lassie.

As Canwell, oozing ambition, took office in 1947, Communists had seized power in Czechoslovakia and cordoned off Berlin. They were advancing relentlessly in China and attacking America by undermining its institutions, Canwell warned. That Harry Bridges was a Communist, intent on controlling the waterfront from Seattle to San Diego, was undeniable, he said. There were Commies "everywhere"—in places you least suspected, even in the Legislature. They had infiltrated a pension union and theater groups. Worse, Canwell charged, they were teaching at our colleges and universities, inculcating impressionable students with Marxist-Leninist dogma. "Not less" than 150 professors at the University of Washington were card-carrying Communists or "egghead" fellow travelers, a Canwell committee member declared.

Canwell's probe was spurred on by three newspaper men—his good friend Ashley Holden, the red-baiting political

Emmett Watson, left, shares a hot story with City Editor Henry MacLeod, center, and investigative reporter Ed Guthman around 1948. *MacLeod Family Album*

editor of Spokane's Spokesman-Review; Fred Niendorff, the Post-Intelligencer's legislative correspondent, and Ross Cunningham, a veteran Seattle Times political writer. The Seattle pair, though competitors, were both intent on exposing subversive elements in the UW faculty. Canwell, who had dabbled in journalism, viewed all three as "outstanding men. ...We had a very amenable relationship." Russell McGrath, managing editor of The Times, thought it too amenable.

Ross Cunningham, 41, had worked first for the Star as an investigative reporter. He hopped back and forth between The Times and P-I two or three times before returning to The Times for "a five-buck raise" around 1939. He was a canny, politically connected newsman. The Blethens liked him. During the 1940 gubernatorial campaign, Cunningham was granted a leave of absence to serve as press aide to the victorious Republican, Seattle Mayor Arthur B. Langlie. He served as the governor's executive secretary for three years before returning to The Times. Things like that weren't altogether unusual in those days. Tough-minded editors like McGrath and Henry MacLeod still didn't like it. MacLeod was unhappy if a political yard sign sprang up within a hundred yards of his house.

In 1944, when Cunningham received the title of associate editor, the attaboy didn't go down well with staffers who questioned Cunningham's objectivity and resented his in with the Blethens.

When Canwell's Joint Fact-Finding Committee on Un-American Activities called its first witnesses in 1948, the chairman declared that legislative rules trumped constitutional rights and due process. It was strictly "Are you now or have you ever been a member of the Communist Party?" No Fifth Amendment; no elaboration; no cross-examination—yet so-called expert witnesses and shady informants were allowed to point fingers with impunity.

Canwell was dismayed that Cunningham was absent from the press table. In his place was Ed Guthman, a tenacious young reporter. Years later, Canwell said with some plausibility that McGrath's decision to replace Cunningham with Guthman was "a point of considerable conflict on a higher level" at the paper. "Somewhere along the line I talked about Guthman to one of those who owned the paper. He says, 'Well, I get a lot of complaints, but it's out of my department. I don't mess with the news end of this thing.' " Frank and Bill Blethen, associate publishers during the interregnum following their father's death, were Chamber of Commerce Republicans and staunchly anti-Communist. They worried that the Post-Intelligencer was pursuing academic subversives with more vehemence. But Elmer Todd was still publisher. His view was that the news end of the operation was best left to the editors. When Todd did offer advice—as he would decisively before the Canwell affair was over—it underscored the depth of his concern that common decency was being trampled.

Canwell claimed Cunningham warned him about Guthman, saying, "Well, we think he's a Commie but we can't do anything without proof." And that meant McGrath might be in on it, too, Canwell surmised.

The things Albert Canwell said without proof fill hundreds of pages of legislative and oral history transcripts. In an interview 50 years later, indignation still palpable, Canwell railed that McGrath had replaced a "great newsman" with a lying, left-wing phony reporter. Guthman was an "ACLUer" at best, a Communist "plant" at worst—out to sabotage his committee's vital work and "cream" anyone who got in the way, Canwell declared. MacLeod marveled at all this vituperation for a decorated World War II combat officer who shared Canwell's concerns about Communism. Guthman said his wartime experiences had instilled "a deep personal revulsion for tyranny in any form."

Some of the 11 UW faculty members called before the Canwell Committee that summer admitted they had once belonged to the Communist Party. To Canwell's disgust, however, they wouldn't name names. Others refused to answer any questions. Melvin Rader, a tall, bespectacled young man who taught philosophy, denied ever joining the party. His father, a Walla Walla attorney, was a loyal Democrat blackballed for defending Wobblies during the first Red Scare. Rader developed a passion for liberal causes and joined the anti-fascist Popular Front during the 1930s. The Communists tried to recruit him. "[W]hat they didn't realize was that he drew a very sharp line between accepting the Communist philosophy and that of an honest liberal," said a fellow faculty member who acknowledged having been a member of the party in the mid-1930s. Communism was a misguided ideology that had degenerated into cruelty, Rader told friends.

He was interrogated at length concerning testimony that he had attended a high-level Communist Party summer retreat in New York 10 years earlier. Not only untrue but virtually impossible, Rader said. He had taught classes on campus until around the first of August that year, then spent six weeks vacationing with his family at a lodge near Granite Falls north of Seattle. Canwell dismissed the story with his favorite adjective–"phony."

The committee adjourned with a flurry of contempt citations. The UW regents and president, hard-pressed by conservatives, fired three professors. Rader kept his job, but his reputation was tainted. When Rader attempted to pursue a perjury charge against his accuser, he learned that the ex-Communist "expert witness" had fled to New York. A judge

Albert Canwell, left, meets with UW President Raymond Allen, center, and Professor Melvin Rader. *Seattle Times* photo

there refused to extradite him to a state he said was squiggling with Communists and fellow travelers.

Elmer Todd was outraged by Rader's predicament. "This is wrong," he told McGrath. "You just don't treat people this way." Guthman long remembered McGrath telling him, "It's obvious the committee isn't going to settle this. And the courts aren't going to settle it. Only one side of the story has been told. It's time for this newspaper to do its job and find out the truth."

Guthman drove to Granite Falls to see if he could find evidence to back up Rader's story that he'd been vacationing with his family when he was supposedly in New York for indoctrination. The Canyon Creek Lodge had burned down, but the former owner lived nearby. "I asked if I could see the register for the summer of 1938. She said the Canwell Committee already had been there." She remembered an investigator saying, "There it is—Rader—1938," as he thumbed through the pages. He'd taken them with him, leaving her a receipt. She showed it to Guthman.

Confronted with this news, Canwell and his investigators said they had a file card from the lodge that indicated the Raders had stayed there in 1940, not 1938. They claimed to know nothing about a register from 1938. Guthman was just "cooking up this phony Rader cause celebre," Canwell said years later.

Guthman needed more evidence. Professor Rader recalled checking out books from the library. He'd made bank deposits and ordered new eyeglasses. Guthman meticulously collected library records, deposit slips and receipts. Professor Rader demonstrably was in either Granite Falls or Seattle all the while he was supposedly in New York absorbing the Party line. Everything Rader told him checked out, Guthman assured his editors.

Months passed. It was a huge story, one that would dramatically elevate the reputation of The Seattle Times. Yet the paper sat on it. If Ed Guthman was frustrated, imagine being Melvin Rader. A cloud of suspicion followed him everywhere as the Cold War heated up. Seattle historian Lorraine McConaghy produced a nuanced analysis of why the newspaper was so antsy:

> Raymond Allen, the university president, was out of town throughout the summer of 1949, and the paper ... delayed publication until his return in hopes that he would take some official action that would provide "a peg" for the Rader stories. Guthman recalls that Todd and McGrath phoned Canwell and informed him of Guthman's evidence, inviting him to visit the Times offices. Canwell did not come. When Allen returned, Todd and McGrath decided to bring the evidence to him, hoping that Canwell would join them there. The meeting was finally set, and Guthman began writing day and night, preparing to publish.

Canwell, prodded by Allen, finally arrived on campus and "spent a tense four hours with Rader, Allen and Guthman." Afterward, the university president announced that the evidence gathered by Guthman convinced him Rader had been falsely accused. Canwell was sullen and unrepentant.

The Times' double-deck banner headlines on October 21, 1949 declared:

RED CHARGES OF CANWELL FALSE, U. OF W. RULES, CLEARING RADER

About two inches lower, readers were also told: "10 U.S. Reds Get 5 Years, $10,000 Fines; Bail Denied 11 Commies On Appeal." If the message was mixed, it was by design. In exposing Canwell, The Times had admirably done its duty. Most American newspapers were intimidated by the red-hunters. Yet in hedging its bets by delaying publication; by artificially "balancing" its front page with a warning that the commies were still out there, and by failing to follow up with editorials accentuating Canwell's reckless disregard for civil liberties, The Times was, at heart, as nervous and conflicted as America in what McConaghy aptly describes as "the perilous climate" of the Cold War.

In 1950, when Canwell sought the Republican nomination to challenge U.S. Senator Warren G. Magnuson, a freewheeling Democrat, The Times found Magnuson "guilty of giving protection to leaders of the Communist line of thought in this state over the years."* The Post-Intelligencer agreed that Magnuson "was following Truman down the path to socialism."

In all, Albert Canwell lost three bids for higher office and slunk bitterly into relative obscurity; Melvin Rader got his life back and Ed Guthman and The Seattle Times won the 1950 Pulitzer Prize for national reporting. Henry MacLeod's son, Alex, who became managing editor of The Times 36 years later, remembers that Guthman "was always referred to at our house as 'Edwin Otto Guthman' as a sign of respect."

---

* "Despite all of their disdain for his politics and [playboy] lifestyle, The Times was not reluctant to call on Magnuson for help of a most delicate nature," Shelby Scates wrote in his 1997 biography of Senator Magnuson. "Elmer Todd ... wanted Maggie's help to 'locate someone off on a spree ...in a bad crowd.' The someone apparently was "one of Blethen's sons, a prodigal." Magnuson told Scates he had done his best on behalf of the Blethen offspring, but did not disclose the result of his efforts. Most likely it was an attempt by Todd to dissuade "Judge" Blethen from his alliance with the Ridders.

Guthman temporarily left journalism in 1961 to become Robert F. Kennedy's spokesman at the Justice Department. They had met while investigating Teamsters union corruption and became close friends. Guthman became national editor of the Los Angeles Times in 1965. During Watergate, he won a spot on Nixon's enemies list, which he took as a badge of honor. Guthman believed McCarthyism could have been derailed early on "if East Coast editors had had half the courage" displayed by Todd and McGrath. "Innocent people were terrified by their own government. It should never have happened."

Frank Blethen Jr. was in kindergarten when Melvin Rader was exonerated by The Times. As Blethen was moving up at the paper, Henry MacLeod told him why Elmer Todd, Russell McGrath and Ed Guthman mattered so much. Blethen finally met Guthman not long before the newsman's death. "When he told the Rader story to an auditorium full of our editors and reporters, it was just magic. Here's a story where a publisher said, 'People shouldn't be treated like that.' An editor absolutely agreed and a great reporter uncovered the truth. We've won eight more Pulitzer Prizes since 1980. People ask me, 'What Pulitzer are you most proud of?' thinking I'm going to talk about the ones on my watch. And I say, 'The first one, because that's the one that took real courage.' Ed Guthman is one of my heroes. He set the standard for our family's commitment to public-service journalism."

7 | The Third Edition

At 76, Elmer Todd understood youth must be served. If he was nervous about relinquishing day-to-day management of the newspaper to the third-generation Blethens in 1949, he kept it to himself. They owned the store. Of his old friend's sons, he judged 36-year-old Bill Blethen, the Yale graduate, readiest by far. Bill became publisher. Bill's half-brother, Frank, older by nine years, was named company president as a consolation prize. Frank's interests centered on the production side of the business. Jack Blethen, 31, became vice president and remained in the newsroom.

Chairman of the board for the rest of his days, Todd was no figurehead. He had arrived with the Gold Rush and would go out with the Space Needle. His snowy mustache was the frosting on a wise smile. When they ignored his advice, bad things usually happened. The newsroom would miss his hands-off policy.

As Bill Blethen was settling into the publisher's office at Fairview and John, the Post-Intelligencer was staking its claim to supremacy closer to downtown at Sixth and Wall. The morning daily's new $4 million headquarters was crowned by an instant icon—a mammoth globe. "It's in the P-I" rotated at its equator and a proud neon eagle was perched atop the North Pole.

During World War II, when the rivals dueled with "extra" editions on big news from the battlefields, circulation was neck and neck. Then as the war was winding down, Todd launched a clever—and prescient—national marketing campaign. "War's end will mark the Dawn of the Era of the Pacific," the eye-catching ads said. The Times was already "the

The Times newsroom in the 1940s: At desks in the foreground, from left: Bob Barr, Chuck Carson, Bob Patterson, Paul Staples, R.H. "Skipper" Calkins. Standing at the teletype machine is Mel Sayre. To his left are Henry MacLeod, Don Magnuson, Leo Sullivan and Fred Earp. Behind Sayre are Molly Sapera and Bob Twiss. *MacLeod Family Album*

preferred newspaper in 7 out of 10 homes in this prosperous city," and Seattle was "just beginning to grow!" By 1950, The Times had a 25,000 weekday circulation lead—it would never again be topped—thanks to its Seattle-centric news product and superior carrier force. Its 3,500 newsboys were rewarded with medals, prizes and picnics and regularly praised in print, the tradition that began with Alden J. Blethen. On Sundays, however, the P-I was 24,000 ahead. Its reach was wider, with circulation throughout southwest Washington and east to Wenatchee and Yakima. Royal Brougham's zippy sports pages and Hearst's popular syndicated features were a big draw. With Emmett Watson and Doug Welch writing witty columns, the P-I was a livelier paper, with more bylines and fewer stuffy rules. Ed Donohoe, whose acerbic column in the Teamsters' Washington state house organ was a must read, famously dubbed The Seattle Times "Fairview Fanny." And it fit. Times editorials, to the chagrin of many in the newsroom, read like

Chamber of Commerce press releases. People of color—other than crossover entertainers like Harry Belafonte, "the popular Negro singer," Japanese "violin prodigies" and "Filipina Beauties on Tour"—were seldom seen in the news columns. The Club Life & Society section, established in the 1930s by the redoubtable Virginia Boren and carried on by Dorothy Brant Brazier, featured page after page of well-bred young brides and social-register matrons boosting Children's Orthopedic Hospital. To borrow a word often used in the chatty "Thoughts While Reading The Times" column by Carl E. Brazier Sr., The Times saw itself as a "responsible" newspaper, a welcome nightly visitor, as it were. In its pages, "mid-century Seattle was white, self-satisfied and affluent."

Puget Sound's postwar economy was on a roll, thanks to Boeing, the Port of Seattle and tens of thousands of newcomers putting down roots. Elmer Todd believed The Times needed a visionary manager who could also do the math. Overtaking the Post-Intelligencer once and for all would require more revenue. He'd had his eye on a sharp young CPA at Touche, Ross & Company, the prestigious accounting firm. Todd liked everything about Weldon J. "Jerry" Pennington. He was smart, confident, competitive and a self-made man. After working his way through college, Pennington became an FBI agent during World War II. He was a man's man who played a ferocious game of handball, jogged daily and avoided the three-martini Washington Athletic Club lunches that often left Frank and Bill Blethen groggy by 1:30. Pennington had a favorite saying for something really good: "That's a 10-strike!" At Todd's urging, the Blethen brothers hired the 32-year-old accountant as their chief financial manager in 1951. As decisions go, it was a 10-strike.

As strikes go, the walkout in 1953 by 250 Seattle Times reporters and editors, backed by 450 members of the mechanical unions, was far more than the Blethens bargained for when they dug in their heels that July. The paper suspended publication for 95 days and the Post-Intelligencer reaped the windfall. The mechanical unions had joint contracts with both dailies, but workers at the P-I stayed on the job while picket lines encircled The Times.

In the 17 years since its landmark strike against the Post-Intelligencer, the American Newspaper Guild had become a robust union, though journalism was still viewed as a craft rather than a profession. Newsroom wages were abysmal at smaller papers and middling at best for experienced reporters on metros. The International Typographical Union, meantime, was engaged in a struggle with publishers over union jurisdiction and job security as automated typesetters began to displace workers. Between 1951 and 1961, 288 American newspapers were impacted by strikes.

At The Times in 1953, the Newspaper Guild sought an across-the-board wage increase of 7.85 percent. The Blethens offered 3.5 for those earning less than $100 a week and 5 percent for their better-paid newsroom workers. Experienced reporters at The Times earned a minimum of $102 per week; senior copy desk editors were paid $110. Times management was aggrieved by the walkout, telling *Editor & Publisher* magazine that "a substantial number of Times employees receive premium salaries, above the minimum," a practice initiated by C.B. Blethen after the 1936 strike. The Guild's rejoinder was that a substantial number were seriously underpaid.*

The Federal Mediation and Conciliation Service entered the stalemate in mid-September. On October 3, the Guild settled for raises of around 6 percent. Twelve days later, the newspapers' joint negotiations with the printers, pressmen and other mechanical unions were finally settled. The reporters' deal looked better than theirs. The International Typographical Union already had the sinking feeling life would never again be the same. The Guild, though, was pleased with its gains, confident it would be a long time before either of the dailies called their bluff again. In the Hearst boardroom there was surely glee over turnabout being fair play. In 1936, C.B.

---

* A legendary newsroom story from the 1953 strike features "Round John" Reddin, the Jackie Gleasonesque police-beat reporter for The Times. Reddin was lounging on a cot at the police station when a cop stuck his head in the door and said, "Hey, John, still on strike?" Reddin yawned and nodded. "What's the strike all about?" the cop persisted. "Better working conditions," said Reddin.

Blethen had expressed outrage that a handful of "radicals" had shut down the city's pioneer newspaper, but he continued to publish. "Now it was the P-I's turn," the Guild would observe. The morning paper's ad lineage in August of 1953 "soared to 1.9 million lines, compared to 932,121 lines in August 1952," and its editions were almost twice normal size.

On October 19, The Times celebrated its return with happy-face hoopla—"the biggest bonanza of comics in Seattle newspaper history." It offered 19 full pages of funnies, and 60 more over the next week, to bring its readers up to date. Did Daisy Mae and Li'l Abner have their baby? In "Terry and the Pirates," had Buck Wing been rescued from the Communists? (Reds *were* everywhere.)

The Blethens expanded their plant to accommodate new color presses, hired more reporters and began to gnaw away at the Post-Intelligencer's Sunday lead. Hearst fought back, and Seattle was treated to a classic circulation war. State Senator Albert D. Rosellini, an ambitious Democrat from Seattle, made headlines by setting out to uncover vice, which was largely out in the open. He was elected governor in 1956. Ed Guthman and his energetic new sidekick, Don Duncan, chased down bid-contract abuses in the state's purchasing department under the new administration. Scandals sold papers. So did sports. At the Post-Intelligencer, Royal Brougham brokered a legendary basketball game between Seattle University's jump-shooting Chieftains and the Harlem Globetrotters. (The collegians won in a stunner behind the play of their All-American O'Brien twins.) Bob McCausland drew wry cartoons about the exploits of "Hairbreadth Husky," the University of Washington's resurgent football team. At The Times, Georg Meyers, a meticulous investigative reporter who also wrote gracefully, was poised to move to the sports page, joining the popular Lenny Anderson, one of the best baseball writers in America.

Duncan, Marshall Wilson and the effervescent Constantine "Gus" Angelos were rising stars in The Times newsroom. There was an undercurrent of frat-house resentment over the notion it was a staid place compared to the P-I, aka "The Pig's Eye." The Times had just as many bottle-in-the-bottom drawer tipplers and merry pranksters as the competition, according to Duncan, who didn't drink but was a connoisseur of newsroom mischief. There were flaming waste baskets, yo-yo contests and bulletin-board howlers clipped from other papers. Cub reporters consigned to the Saturday night shift underwent hazing: They couldn't take a dinner break until they accomplished the practically impossible feat of tossing a paper clip onto a nail hammered atop a doorsill. Though each newsroom was out to scoop its rival, the insult-swapping was mostly good natured. Several Times reporters had worked for the P-I and vice versa, notably Emmett Watson, whose friend Lenny Anderson joined him at the P-I in the 1960s. Over the next 50 years, some couples—married or otherwise engaged—had conflicting allegiances. Some even ended up on opposite sides of picket lines.

Constantine "Gus" Angelos and Don Duncan, in the background, work on stories in The Times newsroom in the 1960s. *MacLeod Family Album*

The Seattle Times' 1,200 employees included a doorman—an old fellow named Roy who provided "a touch of cap-tipping courtesy" as he opened the heavy front doors for women. The Times was a self-contained world, right down to a barber shop. Behind it was a rest room, complete with chaise lounge. Duncan was getting a trim one afternoon in the late 1950s when the barber remarked, "You're sure getting a lot of bylines." To which Duncan replied, "They're working me to death and they don't pay that much!" Bill Blethen, snoozing after lunch, rousted himself from the couch, popped out and barked, "So we don't pay you enough, Duncan?" Duncan recalls stammering, "Well, nobody can pay me enough, sir!"

There was frustration in the newsroom that the news "hole"—the column inches allotted for stories and photos—was too skimpy. Reporters groused to Henry MacLeod that the paper's motto ought to be "All The News That Fits We Print." MacLeod was both city editor and ex-officio chaplain. "Henry" to everyone, he was serious minded yet an apostle of civility. He cared about his troops. When reporters and photographers returned to the office soaking wet after covering a plane crash, MacLeod sent out for dry socks and hot food. He was a great shirt-sleeves editor who relished working side by side with talented reporters but hated dealing with conflict. He gave people long leashes (sometimes too long) and salved wounds.

Some said Duncan's talents as an investigator and breaking-news reporter were squandered because he could bang out a compelling human-interest yarn in nothing flat. Emmett Watson called him "the energizer bunny." The truth was that "Dunc" loved writing about real people and happily accepted an offer to become a daily columnist. "I got tired of seeing the little guys in government lose their jobs or become objects of derision as a result of our stories while the guys at the top were untouched. I also wondered, sometimes aloud, that we seemed to look the other way when private enterprise screwed the public."

That both papers failed to report one of the most storied moments in aviation history might be evidence of Boeing's clout in the mid-1950s when the planemaker employed some 35,000 in King County.

The huge crowd ringing Lake Washington for the 1955 Gold Cup hydroplane race was electrified when Alvin "Tex" Johnston, Boeing's swashbuckling test pilot, couldn't resist making two 360-degree barrel rolls over the course in the prototype of the company's game-changing 707 jetliner. Boeing president Bill Allen told Duncan years later he was "completely startled" the first time it happened. He surmised Johnston had turned too quickly and was forced to roll the aircraft. When it happened again, he concluded his test pilot was either off his rocker or the priceless airplane was in serious trouble. The company's retired public relations man told Duncan his white-faced boss turned to him after the first barrel roll and said, "I don't think we should have anything in the papers about that." Fat chance. There were at least 200,000 eyewitnesses. Nevertheless, the next day's papers failed to mention the incident. Rumor had it that Boeing quashed the story. In 1990, when a long-awaited tell-all book by Tex Johnston detailed the stunt, Duncan talked again with the former PR manager. He insisted "the press just dropped the ball," likely because most reporters were caught up in the story of Seattle's *Miss Thriftway* losing a disputed decision to a boat from Detroit. Duncan scoffs. "It was either pressure on the publishers or the unwritten law" at both papers that Boeing controlled what was news. "That's how much power the company had," Duncan says. When a Times reporter got caught trying to pass off a Boeing press release verbatim as a news story, he escaped with a wrist slap.

Coziness could produce dividends. Bob "Twister" Twiss, the longtime aviation editor, frequently played cards with Boeing's public relations people and came up with scoops on new orders. Boeing executives apparently believed the chunky, cigar-chewing newsman had either a mole in sales or spies at the Olympic Hotel where airline executives stayed when deals were being consummated. "They never figured out who his sources were, and it drove Boeing up the wall," a longtime colleague remembered. Younger reporters and editors resented that Twiss, seemingly "impregnable in his office," pretty much did whatever he wanted, especially with his travel section. Well into the 1970s, Boeing remained "the biggest sacred cow in the State of Washington."

8 | Changing Times

TWO world's fairs, half a century apart, were seminal events in Seattle history and a circulation manager's dream.

Once sold on the idea, Bill, Frank and Jack Blethen boosted what became "Century 21" with the same sort of fervor their grandfather had heaped on the 1909 Alaska-Yukon-Pacific Exposition. Colonel Blethen believed the A-Y-P would showcase Seattle as the gateway to not just the Klondike but the entire Pacific Rim. He was right. The fair drew 3.7 million visitors and broadened the city's cultural horizons. The grounds of the University of Washington, where the fair was held, were transformed by the Olmsted Brothers, America's foremost landscape architects.

Why not do it again, bigger and better, on the 50th anniversary of the first fair? Downtown businessmen were worried about a sense of civic "sluggishness" and competition from the suburbs. Northgate had a new shopping mall with free parking. Ross Cunningham, who'd been at the 1955 luncheon where the idea for a latter-day fair was hatched, often boasted with little exaggeration "that with a quick call or two, he could easily launch a civic movement." With the Blethens' blessings, the newspaper's associate editor headed straight to Olympia to lobby for startup money.

In 1957, the Soviet Union gave the fair its compelling "Space Age" science-and-technology theme when it launched *Sputnik*, the world's first artificial satellite. America got the shivers as the Cold War advanced to outer space. "For the first time," warned U.S. Senator Henry M. Jackson, the hawkish Washington Democrat, "our country is losing a scientific and engineering race which we were determined to win." Jackson and his seatmate, Appropriations Chairman Warren G. Magnuson, opened doors at NASA and the National Science Foundation, secured funds for a U.S. Science Pavilion and prodded Boeing to get with the program. Postponements and squabbling over which site was best frustrated Edward E. "Eddie" Carlson, the dynamic hotel executive who headed the World's Fair Commission. "More than once Ross Cunningham, Carlson's favorite confidant, talked him out of stopping the project," Murray Morgan recalled. "More than once a Times editorial, or a column by [the paper's arts critic] Louis Guzzo defending some aspect of the civic center concept gave new heart" to the organizers. When the Space Needle passed 400 feet, The Times launched a weekly column by the construction superintendent for the steel supplier.

The Seattle Times had a landmark moment of its own as the countdown to the fair captured the city's imagination. For the six-month period ending March 31, 1960, it had overtaken the Post-Intelligencer for supremacy on Sunday—252,614 to 249,151. The Times had pulled ahead to stay on weekdays during the 1940s, but not since 1921, when Hearst purchased the P-I, had The Times led on Sunday. The P-I was one of the few metropolitan morning newspapers losing ground to an afternoon competitor. The Times enjoyed a substantial readership advantage in the city and its growing suburbs, as well as Everett and much of Snohomish County as freeway construction advanced. Advertisers noticed. So fat was The Times on Sundays that some advertisers were kept waiting. It was also happening on Wednesdays and Thursdays when supermarkets ran page after page of ads. Preprinted inserts came later. Knowledgeable observers were amazed that Hearst, with far deeper pockets, was dithering away its morning advantage.

America had been moving toward one-newspaper cities since the early 1950s. "Several developments began the erosion," John Morton, a leading industry analyst, observed in *American Journalism Review*:

Most important, of course, was the

> spread of television, which captured an ever-growing part of the leisure time people had spent reading newspapers, especially afternoon newspapers. Local TV news competed directly with afternoon papers; the rapid growth of local radio added news competition as well. Television and radio also captured a growing share of ad revenue that newspapers need to survive. [Then] with suburban sprawl and traffic congestion, it became difficult to deliver a timely newspaper beyond city limits.

You don't need many reels of microfilm to notice the difference in Seattle's daily newspapers before and after the world's fair, particularly The Times, which had been dowdier than the P-I. The writing in both papers, though still gee-whiz over the celebrity of the day, was brighter. Bylines were everywhere. There was less grip-and-grin and more real photojournalism. Classical music and the other fine arts were covered with more verve. Dueling special sections, replete with color and graphics, catered to regular readers and visitors alike. At 380 pages, the world's fair souvenir edition published by The Times was its largest edition ever.

The "Fabulous Fair in Seattle" was hailed on the cover of *Life* magazine as a coming-out party. It didn't just rain all the time in Seattle. Each day offered a smorgasbord of celebrities. John Glenn and Wernher von Braun rode the Monorail together. (It being curiously lost on most that the first American to orbit the Earth had been sent aloft by Hitler's rocket man, a scientist the U.S. deemed too valuable to be consigned to the dock at Nuremberg.) Billy Graham warned that God—not Russia or America—would "rule the world of tomorrow." And Elvis, exuding pheromones, "blazed a glittering path like a glowing comet across the World's Fair grounds" that September. Dick Moody of The Times and the P-I's Jack Jarvis were nearly trampled by a throng of swooning schoolgirls.

Century 21 ran for six months in 1962 and attracted 10 million visitors. It left Seattle with an iconic landmark and a new civic center that celebrated science, the arts and entertainment. The Seattle Symphony Orchestra acquired a proper concert hall. The former Washington State Pavilion became home court for the SuperSonics of the National Basketball Association, the city's first modern-era major-league franchise. Some, however, saw the fair as a pseudo space-age Potemkin village where winos and low-rent expendables were swept under the welcome mat and minorities relegated to housekeeping and busboy jobs.

In the 1960s, The Seattle Times, like the city itself, had one foot in the future and the other stuck in the past. With the strong backing of both dailies, a group of civic activists led by Jim Ellis, a visionary bond attorney, finally won voter support for a new utility. The Municipality of Metropolitan Seattle—"Metro"—was tasked with cleaning up Lake Washington. Large stretches were off-limits to swimmers. The effluent of unregulated growth—fecal matter, oil, antifreeze and insecticides—had percolated for decades.

So had vice. Mayor Gordon S. Clinton, a clean-cut young ex-FBI agent, took office in 1956 on a progressive platform. He was an early backer of Metro, championed a regional transportation plan and established a human-rights commission. Clinton's promise to root out police corruption collided with the "tolerance policy" Colonel Blethen helped institute half a century earlier. By the 1950s, proponents argued that allowing semi-organized crime was the best defense against organized crime. As Clinton was leaving office in 1964, The Times editorialized that one could "safely assume" pinball machines and other forms of gambling soon would be given "looser rein." There was "widespread belief in political circles that a majority of the citizens of Seattle want it that way" and ample "evidence to support this contention." Ross Cunningham believed his old friend, County Prosecutor Charles O. Carroll, was keeping The Mob out of King County. Carroll flatly denied there was ever any such thing as a tolerance policy, reminding critics that he had launched a probe of illegal gambling when he became prosecutor in 1948. That "crackdown" blew over in a hurry. "If you cleaned this city up," Seattle police joked, "we'd all have to go on welfare 'cause none of us could live on our salary." The wages of sin were substantial. Prostitution, cardrooms, bingo parlors and pinball machines produced profits and payoffs that "exceeded a hundred million dollars a year in Seattle," wrote William J. Chambliss, a sociologist who went undercover during the early 1960s to explore vice in King County.

Henry MacLeod, by all accounts the best-liked man in the building, was elevated to managing editor of The Seattle Times in the spring of 1960 when Publisher Bill Blethen abruptly fired the legendary Russell McGrath. It was a stunning development.

The publisher visited every department almost every day but never stayed long in the newsroom. He relied on Cunningham to keep him in the loop. Bill Blethen's reputation for not interfering with his top editors was burnished by scuttlebutt filtering from the copy desk that he summarily rejected requests by bigwigs to keep their names out of the paper for drunken-driving arrests and other embarrassing incidents. (Blethen, the story goes, said the rule also applied to himself and his brothers.) Others said that when Blethen meddled he took care to cover his tracks. It was rare, in any case, for someone to be fired at The Times, especially someone like McGrath, who had joined the paper in 1919. The Times was family. Typical was the story of an oldtimer who took ill "and was carried for over a year at full salary."

There are two versions of why McGrath got the ax. Don Duncan insists it was because McGrath let the New York Times News Service lapse. When McGrath asked his copy editors why so few New York Times stories made it into the paper, he was told they were "just too damn long," according to Duncan. The local news hole was already tight. Bill Blethen reportedly came unglued over breakfast when he picked up the P-I and read a three-column front-page announcement that screamed neener-neener. Henceforth, the story said, "the vast news-gathering resources of perhaps the greatest reporting staff in the world—that of The New York Times—will be at the service of Post-Intelligencer readers EXCLUSIVELY in the Seattle area." That may have been the last straw. MacLeod's son Alex understood that McGrath was fired for failing to heed an order from the publisher to "play down a story regarding some shenanigans by Governor Rosellini." The Times was taking a lot of heat from Democrats for its coverage of the governor. Bill and Jack Blethen, raised as Catholics, may have blanched at the anti-Catholic, anti-Italian prejudice that coursed through Republican criticism of Rosellini and decided the paper should lay off him for a while. Cunningham had started the long-running feud in 1952 by red-baiting Rosellini. Lately, however, he had written some positive columns about the administration's social-service reforms. (Rosellini acknowledged in later years that Cunningham was an astute "student of state government.") The newsroom was aware, too, that the advertising and circulation departments had been complaining that McGrath's commitment to investigative reporting was causing problems.

A few days after MacLeod moved into the managing editor's office, McGrath appeared in the newsroom. "Mr. McGrath to see Mr. MacLeod," he politely informed the receptionist. "We all watched Henry stand to greet him," Duncan recalls. "You could see what was happening through the glass. They spoke for a few minutes, then shook hands. Mr. McGrath walked out, ramrod straight. I thought to myself, 'What a dignified way to go.' It was a poignant moment. He was a great editor."

9 | Growing Pains

THE newsroom took pride in the legacy of Ed Guthman's Pulitzer Prize, but enterprising reporters were often frustrated by the paper's fiefdoms.

Don Duncan and Marshall Wilson were given free rein to probe the dubious financial underpinnings of Ocean Shores, a beachfront development backed by Washington's former boy-wonder Republican attorney general, Don Eastvold. In 1961, however, when Duncan handed in a piece on the regional influence of the John Birch Society, he discovered that digging was subject to limits. The story was a sidebar to a hard-hitting United Press International series The Times was running. City Editor Mel Sayre, a Lou Grant lookalike, spiked it. "Sayre was a short, bald man with strong arms, and one of the best pencil editors in the newsroom, but *very* conservative," Duncan recalls. "Sometimes I rubbed him the wrong way because when I had a great story I wasn't shy about saying it belonged on Page One. But Mel had his biases and had to show me who was boss. 'Who is the city editor of this paper, Mr. Duncan?' he'd demand. Appropriately chastened, I'd say, 'You are, sir!' "

The Times took a flogging in the letters column for publishing the series and for denouncing the Birchers as a "dangerous extremist movement ...wholly committed to the conspiracy theory of history." The editorial, one of the paper's most forceful in years, presumably was written by Ross Cunningham—or at least had his imprimatur. They all did. Cunningham enjoyed confusing his critics. He was a boater and hiker and supported aspects of the growing environmental movement. He was beginning to have his doubts about Vietnam. He smoked his pipe, maintained his trademark "faint, knowing smile," and kept a finger to the wind. Duncan and others—including Cunningham's successor, the fair-minded Herb Robinson—say they never saw him tell a reporter what to write. But even the copy boys who filled the paste pots knew Cunningham was not just the voice of the establishment. He had the publisher's ear; his name opened doors. The prosecutor's office always "timed big announcements for The Times' afternoon press runs, and secretaries waved Times reporters into Chuck Carroll's office without an appointment."

In 1964, when Jack Blethen wanted to endorse Barry Goldwater because he was mad at Lyndon B. Johnson for sending the contract for the TFX fighter jet to Texas, Cunningham talked him out of it. The Times told readers it could reach "no overriding consensus" on the presidential candidates. Not so in the race for governor. To no one's surprise, given its disdain for Rosellini, The Times was enthusiastic about 39-year-old Dan Evans, scoutmaster to a troop of moderate young Republican legislators. Rosellini, seeking a third term, received the P-I's endorsement and blasted The Times at every stop on the campaign trail. Evans was one of the few major-office Republican candidates to escape the Johnson landslide. Cunningham wrote that Goldwater's defeat and Evans' victory represented a "mandate for moderation."

"After John Kennedy's funeral, you could almost feel the G-forces as history began to accelerate," Seattle historian Walt Crowley wrote in his memoir of coming of age in the 1960s.

Moderation faced a test and flunked it earlier in 1964 when Seattle was embroiled in a pitched battle over an open-housing referendum. Blatant red-lining confined most of the city's 27,000 African-Americans to the Central Area; covenants kept Jews out of upscale neighborhoods. The publishers and opinion-page editors at both daily newspapers were largely AWOL from the fight to end housing discrimination. The Post-Intelligencer wondered whether the proposed remedy—an ordinance prohibiting racial and religious discrimination by realtors, lenders and property owners—was "not worse than the disease." The Times declared that civil-rights demonstrations hurt the cause and worried that the rights of property owners "to sell, rent or lease their properties to persons of their own choosing" would be impaired. Civil rights leaders were bitterly disappointed, though not surprised, when the voters resoundingly rejected the ordinance.

Seattle was a microcosm of America's painful struggle with racism. Sixty-five percent of California voters that same year backed a ballot proposition nullifying a fair housing act adopted by the legislature. Watts was in flames by 1965. Racial tensions in Seattle heightened when an off-duty white police officer alleged to have made racist comments killed a black man after a melee in the International District. Henry MacLeod and his 22-year-old son, Alex, an aspiring journalist, joined a throng of Seattleites in a memorial march for Martin Luther King Jr. They collected Russell McGrath along the way and held hands during the singing of "We Shall Overcome."

Though The Seattle Times and the times were changing, the newspaper kept sending mixed messages. Its coverage of the tribal "fish-ins" on the Puyallup River avoided stereotypes, while the opinion page saw Indians "on the warpath" with "well-publicized" imported allies like actor Marlon Brando. It wondered "to what extent pre-Civil War treaties and the rights or wrongs of that long-ago era should be applicable today."

Given Jim Ellis' track record with Metro, the municipality that resuscitated Lake Washington, The Times and P-I enthusiastically supported his push for "Forward Thrust," a massive public-works program. Ellis envisioned new parks, community centers, a multipurpose stadium and rapid transit system. His challenge to the Seattle Rotary Club on November 3, 1965—one of the landmark speeches in Seattle history—was heralded with a four-column story boxed in the middle of The Times' front page. A movement with "World's Fair zip" could usher in "a golden age for Seattle," Ellis said. And if the dramatic population growth demographers were confidently predicting came true, he warned that the alternative would be gridlock, smog, clogged storm sewers and a city bereft of greenery—a city with few places for kids to play and a county with acre upon acre of cookie-cutter subdivisions. When the Forward Thrust proposals reached the ballot, the only major

Managing Editor Henry MacLeod, rear, and his assistant, Jim King, review the paper in the 1960s. *MacLeod Family Album*

casualty was rapid transit. The measure would have parlayed $385 million in local bonds into a total of $1.15 billion, thanks to federal matching funds. It was "the stupidest 'no' vote the people of Seattle ever cast," says former U.S. senator Slade Gorton, who pushed through the Forward Thrust enabling legislation when he served in the State Legislature.

As MacLeod mentored a new generation of reporters and editors, The Seattle Times began to shed some of the plodding, paper-of-record provincialism that spoiled Sunday mornings for Peter Bunzel, the publisher of KING Broadcasting's sophisticated new *Seattle* magazine. William Prochnau, who became The Times' Washington correspondent at the age of 26 in 1963 and was dispatched to Vietnam two years later, emerged as one of the finest reporters of his generation. (In the 1970s, Prochnau appeared on Nixon's famous Enemies List, together with Ed Guthman.) Lane Smith's coverage of religion and social-justice issues stood out for its insight and persuasive civility. Don Hannula, a wry Finn who grew up working in his family's fish market in Aberdeen, wrote about Native American fishing rights with instinctive fairness. Gus Angelos' work gave new breadth to the paper's education coverage. Lou Guzzo's assistant editor for the arts was Tom Robbins, an offbeat genius dabbling in psychedelics. After encountering a red-headed wino he took to be an oracle, Robbins "called in well" one day and left for New York. He went on to write best-selling novels that captured the turbulent zeitgeist of the 1960s. One wag said a couple of peyote buds might have done wonders for The Times opinion page, which had dismissed advocates for saving wild places as "mountain climbers and bird watchers." The page was still susceptible to bouts of myopia, despite the arrival of Herb Robinson from Seattle's KOMO-TV, where he was an award-winning newsman. The paper refused to embrace the movement to preserve the historic Pike Place Public Market. As a crucial vote neared in 1971, it scolded the market's "so-called friends" that it was time "to face facts" and get out of the way of progress. Otherwise "the blight" would "creep into adjoining areas" and Seattle could be "robbed of its most exciting opportunity for civic accomplishment since the 1962 World's Fair." Fifty-nine percent of the voters backed the initiative.

When The Times' circulation lead accelerated in the mid-1960s, Bill Blethen worried that winning so decisively could backfire. His inclination was "to stay just far enough ahead of the P-I to keep it hopeful and unsold." Given the growing advantages of the morning market, Blethen feared what an aggressive new owner could accomplish with the Post-Intelligencer. In 1965, however, the P-I acquired a feisty new publisher, Dan Starr, who promptly hired away Guzzo.* Starr also

---

* Starr and Guzzo made for a combustible combination that compounded the P-I's challenges. "Want him back?" Starr reportedly once asked Pennington, less than half-jokingly, after Guzzo proved to be a mixed bag as a managing editor. Guzzo's considerable talent was compromised by his fickle temperament. In the 1970s, when he became aide-de-camp, political mentor and biographer to Governor Dixy Lee Ray, their disdain for the P-I was radioactive.

ordered a redesign and beefed up the newsroom. Jerry Pennington, now second-in-command at The Times, convinced Blethen it was time to take the gloves off. Henry MacLeod happily set about recruiting more staff. One of his sight-unseen hires was H. Mason Sizemore, a 24-year-old copy editor who would become president and chief operating officer of the company within 20 years. Sizemore came to Seattle from graduate school at the University of Missouri, one of America's top journalism schools. He had a bashful, disarming smile, precocious maturity and gumption. When he was editor of the student newspaper at the College of William and Mary in Virginia, Sizemore clashed with the college president. "He booted me out of school for an editorial accusing him of abridging academic freedom. The dean of students told him that if he thought he had problems with me, he should be prepared for what the professional press was going to do to him when it found out that he had kicked me out of school late in my senior year." Sizemore received his degree.

Mason Sizemore. *Seattle Times photo*

The pace of change at The Times accelerated when Jim King, an avuncular newsroom veteran, became MacLeod's assistant in 1966. It was clear to both early on that Sizemore was a comer. Another great hire was Richard Larsen, who had done exceptional work for The Wenatchee Daily World before becoming top aide to a young congressman from Spokane, Tom Foley. Like The Times itself, however, MacLeod took pride "in not rushing into things." Larsen grew impatient parked on the copy desk with small-potato writing assignments and began entertaining other offers. MacLeod got the message. He "threw his arms around him and convinced him to stay" with a promotion to chief political writer. Over the next 23 years, Larsen was one of the most astute and readable political writers in America.

June Anderson Almquist, a brassy trailblazer who had

the best Rolodex in the newsroom, spent 15 years striving to elevate the Society section from bridal showers and teas before MacLeod gave her the chance to oversee the women's-news pages. Now there were stories about birth control and women's rights. Though matrons howled over changes in courtesy titles—they *wanted* to be "Mrs. Norton Clapp"—Almquist finessed things by building bridges between the old and new generations of female readers. An imposing woman with a booming voice, she was "un-ignorable," as Jim King put it. On her first day at work, sporting a hat "the size of a beach umbrella," she stopped traffic in the newsroom. Terry Tazioli, one of her protégés, said she could have been an extra in Wagner's Ring Cycle. Almquist would become the first female assistant managing editor in the history of Seattle newspapering.

Jerry Gay, a long-haired kid with one ear glued to the emergency-frequency scanner, was part of a new generation of Nikon-wielding photojournalists. His photo of four hollow-eyed firefighters taking a break against a muddy embankment after an early-morning house fire won the 1975 Pulitzer Prize for news photography. Coming 25 years after Ed Guthman's Pulitzer, the award was the perfect bookend to Henry MacLeod's career as a hands-on editor.

Frank Blethen Sr., a heavy smoker and drinker, died in his sleep at the age of 63 in January of 1967. Thirty-four days later, Bill Blethen succumbed to a heart attack at 53. Jerry Pennington became company president and de facto CEO. His desk was as orderly as his mind.

The new publisher was C.B. Blethen's youngest son, 49-year-old Jack, who had shown considerable talent as a reporter when he returned from World War II. Some saw Jack Blethen as "the brother most interested in the paper," especially early on when his health was still good. He was in the early stages of Huntington's disease, the cruel neurological disorder that eventually took his life. When he moved into the publisher's spacious corner office, his speech was slightly slurred. Outside work, he had "only a few close friends." His primary interest was the newsroom. Herb Robinson told the other editors that while Jack seemed shy, he participated actively in editorial board meetings "and didn't flinch when an editorial ticked off local big shots." He was, for now, the sole holder of the company's voting stock.

It was Jerry Pennington's fiercely competitive nature—he was a standout wrestler in high school and up and at 'em by 5 a.m. each day—that propelled The Times to an improbable 50,000 circulation lead by the end of the 1960s. It was winning the ad lineage war, too. In 1968, The Times carried 3.4 million inches of advertising; the Post-Intelligencer 2.1 million. The Times expanded its plant to accommodate new presses.

With Elmer Todd as a tutor and Pennington crunching the numbers, Bill and Frank Blethen had left their brother a company that was debt free and grossing some $30 million per year. On the advice of Todd and Pennington, the third-generation Blethens in 1956 had made a decision calculated to ensure the newspaper would be the family's lasting legacy: They reorganized the Blethen Corporation as a holding company, with three classes of stock, according to the Harvard Business School case study sanctioned by the Blethens in 2001:

> Voting shares could only be held by male, blood heirs of the founder. The three brothers each held one-third of those voting shares. (This clause was changed in 1976, when female blood heirs became eligible to hold voting shares...) Male and female blood descendants were permitted to own both classes of dividend-paying shares. Non-family members, such as surviving spouses, could own only nonvoting preferred stock.
> The 1956 agreement required that any further change to the Blethen Corporation by-laws be supported by 80% of the voting shareholders. If any two of the brothers were to die, the surviving heir would retain voting control during his lifetime, after which the voting shares would move to the next generation. ...
> The Blethen Corporation and [Ridder Publications Inc., which in 1974 merged with

Knight Newspapers Inc.] owned the Seattle Times Company. The Seattle Times Company had two classes of shares. Class A preferred shares had no voting power and paid a capped dividend of $1 million. Knight-Ridder owned 65% of these shares. [By 2011] seven Blethen family members and a few non-family shareholders owned the remaining 35%. There were also Class B voting shares. Of these, five fourth-generation Blethen cousins owned 50.5% and 49.5% were owned by Knight-Ridder. ...

Each of the five fourth-generation branches of the Blethen family tree would choose their successors on the Blethen Corporation Board from members of the fifth generation. There were to be 10 seats in all, five for Blethens and five for "broadly experienced" Pacific Northwest business people "dedicated to the continuance or re-establishment of The Seattle Times as the dominant Washington State daily newspaper, and familiar with the Blethen family." All 10 board members, moreover, also had seats on the Seattle Times Company Board.

Knight-Ridder, a publicly-traded company, and any of its successors as the minority shareholder in The Times, were out-numbered and out-flanked. When this became increasingly clear, they didn't like it.

A brainy young writer named David Brewster reported for duty on the copy desk at The Times in 1968. Brewster had worked summers on a New Jersey daily while studying for a master's degree in English from Yale. Academics of that era often sniffed that journalism was a trade, not a profession, Brewster knew better. After three years of teaching entry-level literature and writing courses at the University of Washington, he was looking for a way back into journalism. Everyone told him The Times, with its oak cashier cages and quiet corridors, "felt like a bank," but there was an opening and Brewster took it. If he had visited the Post-Intelligencer first and been invited to share a break-time joint on the roof with Tom Robbins, he might have landed there instead. The budding novelist was back in town as part of what P-I writer Mike Lewis recalled as "the most literarily gifted, counterculture copy desk" anywhere in America. Robbins' fellow toilers included Frank Herbert, whose science fiction stories were finding a wider audience, and the legendary Darrell Bob Houston, a disciple of Jack Kerouac. When the Dodgers' Sandy Koufax struck out 18 batters in one game, Houston's headline was "KKKKKKKKKKKKKKKKKoufax!"

Brewster didn't stay long at The Times. But it was long enough to form some lasting impressions and gain entrée to inner sanctums. He offered a rare inside look at "Fairview Fanny" in a fascinating 1969 piece for *Seattle* magazine, where he had become a writer and editor. Brewster told of wandering the building in his free time after mastering the paper's fussy stylebook. He encountered an artist empowered to airbrush Daisy Mae's cleavage or any other "unseemly female exposure" that might otherwise slip into the comics and scandalize a nuclear family. He took note of the fine work being done by Duncan, Hannula and others, but also saw the silos and speed bumps. Doing time on the copy desk, with only a column or two to break the monotony, Brewster and Dick Larsen had chafed at the paper's inertia. The Seattle Times, in fact, was a lot like most metropolitan newspapers—and America itself—on the cusp of societal upheaval. Many reporters were "so tired of all the Eagle Scouts, golden wedding couples, boys and girls of the month, and begonia raisers on Bainbridge," Brewster wrote, "that they are wont to call The Times the 'country's largest weekly.'"

When Brewster made his return visit, he snagged an audience with Jack Blethen. As they moved past pleasantries, he encountered the "touch of peevishness" that would grow more pronounced in the years to come. Ross Cunningham, in contrast, granted Brewster a long, reminiscent interview. When Brewster ventured that some readers believed The Times—and Cunningham himself—were falling behind the times, the opinion page director furrowed his brow, gazed out the window for a moment, and then to his visitor's astonishment agreed that the criticism was justified. "In fact, the whole newspaper industry is out of date," Cunningham said. If that was an epiphany, it probably had something to do with an embarrassing story in the competition that was the talk of the town.

Marshall and John Wilson, who weren't related but soon became known as "The Wilson Boys," had taken up the Guthman mantle as the paper's marquee investigative team. They began digging into the police payoff network and peeled back the covers on a whole series of sleazy relationships. It was the Post-Intelligencer, however, in concert with *Seattle* magazine and KING-TV, that produced the sensational 1968 exposé that spelled the beginning of the end of Chuck Carroll's long political career. A story by Orman Vertrees, one of the P-I's best diggers, revealed that the most powerful politician in King County was cozy with a shadowy figure named Ben Cichy. Cichy was a kingpin of the "non-profit" coalition that had held the master license for pinball operations in King County since 1942. Its profits were estimated to be $5 million a year.

Times reporters and editors were doubly chagrinned at a sidebar by Shelby Scates, a well-traveled reporter whose hard-nosed style personified the P-I. The story detailed Cunningham's longtime friendship with Carroll and revealed that the opinion-page director had brow-beat the Municipal League into upgrading the prosecutor's rating from "above average" to "superior" in a recent election. Cunningham's old-boys-club loyalty to Carroll left a taint on a long career that included praiseworthy work. He had been a strong advocate for Metro, Forward Thrust, Century 21 and an array of charities. Times reporters and editors were reminded of the dangers of entangling alliances long after his retirement in 1977.

When John Hamer arrived at The Seattle Times from *Congressional Quarterly* in 1977 and joined the opinion page staff he was shocked to learn there was no written ethics code. He talked it over with three other young staffers, Mike Fancher, Alex MacLeod and Ross Anderson. They became an ad hoc committee, studying codes collected from major newspapers around the nation before drafting one for The Times. Its tenets are unchanged today: Because a newspaper "is no ordinary business," the conduct of its employees, especially news and editorial staff members, "must be above reproach." Avoid conflicts of interest, the code admonishes, particularly with politicians, other public officials and institutions. Accepting any gift of significant value—notably travel, lodging, meals and liquor—is forbidden. Plagiarism is a grievous matter.

But in the beginning, to the idealistic drafters' surprise, newsroom management and the Newspaper Guild balked. "So we walked it around the newsroom and got at least half the staff to sign it and agree to abide by it," Hamer remembers. "This may have been unprecedented in the history of American journalism." For Fancher, the episode was an instructive preview of issues he would face when he became executive editor. "The fact that the newsroom staff was unionized created serious complications for introducing something like an ethics code," Fancher says. "I didn't understand that complexity when our merry band of ethicists created our code and presented it to Jim King, our editor. There was no way management could adopt a code submitted by union members without any involvement with the union. That would be a form of direct bargaining with the members. Later, Jim agreed that management could adopt a code under the management rights clause of the contract. I was in management by then. We adopted a code that was quite similar to the one staff members had proposed, but we did it without any direct staff input." The most troublesome aspect of the code, Alex MacLeod recalls, was its prohibition on accepting free travel, which would put an estimated $60,000 dent in the newsroom budget. The travel section under the purview of the enterprising Bob Twiss capitalized on free flights and cruises. Enter Jerry Pennington. The Times' president supported the ethics code and assured King he would underwrite travel, just not as much as Twiss was accustomed to. Twiss bitched about all the new "kids" and their rules. "It was just a small part of moving The Times forward," MacLeod says.

10 | An Irrational Decision

In 1967, when the father he never really knew died, Frank Blethen Jr. was more angry than sad. He made what he calls "an irrational decision." He decided he would go to work at The Seattle Times after all, at least for a year.

He was 21 and a senior at Arizona State University, majoring in business, when his father died in his sleep three months after marrying for the fifth time. The last time they'd talked, his father poured himself his third before-dinner cocktail and asked which department he wanted to start in after graduation.

"I'm not going to come to work here."

"What! Are you serious?"

"Yes. I have absolutely no interest in working here."

"Why have you been coming up here to work every summer?"

"Because I wanted to get to know you."

That his father was speechless spoke volumes.

Frank Sr., only four when his mother died of pneumonia in 1908, had never learned how to be a father. His own was indifferent, and his stepmother made no pretense that her boys weren't special. "My father spent his entire life searching for a mother," Frank Jr. says. "His brother, who ended up being disowned, had one reaction to their unhappy childhood. My father's reaction was to be very passive and submissive to his dad, 'The General.' He learned to be likable. He would walk around the newspaper shaking hands and saying 'Hi.' People liked Frank, but he could not develop any interpersonal relationships with his own children. He was a lonely man. He was 63 when he died but looked 83."

Frank Jr. and his sister Diane grew up in Arizona with a nurturing single mom. "We had a *wonderful* mother. I truly didn't know I was supposed to have a dad until I hit my teen years," Frank Jr. says. Kathleen Ryan Blethen and her kids spent time in Seattle practically every summer. Her vivacious sister, Sheila, was married to Dave LeClercq, a Lake Union boat builder who loved kids. Those were the best of times, Frank Jr. recalls. He adored his aunts and uncles and grew close to his Ryan-side cousins. Back home in Arizona, school was often a struggle. During his 30s, when he realized he had Attention Deficit Disorder and was also mildly dyslexic, a lot of things snapped into focus. "ADD people learn in different ways. It was frustrating to have to work so hard for C's. Junior high was when I really started getting angry. I never got a birthday card or Christmas card from my dad; never had a present. When I'd try to call him he wouldn't take my calls."

Jerry Pennington would. The executive who seemed able to absorb spreadsheets at a glance wasn't always all business. He had embraced Elmer Todd's role as caretaker of the Blethen family trust—and not just the money. Now he would become "the closest thing I ever really had to a father figure and a real mentor," Frank Jr. says. "When my father died, Jerry also became my trustee. I think my dad figured the way he'd deal with me by not having to deal with me was to have Jerry as the go-between. Through Jerry, I started working at the paper during the summer, starting when I was 15. My goal was to try to get to know my dad. I had no intention of living up here or joining the newspaper. I had these vague notions about what I was going to become. I was either going to be a social worker or a veterinarian—not quite knowing what either one entailed.

"I think Jerry essentially told my dad, 'You have to talk to your son.' So every summer on my first day at work I would dutifully go into his office, and he would spend his obligatory 15 or 20 minutes with me. Then at the end of the summer I'd go into his office and he'd spend another 15 or 20 minutes with me. He had no clue how to talk to a kid. He wasn't good with adults, let alone kids. The only summer I didn't work at The Times was when my mom was suing him for some additional child support and it was really ugly. I told Jerry I didn't want to see him at all or be there. That's the summer I worked for my Uncle Dave, caulking those old wooden boats. It was the only time in my life I had biceps, and boy did I sleep well at night. Uncle Dave's work ethic was amazing."

Blethen spent a few weeks in every department at the newspaper, with an emphasis on circulation and the business offices. "You start getting the sense that there's something special about a family business, and that the people who work there think there's something special about it. Then you start reading the paper, getting interested in local news. I'd see Henry MacLeod, the managing editor, having his lunch in the cafeteria, no doubt wanting privacy. But I'd go, 'Mr. MacLeod, can I sit with you and ask you some questions?' 'Oh sure,' he'd say, being very tolerant to a kid."

Frank Jr. for the first time also got to know his Blethen cousins, especially Will and Bob, Bill's sons. They were his age. They all spent part of their summers working at The Times. Jack's sons, John P. and Alden J. "Buster" Blethen IV, were a few years younger.*

Frank Jr. stayed with his Uncle Bill when he came to Seattle to attend his father's funeral. "I barely knew Bill Blethen, but he and his wife Ruth were incredibly gracious to me. Bill told me I should come to work at the paper after graduation."

Two months later he was back—this time to bury Uncle Bill. "Jerry Pennington took me aside and really impressed me with my responsibilities to the family legacy. If my father had lived I probably wouldn't have come to work here. My Uncle Jack was now the publisher."

The first year was, in a word, "miserable," Blethen recalls with a rueful chuckle. The future publisher of The Seattle Times, who now drives a Porsche SUV, arrived in town near broke in a battered Volkswagen to take up his duties as the assistant credit manager. It was 1968, and his own credit was

---

* The first "Buster," Alden J. Blethen III, died in the 1930 motorcycle accident at the age of 20. Alden J. Blethen IV, born in 1951, resembled the uncle he never knew—except for the fact that at 6-5 he was about five inches taller.

tenuous. With college loans to pay off, he had borrowed money from The Times to make the move and rent a tiny apartment. He plunged into work, gained confidence, got married, then found himself as acting credit manager in the middle of the 1971 "Boeing Bust." Seattle's mainstay industry laid off 60,000 workers and barely averted bankruptcy. "When two real-estate guys with a dark sense of humor put up the billboard that said 'Will the last person leaving Seattle turn out the lights,' I hadn't dealt with an account value of probably more than four or five hundred dollars. All of a sudden, I'm representing us in bankruptcy court and Dick Balch, the wacky auto dealer who smashed cars in his commercials, owes us $150,000, which was huge money in 1971."

In another department, young Frank encountered "a complete control freak" who resented being burdened with the latest Blethen whippersnapper. When the man returned from vacation and discovered Blethen had had the temerity to take some initiative, he chewed him out in front of another subordinate, fuming, "You won't do this in *my* newspaper!" Blethen quit on the spot, saying, "This is not *your* newspaper. This is the Blethen family's newspaper. And I'll be damned if I'm ever going to work with anybody like you again!" He was cleaning out his desk when he was summoned back to hear an apology. Pennington talked him into staying. Blethen became purchasing manager and also oversaw building maintenance. He absorbed some unappreciated teasing from his cousins when janitorial services were found wanting. "But it was the best, most concentrated two years of learning I think I've had in my career. I learned all the ins and outs of running a newspaper."

Pennington once intimated to close friends that the Blethens seemed to have "a mean streak." He was stunned, however, by Jack Blethen's reaction in 1974 when he suggested that Frank Jr. was ready for a new challenge as associate publisher of the company's recent acquisition, the Walla Walla Union-Bulletin. "Until then, Jerry hadn't realized Jack harbored any animosity toward me," Frank says. "Indifference, yes—to me as well as his other nephews, Will and Bob, and anger with his own son, John. But now he went ballistic and started ranting, 'You're trying to put Frank into my chair! I'm not going to let him go to Walla Walla!' Jack claimed Jerry had never given his son Buster an even break. Jerry told me it was the first time in all their years together that he and Jack had ever had a major disagreement. I'm thinking 'Holy shit!' But Jerry said, 'I think he'll come around. Just hold on.' "

A few days later, Jack Blethen summoned Pennington. "He can go to Walla Walla on the condition that he's never coming back." Told this, Frank Jr. was incredulous. "I do not accept such a condition."

"Fine," his mentor said. "I told Jack I'd relay the news but that he needs to tell you to your face. You need to tell Jack whatever you need to tell Jack."

Blethen recalls entering the publisher's paneled inner sanctum with trepidation. Jack, never making eye contact, mumbled his condition. His nephew, courage buoyed, rejected it. "Fine," Jack shrugged. He had something else up his sleeve.

Frank Blethen Jr. became associate publisher of the Union-Bulletin at 29 and publisher two years later in 1976. "When Jerry Pennington first talked to me about Walla Walla, he said, 'We've got this great opportunity for you.' What he didn't say, I realized later, is 'You're the only one who will do it for such a small salary!' " The 15,000-circulation Union-Bulletin was one of the state's oldest papers, with roots dating to 1869. It seemed to Blethen that it hadn't changed much in 50 years. "I hired another young guy, Chuck Cochrane, as my first general manager. He was one of the best hires I've ever made; an incredibly competent manager. We resolved that we needed an editor who could shake things up. In hindsight, the paper was so bad, so dowdy-looking and dull, that even if I'd screwed up in my first outing as a publisher nobody would have known."

They didn't screw up and many noticed, especially when the new managing editor was only 25. N. Christian Anderson III, had been the boy-wonder city editor of his hometown paper, the Democrat-Herald in Albany, Ore. He was whip-smart, confident and ambitious. "For someone so young, Chris had amazing instincts as a newsman," Blethen remembers. "The day after Christmas one year I rode my bike down to the office, with my son Ryan, who was about 2, in the back seat. On weekends or holidays, I'd pick up my mail, buy him a candy bar from the vending machine and see if anything was happening. Chris was sitting in the newsroom, practically alone."

"What are you doing in here?" Blethen said. "There's not much news today."

"No, it's a great news day," Anderson said, brightening. "We've got reporters out there where everybody is."

"Where's that?"

"Returning gifts!"

Frank Blethen as the young publisher of The Walla Walla Union-Bulletin. *Seattle Times photo*

The Union-Bulletin's lead story that afternoon, replete with photos, was all about what happens in stores on the day after Christmas. "It was a great lesson for me because Chris was right," Blethen remembers. "Good newspapers, big and small, connect with people. They tell what people are doing and why. Some stories that seem routine can be great in the hands of great reporters and photographers. The same holds true for big stories that nobody else has noticed. Walla Walla's claim to fame in that era—long before the wine industry transformed the area—was that it was home to the state penitentiary." When Blethen arrived, he discovered that the Union-Bulletin's coverage of the prison largely amounted to "press releases that were always favorable to the warden, who was very close to the business community." Anderson's small newsroom set out to explore the consequences of a prison "reform" movement that gave inmate gangs so much latitude that they virtually ran the institution. A Union-Bulletin reporter-photographer team spent months documenting the reality that the tail was wagging the dog. The award-winning series was picked up by The Associated Press and published by The New York Times—even by the Post-Intelligencer. Blethen says he offered the stories to

The Seattle Times first for simultaneous publication. Editors there demurred in a haughty tone Blethen interpreted as "if there's a story there *we'll* tell it." "I'm thinking: 'Man! I hope when I get to Seattle I'm never like that.' "

In the 1970s, when many family-owned papers were acquired by chains, they were usually given a corporate cookie-cutter makeover and strip-mined for profits. If they were mediocre before, they usually stayed that way, and if profits dipped below 20 percent layoffs ensued, usually in the newsroom first. "The Seattle Times Company transformed the Walla Walla paper—and later the Yakima Herald-Republic as well—into one of the best small dailies in America," Blethen says. "I learned important lessons in Walla Walla."

Jim King, who had become editor of The Seattle Times in 1975 when Henry MacLeod retired, took full note of what Blethen, Cochrane and Anderson had achieved, and in 1978 hired Anderson as an associate editor of The Times.*

Blethen returned to Seattle the following year as assistant circulation manager. He and Pennington had defied and out-maneuvered Jack Blethen in a high-stakes struggle over the Blethen Corporation bylaws.

---

* Chris Anderson's arrival in the Times newsroom met with some resentment and resistance. Besides being a much-talked-about prodigy with a headful of ideas, particularly concerning design and features, he was the first person in decades brought in from the outside at such a high level. He didn't stay long. After overseeing the first major redesign of the paper in decades, Anderson at 30 became the youngest editor of a metropolitan newspaper in the U.S. when he was named editor of the Orange County Register in 1980.

11 | Bylaws and Bygones

FRANK WETZEL, a wise and witty newsman, spent 23 years with The Associated Press before he signed on as editor of the Bellevue Journal-American in 1977. The new daily was trying to secure a niche as not just the voice of the booming east side of Lake Washington; it wanted to be seen as a full-service alternative to The Times and P-I. Wetzel offered readers an appraisal of the competition:

> **The Seattle Times:**
> Everyone who works there is 55 years old, white and male. The Times would hire people, male and female, in their 20s and 30s and in two years, presto! They would be 55 and male. The typical Times employee lived in a multi-columned house built in the 1890s, filled with eclectic bric-a-brac, some of it lovely and some of it junk. He felt the house's disrepair could be fixed with a coat of paint. His dullness was virulent.
>
> **The Seattle Post-intelligencer:**
> A 47-year-old male married three times, a semi-reformed alcoholic who vacillates between wild sprees and determined respectability. He dreams of regaining his fortune but his wealthy relatives in the East won't send money.

The P-I's newsroom laughed the loudest, though its median age, like The Times', had declined sharply in recent years with the arrival of some young Turks, notably Eric Nalder, Tim Egan and Joel Connelly. Those who understood circulation and ad lineage numbers worried, however, that their wealthy relatives in the East—the Hearst Corporation—wouldn't send more money. In the meantime, they persevered, ordered doubles after work at the Grove, the watering hole across the street, and kept doing what they did best under their crusty editor, Jack Doughty. The former paratrooper was a throwback to the madcap era of "The Front Page" when reporters would do anything for a scoop, including hiding fugitives in rolltop desks. Shelby Scates and Mike Layton, the P-I's ace legislative reporter, exposed a kickback scheme that led to the indictment of state Rep. Bob Perry, who promptly fled the country. In 1979, after 18 months on the lam, the freewheeling Democrat agreed to surrender to Scates, tell all about how he had "whored and sold his soul" and return to Seattle to face the music. Doughty and Scates chartered a plane, flew to British Columbia, got an exclusive on the way back and delivered their man to a federal marshal. People who miss the P-I know that story by heart. Tenacious Seattle Times reporters like Lou Corsaletti and his sidekick, Dee Norton, who scored scoop after scoop as a federal grand jury probed the police payoff scandal, grumbled that the P-I's stories always seemed splashier. Jim King hired away one of the P-I's prize columnists, Rick Anderson, a blend of Breslin and Royko, and gave him a license to prowl. A red-headed kid named David Horsey, destined to become one of top editorial cartoonists in America, was wooed too, but he liked it at the P-I.

In 1987, when Frank Wetzel became the ombudsman at The Times, Fairview Fanny was in the clover—debt-free, with profits on the rise, launching regional bureaus and zoned editions with a creative efficiency denounced as "rapacious" by worried suburban editors and publishers. In a profile of The Times' corporate character, Wetzel set aside bygones in the interest of ombudsmanlike objectivity. He wrote that his old tongue-in-cheek assessments of the rival papers, "if ever accurate, are certainly not now"—especially his take on The Times, where 41-year-old Frank Blethen Jr. was now in charge. He was "a thoughtful, enthusiastic, sincere, friendly," hard-working executive who had placed "young and vigorous" managers in every department. Mason Sizemore, courteous and self-assured with a plummy Virginia drawl, was president and chief operating officer; Mike Fancher, another of Jerry Pennington's protégés, had advanced from reporter to executive editor in the space of eight years on pure merit. Alex MacLeod, Henry's intense son, was now managing editor. They had high expectations and progressive values. The Times had emerged as an industry leader in hiring women and minorities. "The traits valued among its managers—teamwork, nurturing, openness—are often said to be feminine," Wetzel noted. Times people seldom stamped their feet or yelled, "but a mild yelp of indignation was expressed recently ... and everyone agreed that it felt good."

"I have never been around people so unfailingly polite," Wetzel concluded, wishing out loud that he could hear more passion to "kick butt" and right wrongs. "But sometime in the next three years I may hear someone yell in the newsroom. Then I will have hope."

The jockeying that preceded Frank Blethen Jr.'s 1979 return from exile in Walla Walla and rise to publisher of The Seattle Times was not polite. Behind closed doors there had been yelling, tight-lipped threats and expensive lawyering.

Jack Blethen had hoped that having Frank Jr. out of sight, if not out of mind, in a place about as far from Seattle as one could get and still be in the state would strengthen his hand in grooming his son Buster to succeed him as publisher. His plan, which had far broader implications, was subverted by Jerry Pennington.

Elmer Todd, Pennington's mentor, had saved The Seattle Times for the family by securing the Depression-era refinancing of C.B. Blethen's loans. Now, nearly half a century later, Pennington was putting his job as company president on the line by defying an order he saw as not just unethical but injurious to the Blethens' chances of retaining control of The Times for generations to come.

In 1977, Jack Blethen began prodding Pennington, Frank Jr.'s trustee, to sign off on revisions to the Blethen Cor-

Jerry Pennington. *Seattle Times* photo

poration bylaws—changes that also would have jeopardized Frank Jr.'s chances, as well as those of his cousins Bob and Will, to become publisher. Jack was also on the outs with his eldest son, John Prentice Blethen, a free spirit with a ponytail. "Cut it or don't come back!" Jack declared. John left and didn't come back.* John's brother Buster was now the only fourth-generation Blethen Jack saw as publisher material. Alden J. Blethen IV, a University of Washington graduate, stood out in any family portrait. He was 6-foot-5 and movie-star handsome, with a dashing mustache. Only 26 when he was caught up in the divisiveness, Buster was some six years younger than his cousins. Many say he aspired to be publisher mostly because his father aspired for him to be publisher and would have been neither a good choice nor happy in the job. The fourth-generation Blethens found themselves in an awkward position, perhaps none more so than Buster. Until this juncture, he'd been on good terms with his cousins.

Pennington was adamantly opposed to the bylaw changes. He told Jack Blethen's attorney, Willard Wright, the go-between, that he would take no action without Frank Jr.'s approval. Pennington summoned Frank Jr. to Seattle, ostensibly for a performance review. "We met in a private room at the Rainier Club—not at the Times, which seemed curious at first. Jerry said I was doing a great job at Walla Walla. But now there was something else we needed to talk about. He outlined the

---

* "John P. Blethen probably qualifies as the smartest member of our generation of Blethens because he didn't come to work here," Frank says. "He became a successful investor and avid horseman, as well as one of the best board members The Times' has ever had."

bylaw changes Jack wanted. In essence, they would have given Jack control of all the votes. He already had control of Will's and Bob's, unbeknownst to them. And if he was ever incapacitated, his attorney's law firm would have de facto control of the Blethen Corporation. For Jerry and me, the central issue was not whether Will, Bob or I would have a chance to become publisher; it was that Jack's plan was putting us on a path to cede control of the company to an outside law firm and the eventual loss of family control and stewardship."

When Knight-Ridder's top executives, Lee Hills and Bernard H. "Bernie" Ridder Jr., got wind of Jack Blethen's plan to elevate Buster to publisher they registered their disapproval with a formal letter of protest. Frank was a far more capable manager, The Times' minority partners said. "They had great respect for Jerry Pennington," Frank says, joking that given later disagreements with Knight-Ridder over his stewardship of the company "that letter was the only nice thing they ever said about me." Bernie Ridder's son Tony, who became chairman and CEO of Knight-Ridder in 1995, says, "I think Dad felt that if Knight-Ridder hadn't gone to bat for Frank it very likely could have ended up that Buster Blethen would have been the publisher of The Seattle Times."

Jack Blethen had strengthened his hand a few years earlier in a deal involving Seattle Times Company stock claimed by Frank Blethen Sr.'s fifth wife. Though outside legal counsel advised that the widow's case was specious, Jack took the position that any risk was too great. He and the Blethen Corporation paid her $30,000. Pennington, with Frank Jr.'s consent, agreed to the deal. The catch, which became clear when the next shoe dropped, was that Frank Jr. kept only half his father's voting stock. The other half was returned to the Blethen Corporation. The deal significantly diminished his voting rights as well as his future dividend income.

"I made a serious mistake when I advised you to go along with that," Pennington told Frank Jr. as he described Uncle Jack's proposed bylaw changes, "and I'm not going to make the same mistake again. This is your choice. But I wouldn't do it if I were you."

"I agree, but isn't this going to be a big problem for you with Jack?"

"Yeah," Pennington shrugged, "but years ago I wasn't nearly as secure in my career and my life as I am now, so if I get fired I'll be fine. Don't worry about me. This is the right thing to do."

Pennington believed that if he lost his job, Frank Jr. also would be out on his ear—and he was more worried about that than his own future, according to Blethen. "I didn't know it at the time, but Jerry talked with Bernie Ridder, who said I'd have a publisher's job at one of the Knight-Ridder newspapers if Jack fired me."

If there was one thing Jack Blethen knew for certain it was that Jerry Pennington was far too valuable to fire. Hearst would have scooped him up in a heartbeat to resuscitate the Post-Intelligencer. Pennington had rejected just such an offer, as well as an overture from Hearst president Frank Massi to run the company's entire newspaper division, according to Pennington's son-in-law, Robert Merry. The Ridders, moreover, thought so highly of Pennington that he had served on their board prior to their merger with Knight Newspapers in 1974.

The two men at the top of The Times agreed to disagree as the attorneys for each faction began their minuet. That Frank had to borrow money to pay his attorney fees, while his uncle's were paid by the company testifies to how much faith he had in Pennington's instincts. They picked good lawyers, too—Bill Gates* and one of his firm's budding stars, Rick Dodd. It was Dodd who did most of the detail work on the elegantly precise bylaw changes they offered as a compromise.

When Frank, Will, Bob, John and Buster met formally for the first time to discuss the tedious situation, they agreed that if the newspaper was going to remain with their children, their children's children and many more Blethen generations

---

* Gates' brainy namesake son, who could have passed for 14, had dropped out of Harvard to found a software company with his Lakeside School pal, Paul Allen.

The Blethens in the 1970s, from left, Will, Bob, Jack, Frank and Buster. *Nick Gunderson photo*

to come, they had to be "bound together by core values based on trust and stewardship." Buster nodded but said he still wanted preferential treatment on the publisher track. "You're being selfish!" came one of the mildest replies, Frank remembers with a grimace. "The consensus was, 'We're going to settle this now.' We told Buster that if he was going to be publisher he had to demonstrate he was ready to be publisher. And as long as we got the revisions we wanted, we were going to go forward because what mattered was harmony and perpetuation of the family legacy. We said, 'We won't anoint Buster Blethen publisher, but we'll give him preferential treatment provided he completes a multi-year training program.' If ever someone turned a pig's ear into a silk purse it was Jerry Pennington and Rick Dodd, leading us through a process strewn with emotional landmines. We took what typically is a situation that blows up a multi-generational family business and came to a workable solution."

Jack Blethen agreed to the changes, which included criteria for high-quality outside directors for the Blethen Corporation. That was central to Pennington's vision for the future of

The Times. "Businesses like ours traditionally had been pretty much the family sandbox," Frank says. "Often the boards were made up of your hunting buddies. Which is exactly what Jack Blethen picked for his board."

The three most senior directors henceforth would constitute an executive committee with only one formal power—the selection of a publisher. "We created a preference for a Blethen publisher," Frank says. "Doesn't have to be the *most* qualified person to be publisher, but that person has to be *qualified* to be publisher. You may have a non-family member who is more qualified but you'd be looking at a situation where that individual would be your number two person or something like that. We also did some things in stock structure to help my generation in terms of death-tax planning and philanthropic giving. It was all tied into our rule of unanimity on control, which seriously diminishes the ability of one of the voting shareholders to exercise control over the company. We strengthened the buy-back provisions as well. If a family member fails to do good estate planning or runs into financial trouble there's no ruinous fallout to the Blethen Corporation. The only place that stock can go, for a very, very cheap price, is back to the Blethen Corporation. Our old bylaws also said that no female heirs could be involved in the company."

Buster Blethen in due course removed himself from the publisher track and remained in the advertising department. He ended up reporting to Frank. That was awkward for both at first. "But we came to trust one another. I learned that he—like Will, Bob, John and I—had often chafed under his father's expectations. Buster Blethen was a very good man. When I became publisher, Buster approached me about selling his stock to us—his cousins and his brother. It was our belief that he needed the connection to the family stewardship, and that as his health deteriorated he would need a steady income. We talked him out of selling."

Buster and his father carried a tragic inheritance—Huntington's disease. Buster retired from the newspaper at the age of 38, but served for many more years on the Blethen board and became a strong advocate for the family's stewardship of The Seattle Times. Bedridden in his last years, Alden J.

Blethen IV succumbed to Huntington's at 55 in 2006. He had fought its relentless ravages with courage and humor, friends said, "and lived life to the fullest."

Before returning to the Times as assistant circulation manager in 1979, Frank spent several months in North Carolina at Knight-Ridder's Charlotte Observer. He also participated in a three-month Advanced Management Program at Harvard where he read case studies on family businesses and learned more about his family's history of "faltering stewardship and failed parenting." As he delved into the original provisions of the Blethen Corporation, which Todd and Pennington had put together in the 1950s, he concluded it was "absolutely brilliant." They had made the stock "so restrictive among the family shareholders that it was almost impossible to ever sell the company. It really became much more of a stewardship than an ownership. I realized that the changes we had pushed through by resisting Jack's ill-advised plan made things even stronger. If I had been ambivalent about working for the company before, all those feelings were gone now."

In 2001 when the warts-and-all Harvard Business School study of the Blethen ownership was released, one conclusion pleased him the most: "The new checks and balances eliminated the possibility that a single shareholder, like Jack, could damage the family and the business. With this agreement, stewardship, rather than ownership, became a dominant Blethen principle in the operation of the newspaper. Stewardship required that each generation of the family had only temporary control of the company, not ownership, and required that the newspaper business be passed to the next generation in an enhanced condition."

The fourth generation by then had more than an inkling that enhancing the company's condition for the fifth would be the biggest challenge since 1896 when the colonel arrived on Puget Sound with a change of underwear and a pocketful of promises.

12 | The Golden Carrot of Togetherness

Alerted that their publisher was about to arrive for an important meeting, the newsroom at the Seattle Post-Intelligencer braced for more layoffs.

It was the afternoon of January 13, 1981. Though Boeing had rebounded, capturing 60 percent of the jetliner market, it had jettisoned 60,000 workers during the 1970s. America was reeling from high inflation and high unemployment, a big reason why Ronald Reagan was about to become president of the United States. And everyone in the newsroom knew Hearst was unhappy with the P-I's bottom line.

"Don't worry, it's good news," P-I Editor Bill Asbury told Charles Dunsire, a worried longtime reporter, as he passed his desk. When the publisher, Virgil Fassio, entered the newsroom with one arm in a sling and a poker-faced Hearst lawyer in tow, most assumed the news was bad. The sling—Fassio had taken a tumble off a ladder—turned out to be metaphoric. It would have been more apt for Asbury to have said, "There's good news and bad news," which would have left things to the ear of the beholder and covered most of the bases. Fassio certainly didn't look happy.

Reading from a statement, the publisher revealed that the Hearst Corporation and The Seattle Times had reached "an agreement in principle" that The Times would handle advertising, production and circulation for both newspapers if the companies were granted an antitrust exemption under the federal Newspaper Preservation Act of 1970. The newsrooms would remain independent, Fassio said, and the P-I would publish six days a week. There would be one jointly branded Sunday edition. The P-I's portion would be a six-page editorial/op-ed section and Hearst's King Features comics.

Tim Egan, Eric Nalder and Joel Connelly, three resourceful reporters who had been hard at it a few minutes earlier, felt like passengers on a 747 that had dropped a thousand feet in three seconds. "Suddenly, the air went out of us," Connelly recalls. Nalder kicked a file cabinet. Not hard, but everyone heard it because the room was so quiet.

David Brewster's paper, the Weekly, spotlights the controversial JOA. *Washington State Library*

What was the good news? The proposed joint operating agreement—a "JOA"—meant long-term survival for the Post-Intelligencer, Fassio said. The paper had lost around a million dollars a year for 12 years. It would take "more than a miracle" to halt the slide. The litmus test of the Newspaper Preservation Act was that one of the proposed partners was otherwise unlikely to survive.

The publisher apologized for not being able to entertain questions, adjusted his sling, turned on his heel and left. Some reporters scampered down to the lobby and discovered "a kind of lockdown in progress." Others fanned out to take stock of the fallout in departments where the job losses, should the deal go through, were sure to be devastating—advertising, composing, the pressroom and business office. They were mortified to discover that Hearst executives had issued a gag order. They weren't supposed to cover what was arguably the biggest story in the 118-year history of their own newspaper. "The war's over," said reporter Mary Rothschild, "and we're Poland." Other angry P-I staffers called it "V-T Day"—Victory for The Times Day. Someone suggested that "JOA was really more like SOL." An Emmett Watson column headlined "Fear Not, Your Old P-I is Alive and Kicking" appeared atop page one three days later. As morale-boosters go, it was a limp happy-face balloon. Watson's days at the P-I were numbered. So were Bill Asbury's.

There were no high-fives at The Times. Jim King, the executive editor, climbed atop a desk to make the announcement. Everyone listened intently, many with arms folded. Alex MacLeod's dark-bearded face became a stony mask when he heard that if the JOA went through The Times would be required to discontinue the weekday morning edition it had launched a year earlier. When Mike Fancher, who had arrived from the Kansas City Star in 1978, was named night city editor to oversee content of the new edition, he picked MacLeod as his assistant. An odd couple—Fancher became the Zen master of the newsroom; MacLeod the sheriff—they were a tight tag-team for the next 23 years.

    The circulation of the morning edition—Frank Blethen's bailiwick—had grown to nearly 50,000, peeling 6,000 copies off the P-I's circulation, even though the a.m. edition was sold only from newsracks and stores. Further, the Times' circulation leads were at all-time highs—73,000 daily and 127,000 on Sundays. "The announcement felt to us like a tie when victory was at hand," MacLeod remembers. "It felt like we'd been sold down the river." A fierce competitor, he also instinctively understood that to P-I people a JOA felt like surrender. If MacLeod and Fancher, Nalder and Connelly had bumped into one another after work that dispiriting day and resolved to repair to the nearest bar they likely would have agreed that their feelings were neatly distilled by one of the first words that popped into MacLeod's head when he heard the news: "Bullshit." The prospect of a jointly branded Sunday edition was especially mortifying. Hardcore Times people didn't want the P-I's name on their paper. At the other rampart it smacked of a sop. P-I reporters and editors chafed at the realization they stood to lose a showcase for their best work. "I don't have a paper now, do I?" the newly arrived editor of the P-I's Sunday edition grasped, prematurely but presciently.

King fielded a couple of questions. He said the joint operating agreement might take a year or more to win approval from the U.S. Department of Justice. Some two-dozen JOAs were in place across the country, the most recent in Cincinnati, where the endangered Post had entered into a marriage with the Enquirer in 1979. "Is there any way out of this?" someone said. King said the Seattle proposal contained an escape clause: three consecutive years of losses by either partner.

The joint operating agreement was Jerry Pennington's idea. In the mid-1970s, with Jack Blethen's blessings, Pennington met several times with Hearst executives, including Frank A. Bennack Jr., Hearst's folksy yet shrewd chief operating officer. They said his terms, especially a 70-30 profit split, amounted to surrender. The talks broke off. Their change of heart was prompted by escalating losses and the prospect of having The Times as a full-bore morning competitor. The morning edition was a bold strategic move by Pennington. No one was more gung ho than Frank Blethen, who had been named circulation manager in 1980 and was poised to expand the reach of the a.m. edition. Blethen blanched at the irony of a pivotal JOA concession by The Times: It would be forfeiting the morning market, save for weekends and holidays, for 50 years. It seemed to him that they ought to be in it to win it. "Boy, we were kicking butt with our morning edition," Blethen says, all but rubbing his hands together. "It was clear that afternoon papers were an endangered species. The suburbs were growing and the freeways were jammed. Hearst took stock of our morning edition and recognized that if they didn't get a JOA done ASAP they wouldn't have enough circulation left to be a viable negotiating partner."

The tradeoff was palatable to Pennington for several reasons: He worried that Hearst might get serious in Seattle and outspend the Blethens in a morning showdown or try to undermine the family's majority-stake in The Times. "I maintained it was false competition," Frank remembers. "Hearst was subsidizing the P-I. Any other owner would have gone out of business. Bennack knew it was a good deal for Hearst. He is one of the smartest, most competitive newspaper men I've ever met. But it's not like I really had a voice at the table. I certainly respected Jerry's position. It was hard to fault his strategy. In the near term, the next 10 or 15 years, it was going to be the lowest risk decision for the Blethen family and a source of important additional revenue. I've stated that it was a marvelous business decision for The Times and the family. But I sure wish he hadn't done it."

Pennington's point was that other chains, notably Gannett and Knight-Ridder, The Times' minority owner, were increasingly acquisitive. Estate taxes and squabbling over dividends had led to the sale of many family-owned newspapers. The Seattle Times was succeeding in an era of steadily declining p.m. newspaper circulation. But for how long and at what risks? The company's profits—4 to 6 percent—were shockingly puny compared to industry norms, and the dividend stream was shallow. The Times needed to make major investments in new printing technology and presses. If the future held a one-newspaper town, Pennington wanted the survivor to be The Seattle Times. Besides, it was a pretty sweet deal. Sixty-eight percent of net revenues from the joint venture would go to The Times—6 percent of that as a management fee. The Times would sell all the ads and set the rates. Deals like that were "the golden carrot of togetherness," the publisher of Hearst's allegedly failing San Francisco Examiner, wrote in 1965 as his paper pursued a partnership with the surging San Francisco Chronicle. In return for a 50-50 revenue split there, Hearst agreed to switch to afternoon publication.

When he drew the assignment to cover the Justice Department's JOA vetting process for the P-I, Charles Dunsire began to plow through the 22,000 pages of documentation submitted by the prospective partners. Some of it was "surprisingly fascinating," he wrote, including the revelation that the Blethens and Hearst had "explored the possibility of one newspaper buying out the other" at the time of the 1953 Newspaper Guild strike against The Times. The details of the JOA monetary incentives for each were also spelled out:

> Bennack told Hearst's board of directors that the projected profit for the P-I under a JOA in 1982 would be nearly $1.8 million in contrast to an estimated two-million-dollar loss without a JOA. The Times' bean counters, meanwhile, calculated that a JOA would produce an additional $1.4 million a year in income for the Times, based on a projection for 1983. Times President and chief executive officer W.J. Pennington disclosed that operating profits for 1981—without a JOA—were projected at $5.4 million, well below the industry average for newspapers of its size.
> The reason the Times could see additional profits in a JOA with the P-I, financially failing though the latter might be, was that the P-I's morning circulation remained reasonably strong and its share of the Seattle market's newspaper advertising, while well below that of the Times, was significant.

Any way you cut it, "many of us thought JOAs were special interest legislation to make publishers rich, or richer," MacLeod says. "The so-called 'failing newspaper' in most of them was the afternoon paper, and many of them were 'failing' because publishers were starving them in order to continue to pay themselves dividends." The catchphrase at the P-I was "What's failing is our management."

Joel Connelly, a large man with a walrus mustache and encyclopedic mind, was chagrined to discover the Newspaper Guild "was useless, and that we had made it so. The executive director talked down to us; told us not to be emotional. The Guild leadership was largely hacks, mainly because star reporters didn't want to be bothered. I had queasy memories of the scene from *The Caine Mutiny* in which the mutineers' defense lawyer, Lt. Barney Greenwald, talks about Capt. Queeg having done grungy work in pre-war Navy and getting no sympathy from peacocks in his ward room. A good deal of the impetus for saving the P-I came from folks in the advertising department."

Connelly, Dunsire, Hilda Bryant, Shelby Scates, Dan Coughlin and several other Post-Intelligencer reporters and editors helped organize the Committee for an Independent P-I. It found a passionate ally in David Brewster's People Opposed to a 1-Newspaper Town—PO1NT. Brewster wasn't sure whether a JOA would help or hinder his five-year-old "alternative" paper, the Weekly, but he believed the Newspaper Preservation Act was a terrible law and considered it a civic duty to join the fight. Suburban publishers enlisted, too, but only a handful of advertisers had the nerve to publicly support the Committee for a Free Press.*

David Brewster.

Brewster is a slender man with analytical eyes and a jaunty wave of upswept hair. He was one of the young Ivy Leaguers who fell in love with Seattle in the 1960s. Their outward preppiness was deceiving. They set out to be change agents and viewed politics as a contact sport. After his brief stint on the copy desk at The Times, Brewster landed first at *Seattle* magazine, then at the Argus, Seattle's venerable weekly in its last flowering. In 1976, with a $75,000 grubstake from friends and admirers, he launched the Weekly. It made its debut the week the Kingdome stadium opened just south of

---

* James F. Vesely, who came to The Seattle Times in 1991 as associate editor of the opinion page after stops in Chicago, Anchorage and Detroit, closely followed the debate over the Seattle joint operating agreement. The whole focus nationally was on JOA's between rival metropolitan papers, says Vesely. "But a JOA between the afternoon Seattle Times and the morning Bellevue Journal-American would have been both revolutionary and prescient. Would it have worked? Maybe not, but nobody clearly saw the writing on the wall in the rise of the suburbs, other than as secondary markets."

historic Pioneer Square, which was sprouting art galleries and upscale restaurants. By 1981, his paper read more like a sophisticated magazine than a newspaper. It became an influential progressive voice, filling the void left by the demise of *Seattle*. Brewster and a stable of other talented writers focused on politics, arts, entertainment and the restaurant scene. They wrote often about both dailies and found them wanting. The Times had made strides under Henry MacLeod and Jim King, Brewster says, "but it was still too bourgeoisie, suburban, prudish," while the P-I bounced between Hearstian "sports and mayhem and stories that appealed to an audience of the educated elite." Both papers had first-rate reporters who deserved better assignments. Whatever their shortcomings—real or perceived—"we needed them both."

After the announcement, the Weekly took stock of the fallout, hoping it would eventually become clear "whether Hearst deliberately let the paper slide into financial distress—the reward for which can be a government grant of perpetual monopoly—or just bungled its way there. The answer is probably a combination of both: after all, with such an incentive to bungle, the habit can rapidly become addictive." William Randolph Hearst's war-mongering, red-baiting and other editorial eccentricities "ill-suited moderate, sensible Seattle," Brewster wrote. And "in later years, as the Hearst Corporation has found money easier to make in real estate and magazines, the management of its metropolitan dailies has only gotten more erratic." In Seattle, it had squandered a morning niche that should have been increasingly advantageous.

Frank Wetzel, then editor of the Bellevue Journal-American, told the Seattle-King County Bar Association the JOA would put The Times in the catbird seat to set advertising rates. "The Newspaper Preservation Act is a classic case of powerful special-interest forces pushing through legislation when there is no specific, identifiable victim. My contention is that the public is the victim," the future Times ombudsman said.

Twenty-two joint operating agreements were in place in 1969 when the U.S. Supreme Court struck down the pact in Tucson, ruling it amounted to illegal price-fixing and profit-sharing by the Citizen and Daily Star. The law granting antitrust exemptions for "failing" newspapers was passed by Congress the following year after the industry staged a full-court press. Richard Nixon, in his first year as president, initially opposed the act. His change of heart came after a letter from Richard E. Berlin, Hearst's CEO. A veto "would carry political consequences," Berlin intimated, adding that Nixon's support "would conversely help the president and his allies." Every Hearst newspaper endorsed Nixon for re-election in 1972. For that matter, so did The Seattle Times and almost every other newspaper in America—93 percent to be exact. (But Nixon had no inkling in 1969 that his next opponent would be the hapless George McGovern. Even then he was still so paranoid that he sanctioned the Watergate break-in.)

The attorney who took up the challenge to the JOA was one of the finest trial lawyers in the United States, or as Emmett Watson put it, "the kind of attorney that a gunnysack full of graduates from Harvard Law can never hope to be." William L. Dwyer was 34 when he won a landmark libel case—the 1964 verdict against Albert F. Canwell and three other calcifying red-baiters who had smeared a liberal state legislator, John Goldmark. In 1976, Dwyer represented the state in its case against baseball's American League over the underhanded removal of the Seattle Pilots after just one season in Seattle. "We were about 20 days into the trial when the league lawyers realized the jury was going to vote for capital punishment," says Slade Gorton, who was Washington's attorney general when he hired Dwyer to press the case. "Dwyer just shredded them." Seattle was back in the big leagues the next year with the Mariners. Dwyer's trifecta of storied victories was complete in 1978 when he won King County a $12 million settlement from the original contractor for the new Kingdome, home to the Mariners, the Seahawks of the NFL and SuperSonics of the NBA.

Dwyer took the JOA case pro bono. He had considered a career in journalism before opting for law school and covered the Canwell Committee hearings in 1948 as a reporter for the University of Washington's student newspaper. By night Dwyer had filled paste pots in the P-I newsroom. When he introduced Dwyer at a gathering of JOA opponents, Joel Connelly quipped, "Our situation is so serious that we are even enlisting help from onetime P-I copy boys." Their initial fundraiser was a showing of *Citizen Kane.*

"Our argument was that the P-I was not failing; it was cooking its books" with all sorts of fees for features and other accounting jujitsu, Brewster says. "Hearst looked at the P-I as an unimportant paper. It was not in a major market, and probably couldn't make much money regardless. They sent in publishers who were not heavyweights on their way up in the Hearst hierarchy. With Hearst's headquarters in New York, a long way from Seattle, it was kind of like the Spanish Empire: here we are, way over here in the Philippines, so to speak, a long ways from Madrid."

Absent the expedient option of a joint operating agreement, the opponents believed Hearst was likely to sell the Post-Intelligencer, "maybe to somebody good; maybe to somebody bad. It was worth the risk," Brewster adds. "The first thing we found was that very few figures in town, particularly advertisers, would dare to support us because they feared repercussions. Lamont Bean of Pay'n Save Corporation was one of the courageous advertisers who provided some money for legal expenses. We had some unions on our side, and some good government types. But that was it."

They made overtures to The New York Times, The Wall Street Journal and other major publishers, including Rupert Murdoch, then making his first foray into North America, but the publishers' club had its own unwritten rules. It was Catch 22, Brewster remembers. "Privately they said, 'If the P-I comes up for sale of course we'd be interested, and the only way it's going to come up for sale is if you block the JOA. But if we oppose the JOA there's no way that Hearst would ever sell to us. We'd just shoot ourselves in the foot, so good luck to you guys.' We could never figure out a way around that."

It was a two-year roller coaster ride for JOA opponents. They cheered when the Justice Department's Antitrust Division recommended rejection of the Seattle application, saying there appeared to be legitimate prospective buyers if Hearst offered to sell the P-I. They lost the next round when Attorney General William French Smith ruled that the "failing newspaper" test "did not require the absence of willing purchasers." The Committee for an Independent P-I took its case to U.S. District Court in Seattle and prevailed. There could be no JOA, Judge Barbara Rothstein ruled, "without exploring the alternative of sale to a noncompetitor." The U.S. Ninth Circuit Court of Appeals disagreed, holding that Hearst had "met its burden of showing that the alleged alternatives did not offer a solution to the P-I's difficulties." Hearst convinced the court it "had managed the Post-Intelligencer reasonably and that financial failure would be inevitable no matter who bought the paper," wrote John P. Patkus, who analyzed the Newspaper Preservation Act for the *Akron Law Review*. To Connelly, Brewster and the other opponents this was preposterous. During the first JOA hearings before an administrative law judge, former P-I editors Lou Guzzo and Bill Asbury cited a litany of Hearst blunders and unbenign neglect—clunky presses, poor delivery service and the failure to parry The Times' morning edition, as well as price hikes and content changes that generated subscriber blowback. The P-I's talented newsroom was ill-served by ham-handed management, they charged.

As to a possible buyer, Dwyer had quizzed Frank Bennack about Murdoch's reported interest in the P-I. The Hearst executive acknowledged he had met with the controversial Australian press magnate just before the hearings began. But the feeler was tentative, Bennack said, and Murdoch was told the Hearst Corporation had "no present intention" of selling the P-I. Well, Dwyer prodded, what if there was a less tentative offer—one that identified the potential investors and set out their intentions for operating the P-I? "We would look at that," Bennack conceded. "Murdoch had never made such a specific offer," Dunsire wrote, "although it seemed clear he was waiting in the wings in the event the JOA was denied." The P-I writer also chased down a story that Bill Moyers, the highly regarded television commentator, was interested in buying the paper. Moyers flatly denied it. An overture by former Seattle Congressman Jack Cunningham, a one-term conservative firebrand, proved "vaporous."

The last person leaving the press room under the globe at Sixth and Wall turned out the lights in the early-morning hours of Sunday, May 22, 1983. When the JOA went into effect the next day, opponents' hopes rested with the court of last resort. Dwyer had petitioned the U.S. Supreme Court to review the Ninth Circuit's decision, charging that the JOA would make the Post-Intelligencer "a commercial appendage to its dominant partner" and deprive the region of two "diverse and antagonistic" voices.

Defeat came that fall. Without a word of comment, the court declined to hear the plaintiffs' arguments. "We almost won," Brewster said in 2014. It was too long ago to sigh, but he paused for a moment and shrugged: "Dwyer was a fabulous attorney. He told me at the time it was the only case he had lost. We drew a bad panel in the court of appeals, which is always a crapshoot."

Brewster may be surprised to learn he and Blethen were in complete agreement on the folly of the Newspaper Preservation Act and Dwyer's talents as a litigator. "Obviously, at that stage in my career and my location in the organization I had to keep my thoughts to myself," Blethen says. "But I was completely sympathetic with Dwyer and the efforts to thwart the JOA—not only from a competitive, strategic standpoint but also from a public policy standpoint. The Newspaper Preservation Act was one of the worst pieces of legislation I've ever seen. It had nothing to do with saving journalism or localism and everything to do with helping the early aggregators and mercenaries begin their march to the terrible newspaper and media concentration and disinvestment in journalism and public service we have today."

13 | The Margin of Excellence and a Shocking Loss

WHAT The Times billed as "SUPERSUNDAY"—the first joint edition—made its debut on May 29, 1983. Both newsrooms winced at the marketing department's retrograde hype, especially the emphasis on "Twelve pages of funnies—a bundle of fun the whole family will love!"—as if Junior, wearing a beanie, would be sitting cross-legged on the floor chortling over Dennis the Menace and thrilling to the adventures of Prince Valiant instead of playing Pac-Man.

If no substitute for two Sunday newspapers, that first 292-page edition was an impressive package and no flash in the pan. It had a dozen pages of opinion and commentary, quick-read digests, bold graphics, more features and columns and two magazines. The Seattle Times would emerge as a national leader in newspaper design. The revenue stream coursed with huge display ads and 33 pages of classifieds. That was good news for the newlyweds, but the emotional bottom line for P-I editors and reporters was this: only six of those 292 pages belonged to them. Their "Focus" section—an inconvenient stepchild in an arranged marriage—migrated farther and farther back in the voluminous package in the months to come. The P-I published a 250-point manifesto promising to "stay feisty." And it did.

David Horsey, who would go on to win two Pulitzer Prizes for editorial cartooning, feared the JOA would neuter his paper. Now, however, there was more money for ambitious projects and travel. Horsey toured Japan with Evelyn Iritani, the P-I's Pacific Rim correspondent. An eight-page special section ensued. When Joel Connelly became the P-I's Washington, D.C., correspondent in 1985, the job now even included a modest housing allowance.

Under John Owen, a consummate old pro who wrote a delectable food column in his spare time, the P-I's sports pages sparkled with young talent, including Art Thiel, who wrote with flair and wit. The P-I was particularly determined to challenge The Times' vaunted investigative chops. Times reporter Paul Henderson—with an assist to Dick Cheverton for deft editing—had won the 1982 Pulitzer Prize by proving prosecutors had wrongfully convicted a man of rape. His colleague Erik Lacitis was a Pulitzer finalist in feature writing that same year for a compelling first-person narrative of a day in the life of an abortion clinic—the women seeking abortions and a physician whose cause was to ensure the procedure was safe. Meantime, Connelly and John Dodge, a dogged reporter for the 18,000-circulation Daily World at Aberdeen, were scoring scoop after scoop on the meltdown of the Washington Public Power Supply System's inept nuclear power plant program, a story with huge national implications.* The JOA ratcheted up the P-I's we-try-harder competitive pride. That was also added motivation for the rising young editors at The Times. They hated being beaten by the P-I.

The Times had assured nervous advertisers there would be "no increase in present base rates ...solely as a result of the

Joel Connelly. *Seattle P-I photo*

---

* Full disclosure: The author was John Dodge's editor at Aberdeen during the WPPSS debacle. The Post-Intelligencer's coverage, highlighted by Joel Connelly's resolute reporting, was a finalist for the 1983 Pulitzer Prize for public service reporting. Frank Blethen was profoundly embarrassed that The Times was not a "critical watchdog on the whole WPPSS fiasco" and determined that it would never again be caught napping on a major story.

joint operating agreement." The reality was that the Post-Intelligencer, desperate for revenue, had offered so many "specials" and "combo" deals that its rate card was largely window dressing. The Times' ad rates for Sunday jumped 50 percent based on a projected 47 percent circulation gain to 500,000. An estimated 60,000 readers had purchased both Sunday newspapers (combined circulation 540,300). The Tacoma News Tribune, Everett Daily Herald and Bellevue Journal-American beefed up their Sunday editions, hoping to snag defectors.

The next audit certified there were 473,200 customers for the joint edition. The Times had gained 134,600 on Sundays but lost 23,600 on weekdays, 10,000 of that from ending its weekday morning edition. By 1987, the Sunday paper's circulation finally topped half a million. But The Times' daily lead—nearly 64,000 in 1980—was half that at decade's end. Pre-JOA projections that the combined Sunday edition would hit 625,000 by 1992 would fall more than 100,000 short of reality.

As Puget Sound's population soared and newspaper readership declined, Blethen's determination to abandon afternoons grew. It's remarkable, looking back, that The Times was able to maintain its dominance while stuck in the PM position. Afternoon papers were dying all over America.

Emmett Watson returned to The Seattle Times a few months after the JOA began. His 33 years at the Post-Intelligencer came to an end in a dustup over a scathing column about Mariners owner George Argyros, who counted P-I Publisher Virgil Fassio as one of his few friends in Seattle. Among Watson's many friends was Times Editor Jim King, who suggested lunch. Managing Editor Mike Fancher and City Editor Alex MacLeod, son of Watson's old friend Henry, were there to underscore a job offer. "I couldn't help but remember that I had almost dangled Alex on my knee when he was a child," Watson wrote. "It was his idea to hire me. It felt like full circle." When provoked by PC liberals, snug in their Volvos, and sanctimonious "pseudo Christians," Watson could still arch a withering bushy eyebrow. With Watson's best years behind him, however, the real prize catch from the P-I arguably was Eric Nalder, the terrific investigative reporter who had kicked the file cabinet when the JOA was announced. Nalder would thrive in a Times newsroom that allowed its most resourceful reporters the time it took to develop important stories.

Don Duncan had returned to Fairview Fanny in 1979 after six less-than-contented years as managing editor in Tacoma. He was happy to be "the world's oldest general-assignment reporter." All around him now were "a bunch of bright kids" he liked and admired. There was Bill Dietrich, the versatile reporter he helped recruit from The Columbian at Vancouver, Wash.; sportswriter Steve Kelley; art director Steve McKinstry and Terry McDermott, who had few peers in the time-honored art of lead-writing. David Boardman, a copy editor with the uncanny ability to improve everything he touched while preserving the writer's voice, was spotted as a comer early on by Fancher and MacLeod. Duncan observed tartly that under the new generation of managers there were too many meetings and not enough video-display terminals, but their work ethic and goals were beyond reproach. The hiring freeze instituted during the recession was lifted and excellence was expected.

The joint operating agreement "was a watershed event" for The Seattle Times, the Harvard Business School study of the Blethen dynasty concluded. It "solidified family ownership by ensuring a substantial, steady dividend stream to shareholders" and "helped temper" the aversion to debt that sprang from C.B. Blethen's reckless spending in the 1920s. In the years just prior to the JOA, The Times' net profits hovered around 5 percent (about $5.5 million in 1981). Jerry Pennington's projection that the JOA would generate another $1.5 million per year in profits proved far too conservative. Revenue from display advertising soared as Puget Sound became a hub of the high-tech revolution. By the mid-1990s, Times profits topped 14 percent—still less than half what many chains were extracting. The Blethens were investing heavily in high-quality journalism. When the Internet began to change everything, many recalled something Pennington had told his department heads when the JOA profits began rolling in: "Any idiot can manage a company well when times are really good. The real test of a manager is to keep things going well during hard times."

Pennington had risen to publisher in 1982 when Jack Blethen, battling Huntington's disease, kicked himself upstairs to chairman of the board. Pennington's protégés, Frank Blethen and Mason Sizemore, were also advancing, as per his plan. Blethen became vice president for sales and marketing. Sizemore, whose MBA studies at the University of Washington were being financed by The Times, had moved from the newsroom to production director. He was being groomed to succeed old-hand Harold Fuhrman as general manager. Fancher, meantime, had succeeded Sizemore as managing editor, and was also on the MBA track. Mindy Cameron, former managing editor of Idaho's respected Lewiston Morning Tribune, was Alex MacLeod's assistant on the city desk. After 35 years with The Times, Jim King, editor and vice president, relished the opportunity to close out his career harnessing "all that amazing energy" he helped discover.

Pennington declared he wanted The Times to become one of the 10 or 15 best newspapers in America—preferably the top 10. What would it take? King, Sizemore and Fancher told him it would require siphoning some of those JOA profits to the news department.

When the senior editors assembled for a goal-setting retreat at a resort along Puget Sound, Pennington arrived by float plane. He was impeccably dressed, as usual, in a finely tailored wool overcoat, handsome suit and tasteful silk tie. "With his bald head, and the extra million dollars he gave us to create a 'margin of excellence' in our news coverage, we all thought of him as Daddy Warbucks," MacLeod remembers.

As a club man, board member, patron of the arts and philanthropist, W.J. Pennington had few equals in Seattle society. He served on more than 20 boards: PACCAR Inc., Rainier Bank, Safeco Insurance, Goodwill Industries, Rotary and Junior Achievement, as well as the mayor's government review commission. He headed a campaign that raised $28 million for the expansion of Children's Orthopedic Hospital and resurrected the newspaper's 1920s-era Fund For The Needy. "We asked him if he would give those up, now that he was publisher, to avoid conflicts of interest," MacLeod recalls. "He said he wouldn't. He didn't see any conflict of interest because he

Mike Fancher, left, and Paul Henderson, center, congratulate Peter Rinearson, winner of the 1984 Pulitzer Prize for feature writing for his series on Boeing's new 757 jetliner. *Seattle Times photo*

would do nothing to influence news coverage. He was good to his word."

The new team immediately scored a "10-strike," to borrow Pennington's favorite phrase. "Making It Fly," an eight-part series by Peter M. Rinearson on the gestation of Boeing's revolutionary 757 jetliner, won the 1984 Pulitzer Prize for feature writing. Edited by Steve Raymond, the best craftsman on the city desk, the stories narrated Boeing's $1.5 billion gamble with such *New Yorker*-like skill that the judges decided it didn't really fit in the National Reporting category. They moved it to features to ensure it won a prize and resolved to create a new category, Explanatory Reporting, for the following year.

Around lunchtime on Friday, March 15, 1985, the newsroom was stunned by a call reporting that Pennington had drowned within sight of his Whidbey Island summer home. "He was so active and fit that my reaction was that this couldn't be Jerry," MacLeod remembers. "When Don Duncan nodded at me while he was on the phone talking to authorities, it started to sink in."

The 66-year-old publisher had relinquished the duties

of company president to Frank Blethen just two weeks earlier and cut his work week to three days to be able to spend more time on the island with his wife of 39 years, Dorothy. When he returned from his morning jog, she watched him walk to water's edge with the 10-foot aluminum skiff he carried on his back like a turtle. As he rowed out to set his crab pots—freshly baited with what he called his "magic potion"—the phone rang. It was Dorothy's mother. When the conversation ended some 15 minutes later, Dorothy scanned the waterfront. There was no sign of Jerry. The skiff had overturned at least twice before when he was tending the crab pots, but he was a strong swimmer and easily made it back to shore.

She called the marina and was told someone had spotted a capsized dingy and alerted authorities. Others had seen a man waving his arms in obvious distress. Pennington's body was discovered, floating face down, about 50 yards from the skiff. One of the first on the scene was the local marina owner's son, who noted that Pennington had kicked off his jogging pants when the skiff overturned. He was still wearing his sneakers.

The news spread fast. It seemed as if everyone on that side of the island knew Jerry. Men half his age marveled at his fitness; he played a wicked game of handball. On a winter's day, however, in the 45-degree waters of Puget Sound, the cold-shock response induces hyperventilation. He must have expended a lot of energy thrashing to free himself. "If you rowed out just a little too far, you'd hit a big drop-off and you could lose a crab pot," says Jerry's daughter, Sue Merry. "My guess is that he realized he was out too far, grabbed for the crab pot, capsized the boat and became disoriented in the cold water. An autopsy revealed some blockage of arteries, but it was hypothermia that took his life."

"The irony of this whole thing," a neighbor said, "is that he was just starting to think about taking it easy. He'd put out that crab pot a thousand times before. Things like this don't happen to a W.J. Pennington. ... He was strong as an ox." P-I Publisher Virgil Fassio spoke for thousands when he heard the news: "I'm completely shocked."

"At first, I was numb," Frank Blethen remembers. "Jerry was like a father to me—the father I'd never really had. He was my trustee and my mentor. He put his job on the line to ensure I would have a chance to become publisher. He was the hardnosed visionary who wanted The Times to become a great newspaper and remain in the family for generations to come. And now he was dead."

Three days later, 39-year-old Francis Alden Blethen Jr. became a director of the Blethen Corporation, chief executive officer of The Seattle Times and its seventh publisher. He didn't need the Knight-Ridder votes but he got them. Sizemore, 43, the sure-handed general manager whom Pennington had groomed, was elected company president. With William K. "Will" Blethen, 38, serving as company treasurer and his brother Bob, 37, as promotions manager, the fourth generation was now in control. Will was shy; Bob gregarious. Two nice guys. Some said too nice.

The fears of Frank's Uncle Jack, who had declared he could go to Walla Walla if he never came back, had come true. His nephew was now publisher, while his son Buster was parked in national advertising, a member of the board but no longer interested in being publisher. Jack was still chairman, but too ill to do much but nod with as much equanimity as he could muster as Frank assumed control.

14 | Core Values

When 40-year-old Michael Reilly Fancher succeeded Jim King as executive editor of The Seattle Times in the summer of 1986 someone wrote that it was the end of an era. King had joined the paper when Fancher was in diapers. With his handsome, friendly face, gray-streaked temples and Dunhill briar pipe, King resembled an editor-in-chief rolled in on casters from the back lot at MGM. In his own gentlemanly way, however, King had been a change agent, not old school—"an idea guy who liked to try new things," his successor said. King hired women and minorities, installed an ombudsman and enjoyed tinkering with page design. He was self-effacing and wry. "A newspaper editor," King once observed, eyes twinkling, "has more opportunities to make people unhappy than anyone else you know."

Fancher, who rose from reporter to executive editor in eight years, had a disarming smile and a close-cropped beard that was beginning to go gray. It was Alex MacLeod, Fancher's newsroom running mate, who dubbed him "The Zen Master." Though a head shorter than Phil Jackson, the NBA coach who sometimes burned incense in the locker room while urging his players to visualize victory, "Fanch" gave off the same vibe. He was a thinker. His newly acquired master's degree in business administration was seen by some as part of an insidious movement to commodify news with productivity charts, marketing plans and focus groups. When Fancher briefed Blethen on his annual goals, "he sounded like any other striving young organization man on the fast track," wrote Doug Underwood, a Times reporter-turned-professor, in a book called *When MBAs Rule the Newsroom*. Fancher was part of a "brave new

Five managing editors: From left, Henry MacLeod, Jim King, Mason Sizemore, Mike Fancher and Alex MacLeod in 1989. *Seattle Times photo*

world of marketplace newspapering," Underwood wrote. "[He] installed a large and pervasive bureaucracy of midlevel editors, tightened the reins on reporters, redesigned sections of the newspaper based on readership surveys" and drove away great reporters who balked at being cloned.

Blethen scoffs. "I drafted goals for each department. Then we would discuss and prioritize. It was nothing like Underwood's fantasy of some corporate MBA PowerPoint routine. We added editors and tightened the reins because changes were badly needed. Reporters were accustomed to having too long a leash. It really bothered me that our headlines were so often inaccurate and sophomoric. Fancher and I insisted on more professionalism. Alex was the instrument."

"When I succeeded Fanch as managing editor, he gave me room to be myself and make change happen," MacLeod says. "Journalism is his heart and soul, but day-to-day command and control is not his thing. He is an intellectual who practices the power of trust to get the best out of people. Fanch was a transformative figure in the history of The Seattle Times."

Ross Anderson, a former Times reporter, remembers standing beside Fancher in the newsroom early on, "looking across that sea of people and desks and paper and telephones and realizing: Fancher sees things I do not see. I see people and desks and paper and telephones. Fancher sees organizational charts, flows of energy and invisible lines of influence, interactions between people or the absence of interactions. I don't know what he saw, but whatever it was made him an executive editor while I remained a city-hall reporter. ..."

In MacLeod, Fancher saw a loyal, fiercely competitive editor with high standards and expectations. Or as he famously put it less decorously, "MacLeod may be an asshole, but he's my asshole."

A broad-chested man with a dark beard, Alex MacLeod squinted over each edition. He had a low threshold of tolerance for errors and omissions. Some said he was tyrannical. He made people tremble, even cry, when he demanded to know why the competition had a story The Times didn't. When the Weekly polled the newsroom soon after he became managing editor, a black and white picture developed:

"He's real good at saying no. ... He has some kind of control fetish."

"If he doesn't like you, you're sunk, and he doesn't like people who talk back."

"He's a person with extremely good news judgment."

"He cares a hell of a lot."

"It's important to have him in the newsroom."

It was important to Fancher to have MacLeod in the newsroom. They had been upwardly mobile teammates since their days together editing the morning edition. Fancher's vision revolved around "a better accounting of reporters' time, greater cooperation with graphics people and a more intense effort to get as much news and information into the paper as fast as possible" while their best investigative reporters worked on important, meticulously researched projects. MacLeod's job was to make it happen with a cast of 266 highly creative, individualistic people. There were self-inflicted pressures, too, for the son of a legendary managing editor. Staffers he respected told him he needed to take more deep breaths and work on his people skills. He turned down his thermostat and became a better listener—and a better manager for it. But no one ever accused Alex MacLeod of being laid back. If you'd done good work, you had a staunch defender when the proverbial shit hit the fan.

In promoting Mindy Cameron to city editor and Cynthia Meagher to associate managing editor, Fancher and MacLeod were also serving notice that the newsroom was serious about diversity—though those two bright, experienced journalists were promotable on merit alone. Millie Quan, who became assistant managing editor for administration in 1989 when the trailblazing June Anderson Almquist retired, scoured the country for bright prospects. A special internship program gave fledgling minority journalists a year's worth of experience between The Times and its other papers. After Quan departed for the Los Angeles Times, Patricia Foote, the can-do longtime assistant managing editor for features, took over the role of recruiter. In 1990, when Cathy Henkel was promoted to sports editor, only three other women in the nation were overseeing sports sections at metropolitan newspapers. The daughter of a high school coach, Henkel was a gamer if there ever was one. She endured catcalls from the stands during the 1970s while covering prep football for the Register-Guard in Eugene, Ore. When she was promoted to cover college sports, she was booted out of an Oregon State University locker room. "It was like the world came to an end. I didn't realize it was me" until someone grabbed her by the arm and pushed her out the door. With her passion for sports, sense of humor, diplomacy and the courage to take on tough stories, Henkel elevated The Times' sports sections to the nation's top 10. And when she retired in 2008, a male reader declared she had done a "kick-ass" job.

A newsroom that was an industry leader in diversity was the most public face of a company-wide effort to hire and promote women and minorities. Under Frank Blethen, Mason Sizemore and Jim Schafer, the company's industrial relations executive, The Times was changing from an old-boys club. Carolyn Kelly, who joined the company in 1977 as a 25-year-old CPA, had played a key role in ironing out the operational details of the joint operating agreement. She was now the marketing director and soon would be the newspaper's chief financial officer. The human-resources manager was Phyllis Mayo, an ebullient African-American with a master's degree from Harvard. The Times created a subsidized day-care center for employees' children and was named to *Working Mother* magazine's top 100 companies for nine consecutive years. "We saw diversity in two ways," Blethen says. "First, it was the right thing to do. We were reporting on diversity and editorializing on diversity, so we should be practicing diversity. When I became publisher and started talking to our board about how important diversity was, all I got was blank looks. Then I started talking to other people in the industry. It didn't take long to realize that most companies were talking about diversity mainly because they wanted to avoid lawsuits. A lot of smart, qualified minorities and women were being overlooked. Hiring them gave us a competitive advantage and we also gained a reputation as a great place to work."

"Maximizing the workplace satisfaction of all employees" was one of four core values Blethen and his cousins adopted in 1985 after they gained control of company. The other three—also still in place—are these: "Remain family-owned, private and independent; serve the community through quality journalism" and "be the country's best regional newspaper." MacLeod challenged the wisdom of trumpeting the last goal. It was aspirational, all right, "But how can we prove it?" "We don't have to prove it," Blethen said. "We'll *know* when it's true." Goal-setting retreats, affirmations and values-based mission statements were all the rage in the '80s, but The Seattle Times also declared, "Cash flow, not net income, is our standard of efficiency."

Cash flow *and* net income were rising steadily as Seattle's stock rose. Bill Gates and Paul Allen were becoming billionaires, Microsoft having revolutionized personal computing. The city was sprouting skyscrapers and high-tech start-ups; the Fred Hutchinson Cancer Research Center was a national pacesetter; biotech and cellular were growing; Starbucks was poised to go national, and Bellevue, with high-rises of its own and the toniest shopping mall in the Northwest, was now the state's fourth largest city.

The Times added a dozen talented reporters and editors. It set out to print more insightful features, burnish its reputation for investigative reporting and become a national

Seattle Times news staffers watch TV coverage of the explosion of the Space Shuttle Challenger in 1986. *Seattle Times photo.*

pacesetter in newspaper design. Never again, it resolved, would it be beaten on big, breaking news stories. When Mount St. Helens erupted like a hydrogen bomb on May 18, 1980, in one of the worst natural disasters in American history, Jim King had asked the paper's tight-fisted general manager, Harold Fuhrman, for the go-ahead to hire a helicopter. Fuhrman refused, while Ted Natt, publisher of the 26,000-circulation Daily News at Longview, pulled out all the stops. "Ted's paper won the Pulitzer, and deservedly so," Blethen says. "Their reporters and photographers were in the air and on the ground. They knew it was the story of a lifetime. And we couldn't afford a helicopter! One of the first conversations I had with Mike Fancher after I became publisher was that I didn't want them ever going to a general manager or trying to find me to ask if it was OK to do whatever it took to cover a major news event."

The Times' Tomas Guillen, Carlton Smith and Natalie Fobes were Pulitzer Prize finalists in 1988—Guillen and Smith for an analysis of the baffling Green River serial-killer investigation, and Fobes for a series documenting the Pacific salmon's struggle to survive a gantlet of man-made obstacles. A seven-part series on the catastrophic 1989 *Exxon Valdez* oil spill in Alaska won the paper's fifth Pulitzer. Ross Anderson, Bill Dietrich, Mary Ann Gwinn and Eric Nalder documented the devastation. It was a cautionary tale. On average, an oil tanker laden with crude cruised into Washington waters every 14 hours.

Some observers said the paper seemed "feminized," which Blethen readily acknowledges was partly strategic. "As an afternoon newspaper we had a very significant female audience that was leaving a.m. papers." He also believed newspapers were dowdy and dull. Fancher's team redesigned the paper to make it brighter and better organized, putting new emphasis on writing that sparkled, first with Cyndi Nash, then Arlene Bryant, as news features editors. When the ebullient Terry Tazioli, former producer of KING-TV's "Top Story," became editor of The Times' "Scene" section in 1986, it became bolder and more topical. Tazioli met Robert O'Boyle, a remarkable young man afflicted with AIDS, and offered him a column. "We were one of the first major dailies in America to give readers insight into what it was like to live with a death sentence," Tazioli recalls. "When Robert died, the newspaper provided a phone number for readers to call to offer condolences. We got so many calls in the first hour that it shut down the system." The Times won so many Penney-Missouri Awards, the Pulitzer Prizes of lifestyle writing, that "they kicked us out of the competition for a couple of years," Tazioli recalls.

The event that knocked Seattle's political pundits for a loop was The Times' endorsement of Michael Dukakis for president. That the largest newspaper in a swing state was backing the Democratic nominee for the first time since 1900 generated national headlines.* Local cynics chalked it up to Blethen, in his editorial page coming-out party as publisher, putting a moistened finger to the wind and deducing it would be a good time to grab attention for himself and his paper. Seattle, with its growing number of young professionals, educators and still formidable unions, had been turning left since the late 1970s. The Times' opinions grew a shade more liberal after Herb Robinson succeeded Ross Cunningham as editorial page editor in

---

* Previously, the last Democratic presidential candidate endorsed by The Seattle Times was the party's 1900 standard-bearer, William Jennings Bryan. Frank Blethen's great-grandfather adored the silver-tongued populist. The Times sat out the 1916 contest between Wilson and Hughes and the 1964 Goldwater-LBJ race.

David Boardman pours champagne on Bill Dietrich, Mary Ann Gwinn and Eric Nalder in 1990 to celebrate The Times' Pulitzer Prize for coverage of the Exxon Valdez oil spill and its aftermath. *Seattle Times photo*

1977, but Blethen saw the page as boringly conservative.

In 1988, when Robinson returned from his daily meeting with Frank and informed the opinion page staff that The Times would endorse Dukakis, it was a surprise but no bombshell, according to John Hamer, a right-of-center editorial writer in those days. "Herb had assembled a diverse editorial board that included me, Dick Larsen, Don Hannula and Patricia Fisher, an African-American whose career would be cut tragically short by multiple sclerosis." The editorial board, then as now, interviewed candidates, weighed the issues and strived for consensus, Hamer says, but presidential endorsements traditionally were the publisher's prerogative. To no one's surprise, the Post-Intelligencer, a Hearst newspaper, endorsed George H.W. Bush. America's destiny was at stake, William Randolph Hearst Jr. declared. The Times' endorsement of the Massachusetts governor was one of the earliest by a major newspaper.

"When Frank took over as publisher, he called the editorial staff together for a half-day retreat," Hamer remembers.

"He said he wanted to get to know us and talk about our editorial philosophies. 'I want diverse voices and opinions,' he said, 'and if you disagree about a stand we're taking feel free to write a column.' So I wrote a column saying that endorsing Dukakis was a mistake. I think that was the beginning of the end for me at The Times. Herb Robinson told me, 'Don't ever cross him. He never forgets.'"

"The real issue" between the two at the time, according to Blethen, was not Dukakis or Bush or "my policy of encouraging cogent, thoughtful columns contrary to the paper's official endorsement. As I set out to rebuild our editorial page staff, I had no respect for Hamer as a thinker or journalist, so I guess the feeling is mutual." They would clash bitterly when Hamer went on to co-write CounterPoint, a newsletter that reviewed the state's news media. It spotlighted the celebrated 1996 incident where Blethen wounded his neighbor's allegedly pesky dog with a pellet gun. (Blethen dismisses CounterPoint as a "vile, mean-spirited, right-wing" creation, while Hamer says it was then that people began to realize Frank was morphing into his mercurial great-grandfather.) When Hamer headed the independent Washington News Council, there was more bad blood, this time with Fancher and MacLeod.

If the Dukakis endorsement was construed as a sign The Seattle Times was no longer predictable old Fairview Fanny, so much the better, Blethen says. "But I was genuinely concerned about Bush. He was parroting the Reagan line about the dramatic growth of the U.S. economy, while blithely ignoring the soaring federal deficit. Dukakis was hapless, but he was by far the stronger candidate in terms of support for education and civil rights. Reagan and Bush had been savaging student financial aid and affirmative-action programs at colleges and universities." The Times announced its endorsement five weeks before election day and two weeks before Dukakis' debate gaffes eroded the last vestiges of his 17-point, post-convention lead. The paper stuck by him while angry calls and letters poured in and some readers canceled their subscriptions. The rest of The Times' slate that year defied pigeonholing. It backed Republican Slade Gorton for the U.S. Senate over Mike Lowry, a pluperfect liberal, and supported raising the minimum wage. "That Frank went left for Dukakis didn't help him much in Seattle's political orthodoxy because day to day, the P-I was the left's darling," says Jim Vesely, a retired Times opinion page editor. Dukakis narrowly won the state that November, thanks to a 60,000-vote margin in King County. Washington and Oregon were the only western states he carried.

When Lance Dickie, who wrote with passionate civility, arrived at The Times in 1988 from The Statesman Journal in Salem, Ore., Blethen saw him as "the first building block" in the creation of what he envisioned as the region's most progressive editorial page. Opinion page editors came and went. Dickie was an anchor for the next 26 years.

Since Dukakis, The Times has backed every Democratic presidential nominee except Al Gore. It abandoned George W. Bush in 2004, and was solid for Obama. Conservatives have branded it the most liberal newspaper in the state, while liberals decried its call for Bill Clinton to resign during the Monica Lewinsky scandal. They were outraged in 2004 when the newspaper backed Republican Dino Rossi for governor over Chris Gregoire. Two years later liberals said "See!" when the paper endorsed Mike McGavick, Slade Gorton's former chief of staff, for the U.S. Senate against Maria Cantwell. And in 2012, The Times' wholesale advocacy of Rob McKenna, the GOP's candidate for governor, ignited a firestorm we'll get to later.

In the 1990s, Frank Blethen's emergence on the national stage as a passionate advocate for repeal or reduction of the estate tax became an endorsement litmus test. "It was a deep and sincere belief on his part that the 'death' tax was ruinous to farms, medium-size family businesses and even such family enterprises as black-owned funeral parlors across the South that were being consolidated under single ownership," says Vesely. "Keep in mind also that it was often the estate tax that allowed Gannett to grow to some 90 formerly family-owned newspapers. But The Times could hardly endorse candidates who did not favor the overriding issue of the publisher's key agenda—the estate tax—even if we did not cite that as a reason. And because the issue leaned GOP rather than Democratic, we were fenced in on some endorsements."

Blethen gave his cousins, Will and Bob, seats on the editorial board to heighten family involvement in editorial policy, but they were never major players like Cameron, Vesely, Dickie, Richard Larsen, Don Hannula, Casey Corr, Bruce Ramsey, the brainy Terry Tang, who went on to become deputy editor of the editorial page at The New York Times, and in recent years Frank's son Ryan and Kate Riley. The Times periodically attempted to "balance" its op-ed page with a true conservative. John Carlson, the state's foremost young Reaganite, wrote a lively op-ed column from 1993 to 1995 on a freelance basis. When he became the afternoon host on KVI radio, he got the boot and was succeeded by a capital C Conservative firebrand, Michelle Malkin. That she was a first-generation Filipino-American and sizzlingly bright confused and angered Seattle liberals, not to mention the newsroom. "Frank believed KVI's confrontational format coarsened debate, so they hired Michelle," Carlson says. "Talk about scorched earth!" Malkin was an equal-opportunity provocateur who soon moved on to New York to write a nationally syndicated column and join the Fox News stable of commentators.

When Mindy Cameron, then city editor, succeeded Herb Robinson as opinion page editor in 1990—becoming the first woman to hold that post at The Seattle Times—many were surprised. Most figured Larsen, whose political column was a must-read, would get the job. Given that Cameron had never been a fulltime editorial writer, it was an outside-the-box choice. Blethen respected her instincts, wanted to send a message and in the years to come gave her considerable leeway. In a gripping 1992 column headlined "An intensely personal, private decision," Cameron revealed she had had an abortion as young woman, only two years after the landmark Supreme Court decision that made it legal. Now, writing in the aftermath of a ruling that upheld Roe v. Wade by the narrowest of margins, she warned that centrists on the high court, in a search for compromise, had sold out on a "fundamental liberty." They had endorsed government intrusions into a woman's life "at a time when she is making the most private and sensitive of decisions—whether or not to bear a child." The reaction fell along the usual political/religious fault lines but it was strongly pro-Mindy. "There was a groundbreaking aspect to it," Vesely remembers. "We always read one another's stuff before publication, but I read that column twice. I told her it was a remarkably poignant piece. But it was so confessional, so personal, that it made me cringe a little for her. I was a strong proponent of a woman's choice, but only a brave woman could have written that column."

When Vesely, a personable, savvy old pro, succeeded Cameron in 2001, he too had a wide berth, though he was more conservative. However, if push came to shove, Cameron says, summing up both their experiences, "we either agreed or Frank had it his way." Then with a little chuckle, she adds, "He owns the place. He's very bright but no model of political consistency, which made things interesting." Vesely puts it this way: "Ask practically anyone who has worked for Frank and they'll tell you he is a remarkable and stalwart friend of news and editorial. He thwarted with a smile attempts to get me fired, and was remarkably open about a thousand other issues of the region and the state. But he knows exactly what he wants, even if it is only for the afternoon. His mish-mash of opinions equates in my mind to independence rather than ideology. Unlike The New York Times and Wall Street Journal, The Seattle Times does not have an ideology. It has a vivid publisher instead of a set of political and social concepts. And, like myself who can often vote Republican, Frank is the first to embrace social equality, both in his heart and on his pages. He's unpredictable, but not intellectually lazy."

Whatever the Dukakis endorsement really said about Blethen and his newspaper it cast him in a new and different public light. During his rise to publisher, other media had profiled him as "soft-spoken, maybe even shy"—a "nice guy" whose only management weakness seemed to be "that he is sometimes impatient." The Weekly's J. Kingston Pierce predicted in 1985, "Frank Blethen is not likely to ever compete with his great-grandfather for notoriety."

If "notoriety" seems a reach, except for the most vociferous Blethen haters, no one could dispute that he has raised a lot of hell of his own in the past 30 years.

15 | Fiduciary Duties

Fairview Fanny's fearlessness was surprising—and angering—a lot of people.

An explosive investigation by Susan Gilmore, Eric Nalder, Eric Pryne and their city editor, David Boardman, prompted a U.S. senator to abandon a bid for re-election and generated a national debate on the use of unnamed sources.

Brock Adams' charmed political career ended on March 1, 1992, a cloudy Sunday in Seattle. Eight women who shared their stories after being promised their names would not be published told of being sexually harassed and molested by a liberal Democrat once dubbed "the young prince of politics." Adams had never lost an election. The allegations, including outright rape, gave new credence to a story the paper had published 3½ years earlier when a former congressional aide publicly claimed she had been drugged and molested by the senator. Adams asserted the young woman, a family friend, had fabricated the story to extort money. Authorities in the District of Columbia declined to prosecute. Adams' new accusers alleged a pattern of predatory abuse of power that stretched back 20 years. The stories were "created out of whole cloth by people who hate me," Adams said at a hastily called news conference. He flogged The Times for "the worst kind of journalism—anonymous vilification," and pronounced it the "saddest day of my life." The state Democratic Party chairwoman said he ought to consider resigning. Adams served out the final 10 months of his term under a cloud and never again sought elective office.

Journalists, ethicists, professors and public figures weighed when, if ever, a news story justified the use of anonymous sources. George Will said the Adams story amounted to "an open license for character assassination." Fancher, MacLeod and Boardman believed Adams' behavior was so malignant that The Times would be almost an accessory to crime if it sat on the story. P. Cameron "Cam" DeVore, one of the foremost First Amendment attorneys in the nation, vetted the story for The Times.* Still, Fancher warned his publisher that the story would end Adams' career—and that the newspaper would immediately become a big part of the story. The linchpin for publication, Fancher says, was that Adams' accusers were willing to sign statements agreeing to testify if the paper were sued. "The choice we faced was no story or this story. I told Frank we wouldn't run it if we weren't sure." Blethen listened intently, also aware that a defense could cost millions if Adams took them to court. Then he said, "How could we know this and not publish it?" *Time* magazine called the investigation a textbook example of "meticulous, convincing journalism." The Seattle Times was a 1993 Pulitzer finalist for Public Service Journalism and won the prestigious Goldsmith Prize for Investigative Reporting.

That allegations of misconduct by the University of Washington's football program generated more condemnation of The Times than the Brock Adams controversy italicized the sacred-dog status of Husky football. Under Coach Don James, the revered "Dawgfather," the UW won four Rose Bowls and a share of the 1991 national championship. An exhaustive Times investigation in 1992 revealed recruiting violations and a $50,000 loan to a star quarterback. When the Pacific-10 Conference imposed sanctions, the winningest football coach in UW history resigned and the Husky faithful were outraged over the media's "character assassination."

---

* DeVore, who died in 2008, advised The Times for 30 years. He was secretary to its board of directors, helped craft the joint operating agreement and played a key role in at least three Pulitzer Prize-winning stories, according to MacLeod. Thanks to DeVore, The Times was able to publish stories "that were above reproach even though there was considerable risk to the paper in terms of our reputation or just plain legal jeopardy in all of these articles," MacLeod says.

In the middle of the recession that doomed George H.W. Bush's bid for re-election, The Seattle Times Company purchased the 40,000-circulation Yakima Herald-Republic for $60 million. "You may ask how we can afford to buy a newspaper in tough economic times. The answer is simple," Mason Sizemore and Blethen said in a statement. "The financial performance of the Herald-Republic will cover our cost of owning the newspaper, meaning that the purchase will have virtually no impact on the resources available to operate The Seattle Times newspaper." They emphasized that the Yakima paper would be treated as an editorially independent "self-sustaining entity."

Under Houston-based Garden State Newspapers, headed by the controversial William Dean Singleton, the Yakima paper had been producing profits that topped 35 percent. Blethen and Sizemore viewed that as journalistic malpractice. ("If you're making less than 10 percent you're cheating your shareholders and if you're making more than 20 percent you're cheating your readers," Andrew Barnes, chairman and CEO of the St. Petersburg Times, observed during the 1990s.) When Sizemore told the Herald-Republic's publisher he should invest more in his news product, he thought he had died and gone to heaven. Yakima was about to have a dramatically better newspaper. Revenues from the Herald-Republic and Walla Walla Union-Bulletin—which had been judged the Northwest's best small daily two years running—would prove crucial for The Seattle Times Company in the choppy years to come.

The bottom line, according to Tony Ridder, who as president of Knight-Ridder was emerging as Frank's nemesis, was that "they paid way too much for Yakima, and that was part of a pattern. We didn't say, 'You shouldn't buy it.' We said, 'You don't need to pay that much.'"

Knight-Ridder had no objections, however, when the Blethens invested $200 million in a new printing plant at North Creek in Bothell, northeast of Seattle. "That made sense," Ridder says. "New presses and mail room equipment—I was all for that. That was the lifeblood of that newspaper." At the time, the North Creek facility was the largest investment in the history of The Seattle Times Company. Another suburban production facility was planned for Renton to the south. In 1991, The

Times purchased Rotary Offset Press in suburban Kent, which prints a number of weekly newspapers as well as The Times' total-market-coverage mailer, pamphlets, brochures and magazines. It began printing the Northwest edition of The New York Times in 2002 after a new high-tech press was installed.

Bill Clinton, The Times' pick for president, would preside over the longest economic expansion in U.S. history. But the recovery from three straight years of declining advertising revenues had only just begun in the summer of 1993 when Blethen and Sizemore announced that effective January 1, 1994, The Times would no longer run tobacco advertising. The evidence that tobacco use caused cancer and heart disease was irrefutable, they said. Critics called the decision an infringement of free speech, tobacco being a legal product. "So are handguns, escort services and X-rated movies," Blethen said. "We're not running ads for those either." The Times was the largest paper in America to take the step—one that would cost the company upwards of $125,000 a year in revenue. "As a percentage of our ad base, which is at about $200 million, it's insignificant," Sizemore said, "though in these times, when ad revenues are down, any decision like this is a weighty one. We just couldn't in conscience be a part of it any more. These ads were designed to kill our readers."

Knight-Ridder, two years later, urged its publishers to start refusing ads that made smoking seem cool or sexy. But the ban wasn't mandatory. Unhorsing the Marlboro Man in a burst of headline-making altruism struck some in the newspaper industry as foolish grandstanding. During the recession, The Times also eschewed the steep layoffs imposed by most newspaper chains, trimming instead through attrition. Frank Blethen, moreover, had earned around $900,000 in salary, bonuses and dividends in 1992, according to a story in his own newspaper. So all the high-minded talk about "excessive" profits and the baleful concentration of media ownership didn't go down well with Knight-Ridder, a publicly-traded company. "They kept telling us about our 'fiduciary responsibility' to the shareholders," Blethen remembers. There was something about the way the Knight-Ridder people said that word—"fuhdoosh-ee-airy," enunciating every syllable—that irritated the hell out of him. "The inference was that we were cheating them by running a newspaper that was too good. We believed their profit expectations were obscene and unsustainable."

Hearing this, Tony Ridder seemed to measure his reply for several seconds. Then he said, "The Seattle Times always underperformed financially. We never thought they did what they could do from a revenue standpoint, and I think it would be fair to say that on the expense side we didn't think they did either ... comparable to other newspaper operations of about the same size. ... We were very disappointed in the performance of the Seattle newspapers. One of the things that used to drive me up the wall was that I would read Frank was saying I was saying 'He's spending too much money on his newsroom.' I never said 'You're spending too much money on your newsroom.' There were times when we said, 'We think you could do a better job of controlling costs.' Or maybe 'Your costs don't need to go up 10 percent next year. You should shoot for 6 percent or something like that.' But we never ever said, 'You're spending too much money on your newsroom.' "

In the spring of 1993, to mark the tenth anniversary of the joint operating agreement, The Times' Terry McDermott took stock of what was predicted and what had actually happened. It was a remarkably candid Sunday think-piece, replete with observations about his publisher's $1.6 million waterfront home, Lexus sports coupe and Range Rover—as well as a prescient prediction that in another 10 years all bets were off.

The "untold disasters" forecast when The Seattle Times and Post-Intelligencer merged business operations ranged from "mass extortion of advertisers and Orwellian manipulation of public opinion" to speculation that the P-I's landmark rooftop globe would be sold. [It now graced the P-I's new waterfront offices.] "Some of what was predicted came true," McDermott wrote. "Some of it did not. But the worst was never imagined. It was this: In the long run, very few of the effects of the JOA seem likely to matter. The future of newspapers in Seattle has much less to do with what the two dailies do with, or to, each other than with what the market does to them. ...

A Blethen family photo in the early 1990s: Back row, from left: James and Ryan (Frank's sons), John, Buster, Kerry (Buster's daughter). Middle row, from left: Will, Bob, Frank, Barbara "Bobbi" Blethen (John and Buster's mother), Sue (Bob's wife), Rob (Bob's son). Front row, from left: Trace (Will's son), David (Bob's son), Courtney (Buster's daughter), Jessica (John's daughter) and Christine (Bob's daughter). *Seattle Times photo*

The whole notion of having mass media depends foremost on having mass audiences, and the market for that audience is fragmenting even faster than the market for advertisers. ... Circulation of the two newspapers is only marginally greater than it was a decade ago. And their combined share has declined precipitously," despite the fact that King County had added 250,000 people since 1983. "A JOA purposely ignores the dynamics of the information market and tries to capture the past," McDermott wrote. "The newspapers, frozen in their tracks, try to be all things to all people. The danger is they might end up being nothing to anyone."

David Brewster, whose alternative paper, the Weekly, closely covered the media, was glad Seattle was still a two-newspaper town, yet underwhelmed by the dailies' combined output. The Hearst Corporation now had a profitable property—at least $8 million a year—while The Times' profits were estimated at $20 million. It had spent millions to launch tailored-content zoned editions to burgeoning Bellevue and the suburbs to the north and south. And what was the readers' return on investment? The Times' investigations were laudable, Brewster allowed, but all those awards disguised the paper's "ordinariness." And the once-sassy P-I—to the distress of its newsroom—now seemed to be the voice of the business establishment. "The editorials almost worship authority. It's almost a parody of the old Seattle Times," Brewster said.

Bob Brown, the local media director for McCann-Erickson, a national advertising agency, sniffed that none of that mattered much. "Newspapers are the dinosaurs of the media business and The Seattle Times is Jurassic Park."

Blethen said the secret to survival was "adaptation."

The centennial of the Blethen stewardship of The Times was just three years away. It was time to take stock of the past and the future. Frank was devoting a substantial portion of every week to family matters, working with his cousins to imbue the fifth generation's sons and daughters with their responsibility to the Blethen legacy. "We're not publishing newspapers to make money," he said. "We're making money to publish newspapers."

Jack Blethen died at 74 in the spring of 1993 after his long battle with Huntington's disease. Knight-Ridder saw an opening.

Bernard H. "Bernie" Ridder Jr., the 76-year-old retired chairman of the Knight-Ridder board (He was Tony's father), invited Frank to breakfast when he arrived in Seattle for the funeral. The Times was in the late stages of crucial labor talks. Strike-phobia from the 1953 walkout that cost the company 95 days of revenue had made management squeamish about hard bargaining. "We had to get our costs under control," Blethen remembers. "Our chief negotiator was Jim Schafer, one of the best hires Jerry Pennington ever made. Schafer had worked in labor relations in the volatile forest products industry. We needed to change the labor culture at The Times. This was our chance to make some real progress."

Bernie Ridder was literally and figuratively a big man—6-foot-5, with a passion for football and golf. Blethen was startled when he urged him to be less aggressive.

"Why would we do that?"

"Because you're not Jerry Pennington," Blethen distinctly remembers Ridder saying. "We know you're pushing for some pretty dramatic changes that need to be made. But if you fail, people are going to see you as a failure. If Jerry had failed, people would just say, 'Well, that's too bad.' "

"Maybe they were thinking the unions would think I was inexperienced or didn't have the cojones to be tough—and that they'd take a strike just to have a strike, which would hurt Knight-Ridder's profits too. Who knows? I thought long and hard about what to say because this was a big pucker factor for me. Finally, I said, 'Bernie I would love to be off the hook on this. I don't know what's going to happen but I know that if we don't get all or some of these concessions and start down a different path you and the board are going to want my head in three or four years anyway because we can't operate the company with the kind of expenses we'll have going forward.' "

Blethen sensed he was being subjected to a good cop/bad cop routine.

"Bernie may not have had any ulterior motives. Maybe he was just being fatherly. But a very definite pattern emerged. His son, who sat on our board, was the president of Knight-Ridder, and they were obviously intent on gaining control of The Seattle Times. Tony certainly didn't like what he saw happening in Seattle. The first part was 'Play nice with Frank. He's in over his head and all family businesses fail sooner or later.' But then they saw clearly that we were improving our journalistic product; that we had an aggressive young management team; that we had succeeded in securing better contracts with the unions, which was huge. I think they concluded that everything we were doing was shoring up the Blethen family's control of The Seattle Times."

The Blethens were busily acquiring more real estate in the South Lake Union neighborhood around the Times Building at what Frank remembers as the "ridiculously low" pre-bubble land values of the early 1990s. Then, he says, Knight-Ridder board members started strenuously objecting to any purchase that wasn't immediately contiguous to the newspaper's headquarters. If not for that, "we probably would have had another billion dollars' worth of property we could have sold" when things got rocky in the 21st century. "But after Jack died, it was stir-the-pot time, creating dissension among the board members. Talk about fiduciary responsibilities! Knight-Ridder members of our board were not fulfilling their fiduciary responsibilities to the Seattle Times Company. Sitting as Seattle Times Board members they had fiduciary responsibilities just like I do."

Tony Ridder says, "I felt like they were just trying to acquire a lot of property around the plant for a purpose Frank couldn't explain. I said, 'Look, if you're acquiring it because you've outgrown this building, or this building isn't safe [that would make sense], but *why* are you buying up all this property?' 'Well, because it's available. ... It's going to be increasingly valuable.' ...It was like a rainy day fund. That *was* smart [given their later difficulties]. There's no question about that, but I just thought it was not a good use of their money because they had all this other debt as well."

One observer saw Frank Blethen and Tony Ridder as "two young pit bulls" staking out their turf. "I must admit I ratcheted it up," Blethen says with a chuckle. "It was pretty easy to bait Tony Ridder. I got some counseling from my outside directors to take it easy, but my point to them was that as Knight-Ridder came to the realization they weren't going to get control of this place it was just a matter of time until they became more confrontational."

"He exaggerates," says Ridder. "He cares about the quality of his paper, and for that I give him credit. But he's arrogant."

16 | The Stare-Down

Tony Ridder and Frank Blethen are the great-grandsons of self-made men from the golden age of newspapering. Five years older than Frank, Tony was 53 in 1993 when they had their first stare-down. Ridder was a tall, athletic man with a confident smile. His silver hair, thinning on top, was swept back suavely at the sides. Ridder's career had taken him from the newsroom of a small daily in South Dakota to the publisher's chair at the San Jose Mercury News. On his watch, it became "The Wall Street Journal of Silicon Valley," doubled its circulation, banked millions upon millions from classified ads and won a Pulitzer Prize. *AdWeek* magazine named him Newspaper Executive of the Year in 1991. Now he was president of Knight-Ridder Inc.

When Knight Newspapers and Ridder Publications merged in 1974, both having gone public five years earlier, Knight-Ridder became one of the largest newspaper companies in America—"and one of its best," the *American Journalism Review* noted, "second only to the New York Times in the number of Pulitzer Prizes won by its papers." In the early 1990s, however, with the recession crimping profits, the price of newsprint on the rise and readership declining, Ridder was under pressure from shareholders to cut costs. It was unpleasant business, but Tony got on with it, proved good at it, in fact. Some Knight-Ridder workers later took to calling him "Darth Ridder." One Knight-Ridder editor believed Tony still cared deeply about quality journalism, "but it's as if we made a Faustian bargain when we went public." Another observer is Davis "Buzz" Merritt, a retired longtime Knight-Ridder editor who dissected the company's profit expectations in a book called *Knightfall*. Budget sessions with Tony Ridder were "like being in the presence of a machine," Merritt remembers. "He was not interested in conversation about anything else. He just wanted to run the numbers."

After Jack Blethen's funeral in the spring of 1993, Frank felt certain he and Tony were on a collision course. Tony's back stiffened when Frank vowed there was no way he would make company-wide cuts for short-term returns and have his paper become "mired in mediocrity" like the chains, beholden to faceless institutional investors. "You sell your soul to the devil once you go public," Blethen said. Ridder and Bob Singleton, his tough-talking chief financial officer (no relation to William Dean Singleton), took umbrage at the notion they were pawns of Wall Street. It was Frank's grandfather, after all—the yacht-buying spendthrift—who had surrendered 49.5 percent of the company to keep The Seattle Times afloat during the Depression. It was time for the Blethens to stop denying Knight-Ridder shareholders "a decent return on their investment," Singleton said.

Tony Ridder. *Knight Ridder photo*

Did Knight-Ridder have "the nerve to go for the jugular?" a reporter asked.

"Oh, they have the nerve," Singleton said. "Tony has the nerve. Don't stare him down. You won't win."

Blethen was determined not to lose.

"Next, we received a letter from Knight-Ridder accusing us of mismanaging The Times," Blethen remembers. Then all of the shareholding family members, including Buster Blethen, whose health was failing, received letters from Knight-Ridder offering to buy them out. "It was a classic end-around," Blethen says.

"Ultimately, economics will control," Singleton predicted from retirement three years later as the stalemate continued. "Dangle enough money, somebody'll get greedy and the Blethen family will cave." In that event, however, there was cave-in insurance in the Blethen Corporation stock ownership rules, which were strengthened during Frank's dustup with his Uncle Jack over lines of succession. If a family member wants to sell his or her stock, the other shareholders have first option.

The accusation of financial mismanagement incensed Blethen and Mason Sizemore, his chief operating officer. Blethen was "fed up with their complaining and mucking around—especially the notion that we were running the business into the ground." He commissioned Davis Wright Tremaine, a Seattle law firm with a nationally recognized media practice, to oversee an audit of the newspaper's finances. Davis Wright found The Times' management beyond reproach, Blethen says, but recommended a second opinion. Skadden, Arps, a prestigious East Coast law firm, agreed with the first.

When Knight-Ridder's chairman and CEO, the courtly James K. Batten, was ushered into the 1993 Blethen board meeting, he read a formal statement expressing the minority partner's concerns about management of The Seattle Times Company. "We welcome any actions you choose to take," Blethen said crisply as he revealed the audits. "Batten was a distinguished journalist, a Southern gentleman straight from Central Casting," Blethen remembers. "His hands were shaking when he read the statement. Tragically, he was dead within two years from a brain tumor. I don't think his heart was in the attempt to undermine us. They stopped talking about fiduciary responsibilities after that. I redoubled my efforts to make sure the other family members were on board. My cousins were resolute that this is a family legacy."

Blethen made the next move later that year. After gathering estimates on the value of Knight-Ridder's minority position, he arrived at their headquarters in Miami, together with Sizemore and Carolyn Kelly, The Times' chief financial officer. They were there, Blethen announced, to offer $25 million for Knight-Ridder's share of The Seattle Times. Given that the Blethens held the majority of the voting stock, their position buttressed by the corporation's bylaws, Frank asserted that Knight-Ridder's stake in the company was the present value of future dividend flows.

Ridder rejected it out of hand. "I thought $25 million was just insulting," he says. "I don't remember what I countered with, but it was a far higher number, and I emphasized that we were interested in buying, not selling."

"This will be the last and best offer you'll get from us," Blethen recalls saying with solemnity. "If you're not willing to sell, we're going to invest that money in our company. Here's your window of opportunity."

A Knight-Ridder executive with a droll sense of humor walked over to a bank of windows, gazed out for a moment, then allowed, "So you're saying we just open this window and step out from the sixth floor?" That broke the tension. The room erupted in laughter. But the meeting was over. "In essence, they kicked us out of their offices and we were left standing in a parking lot in a not-so-great part of Miami before wide use of cell phones, trying to figure out how to get a taxi," Kelly remembers.

And that was that for then. The ongoing Ridder-Blethen stalemate—featuring as it did the quotable scions of famous publishers—was the subject of national media attention. Family-owned newspapers fractured by internal squabbling were selling out to chains dangling irresistible amounts of money.

Back home on Mercer Island, Blethen found himself embroiled in an embarrassing neighborhood dispute.

"Red" was a young Labrador Retriever with big brown eyes. On May 10, 1996, he allegedly strayed next door into Blethen's yard and began pawing up the shrubbery and chasing the publisher's cats. It wasn't the first time either, Blethen would say, adding that he'd been dealing with "neighbors from hell" for two years. When Red returned home acting out of sorts, his owner discovered a bleeding wound and confronted Blethen. The publisher admitted to shooting Red, the neighbor told police, but Blethen stated he had fired a pellet gun only to shoo away the pooch, aiming at the ground behind the animal. Red's owner, an attorney, categorically denied his dog was mischievous and asserted that Blethen had initiated their previous run-ins. Blethen blithely described the incident as "Doggate" to a pair of inquiring reporters—none other than ex-Times editorial writer John Hamer and Mariana Parks—who broke the story in David Brewster's Eastsideweek. Pressed, Blethen flatly denied responsibility "for those pellets" and said a neighborhood dispute was being blown out of proportion. It seemed he had yet to fully grasp that being the outspoken publisher of the state's leading newspaper made his every alleged transgression fair game, especially since Times editorials were decrying violence. Blethen was pilloried by animal-rights activists who paraded outside the Times Building and featured on the 5 o'clock news. He also caught hell from his cousins as talk radio and papers all over the state picked up the story. Finally, he was charged with misdemeanor cruelty to animals, ordered to pay Red's vet bills and sentenced to 20 hours of community service working with dogs.

David Goldstein's parody of "Doggate." horsesass.org

Blethen says he accepts that it's always open season on publishers, but the incident still rankles: "Red, this so-called puppy, was a big, aggressive dog. And before he showed up on the scene the neighbors had two huge St. Bernards. At one point, both dogs, in our yard, came after me and my two-year-old granddaughter. Being able to jump into a car saved us from what probably would have been a pretty vicious mauling. That was the last straw. I called Animal Control. That part of the story is lost in the saga of 'Doggate.'"

The incident occupies a secure niche in the annals of Blethenology, popping up regularly. In 2006, David "Goldy" Goldstein, a dogged Times critic, posted a parody of a famous

National Lampoon magazine cover on his popular blog, horsesass.org. Beneath The Seattle Times nameplate a dog cowers, a pistol to its head: "If You Don't Repeal the Death Tax," the headline says, "We'll Shoot This Dog."

When Blethen observed that there were "a lot bigger" stories out there, he was trying to call off the dogs. It was also the truth. Jerry Pennington's million-dollar investment in a "margin of excellence" for the newsroom, perpetuated by Blethen and Sizemore, was still paying major dividends in public-service journalism a decade after his death.

In 1995, the Seattle Fire Department was in denial, insisting all safety procedures had been followed at the scene of a warehouse arson fire that killed four firefighters. Eric Nalder and Duff Wilson revealed those statements were smoke and mirrors. "If not for human error, official disregard, malfunctioning systems and misguided policy," they wrote, the tragedy might have been prevented. Faced with the newspaper's revelations, fines for safety violations, lawsuits by families of the dead firefighters and soul-searching of its own, the department instituted new fire-scene safety rules.

The Times was in select company in 1997 when it won two Pulitzer Prizes. Byron Acohido's meticulous investigation of rudder control problems on Boeing's 737, the world's most widely used airliner, helped prompt new Federal Aviation Administration requirements. Nalder, Deborah Nelson and Alex Tizon won for their scathing investigation of a federal program ostensibly dedicated to helping Native American families secure adequate housing. They discovered instead a program so "riddled with fraud, abuse and mismanagement" that tens of thousands of people were "sleeping in dilapidated cars, teetering trailers and rotting, one-room shacks." It was the second Pulitzer for Nalder, one of the best investigative reporters on the planet, and a well-received honor for Nelson and Tizon. Nelson was a national advocate for investigative journalism; Tizon was only the second Philippine-born journalist to win journalism's Oscar. Don Duncan, who had known a lot of great storytellers, spotted Tizon early on as one of the finest writers The Seattle Times had ever seen. Media critics who observed that many newspapers seemed to be designing stories more

From left, Deborah Nelson, Eric Nalder, Alex Tizon and Byron Acohido celebrate their 1997 Pulitzer Prizes. *Seattle Times photo*

to win awards than right wrongs acknowledged that a pair of Pulitzers for stories of such national importance was a singular achievement. Times reporters and photographers were Pulitzer finalists nine times over the next nine years. Duff Wilson's stories revealing that toxic industrial wastes were being recycled as fertilizer was a finalist in in 1998. The practice was legal, and in some cases laudatory. The problem was that cadmium, lead and other dangerous heavy metals often remained. The U.S. had no national regulation of fertilizers. The series led to changes in state laws. Tom Brune was a Pulitzer runner-up in 1999 for an 18-month investigation on the impact of affirmative-action measures. Ensuring equal opportunity was far more complicated than most people realized. Sometimes there were negative consequences to being affirmative.

A dozen Times staffers in all—copy editors, researchers, page designers, photographers and graphic artists—were involved in the prize-winning projects. The common denominator, according to Alex MacLeod, was David Boardman's leadership and deft touch. Everyone saw it. "I watched him take like 60 inches of a reporter's notebook dump and turn it into a gem on deadline," says Chuck Taylor, a former Times reporter who once worked side by side with Boardman on the news desk. "He's a remarkable hands-on editor."

For all the controversy over Frank Blethen's persona as "the last of the buckaroo publishers" pursuing a slew of pet causes, he has been remarkably hands-off with his newsroom, according to Fancher and Boardman—not that he doesn't have a long memory if he's unhappy with someone. John Hamer for instance. There's an unwritten do-not-hire list, headed by Art Thiel, the burly, outspoken former P-I sportswriter. Blethen doesn't seem to care what the Seattle establishment thinks of him. When he notes that he grew up in Arizona and jokes that he's "a runt" with a sense of mission, you get the feeling he's also saying "Don't tread on me."

As Boardman's investigative team took on Boeing, with its 80,000 workers on Puget Sound, the renowned Fred Hutchinson Cancer Research Center and home-grown retail icon Nordstrom, Blethen told his editors he would handle the flak—and the fallout—if they had their ducks in a row. Sometimes there were economic consequences. Nordstrom called The Times' coverage of the controversy over its labor practices "horrible—the worst in the nation ...," and dramatically reduced its advertising, denying it was retaliation. "People can talk all day long about my personality and causes, but no one can deny that this newspaper has had few peers for public-service journalism over the past 30 years," Blethen says.

In the Post-Intelligencer newsroom, The Times' new Pulitzers generated a complicated mélange of emotions tangled up in hard feelings dating to the dawn of the joint operating agreement 14 years earlier. Eric Nalder, Duff Wilson and Casey Corr were their former teammates—defectors as it were, with mixed emotions of their own. It was Nalder who had kicked a file cabinet when the JOA was announced to the P-I newsroom—and who one day would return to the fold.

Angelo Bruscas, the night city editor at the P-I when the joint operating agreement began, recalled how The Times had clamped down on the P-I's puny "Focus" Sunday section. It happened early on after James Wallace, the section's editor, began to infuse the allotted six pages with punchier stories, including a Casey Corr-John McCoy series on charity scams. "Then Frank Blethen and his lawyers invoked the JOA, declaring that what we were doing was violating a stipulation that the section be used for strictly opinion and criticism," Bruscas says acidly. "We were told we could no longer put anything that resembled news in our own section of the newspaper. Then, when we moved into the Internet era, we fought those same philosophical battles over our website. Many of us were bitter. Many of us still are."* But jealousy was never part of the equation, Bruscas emphasizes. To P-I people, their rivals' work was unbegrudgingly exceptional—the byproduct of a talented but also far larger staff—170 vs. 320. The latter was the enviable part. An old joke at the P-I asked, "How many Times reporters does it take to change a light bulb?" "Six—one to change the bulb and five to write about how they did it."

The P-I fielded its own lineup of first-rate writers during the 1980s and '90s, under two remarkable and remarkably different editors—the blunt, old-school newsman, J.D. Alexander, a connoisseur of spirits, food, jazz and ideas, and Ken Bunting, a charismatic African-American from Texas with a booming laugh and a full calendar of speaking engagements. Among the standouts were Wallace, McCoy, Corr, Shelby Scates, Joel Connelly, Solveig Torvik, Evelyn Iritani, Ed Penhale, Caroline Young, Jane Hadley, Steven Goldsmith, Andrew Schneider and Carol Smith—and Art Thiel and Steve Rudman in sports with Bruscas. Besides Connelly's WPPSS stories, which many believed should have won a Pulitzer, Post-Intelligencer stories prompted the Legislature to strengthen child-abuse laws; prodded new trucking regulations by disclosing that long-haul tankers were freighting industrial chemicals and corn syrup on the same round trip; revealed that foster-care kids were being overdosed with mood-altering drugs and documented that asbestos-tainted ore had killed more than 200 people in a tiny Montana town. Connelly tells a story that sums up the frustrations of competing against The Times. The news that Sena-

---

* Blethen's rejoinder is that Hearst was losing an average of $1 million a year at the P-I before it "freely entered" into the joint operating agreement and well understood its terms, including limitations on electronic publishing by the Post-Intelligencer. "And we had to abandon our morning edition."

tor Brock Adams was an alleged molester was broken by the P-I, Connelly recalls. Whereupon The Times launched an exhaustive three-year investigation that documented a pattern of abuses. Connelly and The Times' Eric Pryne, whose reporting played a key role in the exposé, were once rival Washington, D.C., correspondents. Connelly was flying back to the capital one day when he encountered Pryne, headed east to collect an award for the Adams story. "A little bit of enamel ground off my teeth in that flight."

While there was no denying the allure of The Times' impressive news and editorial budget (Corr jumped ship in 1990 after bringing down the executive director of Seattle Metro), David Brewster and others found the P-I's coverage of the arts superior to the "puffy" stuff he saw in its rival. Nor did The Times feature serious architectural criticism, the former Weekly publisher says, "since that offends the business community and seems too esoteric to draw readers. The Times seemed defiantly middlebrow and middle class, which made it go down well in the burbs."

The Post-Intelligencer acquired another nationally respected journalist when Joann Byrd, a former ombudsman at The Washington Post, was named editor of the P-I's opinion page in 1996. It already had perhaps the best editorial cartoonist in the world. David Horsey in 1999 would win his first Pulitzer Prize—the P-I's first as well—and another in 2003. The affable redhead was a masterful caricaturist who could wield a stiletto or a butterfly net with equal dexterity. He rendered Fairview Fanny as a preening bleached blonde with huge bazooms.

There was a conviction at the P-I that when it came to Pulitzers they'd been out-gunned; certainly not outclassed. Those who had worried that the JOA would geld the P-I had underestimated its deep-seated competitiveness. In the 1990s, the rival newspapers produced the finest run of important reporting in Seattle history. Horsey is now inclined to believe the JOA substantially extended the life of the Post-Intelligencer.

The Internet was changing everything.

Nevertheless, in 1996, the year of its centennial, The Seattle Times was still clinging to a 25,000 circulation lead over its morning rival, despite the acceleration of "death in the afternoon" practically everywhere else and a sharp national decline in newspaper readership. The Times had twice as many reporters, provided better coverage of the growing suburbs and owned the morning that mattered most: Sunday. That it was a home-owned paper—"a values-based company," the marketing department constantly reminded readers—was added cachet. There was some lingering reader antipathy, too, over Hearst's yellow journalism/anti-labor past. P-I people complained that their paper was getting short shrift in promotions and distribution, especially after The Times repainted many of its delivery trucks in a centennial theme and removed "Seattle Times/P-I."

17 | Roots and Branches

Television news crews were jockeying for position when Seattle Times photographer Tom Reese arrived at Kurt Cobain's imposing vintage home overlooking Lake Washington. It was April 8, 1994. Reese took a stairway to the hillside behind the house. Looking down, he squinted through a telephoto lens into a room above the garage and saw a detective crouching next to a body. A rigid right leg, a clenched fist and a tightly tied sneaker filled the viewfinder. "I couldn't believe what I was seeing. It was awful to be there," Reese recalled. Nevertheless, photojournalism was his job. The shutter clicked.

A TV reporter said the news "spread exponentially." Relatively speaking, that was so. When Cobain, a troubled soul whose cathartic music was Nirvana to generations, took his own life, e-mail was in its infancy. Facebook and YouTube were a decade away. There were only about a thousand Web sites in the world. A freshman at Swarthmore College had just launched the world's first blog.

The Times, which rarely showed dead bodies, printed Reese's photo on its front page. Many readers called it tabloid journalism. Mike Fancher, the executive editor, wrote that what motivated the paper to print the photo was the importance of documenting the grim reality of the sad choice the 27-year-old musician had made.

If the tragedy had occurred in 2014, Nirvana fans with iPhones would have scooped everyone with photos and tweets. And the muted image of Cobain's body now pales in comparison to a YouTube video purporting to show Michael Jackson "in full death mask on a gurney."

When Marshall McLuhan, the visionary philosopher, predicted in 1964 that advances in communications technology would lead to a "global village" even he may not have fully grasped that the medium would become a messenger of almost instantaneous connectivity, with dial-up AOL chirping, "You've got mail!" There were 16 million Internet users in December 1995, 0.4 percent of the world's population. A year later there were 36 million, then 70 million, then 147 million, then 248 million—4.1 percent of the world in the space of four years. There were a billion users by 2005, two billion by 2010 and more than three billion in 2015—42 percent of the people on planet Earth.

When he took his first job at The Seattle Times in 1967, Frank Blethen saw the hulking old "hot metal" Linotype machines—19th century technology—being trucked to the scrapyard. Tall gray tape-fed phototypesetters took their place. In the 1980s as Blethen, Sizemore and Fancher took control of the newspaper, they were shocked by how quickly newly-installed technology became old. When they met Bill Gates, Paul Allen, the McCaws and other high-tech innovators it became even clearer that the future of the franchise hinged on The Times keeping up with the times.

In 1992, when Nintendo's Hiroshi Yamauchi wrote a check to keep the Mariners in Seattle, Blethen was impressed. An avid baseball fan, he got to know Howard Lincoln, chairman of the video gamemaker's American operations. Through Lincoln, he met Jim Clark, who together with Marc Andreessen developed the first popular web browser, Netscape Navigator. "It was still hard to visualize where all this would lead—how search engines and hyperlinks would change everything," Blethen says. "Things were happening so fast."

The Times dabbled in audiotext and a digital bulletin board. Then, in the summer of 1995, the same week Microsoft launched Windows 95 and The Microsoft Network, it became one of the newspaper dot.com pioneers. "WebEdition/Education" was designed to engage students and teachers in the newspaper's special reports. The first focused on the 50th anniversary of the atomic bomb. Soon thereafter "Seattle Times

Extra," a website featuring news and classifieds, debuted. Jack Williams, the vice president of sales and marketing, was tasked with developing a workable business model, a tall order. "We all loved newspapers and newsprint and believed they'd be around for many years to come," Blethen remembers. "We also knew that if we didn't keep pace in cyberspace by experimenting to see what worked we could be in trouble."

Tony Ridder knew it too. With few regrets, Knight-Ridder and AT&T had invested $50 million in an online subscription news service called Viewtron that folded in 1986 after never turning a profit. Not long after he became chairman and CEO of Knight-Ridder in 1995, Ridder fielded questions at a gathering of his editors. "Tony," one said, "what keeps you up at night? What do you most worry about?" He thought for a minute, then said, "Electronic classified."

"The classified ads ... are the bedrock of the press," McLuhan had written in the '60s. "Should an alternative source of easy access to such diverse daily information be found, the press will fold."

Craigslist, the free classified ad website, caught fire in San Francisco and began spreading across the country. eBay, a garage sale on steroids, went public, then global. Jeff Bezos, Amazon's founder, read Sam Walton's retail gospel, cribbed the best of Costco and set out remorselessly to become king of the dot.com retail jungle—from books and music to the "everything" store. Google was launched as a noun and became a verb, seemingly overnight.

Newspapers' clunky, conflicted first attempts at building their own websites produced little revenue. Those that charged non-subscribers an access fee—"paywalls"—usually fizzled. Arthur Ochs Sulzberger Jr., the fourth-generation publisher of The New York Times, told a gathering of editors, "I fear we are raising a whole generation of readers who expect quality information for free."

By the 1970s, the beleaguered U.S. Postal Service, which Washington, Jefferson and Franklin saw as a vehicle to promote widespread dissemination of periodicals, was in competition with newspapers. "They used their marriage mail rates to steal our advertising insert business by offering rates that were below their cost of doing business," Blethen says, his neck turning red. "It was a double whammy: an institution created to promote newspaper and information distribution was now competing with it—subsidized by the government and allowed to charge what would be anti-competitive rates in the private sector." Craigslist, moreover, blatantly ran ads that violated federal fair employment and housing act laws. "Before crackdowns reduced their take, it's been estimated that Craigslist made about 60 percent of its revenue off discriminatory ads and other activity that would be illegal in a newspaper," Blethen fumes.

Those concerns were far from mind when Blethen stood on a windswept hill 2,500 miles from home and surveyed his ancestors' headstones. Beside him was Basil Blethen, a newfound distant relative with a Maine accent so thick a translator would have helped during their first meeting. Basil lent a hand as Frank attempted to stabilize the marble ball atop a monument erected by his great-grandfather. Then they were quiet for a long moment, listening to the wind.

It was a sentimental journey that began four years earlier, in 1993, when Frank, Bob and Will Blethen resolved to make The Seattle Times' centennial more than a birthday party. To commemorate the 100th anniversary of Alden J. Blethen's 1896 purchase of The Seattle Times, Sharon Boswell and Lorraine McConaghy, two versatile Northwest historians, were commissioned to compile a history. They began sorting through old filing cabinets filled with letters, ledgers and yellowed clippings. To their delight, they discovered a cache of Blethen family home movies of picnics and Lake Washington cruises. "We were amazed by the depth and breadth of materials," Boswell says. Next came oral history interviews. "Some of the stories we'd heard about my great-grandfather were so outrageous we weren't sure what was true and what was legend," Frank remembers. "We really knew very little about his youth growing up in Maine. Sherry and Lorraine set out to uncover the roots of the Blethen family tree and follow the story to Kansas City when he became a newspaperman, and then to Minneapolis where his luck went bad."

They found the original Blethen homestead in Waldo County, Maine, and eventually the family graveyard on that rocky hillside surrounded by cornfields. "The country was high, wild and empty; there were sheep in the road," McConaghy remembers. "When we came literally downhill to Augusta to visit Kent's Hill school where Alden J. Blethen became a star debater, and then on to Bowdoin College, Farmington and Portland, I felt relieved, as we left behind the real-life experience of the mid-century Blethen family in that unforgiving place. It was one of those experiences of place-based history where you couldn't imagine the story any other place." Boswell agrees: "It was so evocative and essential, as biographers, to be able to walk the countryside and streets ourselves. Alden J. Blethen's life was always study in contrasts, but none more extreme in my mind than the difference between this backcountry Maine birthplace and the mansion where he ended his days on Queen Anne Hill in Seattle."

Meticulously rinsing facts from the fiction, Boswell and McConaghy converted their research into a book, *Raise Hell and Sell Newspapers*—a biography of a bigger-than-life self-made man. They also chronicled the story of the newspaper and its region. Each Sunday in 1996, The Times featured a special page spotlighting how the newspaper covered Seattle's changing times—from the Gold Rush and Wobblies to Boeing, Microsoft and the Mariners. A Newspapers in Education program for school children was tied to the topic of the week.

At one meeting of the centennial planning committee, the historians showed the Blethen cousins a photo they'd never seen. It featured their great-grandparents and grandparents, together with the children who would become their fathers and uncles, all gathered on the lawn of the colonel's Highland Drive mansion. Another photo, disquieting in its solemnity, depicted the widowed Mrs. Blethen with her eight grandchildren around 1925. Frank Blethen Sr. has his arm on the shoulder of his half-brother Bill, who would father Will and Bob. Clarance B. Blethen II—"Judge"—appears the embodiment of his nickname, staring straight ahead though wireframe spectacles.

When Boswell and McConaghy returned from Maine

they had photos of headstones and what remained of the Blethen homestead. "I need to see these places," Frank told his wife, Charlene. "As soon as our centennial is over, we're going to Maine." They made the pilgrimage in the spring of 1997. "It was an incredible experience," Frank says, his voice tinged with emotion. "We connected with Basil Blethen and other family members we knew nothing about. They embraced us; they took us everywhere. We soon found out what the farmers meant when they joked that their main crop is rocks. It's so rocky that every winter the freeze and the frost push rocks up through the cornfields. Then they have to clear them off all over again."

That fall, Frank and Charlene returned, this time with Bob and Sue Blethen, Will Blethen, Mason Sizemore, Mike Fancher and his wife, Elaine. They piled into a van, with Frank at the wheel, visited the graveyard, saw the foundation of the family farmhouse and talked with faculty and students at the school the colonel loved. Its headmaster lived in Blethen House, part of an endowment by the colonel. Next, Frank made the trip with the twentysomething members of the Blethen fifth generation—his sons, Ryan and James, and his cousins' children, Christine, Rob and Trace. Ryan, a history major at Washington State University, had always been fascinated by family lore. "I told my dad it would be wonderful if we could buy a newspaper in Maine."

A few months later, the Blethens learned that Guy Gannett Communications, a fourth-generation, family-owned company, had decided to sell its Maine newspapers, including the Portland Press Herald and its Sunday edition, the Maine Sunday Telegram.* At 74,500 daily and 124,500 Sundays, they were the state's largest newspapers. The Kennebec Journal in Augusta and the Morning Sentinel in Waterville were also part of the package, together with the Coastal Journal, a weekly newspaper in Bath. Blethen and Sizemore set to work preparing a bid. Their offer of $205 million was accepted.

---

* Guy Gannett was unrelated to the Gannett Company Inc., which publishes USA Today and other newspapers.

The Seattle Times Company borrowed $213 million to consummate the deal. Guy Gannett Communications had entertained offers from newspaper groups in nearby states, a spokesman said, but "of all the companies in the newspaper business, The Seattle Times is one most like our company in the sense of independence, of family ownership and commitment to the community." John Morton, a leading newspaper industry analyst, observed that given the burgeoning competition, especially electronic classifieds, "most newspaper acquisitions today are driven by cold financial calculations. It's an exercise in which sentiment and other human qualities rarely intrude."

Tony Ridder, following the events closely, groused that the Blethens paid far more than the papers were worth. Thirty percent more, by Morton's estimate. It was true that several other newspaper companies had expressed interest, Ridder said, but the only formal bid was The Times'. Guy Gannett's bankers had shrewdly convinced the other companies to speculate on what they might bid, according to Ridder, then relayed that information to Blethen and Sizemore. "The Blethens ended up bidding against themselves," Ridder declared. Morton wrote that the Guy Gannett family "insisted the deal be structured like a stock sale rather than an asset sale. This meant the buyer would inherit the papers' numerous and restrictive labor contracts and would not be able, as often happens in asset sales, to tell union members, 'OK, tomorrow we take over. You can all reapply for your jobs and start negotiating new contracts.' That limited the amount bidders were willing to offer. It did not deter the Seattle Times Company. The firm has, from a management viewpoint, what might be termed 'the full catastrophe' in the number and aggressiveness of craft unions it must deal with. So, the Guy Gannett contracts were not daunting." Morton added:

Mason Sizemore. *Seattle Times photo*

> As Frank Blethen said in an interview, his firm could afford to take a long view. Some companies, including publicly owned companies answerable to institutional investors, feel the need "to extract a pound of flesh right away." The Times Co., Blethen added, is willing to accept earnings temporarily reduced by the acquisition's costs in interest and principal payments. ...
>
> However the deal turns out for Seattle, it's comforting to know that—in this era of buying, selling and swapping newspapers—sometimes imperatives beyond the strictly financial can make a difference.

Sizemore said the purchase would boost The Times' revenue base by 20 to 25 percent, while cash flow from the Maine newspapers would pay back the debt incurred in the transaction. Chuck Cochrane, publisher of the Times-owned Yakima Herald-Republic and Frank's trusted friend since their days together at Walla Walla 24 years earlier, was named to oversee the Blethen Maine Newspapers.

When he returned from his first pilgrimage to his great-grandfather's birthplace, Frank told Fancher and MacLeod his commitment to family ownership was stronger than ever. "It gives my generation and the next generation a touchstone and tradition we didn't have before." The next generation also acquired a new place to learn the ropes. Ryan Blethen and his cousin Rob would gain valuable experience in Maine, not all of it pleasant.

The Blethen "fifth edition" would soon influence a landmark shift in editorial positions.

In the spring of 1996, The Seattle Times agreed with President Clinton that America wasn't ready for same-sex marriage. It was a view "steeped in the pragmatism of realpolitik," as Mindy Cameron, the editorial page editor, later put it. The Times argued that a protracted battle over the Defense of Marriage Act could undermine hard-won gay rights victories and offend millions. A Gallup Poll found that 68 percent of Americans opposed gay marriage, the Times noted, "but people under 30 are far more comfortable with the idea. A generation from now, the question may not even be controversial."

One of Cameron's most persistent critics once admitted she "at least shows the capacity to change her mind." Never perhaps with more impact than in a column published that Thanksgiving. It was headlined "A time to celebrate family; A time to widen our circles." Cameron thought back to the torrent of letters for and against same-sex marriage. She recalled the joy of her son's wedding. Now with the approach of the holiday season, she reflected on the concept of family and shared an epiphany:

> It all comes down to a simple idea: Who am I (or my elected representative) to tell anyone they cannot marry the person they love and enjoy the full legal as well as emotional benefits of that bond? ...
>
> The nation's discomfort with same-sex marriage is really about fear—fear of people we don't know. That fear is now part of our political culture, thanks largely to the deliberate perpetuation of myths about a gay lifestyle. Whoa. There is no more a gay lifestyle than there is a heterosexual lifestyle. ...
>
> Holidays are a time for inclusion, for widening our circles, not tightening them.

Frank Blethen thought it was "one of Mindy's best-ever columns." He still worried, however, that moving too fast could backfire. Then in 2000, when his sons and the other Blethen offspring gathered for their annual training exercise, a seminal generational moment occurred in the old Seattle Times boardroom. Ryan and James, Frank's sons, and their cousins, Christine, Rob, Trace, Cal and Kerry, were given an assignment. "We always had an exercise involving issues or management concepts," Ryan recalls. "Mindy and Jim Vesely, the associate editorial page editor, split my generation into two teams. One team had to support marriage equality; the other had to come up with arguments against it. Then we'd have a debate. The fourth generation was just there to watch. To a person, everyone in our generation—ranging in age from 21 to 30—supported marriage equality. It seemed odd to us that the fourth generation running the paper was opposed to it. It just seemed like such a fundamental civil right. I was on the team picked to oppose it, which we half-heartedly did."

Afterward, they turned to Cameron and, almost as one, asked about the newspaper's position.

"Well, we're opposed to it," she said.

"*Why?*" one of the cousins implored.

"Ask him!" Cameron said, laughing as she pointed toward Frank at the head of the table.

"I'll never forget that moment," Frank says. "I think I hemmed and hawed for a few seconds. Then I said, 'Well, we're not against it any more. This is your first editorial position as the next generation of leaders in this company.' I'd never had anything against gays. We were one of the first papers to grant benefits to same-sex partners. I was thinking, 'If we do this, are we going to be so far ahead of the community that it's not really going to be constructive? Do we need more time for things to percolate?' It was a journey. And I got there far quicker than I would have because of Ryan, James and their cousins."

"I was very proud of these young people and what we were about to do," Cameron remembers. In a Sunday editorial, the newspaper urged the Washington Legislature to follow Vermont's lead in authorizing civil unions for same-sex partners. Cameron explained the genesis of the newspaper's change of heart in an accompanying column. The headline said, "And the next generation shall teach—and lead."

The Times moved to the forefront of the long campaign for domestic-partnership rights and marriage equality. Washington voters approved same-sex marriage in 2012; nearly 54 percent were in favor.

18 | The Battle for Seattle

For Frank Blethen, February 2, 1999, was a long time coming. He was fizzing with glee as Alex MacLeod told the newsroom the publisher had an announcement to make. Blethen was flanked by family and wearing a prized souvenir from the 1980 rollout of the short-lived morning edition, a ball cap that said "Good Morning" above a rising sun and The Seattle Times logo. Surrendering mornings in 1983 in exchange for the joint operating agreement had rankled for 16 years. "This is truly a historic day," Blethen said. "Within two years, we're going to be a morning newspaper!" Then, to cheering, he pulled on a T-shirt MacLeod had cooked up with the graphics department. It featured The Times' eagle savaging the Post-Intelligencer's landmark globe. The Hearst Corporation, which had agreed to go head-to-head only after hard bargaining, was not amused when a photo of Frank modeling the T-shirt appeared on the front page of The Times. "I knew it would piss them off and fire up our people," MacLeod says. "And for some of us it was a return to the morning, where we'd already kicked P-I butt with our newsrack edition."

No one cheered at the P-I when management handed out coffee cups and T-shirts that said "first in the morning," but the newsroom picked up the gauntlet. "When they discover news, they will be confused," said J.D. Alexander, the P-I's pugnacious editor and publisher. Hardcore newsmen like Joel Connelly, Bruce Ramsey, Steve Goldsmith and Andy Schneider relished the prospect of a head-on collision. "It's almost as good as sex!" Schneider said. Hearst pledged more staff and new computers.

Lee Rozen, who had overseen the creation of seattlepi.

Frank Blethen, sporting a T-shirt that features The Seattle Times eagle savaging the Post-Intelligencer's landmark globe, announces that The Times will go head-to-head with the P-I in the morning market. *Seattle Times photo*

com as manager of new media initiatives, was juiced that the amended joint operating agreement would give the P-I the sorely needed right to expand its website with live news and links to other Hearst publications. "After four frustrating years of incomprehensible delays and several false starts, we suddenly realized The Times had been holding the website hostage for the right to publish in the morning," Rozen remembers. "But it was exciting for Brian Chin and me because we were suddenly getting the go ahead to hire a staff and build a competitive news website." Exciting for beat reporters, too. "Because we did not have an online presence, senior Boeing executives felt we had become 'marginalized' as a paper, so why spend time giving us interviews?" says James Wallace, the P-I's former aviation reporter. "They wanted a paper with a wide online audience to reach more of their employees."

Most in the P-I newsroom also understood, however, that surrendering their monopoly on weekday mornings was a huge takeaway. Wallace saw it as "a bonehead decision and the beginning of our end."

There were several significant sweeteners for Hearst. The linchpin was gaining the first opportunity to purchase The

FAIRVIEW FANNIE GREETS THE DAWN...

"IMAGINE! *ME* IN THE *MORNING!* I'LL HAVE *ALL DAY* TO TELL PEOPLE HOW *WONDERFUL* I AM!"

P-I cartoonist David Horsey's response to Blethen's announcement. *Courtesy David Horsey*

Seattle Times should the Blethens ever decide to sell their majority interest.* The Times was also reducing its share of the profits from 68 percent to 60 percent. Another amendment, an updated "loss notice" clause, would loom large in the next few years. If either partner lost money for three consecutive years, the hard-pressed partner could initiate negotiations to close one of the newspapers "as expeditiously as possible." If no agreement was reached within 18 months, the joint operating agreement would terminate immediately, with no monetary penalties. However, if one partner or the other voluntarily moved to suspend publication, and the Justice Department approved, the profit split would revert to 68/32. In other words, if the P-I ceased publication, Hearst would receive 32 percent of The Times' profits until December 31, 2083. And if The Times

---

* Hearst agreed to pay the Blethens $1 million a year for the next 10 years to secure that right. Some lawyers believed the purchase option went beyond the scope of the Newspaper Preservation Act's antitrust exemption. The agreement apparently took effect without objection or formal approval by the Department of Justice.

suspended publication, the oddest odd-couple marriage of all would ensue: The Post-Intelligencer would be Seattle's daily newspaper. The Blethens would oversee advertising, printing and circulation and collect 68 percent of the profits.

"SUICIDE PACT: Times and P-I set the stage to put one of them out of business," was the headline in Seattle Weekly. Doug Underwood, the former Times reporter turned university professor, commented, "Up until [this announcement], you could have argued that The Times and P-I had the last successful JOA in the country." There had been 28 joint operating agreements at their peak. Now there were 15, and many of those were shaky.

The mayor, advertisers and others ostensibly in the know expressed surprise over the announcement. Industry analysts wondered why it had taken so long. Frank Blethen and Frank Bennack Jr., chief executive officer of the Hearst Corporation, had been discussing the deal for a decade. The rise of the Internet and ever-worsening traffic hastened the decision. While Seattle Times delivery vans grappled with afternoon gridlock, thousands of well-educated newcomers accustomed to digesting their news with breakfast were migrating to online news sources and using free classifieds to sell their stuff.

That The Seattle Times still led the Post-Intelligencer by some 31,000 daily was remarkable—a testament to "a superior product," Blethen asserted. The trend lines told the rest of the story: Circulation at both papers was essentially flat despite good times as Puget Sound grew by 200,000 during the 1990s. The Times' daily circulation had declined 10 percent since 1983 when it was forced to abandon its weekday morning edition. Over the same period, the Post-Intelligencer had posted a 5.5 percent gain. Mornings and the joint operating agreement were keeping the P-I afloat. The Seattle Times, stuck in the afternoon, was dog-paddling against the currents of change, clinging to its distinction as the largest-circulation, market-dominating evening paper in America. Only five of the nation's top 100 dailies published exclusively in the afternoon.

Peter Horvitz, publisher of two suburban morning dailies, the

Eastside Journal and South County Journal, called it "a fake war because there are no economic consequences to their competition." Strictly speaking, that was so. If the P-I survived and thrived it meant more money for both partners—the "agency"—while their competitors absorbed the consequences. The two Franks, Blethen and Bennack, absolutely understood what was at stake. Horvitz said something pithier when he suggested that "both The Times and Hearst would make more money if they stopped publishing the P-I and they had one newspaper—The Times—in the morning. If they eliminated the newsroom at the P-I, that would be pure savings. Basically, The Times would write [Hearst] a check every year." Horvitz predicted Seattle would be a one-newspaper town as soon as the Post-Intelligencer could string together three money-losing years. Professor Underwood said both papers might survive if Seattle's economy kept growing. "My guess is, the first major economic blows that come to these papers …that's when the real soul searching will begin."

To Mei-Mei Chan's circulation department fell the crucial task of placating with freebies, coupon books and other incentives some 30,000 loyal Seattle Times subscribers who were unhappy—many vehemently so—at the prospect of losing their evening paper. "We have subscribed for 25 years," one reader wrote. "If we had wanted a morning newspaper, we would have taken the P-I. Please reconsider this decision."

Since The Times handled circulation for the P-I and would still collect 60 percent of the profits, the change carried other risks. Those who subscribed to both papers accounted for around 7 percent of their combined home-delivery circulation—some 25,000 copies. Further, some 20 percent of the Post-Intelligencer's circulation was in single-copy sales, vs. 10 percent for its rival. Some said the P-I ought to be very worried that The Times, no longer hamstrung by the afternoon delivery cycle, would now have a shot at winning away a sizable chunk of the 30,000 readers who purchased the P-I in outlying areas. The cost-benefit numbers told a different story: the outlying circulation was increasingly unprofitable.

"We were gambling," Blethen says. "But the odds were a lot better than the alternative, which was staying in the afternoon and kidding ourselves that we wouldn't die on the vine."

The battle for Seattle officially began 13 months later after intense planning. Bob and Will Blethen looked on as Frank pushed the button to start the press at North Creek around midnight on Monday, March 6, 2000. The first copies of the morning Times clacked down the conveyor with the latest news: a bitter strike at Boeing; wrangling over Tim Eyman's new transit tax initiative; Amazon's patent on one-click shopping and word that the number of million-dollar homes sold in King County had increased tenfold in the space of four years. Barely noted was an historic moment in the history of Seattle newspapering. With the switch to morning delivery, the last of The Seattle Times' young carriers—a thousand in all—lost their routes to grownups. Among them might have been a descendant of one of the intrepid newsboys feted annually by a grateful Colonel Alden J. Blethen.

"Good MORRRRNing Seattle!" Jean Godden wrote in her popular column, relishing being back for breakfast. She had joined The Times nine years earlier after 17 years at the Post-Intelligencer. Susan Paterno, a senior contributing writer for *American Journalism Review*, bopped between the two dueling newsrooms and was surprised by what she heard:

> Perhaps most conspicuous at the first morning news meeting at The Seattle Times after it became an a.m. paper was what was missing. Amid the jolly banter and the brainstorming and the huzzahs for having put out one helluva great paper that day, no one uttered a single word about The Competition .... It was quite a different matter across town. Editors at the Post-Intelligencer ... were reacting to the Times' coverage at their news meeting with the relish of frat boys Monday morning quarterbacking the previous day's intramural football game. The P-I had that story a week ago, it wrote about this guy months ago, it was loaded with so much more news. "This is war.

Absolutely. No question," says P-I Senior Editor David McCumber afterward, explaining why he came out of daily journalism retirement to help lead the P-I's troops into battle. "We're competing for readers and news supremacy."

If this is war, did somebody forget to invite the Times? It's not as though the Times circulation is so far ahead of the P-I it can afford to be blasé. ... But to the Seattle Times' top editors, there is no competition. "Our strategy is not to be a better paper than the P-I," says Times Executive Editor Michael Fancher with a confident smile and steely stare. "Our challenge is to be better than the Seattle Times."

Though his team was outnumbered nearly 2 to 1, Art Thiel, the P-I's linebacker-size sports columnist, sniffed, "There is an art to turning out well-crafted stories on tight deadline, and The Times is in the finger painting stage of this art." Blethen had given the P-I its own bulletin-board material by telling *Editor & Publisher* the Post-Intelligencer was "a headline service" with "a terrific puzzle page."

Henry MacLeod, one of the most revered editors in the history of The Seattle Times, succumbed to pneumonia at 88 two weeks before the conversion. Alex MacLeod seemed to be channeling his avuncular father, wandering from desk to desk, cheerfully pumping people up while discounting "all the blather about whether we could ever figure out how to be a morning newspaper after all these generations as a slow-footed, long-winded PM."

At the P-I, Hearst's decision to unload its struggling San Francisco paper, the afternoon Examiner, and purchase the morning Chronicle for an estimated $500 million was viewed as a good omen. "This demonstration of Hearst's deep corporate pockets and determination to stay in the West Coast newspaper biz did far more for morale than new desks and Internet access," James Bush wrote in Seattle Weekly. The elevation of the stalwart yet sweet-tempered Ken Bunting to executive editor of the Post-Intelligencer was also welcomed. ("He always had your back," Joel Connelly remembers.) Roger Oglesby, a former Los Angeles Times executive, was the new editor and publisher, J.D. Alexander having moved to Hearst headquarters. Hearst had spent $4.7 million to upgrade the P-I's newsroom, ordered a redesign of the paper and commissioned readership surveys. "Why would Hearst spend that kind of money only to turn around and shut down the paper?" said Kathy Best, the P-I's metro editor. She was emerging as one of the most nimble breaking-news editors in the business. Given greater Seattle's booming high-tech economy and steadily rising median income, Best said it seemed strange that the P-I's circulation wasn't higher: "There's a lot of suspicion on this side that if the [subscription] checks say 'Seattle Times Co.' then maybe the P-I comes second.

"No one in newspapers can say if they'll be here in 15 years," Best said, "because who knows if papers will survive at all?"

Six months later, in the first circulation audit since The Times' shift to mornings, its circulation was up nearly 3 percent; the P-I's was down 8 percent.

And 15 years later, Kathy Best was editor of The Seattle Times.

19 | Momentum Meltdown

In a handsome booklet entitled *Momentum, A Decade of Accomplishment,* The Seattle Times celebrated a string of successes in the 1990s. The decade saw growth "unprecedented in our 104-year history as the plans and dreams of the 1980s found full expression. Journalistic excellence hit new highs. Financial growth was extraordinary. The accomplishments formed a foundation for continued success in the century to follow."

The company had grown from 2,833 employees to 4,140. Cash flow was 33 percent higher than in 1990; assets grew by 217 percent. At decade's end its annual revenues topped $400 million; $13 million in back dividends had been paid to the Blethen Corporation and Knight Ridder. "That accomplishment was particularly meaningful," a Harvard Business School study said, "because only 20 years earlier, the Blethen Corporation had received no dividends and had little hope of receiving any in the future."

Further, the company had acquired the Yakima Herald-Republic and given it the resources to stand out; saw its Walla Walla paper excel as well; built a new production plant at North Creek; capped its centennial by branching out to Maine; launched one of the first newspaper websites; opened a $1.3 million child-care facility; became an industry leader in hiring minorities and women; provided benefits to same-sex partners; rejected tobacco advertising; led record-breaking United Way campaigns; won three Pulitzer Prizes and was a finalist for four more; renegotiated the joint operating agreement; converted to morning publication with no loss of circulation—a gain, in fact. *American Journalism Review* had just ranked The

Frank Blethen, Mike Fancher and Alex MacLeod celebrate "A Decade of Accomplishment." *Seattle Times photo*

Seattle Times Number 14 on its list of the top 20 newspapers in America. These were "the ever-increasing rewards of being a values-based company," the company said, emphasizing that the fifth-generation Blethens were being imbued with their legacy to carry it on. "By sharpening our professional management skills, we will be financially successful. By choosing reasonable profitability based on cash flow, we will deliver better journalism and better community service. And by respecting employees and encouraging diversity, we will serve as a model for independent newspapers in particular and family-owned businesses in general. ... We've done much. But the best is yet to come."

The worst was soon to come. Mo Mentum, as old sportswriters like Royal Brougham used to say, swapped jerseys. First, however, there was an offer Tony Ridder thought the Blethen shareholders wouldn't refuse. In October of 2000, surfing the last wave of newspaper prosperity, Knight Ridder's chairman offered $750 million for The Seattle Times Company's newspapers. Part of the deal was the assumption of some

$200 million in debt the Blethens incurred to purchase the papers in Maine. In 1993, when Ridder offered $500 million for a majority interest in The Times, Buster Blethen's wife Debbie thought, "Yeah, wow, let's do this." Then they talked it over with Frank, who counseled that the paper was a family legacy. This time, even though her husband was losing his battle with pitiless Huntington's disease, she tossed the offer in the trash when it arrived in the mail.

A few weeks later, on November 21, 2000, a thousand members of the Pacific Northwest Newspaper Guild launched a strike against The Times and Post-Intelligencer.

"It feels like a death in the family," Alex MacLeod said, surveying the picket line outside The Times. The building's first-floor windows were sheathed with plywood; chain-link fencing cordoned off adjoining property. Black-clad security guards the strikers called "ninjas" soon took up posts. It was two days before Thanksgiving.

On the outside looking in were Pulitzer Prize-winning Seattle Times reporters Mary Ann Gwinn and Ross Anderson. "When I had my children, they let me take off nine months," Gwinn said, her voice quavering with emotion. "They let me work part-time for seven years. These things mean a lot. So it makes me sad to be out here." Anderson, unable to choke back tears, was one of several strikers uniquely conflicted by the walkout. His wife, Mary Rothschild, an assistant metro editor at The Times, was management. "We had somewhat awkward moments at their house as Ross hosted morning angst meetings of striking reporters," Joel Connelly, the longtime P-I newsman, recalls. Sometimes Mary was leaving for work just as they arrived. Connelly and Rothschild had worked together for years at the P-I before she joined The Times. Between them there were no hard feelings, just the mixed emotions that punctuated the first Newspaper Guild strike in Seattle in half a century. Anderson feared that when it was finally over many good people would be gone, whether by choice or financial fallout.

Newsroom people at both papers were a large part of the minority favoring a federal mediator's call for a 48-hour cooling off period. "Several of us were mystified that a strike

Art Thiel, the P-I's popular sports columnist, was the face of the strike in more ways than one. *Adam Weintraub/Seattle Weekly*

was called when it needed a lot more time in the oven," Connelly remembers. "The wider community was in no way told of our grievances, and didn't understand why we were striking." At the outset, for that matter, many journalists at The Times didn't understand why the people in their advertising and circulation departments were so intent on striking.

Guild members at the Post-Intelligencer, who arguably had the least to gain and the most to lose, were unified in their distaste for Frank Blethen. One picket sign featured a photo of him gleefully wearing the attack eagle T-shirt. Art Thiel, the popular P-I sports columnist who had scoffed at The Times' vaunted journalistic prowess, emerged as a Guild spokesperson, together with Ron Judd, a Times sportswriter. Judd, the son of a Boeing machinist, was a staunch unionist, yet a model of restraint compared to two veteran Times copy editors who were oblivious to "the ever-increasing rewards of being a values-based company." For Emmett Murray and Ivan Weiss the strike was a long-deferred showdown. "It all started in 1987" with a pay-for-performance demand that was anathema to the

Guild, according to Murray, who had been one of the union's top leaders for decades. The Times and P-I had been intent on giving managers wide discretion to boost salaries. Poised to strike, the Guild was forced to capitulate when Teamsters and the Typographical Union said they couldn't guarantee their members would honor Guild picket lines. "We were beaten and beaten bloody in '87," but survived to fight another day, Murray said.

Another day came in the 1990s when the contracts were set to expire. The Times erected security fences and served notice it was prepared to continue publishing in the event of a strike. The Guild once again swallowed unpalatable concessions, including lower pay for journalists in suburban bureaus and commission-only compensation for ad salespeople. Now, in 2000, it was payback time. The Guild wanted an across-the-board raise of $3.25 per hour over three years, contributions to workers' 401(k) plans and an end to two-tier wages. The papers' final offer was $3.30 over six years and a phase-out of the two-tier plan. The largest Teamsters local quickly settled its contract. Eighty composing room workers voted to strike, which helped energize the Guild.

The underlying issue for union leaders was putting an end to "pattern" bargaining. Over the previous 15 years, after jawboning a pact with one union, Jim Schafer, The Times' senior vice president for employee relations, would tell the next on deck that the same offer was the absolute best they were going to get; anything beyond that could put an end to independent journalism and bring plagues of locusts. "This time we didn't flinch," Murray said. "We said, 'The hell with you too!' "

"We had almost a half-century of experience that said we weren't going to have a strike," Mason Sizemore, The Times' chief operating officer, said after it was over. "Even when the Guild people started talking about a strike [back in July] it was hard for us to accept that this was a serious possibility." Blethen, however, says, "I always thought the chance of Guild strike was a pretty strong possibility. That's why we did such extensive planning."

For the Blethens and Hearst, the timing could not have been worse, which the Guild well understood. Retailers kicked off the Christmas shopping season on the day after Thanksgiving. The fourth quarter was also money time for newspapers. The Times and Post-Intelligencer would lose millions in advertising and circulation revenue in the weeks to come. Home-delivery subscribers and newsstand customers received thinner free papers for most of the strike. "It was one of the most unnecessary strikes" in the history of the industry, Blethen says, shaking his head. "It cost us *a lot* of money and hurt the Guild even more. No one won and everyone lost." The problem with unions, Blethen maintains, "is that so often the lion's share of the members don't go to the meetings. It's not a big deal to them, so you end up with a small group controlling things. The Seattle Guild local was very much controlled by P-I employees. This was their strike—together with some Times circulation employees just waiting for their opportunity to stick it to the company. And although Hearst was losing money, too, it could absorb the losses better than us. They stood to gain because if we got in financial trouble they figured they could get control of us" under the terms of the renegotiated joint operating agreement.

The walkout featured a striking role reversal. The unions styled the home-owned Times as a hypocritical cheapskate, while the giant Hearst Corporation—once the archenemy of labor—came off as more conciliatory. Roger Oglesby, the P-I's new publisher, seemed mellow in comparison to Blethen, especially after a legendary incident on the fourth day of the strike. Peter Horvitz, publisher of the Eastside Journal, had printed the first hard-copy edition of the Guild's strike paper, the Seattle Union Record. Blethen was livid. Unable to reach Horvitz by phone, he sent him an e-mail that went viral by the standards of the day when it leaked out: "Fuck you to death. Your ex-friend Frank." When Horvitz told fellow publishers he hadn't realized it was a strike paper until it was too late to cancel the job and would not print it again, Blethen was having none of it. "What part of 'fuck you to death' don't you understand, Peter?"

Rowland Thompson, the adroit director of Allied Daily Newspapers, attempted to broker peace. Blethen was unrepentant, especially after receiving attaboys from other publishers.

He celebrated his feistiness, telling the Wall Street Journal the company psychologist had advised him "to be careful as I'd occasionally want to kick a door down just to see if I could kick it down." That the strikers would make Blethen the boogeyman was predictable. They were wrong, however, to assert he was their only antagonist. Schafer and Sizemore were equally resolute. "We all felt we had put a good offer on the table," Blethen says, "and we were not going to give away the store." The Hearst Corporation, despite Blethen's suspicions about its true intentions, also held fast on the baseline offer of $3.30 over six years. It brought in replacement workers from its other newspapers.

Most of the Times reporters on the picket lines were earning $50,000 a year, many considerably more, thanks to the performance pay program. The merit pay average was set to increase at least 5 percent to $63,000 before year's end. Many of the highest-paid reporters said they were striking for the suburban reporters and the classified, advertising and circulation workers earning far less. The cost of living in King County zoomed during the high-tech '90s. A circulation supervisor at The Times complained that the mileage reimbursement rate had been slashed by 24 cents in recent years. Single mothers with a couple of kids were making $500 to $550 a week, said Times reporter Sally McDonald, who finally decided to cross the picket lines. She was also troubled "by the union's refusal to allow a vote on the papers' contract offer." Art Thiel said the union's discretion over whether to vote on a contract was crucial leverage in negotiating with the company.

Ian Ith, a reporter in The Times' Eastside bureau at the time of the strike, started at around $26,000 despite four years of award-winning work at smaller dailies. He believed the two-tier pay scale was unfair but didn't think it was worth striking over. "I think it was an issue inflated by the Guild leadership to drum up enthusiasm among the news staff. For me, the real issue became clear when we talked with Guild members we had never before associated with professionally or personally—ad guys and distribution and press guys, many of whom really were getting raw deals. We all were together in a sink-or-swim moment, and, frankly, we were not the kind of people who would turn our backs on them. As regrettable as it was, the strike brought a lot of collective spirit and realization that a lot of people worked really hard for crappy pay to produce the papers and put them on doorsteps so people could read our stories." Ron Judd agrees: "The circulation and advertising department people at The Times were the ones most aggrieved. They were a huge chunk of our membership, and they propelled the vote to strike. People in

Carriers and Teamsters on the picket line.
Adam Weintraub/Seattle Weekly

the newsroom who had benefitted from Frank's commitment to quality journalism had no clue that these other folks were so poorly compensated." Chuck Taylor, who organized the Guild's strike paper, loved working for The Seattle Times. "When I got hired there in 1985 I thought I had won the lottery. The place was lousy with talent—smart, progressive journalists. It was really the place to be. I thought I would retire from that paper." His wife, Anne Koch, was a reporter there too. Taylor, now an assistant city editor at The Daily Herald in Everett, believes the strike easily could have been averted. "I think some of us had our hearts broken over Frank's intransigence. There was a lot of wage disparity. But they just weren't going to negotiate. If they had upped their offer 10 cents an hour we would have settled. Instead, getting through the strike cost him at least $26 million in lost revenue and expenses. If McClatchy had been in that situation they would have looked at it in a cold, cost-benefit analysis and they would have said 'Let's find a way to settle.' "

Those attempting to cover the strike with objectivity encountered a pronounced Rashomon effect that seems to have intensified with the passing years. While most blame Blethen to one extent or another, some believe Hearst was playing both ends against the middle, all the while making nice. Some P-I people believe Blethen dug in his heels when he saw the strike was damaging their already hard-pressed paper, a notion he finds absurd. Likewise the suggestion he wanted to break the unions to get an even better offer from Tony Ridder. Among those who crossed the picket line at the P-I are several who say they did so because they feared the strike could be the death knell for their paper. And some P-I strikers told their Guild brethren at The Times they were out there for them because they had to work at a place where management was leaving messages on answering machines, warning strikers they were damaging their careers. Judd was appalled when some well-paid people crossed the picket lines. "Others who had hungry kids at home" could be excused. There was comradery around the burn barrels on drizzly December nights, Judd remembers. "A lot of Times and P-I people became friends for the first time. There was a sense of being together in the same leaking boat."

As the U.S. Supreme Court was casting the five votes that made George W. Bush the 43rd president of the United States, The Times was beginning to hire "permanent" replacement workers. The Guild filed unfair labor charges with the National Labor Relations Board. The Stranger, Seattle's impertinent alternative weekly, nevertheless accused union leadership of "wussyness" and stirred the pot with a "Scab Watch" outing strikebreakers. Times editors Mike Fancher and Mindy Cameron were bashing the Guild with requisite management vigor, yet the strikers' Union Record seemed more like "the senior project of an earnest high-school journalism class," Dan Savage and Josh Feit wrote. They concluded that the union was more concerned with avoiding "going negative" than winning the strike. That stance compounded the strikers' "real problem"—the lack of deep public support. "While liberal, pro-union Seattleites want to support the strike, their commitment runs about as deep as the sentiment of folks who 'want' to ride the bus (but don't, because it sucks) or send their kids to public school (but don't because they suck.) Face it, this isn't a union town in the same way that Detroit is a union town. That city's gory 20-month newspaper strike drew massive public support."*

Judd concedes "Seattle isn't Detroit" but says the strikers received gratifying, underestimated support from other unions and the Church Council of Greater Seattle.

Blethen was angry with the journalists—editorial writers in particular—who joined the picket lines or stayed home. "It does hurt that people don't appreciate what they've been given. I don't mean that paternalistically, but in terms of the unusual environment for excellence we had created. We had given the editorial staff opportunities and privileges, such as writing columns that took issue with the paper's positions. And how did they thank me? They go on strike. Or worse yet, the ones who stayed at home and said, 'Oh, I didn't want the picket line. I wasn't going to support the strike, but obviously I had to stay home.' Bullshit you had to stay home!"

Bruce Ramsey, a libertarian-conservative, was the only Times editorial writer to cross the picket lines. His colleague Casey Corr, motivated in part by "a sense of Irish affinity with workers and their families," carried a placard. "I liked Frank a lot more than the Hearsts. And I was picketing not out of a belief that the strike was a good idea; it wasn't. I just thought I needed to participate in the hope that a united front would force legitimate discussions that would lead to an early conclu-

---

* The strike in Detroit cost Gannett and Knight Ridder $300 million. The combined circulation of their newspapers declined by nearly 285,000. Industry analyst John Morton believes the unions lost even more. By walking out they "handed management on a silver platter what it would have taken a decade to negotiate—the elimination of hundreds of union jobs unneeded since the earlier merger of the two Detroit papers into a joint operating agency."

sion. The strike engendered a lot of complicated feelings. Day by day people began to cross. Our daily meetings of strikers felt like wakes during a pandemic."

As Christmas neared, Sizemore became the Grinch. Neither paper would budge on the $3.30 raise, he said. They were willing, however, to phase out two-tier pay in three years rather than six and better compensate some circulation and advertising department workers. Settlement or no settlement, escalating losses from the strike would require workforce cuts of at least 10 percent at The Times, Sizemore said, and 68 replacement workers would be offered permanent jobs. "We're going to find a way to be profitable in the future, with or without the Guild." Linda Foley, president of the International Newspaper Guild, called it "an incredibly cynical ploy to try and break this strike."

Hearst, contending with only about 130 newsroom and business department workers at the P-I—there were 800 Guild members at The Times—made a new offer that amounted to fewer paid holidays and better health-care premiums. Oglesby for the first time sounded cross. The Guild's appeals to readers to cancel their subscriptions and pressure retailers to withhold ads amounted to "an assault on the newspapers as businesses" and "puts jobs at risk," the P-I's publisher said.

Promised they'd get their old jobs back, Guild members at the P-I settled on December 28. The vote was 88-29. They hadn't won much. Still, "the strike was necessary," wrote John Levesque, the P-I's television critic, "if for no other reason than to let everyone see the real Seattle Times behind the warm and fuzzy artifice created by the paper's enormously effective marketing machine." Two days later, newsroom, advertising, circulation and composing room workers at The Times voted 399-93 to continue their strike. "We're still here, Frank!" a crowd of strikers chanted outside the Times Building, goading the security guards to "Film this!"

The Clinton administration's top federal mediator, C. Richard Barnes, was hailed by all as a model of persistent civility. But it was U.S. Senator Patty Murray, the five-foot-tall Democrat once dismissed as merely "a mom in Tennis Shoes," who brokered the breakthrough. Respected by both sides, the senator had intervened in late December, fearing Seattle stood to lose one of its newspapers if the losses continued to escalate. (Murray supported Blethen's campaign to phase out the estate tax, but she also had strong ties to labor.) Now, with things in danger of "spinning out of control" at The Times, she summoned Barnes, Blethen, Sizemore and union leaders to her office in Washington, D.C. Over the course of 13 hours, she and Barnes kept them caffeinated and talking. The senator herself fetched sandwiches when people got tired and hungry.

On January 4, 2001, they reached a tentative agreement overwhelmingly ratified four days later: The Times held fast on $3.30 an hour over six years; two-tier would be phased out over three years. Nor would it match 401(k) plans. The Guild won concessions that within six months all its members would be back on the job, that the "permanent" replacement workers would be removed and that layoffs necessitated by the company's losses would be made according to seniority. The company's health-care contribution—previously 66 percent—would be bumped to 75 percent; some lower-paid slots would be upgraded. Sizemore, looking drained, said the company expected to cut at least 160 union jobs, mostly through attrition, early-retirement buy-outs and severance packages. Ron Judd, speaking for the Guild members at The Times, said, "This is the first contract since 1987 that we haven't given anything up."

Time would tell—and quickly.

Eli Sanders was a 23-year-old intern at The Times when the strike started, "excited about being involved in something bigger than myself." By the time they began distributing picket signs he had a better understanding of the value of his labor and the meaning of solidarity. Nine years later, reflecting on Seattle's deep labor history and the state of the unions, Sanders wrote:

> What none of us realized then was that the industry we were demanding more from was on the verge of a huge change that would make our strike look, in retrospect, poorly timed

and even more poorly executed. Neither did we have a clear-eyed view of the long change that Seattle itself was undergoing. ... Today's non-union programmers, espresso makers, and lab-coated gene manipulators didn't—and would never—shut down the city in solidarity with striking newspaper workers (or striking Boeing employees, for that matter) in the way that Seattle's trade unions collectively shut down a far less high-tech version of this city in 1919 out of solidarity with striking shipyard workers. ...

I was certainly happy for those helped by what we'd all "won," and I was grateful for the time I'd spent standing around the burn barrel and arguing in the union hall... . But the atmosphere at the Times after the strike was strained and unpleasant; I'd lost a work environment that I hadn't realized was exceptionally nice. Over the next year and a half, I paid $671.46 in union dues (further increasing my net financial loss from striking), and after a series of discouraging events ... I decided to try a different way of doing journalism, and I quit.

Sanders, a wonderfully talented writer, went to work for The Stranger. In 2012, he won the Pulitzer Prize for feature writing, an achievement that underscored the growing influence of all manner of "alternative" media. The 49 days Sanders and some 800 other Times workers spent on strike—exhilarating, confusing and, for some, disillusioning—were part of a sea change in traditional journalism. The battle in Seattle may have marked the beginning of the end of walkouts as an effective tactic against publishers. A bitter, nine-month Newspaper Guild strike at The Vindicator in Youngstown, Ohio, ended in the summer of 2005. Many in the industry believe there will never be another.

John Morton, a leading industry analyst, wrote that a striking Seattle reporter told him early in the dispute that there was "sentiment within the Guild that employees might be better off if Knight Ridder took over. I told him that if the strikers thought the Blethens were difficult to negotiate with, they would be in for a shock if Knight Ridder were in charge. Another of the Guild's dubious achievements in Seattle is that this may no longer be true."

As things returned to some semblance of normal at Seattle's two daily newspapers at the dawn of the 21st century, retailers reported the worst holiday sales in a decade. Sears planned to close 89 stores and cut 2,400 jobs, Wall Street was nervous about declining profits and the slowing economy. High-tech stocks had been declining since Labor Day. Though the dot.com bubble had burst and the forecasts from Microsoft and Intel were disappointing, Google's ad revenues were growing and Craigslist was advancing from San Diego to Seattle. The Sunday Times featured a profile of a Saudi millionaire turned terrorist who was seen beaming during Al-Jazeera's broadcast of his son's wedding. Few Americans knew his name. It was Osama bin Laden.

20 | Joint Operating Angst

While P-I Publisher Roger Oglesby greeted his returning employees with hugs, Happy New Years and free espressos, there were chilly moments in the hallways at The Seattle Times. People who'd been on opposite sides during the strike passed one another without so much as a nod. Alex MacLeod found it difficult to just forgive and forget. Frank Blethen wasn't in a hugging mood either. Ron Judd was surprised and gratified, however, when Blethen sought him out for "some long and candid conversations—mostly about other personal stuff, like he wanted to find out what made me tick. I sensed that he was trying to come to grips with the strike and get to know his people better." It was also clear that things had changed.

The losses The Times incurred during the 49-day strike—an estimated $13 million in advertising revenues and another $19 million in direct expenses—were compounded by the slowing economy and increasingly worrisome competition from the Internet. The company was also in arrears on the loan covenants for the Maine newspapers. The bankers forgave that transgression during the strike but would assess penalties for the first two quarters of 2001. The Times implemented a hiring freeze as part of a 15 to 20 percent workforce reduction. The outcome would be "a more focused newspaper," Blethen said. The "entitlement mentality" was over.

Blethen was in an especially reflective mood when he sat for an interview in January with the *Puget Sound Business Journal*. "It never occurred to us," he said, "that there could be a threat from within; that there could be a circumstance under which our business base could be destroyed by a large group of our employees turning against us and then receiving support from a large segment of the community." At one point during the strike, Blethen said he entertained a notion he would have been "almost pathologically incapable of even suggesting" before then—"that there could be financial circumstances that would cause us to get out of the business." He was counseled by his cousins to remember his own mantra: "The Times is a trust."

February ended with one of the largest recorded earthquakes in Puget Sound history. And March brought a jolt to Seattle's psyche when Boeing announced it was moving its corporate headquarters elsewhere. At the spring meeting of The Seattle Times Company Board, Blethen pledged that the loan covenants would be met, predicted profits of 12.5 percent for the year and, despite Knight Ridder's vocal objections, won the board's approval to boost the company's $6-million annual dividend pool by $1 million. The notion that if a company had debt it shouldn't pay dividends was ridiculous, Blethen said. Further, the company was pushing ahead with the purchase of a new high-tech German press to ensure its Rotary Offset Press subsidiary remained competitive.

Then came the 21st century equivalent of World War III. On the morning of September 11, al-Qaeda terrorists hijacked four Boeing jetliners and flew two into the twin towers of the World Trade Center. When the stock market reopened after a week's hiatus, investors lost $1.4 trillion in the space of five days. Though the market rebounded in the surge of resolute patriotism that followed the attacks, consumer confidence was shaken; advertising in mainstream media slumped. As wariness and tedious new security measures took their toll on air travel, Boeing announced it would lay off 20,000 to 30,000 workers. "Nothing will ever have the impact that 9/11 had on Boeing and on the world. It just changed things overnight," says Alan Mulally, former CEO of Boeing's Commercial Airplanes division. It was the beginning of a calamitous decade.

Six weeks after 9/11, Mason Sizemore, the widely respected president and chief operating officer of The Seattle Times for 16 of the most eventful years in the company's history, was gone in the space of 24 hours. The company called it a retirement. No one in the know, however, was buying the notion that after 36 years with the company, Sizemore, at 60, just up and decided he was out of there without a word of goodbye. "There are just some things best left unsaid between two old friends," says Blethen. For his part, Sizemore will talk about practically anything except The Seattle Times. The leading theories revolve around the stress accrued over the previous year and mutual exasperation. Familiarity, as the aphorism goes, breeds contempt. Sizemore clearly was either fired or fed up. The consensus is fired.

Sizemore was succeeded immediately by Carolyn Kelly, general manager of The Times and a senior vice president since 1997. The 49-year-old was a cheerful, adroit manager and long a Blethen favorite. They first met in the 1970s when she was a CPA fresh out of Gonzaga, auditing the books at the Walla Walla Union-Bulletin. Kelly, with very full plate, was now one of the top female executives in the newspaper industry. The position of general manager was eliminated as part of the downsizing. "Nothing focuses you on a mission like this kind of challenge and this kind of adversity," she said.

Other notable departures included Mindy Cameron, who had announced her retirement before the strike. Sixty-year-old Jim Vesely, the well-traveled newsman Blethen respected, moved up to editor of the editorial page. Ace investigative reporter Eric Nalder signed on with Knight Ridder's San Jose Mercury News. Casey Corr took a job with a tech company startup. Chuck Taylor took a buyout and landed at Seattle Weekly. Ivan Weiss, the truculent Guild shop steward, filed a complaint with the National Labor Relations Board when he wasn't recalled to work within six months—surprise—and eventually extracted a settlement. His parting shot was "I'll never work in journalism again, if I can help it." That was fine with Frank.

Still smarting over Mayor Paul Schell's refusal to talk with Times reporters during the strike, Blethen threatened to move the newspaper's headquarters to the suburbs unless City Hall started to appreciate that business wasn't the enemy. He was fed up with the city's "ultraliberal, pro-labor stance" and penchant for making "zoning changes at the whim of whoever is in charge."

When the books closed on 2001, despite reducing its workforce by 450 while slashing $40 million from its operating budget to assuage its lenders, The Seattle Times reported it had lost money for the second year in a row. Its weekday and Saturday circulation had rebounded to pre-strike levels. Sunday circulation, however, was off five percent and below 500,000 for the first time since 1986. The week's big edition—joint in name only—was noticeably smaller, with far fewer full-page ads and inserts. The Post-Intelligencer's circulation, down nearly 12 percent since 1999, was harder hit—in raw numbers at least—when The Times curtailed home-delivery and single-copy sales of both papers in a large swath of Southwest Washington to save around $1 million. The P-I lost 3,400 readers; the weekday and Saturday Times only 475. It was yet another move to kill the competition, critics said. Carolyn Kelly countered that the outlying circulation was not cost effective, adding that the decision reduced The Times' Sunday circulation by 5,600.

Seattle still had two newspapers, David Brewster said, but anyone could see they were much diminished.

Frank told his cousins they were at a crossroads: Hunker down or double down. They could keep cutting and try to ride out the downturn, hoping they'd still have a viable reader base when it was over. Or they could take advantage of low interest rates to refinance their debt, acquiring in the process even more debt but also $20 million to shore up the paper. Either course was risky, Frank remembers, "so when we decided to refinance it wasn't so much a gamble as an act of faith."

The newsroom's signature trait—great investigative reporting—gave The Times something to celebrate. A series headlined "Uninformed Consent" revealed that patients who received experimental bone-marrow transplants at Seattle's renowned Fred Hutchinson Cancer Research Center were not fully informed of the risks. Nor were they advised that some of their doctors and the center itself had a financial interest in the experiments. The series by Duff Wilson and David Heath won practically every major journalism award in 2002 except the

Pulitzer Prize. A full court press by friends and allies of "the Hutch" may have had something to do with that. Strongly denying any breach of ethics, the Cancer Research Center hired a public relations firm to combat the fallout. Then, just before the final vote by the Pulitzer judges, The Wall Street Journal printed a column attacking the series as a "textbook case" of sensationalism. The author, one of the Journal's editors, had been treated for cancer at the Seattle clinic and was among its leading supporters. When the controversies subsided, the Cancer Center's trustees formed an advisory committee that recommended new conflict-of-interest rules and patient consent procedures.

Even more gratifying to Blethen and his editors were the two near-wins in 2003 when the entire news staff was recognized by the Pulitzer Prize judges for breaking news coverage and investigative reporting. The stories revealed the local ties of two suspects arrested in the D.C. Sniper case and documented the chilling backstory of a would-be terrorist headed for Los Angeles with a trunk load of bomb paraphernalia before he was captured at a Washington State point of entry.

The following year, Christine Willmsen and Maureen O'Hagan were finalists in the public service category for "Coaches Who Prey," the revelation that no less than 159 girls' sports coaches had been reprimanded or fired for sexual misconduct in the previous decade. Nearly a hundred were still coaching or teaching in the Northwest. In all, 17 staffers worked on the series.

The Times and Post-Intelligencer, meanwhile, were embroiled in the messiest, most expensive divorce case in Seattle history. The underlying issue in Blethen v. Hearst was whether both newspapers—community property in a sense—could survive a split.

In the first week of January 2003, The Times announced a third consecutive year of unprofitability, a total of $10 million in losses since 2000. Blethen said he was weighing whether to invoke the loss-notice provision in the joint operating agreement. In truth, he had already made up his mind, telling a group of staffers, "If the P-I doesn't invoke it, we will."

The Times made its intentions clearer yet by hiring freelance writer Bill Richards, a tenacious former *Newsweek* and Wall Street Journal reporter, to cover the impending divorce proceedings. Richards' contract was perhaps unique in the annals of journalism in that it insulated him from interference. Any major disputes over his reportage would be mediated by the Poynter Institute, a nationally respected journalism think tank. The 61-year-old newsman called the pact "creative and gutsy on their part." The head of the Society of Professional Journalists was impressed as well, though Jeffrey Philpott, chairman of the Communication Department at Seattle University, smelled trouble. "It sets up an adversarial relationship with the paper," he said. When Tony Ridder and Hearst insiders proved to be among Richards' best sources, Blethen believed the reporter was veering off the path of objectivity and blew his stack. If there were "lies and exaggerations," as Blethen claimed, Richards said the publisher was part of the problem for "stonewalling" him. Richards' three-year contract was not renewed.*

The escalating adversarial relationship between the JOA partners was underscored by a terse Hearst statement questioning whether The Times' losses could be substantiated (the Department of Justice reportedly received a hand-delivered copy) and a not-for-attribution comment by a Hearst executive that they were "not going to be chased out of Seattle" by Frank Blethen. Hearst observed that since 2002, while newspapers around the nation were making wholesale layoffs and freezing salaries, Blethen had added 71 journalists to his newsroom. Though it pained him to agree with Brewster, Blethen said the scope of the news and editorial content The Seattle Times offered in the year after the strike was "not up to our standards. ...You can't keep your reader base in the face of new competition unless you're willing to invest in your product. That's why we refinanced our loans, and that's why we're different from the giant media companies owned by faceless investors, the ones busy laying off journalists to preserve their excessive prof-

---

* Richards died of a heart attack at 72 in 2014 while exercising on a rowing machine.

its." King County Journal publisher Peter Horvitz, who had angered Blethen during the strike, told Richards it was "inexcusable" for The Times to go on a hiring spree in the middle of a major downturn. Frank figured two fuck-yous sufficed.

The Times' circulation was up nearly 5 percent; the P-I's had atrophied another 5 percent to its lowest level since the 1940s. The Times was winning the head-to-head battle but losing subscription revenue. It was also losing its veteran managing editor.

After three years of relentless stress—his dad's death, the move to mornings, the "stupid" strike, the loan-covenant crisis, plummeting revenues and the battle over the JOA—56-year-old Alex MacLeod realized it was time to go. He'd been sending not-so-subtle signals since 9/11 when he didn't abandon a leave at his Shaw Island getaway and rush back to the newsroom. While his absence also said he trusted his staff, the deeper truth was that he was burned out, a bit bored after 17 years as managing editor and incapable, more than ever, of suppressing what was on his mind. During a budget-cutting discussion at a management retreat after the strike, he observed archly that Blethen and Sizemore were still driving Lexus sports cars. Blethen was not amused.

MacLeod told friends he wanted Dave Boardman, his popular and talented deputy, to have his chance to run the show. MacLeod snapped up an enhanced early-retirement package and decamped to the tranquility of the San Juans.

Negotiations between Blethen and Victor Ganzi, Hearst's president and chief executive officer, over the possibility of modifying the 60/40 profit split stalled. At one point, Blethen says, the Hearst Corporation offered to assume $165 million in Times debts if he would back off. What Hearst characterized as "an upfront inducement payment" of $50 million was also rejected. The strings attached were always unacceptable, Blethen says. "They told us we were facing the most expensive litigation in the history of the industry if we persisted."

The battle was fully joined in the spring of 2003. Asserting that the joint operating agreement as currently configured would "yield substantial losses for the foreseeable future," Blethen informed Ganzi that The Times was invoking the stop-loss provision. The partners now had 18 months to work things out.

Hearst filed suit in King County Superior Court to stop the clock. Ganzi, a former tax attorney, charged that the previous three years were not a fair test of the JOA's economic viability. Blethen fired off a memo to his staff. "It's hard to understand Hearst's motivation in filing suit," he wrote, "unless it is, in fact, based on a strategy to bleed The Seattle Times until we are forced out of business, presumably through a forced sale to Hearst." Seizing the theme, Hearst's lawsuit said it wasn't going to stand by while the Post-Intelligencer, Seattle's pioneer newspaper, was forced out of business by a company whose CEO "had long sought a monopoly." The Times was now citing losses triggered by extraordinary events and inflated by millions in overspending to invoke the escape clause, Hearst's attorneys said. Losses like those caused by the holiday-season strike and terrorist attacks shouldn't count under the terms of the joint operating agreement, they argued. Those were "force majeure" losses caused by circumstances beyond reasonable control. Many in the industry said the smart money was on Hearst, a media conglomerate with annual revenues topping $5 billion. Hearst had outlasted its JOA partners in San Francisco and San Antonio. In Seattle, however, the Blethens owned the plate-making equipment, printing presses, inserters and delivery trucks—all the hard assets required to publish a newspaper. If Hearst threw in the towel it could collect 32 percent of The Times' profits for the next 80 years. But if Blethen prevailed, he might end up with the Get Out of Jail Free card. "The chances of the P-I's owners letting the 18-month clock end without a way to salvage their business interests in Seattle are slim to none," *Editor & Publisher* concluded. "Simply stated," Ganzi said, "the P-I is not financially viable outside the JOA."

The Department of Justice announced it was sending investigators to Seattle to examine issues surrounding the breakup and take a fresh squint at the fine print in the revised JOA. Hearst's lawyers filed with the court copies of internal Times Company documents they said demonstrated accounting jujitsu related to interest expenses on the loans for the Maine newspapers. "The reality is they are making money," said one Hearst lawyer. It was then, Blethen says, that he fully grasped "that Hearst had sicced the Justice Department on us. They were using accounting documents prepared for our board but never submitted to lenders."

The dumpster-diving of the pre-trial discovery process also yielded a recent Times memo indicating Blethen had designs on ending the JOA from his first day as publisher in 1985, which was the gospel truth, as well as a Hearst memo, circa 1993, documenting that while the P-I was now turning a profit, the company was weighing whether it would be better off to just close it down and continue collecting an annual satchel of money from The Times. If Blethen had deliberately overspent to engineer losses, as Hearst alleged, were its own hands entirely clean?

Judge Greg Canova, a quick-witted former prosecutor, granted intervenor status to the Committee for a Two-Newspaper Town, a citizens group supported by the Newspaper Guild and leading liberal politicians, including Congressman Jim McDermott and former governor Mike Lowry. The committee was headed by Phil Talmadge, a former state senator and Washington Supreme Court justice with sharp elbows, and Anne Bremner, a high-profile attorney.

All three factions were in court for the first time that September. The arguments presented that day framed a debate that would take four years to resolve. Hearst's local attorney, Kelly Corr, told Canova his ruling would be "crucial to the future of the P-I" and asserted that The Times' losses from the strike didn't fit the market-change exigencies the loss notice provision was designed to address. Douglas Ross, The Times' attorney, countered that when the JOA was renegotiated in 1999 the partners had discussed losses related to strikes but took no action on exempting labor disruptions from the calculus. Ross said Hearst's arguments amounted to "trying to force a square peg into a round hole."

Labor law expert Dmitri Iglitzin, a high energy lawyer given to cutting the air with his hands, represented the Committee for a Two-Newspaper Town. Iglitzin encountered a speed bump when Canova ruled that at least for the time being the committee could not argue that the JOA constituted a restraint of trade. The judge did allow Iglitzin to argue a perhaps more telling point, namely that the joint operating agreement's voluntary closure provision violated state law and the intent of the Newspaper Preservation Act. The act was designed to preserve two-newspaper towns, Iglitzin said. This pact gave the weakest partner no financial incentive to carry on. The value of two independent newspapers to a community was incalculable, Iglitzin said. The Times and P-I took different positions on the Iraq war, Bush vs. Gore, the estate tax and extending Seattle's landmark monorail. "In all those issues," he said, "it was vitally important to hear both of those voices."

Judge Canova promptly ruled that 2000 didn't count as the first of three consecutive years of losses, noting that in 2001 Blethen had described the strike losses as "an anomaly" in a presentation to bankers. To the delight of the Committee for a Two-Newspaper Town, the judge also cited the JOA's preamble, which declared it was "of paramount importance to the citizens of Seattle and its environs" to have two newspapers.

The Times filed an appeal. Attorneys for both companies agreed to a truce of sorts that stopped the clock on the 18-month countdown to possible dissolution. The state Court of Appeals agreed to expedite a ruling.

The three judges who reviewed the case found for The Times in March of 2004 with a note of regret. "The Times' loss notice represents a sad moment for Seattle and for journalism," Judge Anne L. Ellington wrote for the panel. "The advantage of two daily newspapers is a rare state of affairs today, and the temptation is great to rewrite the JOA, in the hope we will somehow preserve both. But this we may not do. Whatever the ultimate outcome of this litigation, on this question, the agreement is clear and not subject to the interpretation urged by Hearst." Judge Canova was directed to allow The Times' losses in 2000 and 2001 to count toward the stop-loss clause. Hearst vowed to challenge the 2002 loss as well and take its case to the Washington Supreme Court.

Blethen said it was time to get serious about renegotiating the profit split. Given the weak regional economy, contributing to a sharp decline in help-wanted ads, the outlook for the rest of the year was more of the same. "It has to stop," Blethen said. David Brewster, now heading Town Hall, a new cultural center, believed it was inevitable one of the dailies would fail. The survivor would be scooped up by Knight Ridder or another media conglomerate. "The price will be so high that even Hearst and Blethen will sell."

What the Blethens began to sell was real estate. The 34 acres in suburban Renton once considered for a second printing plant fetched $9.6 million. Paul Allen, Microsoft's co-founder, acquired six acres surrounding The Times' headquarters for $31 million as part of his plan to transform South Lake Union into a "new-world melting pot of ingenuity and growth."

Frank feared his world was just melting down.

21 | A Surprising Call

Contemplating another unhappy new year, even Frank Blethen was ready to do the unthinkable. Tony Ridder vividly remembers the surprising call in January of 2005. "Frank said, 'I think we are now ready to sell The Seattle Times. And if you will give me an attractive offer, I will convince my family to sell to Knight Ridder.' He was very cordial. I kind of rushed it through our January board meeting. But then our offer [$500 million] just sat there with him through all of February and all of March. From time to time I'd say, 'Frank, what's going on?' And he'd say, 'I think your price is fair. We're going to get there, Tony. I just need to do more work with the family.' I was lucky …because if Frank had turned around in the middle of February or the middle of March and said, 'We accept it,' I had made a good faith offer we couldn't take back. Business was getting shakier and shakier, and I was getting more and more nervous about the whole deal. Advertising really wasn't picking up. Newspaper stock prices were falling, including ours, so I just got more and more concerned. I think it was around the end of April that I finally told him I was withdrawing the offer. I said, 'I'm sorry, Frank.' He didn't try to talk me out of it. He just said, 'Well, that's fine.' I've always wondered why he changed his mind."

He didn't change his mind. Someone else did.

"We were mired in a hundred-year perfect storm—the strike, 9/11, Craigslist, bank debt and the litigation with Hearst. It was scary and painful. I met with my cousins and explained that for the first time in my career I could not look them in the eye and say I was certain we would survive. The changes were structural, not cyclical. I worried that our children would not have a future with The Seattle Times and that their shares in the Blethen Corporation would be greatly devalued. I said I wanted to stay the course but I had fiduciary and moral responsibilities to them and their families. The one option that would give them and their families some financial security was selling to Knight Ridder. My estimate was that each of the five family segments would garner up to $100 million pre-tax. With my cousins' blessings I approached Tony."

When the offer was on the table, Frank admits his "selflessness" changed. It still rankled that his Uncle Jack had acquired half of his father's voting stock "for a measly $15,000" after Frank Sr. died in 1967—a mistake Jerry Pennington rued even more because he blamed himself for letting it happen. Frank told the shareholders that during his 20 years as publisher they had received record dividends as revenues soared. He believed his efforts entitled him to $120 million from the sale; the other four family-member trustees should receive $95 million.

"We had four votes but needed all five. One Blethen Corporation shareholder insisted everyone should get the same amount. There had to be unanimity. That's why I couldn't give Tony an answer. I would be dishonest if I didn't admit I was pleased with the outcome—still scared but pleased. A sale was anathema to me. But I had worked very hard to try and make it happen and felt I had fulfilled every responsibility I had to my family."

He won't say who derailed the deal because "what's done is done, and it's all OK now."

Things were looking up. Blethen scored back-to-back victories in the space of seven weeks. First, the Justice Department announced there was insufficient evidence to conclude The Times "engaged in improper conduct ... likely to lead to monopolization of the Seattle newspaper market." (Some said the Justice Department just didn't dig deep enough—that was the insufficiency.) Then, on June 30, 2005, the state Supreme Court unanimously upheld the appellate court decision allowing The Times to count its losses in 2000 and 2001. "By the plain terms" of the joint operating agreement, labor costs, "including those occasioned by strikes," could be calculated toward losses, Justice Tom Chambers wrote for the court. "We recognize this day is not a happy day in the ongoing story of Seattle as a two-newspaper town. We genuinely hope that both The Seattle Times and the Seattle P-I will continue to serve our communities and prosper."

Blethen said he hoped the Hearst Corporation would now agree to modify the JOA contract "to reflect today's difficult newspaper economics so that The Times has a fair chance to become profitable again."

"This case," Hearst said from New York, "is far from over." In Seattle, Kelly Corr was more militant. "After the strike years, The Times spent money like a drunken sailor to manufacture that magical third year of loss," Hearst's local attorney said. "We're going to closely examine the losses from 2000 and 2001 aside from the strike as well." Blethen shot back that his paper lost more than $12 million in 2004, despite laying off more than a hundred workers and reducing the size of its editions to save on newsprint. The Newspaper Guild agreed to a wage freeze in a new two-year contract after Blethen allowed the union to audit his books. In Maine, where the Guild represented practically the whole Portland plant, the union was digging in its heels after a hiring freeze, three rounds of layoffs and widespread speculation that the papers soon would be for sale.

On March 30, 2006, the JOA combatants announced they had agreed to settle their dispute through confidential binding arbitration, with a "non-appealable" decision to be made by May 31, 2007. Before it was over, the case would comprise 3½ million pages of documents and thousands of billable hours by the dueling teams of attorneys.

Bill Richards, writing for Crosscut, Brewster's new online news site edited by Chuck Taylor, drilled deeper into shadowy charges and counter-charges involving the JOA. The most incendiary appeared to be a deposition given under oath to antitrust investigators in 2004 by Stephen Sparks, a former Seattle Times vice president. Sparks, who oversaw circulation for both papers from 1993 to 1997 under the joint operating agreement, asserted that Blethen and Sizemore propped up their newspaper's circulation by appropriating the lion's share of the money allocated to recruit new subscribers for both papers. Then, Sparks said, they concocted a "ruse" to wriggle their way into the morning market, telling Hearst that if the JOA wasn't revised The Times would build a second suburban printing plant to expedite delivery of the afternoon paper and extract from its outflanked partner an annual assessment for its upkeep. Carolyn Kelly and Mike Fancher were in on the phony story, Sparks said. The Times flatly denied the charges, noting that the Justice Department's antitrust division had reviewed Sparks' claims before ending its two-year investigation. Hearst sources told Richards the depositions would be part of the case they presented to the arbitrator.*

Taylor was incensed that all this was happening behind closed doors: "It's downright cockeyed given all the sanctimonious talk we hear from newspapers about fighting for public access to courts and government, about how much they care about readers, about how vital their businesses are. In the end, none of us readers gets to know what's going on."

Blethen's pugnacious personality and The Times' growing circulation lead gave the P-I the advantage in the public relations war. Never mind that Hearst was the media behemoth while The Times was a century-old family institution; the public largely perceived Frank Blethen's Seattle Times as the John D. Rockefeller to the P-I's scrappy Ida Tarbell.

The arbitrator agreed upon by both sides was Larry A. Jordan, a 62-year-old former King County Superior Court judge who had seen it all—from salacious divorces to toxic torts over asbestos. Jordan had conducted more than a thousand settlement conferences as an appellate court commissioner before spending 10 years on the bench. Jordan was a blend of crusty and congenial. He had Teddy Roosevelt's mustache and winning smile. Now he had a big stick to settle the battle over the JOA. He'd never get to use it.

---

* When the time came, Sparks was not on the witness list for the arbitration hearing. Sizemore, under oath, had been an unflappable witness for The Times, some sources said. Others said Hearst's lawyers just didn't ask the right questions.

22 | A Brief Reprieve

On the third floor of a downtown Seattle office building, an ad hoc courtroom stood ready. It featured a raised bench for the arbitrator, tables for the lawyers and sophisticated electronic equipment to display their exhibits. Kelly Corr, one of Hearst's Seattle attorneys, was working on his opening argument. It was 8 a.m. on Monday, April 16, 2007. After four years of trading punches in public, Hearst and Blethen were poised to settle their fight over the joint operating agreement in a private ring. Larry Jordan, the arbitrator, anticipated four weeks of forceful testimony. Each side was expected to call dozens of witnesses. Jordan's decision, due by June 7, would be binding and final. The future of the Seattle Post-Intelligencer might hang in the balance. Barred from the hearing room, reporters roamed the hallway, eyed by a security guard with a clipboard. "The informal word was that it might be settled, but as far as I was concerned it was all green to go," Jordan remembers. Then Doug Ross, one of Blethen's attorneys from Davis Wright Tremaine, arrived with the news that Jordan's services were no longer needed. Jordan has always wondered what prompted the eleventh-hour settlement.

Many believe Hearst had a smoking gun; perhaps a compelling new witness prepared to offer additional evidence The Times had sabotaged the P-I's circulation. That theory gained credence when it was revealed that part of the settlement called for Hearst to drop such claims. The real turning point, according to Hearst sources, was Blethen's agreement to defer until 2016 any further efforts to dissolve the joint operating agreement. Even if Hearst had prevailed in the arbitration, they say Blethen could have cited continuing losses to start the dissolution clock all over again.

Hearst agreed to pay The Times $25 million for the nine-year deferment. Simultaneously, however, The Times agreed to pay Hearst $49 million for relinquishing its right to continue collecting 32 percent of The Times' profits through 2083 even if the P-I ceased publication. The net effect was that Blethen now owed Hearst $24 million. The Times pledged to give Hearst more oversight on expenses and agreed to appoint a senior manager to nurture the P-I's circulation.

What did The Seattle Times Company gain? A dramatic reduction in legal bills and the likelihood the P-I would still fold before 2016, Blethen says. "When it did, we'd be off the hook to keep giving them a major share of our profits for another 60 or 70 years. And even if we had won the arbitration, it appeared that the Committee for a Two-Newspaper Town was going to keep us tied up in expensive litigation for several more years. When Doug Ross told us we were still in legal danger, it was like a gut punch. If it hadn't been for that, I don't know if we would settled."

The committee still suspected Blethen and Hearst might have made an under-the-table deal to close one paper. It wanted to subpoena documents and question the principals under oath. When Judge Canova wouldn't allow it, the committee dropped its claims. "Hopefully our work is done," Anne Bremner said a few weeks after the settlement. "We will rise again if we have to, in a heartbeat."

Hearst and Blethen weighed the uncertainty of a trial vs. the certainty of a negotiated settlement and opted for the latter. "Hearst is the one that blinked, not Blethen," said David Brewster. Blethen disagrees: "Neither Frank Bennack nor I are very good at blinking. I've got my differences with Bennack, but he is one tough sonofabitch, and I mean that as a compliment. As Hearst's CEO, he took a relatively small and not very well run company and turned it into a behemoth. It was pretty amazing what he did. I think he concluded that the Committee for a Two-Newspaper Town was going to be a problem for them, too."

What was certain was that uncertainty wasn't going away. The Internet was eating the industry's breakfast, lunch and dinner. Could newspapers gain enough revenue from their own web sites to stem the tide while preserving significant print readership with exceptional local news and commentary? "I don't know if newspapers will survive, period," Blethen said. The King County Journal had folded three months earlier. Much of the blame belonged to "the damned JOA," said former Times ombudsman Frank Wetzel, who once edited the Journal's predecessor. "Instead of competing full-scale with the P-I," the deal gave The Times another incentive to open a formidable Eastside bureau and launch daily zoned editions for the booming suburbs, Wetzel said. Others pointed the finger at former owner and publisher Peter Horvitz for a "terribly flawed" business plan.

There was jubilation in the P-I newsroom when Roger Oglesby, their editor and publisher, outlined the settlement. They cheered and whistled when he said there was one more detail: the P-I's name would be restored to The Times' fleet of delivery trucks. "I don't know what the future holds," said reporter Lisa Stiffler, "but for right now I'm just happy to be happy." A limo load of her colleagues concluded an evening of celebratory revelry by relieving themselves on the lawn at The Seattle Times Building, an incident instantly enshrined in Post-Intelligencer lore as "Revenge of the Pee Eye."

To David Boardman, the new executive editor at The Times, fell the tedious duty of explaining the deal to his stunned newsroom. There were "a lot of very direct and skeptical questions about how it is that a failing business model one week is something we can live with the next week." After 24 years with The Times, Boardman was good at explaining things. "Congratulations. You've got your dream job," Blethen told him when Mike Fancher moved to an editor-at-large slot in 2006. "The bad news is that your dream job no longer exists. You've got to go out there and keep morale up while making serious cuts. You also have to make sure we still have a quality paper that's connecting with readers."

On Fancher's watch—30 years by the time he retired in 2008—The Seattle Times had become one of America's best newspapers. Boardman's skills as a copy editor, investigative reporter and office diplomat had propelled him to the top. Over the next seven character-building years, he would need to muster his own zen to fulfill his exasperating boss's marching orders while rallying a shrunken newsroom to do exceptional public-service journalism.

A major loss was David Postman, The Times' chief political reporter, whose "Postman on Politics" blog was a must-read for thousands. He joined Paul Allen's Vulcan Inc. as media relations manager in the fall of 2008 after 14 years with the newspaper.

Frank Blethen always seemed so self-assured, so quick with a quip or comeback, that few grasped it was sometimes just how he coped with stress. At 62, the publisher was in the biggest pickle of his life. If he closed his eyes he could hear Jerry Pennington saying, "Any idiot can manage a company well when times are really good. The real test of a manager is to keep things going well during hard times." From the day in 1974 when his Uncle Jack snarled that if he went to Walla Walla he was never coming back, Frank had been determined to make good and unify his family in the process. Even Peter Horvitz acknowledged, "No one is more determined than Frank Blethen in keeping a newspaper together. The question becomes, Can that be transferred to the next generation?" Now, facing a brutal economy, daunting debt and a sea-change in the newspaper industry, the question became, Will there be a newspaper to transfer?

Alden J. "Buster" Blethen IV died of Huntington's disease at 55 in 2006. Robert Blethen, the company's vice president for corporate marketing, interpreted a heart attack as a wakeup call and retired at 60 in the spring of 2007. His brother, Will, 62, the company's treasurer for 33 years, retired a month later, saying Bob had the right idea.

"We must adapt or die" could have been the pull-quote for Frank's sobering year-end message to Seattle Times employees. The economic model that led to the rise of the modern-day metropolitan newspaper was imploding. Since 2000, The Times had seen its print revenue base decline by $70 million—25 percent. Times managers "amazingly" had found

$21 million in cost reductions "but we still need another $6 million to ensure stability next year," Blethen said. The industry had seen nothing like this since the 1930s. In 2006 when the McClatchy Company acquired Knight Ridder and its 49.5 percent share of The Times, Knight Ridder valued its stake in Seattle at "well over" $200 million. "It has since been written down twice," Blethen wrote, "and as of last month McClatchy valued it at only $19 million." McClatchy, which paid $6.5 billion for Knight Ridder, had lost 70 percent of its value in recent months. (Tony Ridder had been a reluctant seller, but he got out in the nick of time.) The New York Times' value was down 31 percent; Gannett 30 percent. "These are shocking losses; they reinforce the naysayers' view that newspapers are going the way of buggy whips," Blethen said, adding:

> This has been a painful time to be a newspaper employee or owner. However, if The Seattle Times can adjust to the lower revenues quickly enough and survive through this period, I believe we are on our way to creating the metro newspaper model of the future: A multiformat (print and online) news, information and advertising company based on our unique foundation of journalism and community service. ...Online is one of the keys to our future but it is not a short-term savior. Our online revenue growth is among the best in the country, but it is still only about 10 percent of our print revenue. And while the online growth percentage looks good, it is computed on a small base and the magnitude of growth has begun to slow here and nationally. ...
>
> The options are: sell out for whatever market value might be left; close the doors and liquidate, or keep a laser focus on transforming the business to a smaller, more focused organization... .
>
> For better or worse, my family has chosen door number three.

Blethen said he hoped the transition would be complete by 2015 for "the final hand-off to the next generation of family leaders and stewards." To those young Blethens would fall the challenge of beginning "to grow value again while perpetuating a company practicing journalism with integrity and independence."

The leaders of the family's "fifth edition," Frank's son Ryan and Cousin Bob's son Rob, were sent to Maine in 2001 and 2002 to learn the ropes. Ryan signed on as a reporter for the Portland Press Herald; Rob went to advertising. The publisher was Chuck Cochrane, one of Frank's oldest and closest friends.

Ryan Blethen, born in 1972, is three months older than his cousin. Ryan was a history major at Washington State University, gravitating to the newsroom after spending time in each department at The Times. He spent a year at the journalism graduate school at the University of Kansas. After a brief stint at the family's Yakima paper, he covered a wide range of stories at the Spokesman-Review in Spokane for nine months before heading to Maine. "It was contract negotiations time when I arrived. The Guild was in the middle of a byline strike, so I was one of the only reporters who had a byline. Earlier they had distributed bumper stickers that said 'Make Frank Blethen Keep His Promise.' One member invited me to join the union, which I thought was very polite," Ryan remembers with a laugh. "I respectfully declined." A reporter who worked with him at the time says Blethen struck most people as "a decent guy who could have been an asshole, given the heat his father was taking over the cutbacks, but he wasn't."

Ryan's nemesis was Portland's alternative weekly, the Phoenix, which saw his rise to regional editor in under two years as "nepotism personified." Ryan found himself in the national media spotlight in 2004 as part of a controversy that began before his arrival at the Press Herald. A veteran reporter named Ted Cohen said young Blethen was helping management harass him out of his job because he wouldn't keep quiet about an embarrassing episode. It began in the summer of 2000 when Cohen unearthed George W. Bush's 1976 drunk driving arrest in Kennebunkport. A regional editor—Ryan's predecessor—spiked the story, discounting it as old news, reportedly with Cohen's assent. Nothing came of it until a Portland TV reporter learned that people in the courthouse had been overheard discussing Bush's DUI. She chased down the story, which broke five days before the presidential election. When it leaked out that the Press Herald had sat on the story, Cohen told the media he only wished he had been more assertive. That's when Cohen says things got chilly. By 2004 he was threatening to sue the Press Herald. He cited Ryan's decision to yank him off the Kennebunkport beat he'd had for a decade as part of a pattern of management retaliation. Ryan flatly denied it, saying he "just wanted to move people around, shake things up a bit."

Ryan was summoned home in 2005 to apprentice Jim Vesely as assistant editor of The Times' editorial page. Bloggers promptly launched a "Baby Blethen Watch." The Stranger critiqued his every utterance. One wag said his editorials were reminiscent of "Pat Boone trying to sing Tutti Frutti." He laughed it off and said he admired the alternative paper's edginess. "They understand their audience." At 6-1, with dark curly hair and an easy grin, Ryan in no way resembles his father. It will be a long time, however, before he stops being Frank Blethen's son.

Rob Blethen, a boyishly handsome University of Washington communications graduate, managed classified advertising at The Times during the strike. As he advanced to advertising director of the Portland papers, he won praise for his professionalism and good manners. In the summer of 2008, he became associate publisher of the Walla Walla Union Bulletin, the congenial spot where Frank first made his mark, about as far from the family fishbowl as one can get and still be in Washington State.

A few months earlier, Frank had announced the beginning of the end of the family's sentimental stake in Colonel Blethen's birthplace: The Maine newspapers were for sale.

The precursors of the worst downturn since the Great Depression were the dotcom crash and 9/11. "In response, central banks around the world tried to stimulate the economy," says

Seattle-based investment analyst Eric Petroff. "They created capital liquidity through a reduction in interest rates. In turn, investors sought higher returns through riskier investments." Lenders cutting corners to achieve their own higher returns granted mortgages to borrowers with poor credit. Those subprime loans were like a cancer that grows slowly at first before suddenly metastasizing, seemingly everywhere—in this case, globally. "Consumer demand drove the housing bubble to all-time highs in the summer of 2005." When it burst a year later, foreclosures accelerated. By the fall of 2008 storied financial institutions were failing in the U.S. and Europe, even Iceland. Washington Mutual, Seattle's 119-year-old "friend of the family," was seized by federal regulators in the largest bank failure in American history. Then, in a sickening week of panic selling, the Dow Jones Industrial Average fell 18 percent. Millions of Americans with 401(k) plans were shocked at their losses. The Seattle Times Company's pension plan assets were hammered. Practically overnight, the previously overfunded plan was 23 percent under water—$40 million. Unemployment soared. Auto dealers—major buyers of newspaper advertising—cut back dramatically. By Christmas, The Times had cut its payroll by nearly 500, reduced its weekday edition to three sections, closed its suburban bureaus and pledged most of its remaining South Lake Union real estate as collateral to secure $91 million in loans. An investor group had signed an agreement to buy the Maine newspapers for an estimated $30 million, contingent on securing financing. Newspaper prices were in freefall.

23 | Swift, Surgical & Sad

Being scooped on the news that their newspaper was now officially on life support added insult to injury for the staff of the Seattle Post-Intelligencer. At 5:15 p.m. on January 8, 2009, Managing Editor David McCumber was telling his stunned newsroom that the lead story on KING-TV's 5 o'clock newscast, attributed to a knowledgeable source, sounded like "a bunch of rumor." The next morning they learned it wasn't. Steven R. Swartz, the new president of Hearst Newspapers, arrived from New York to confirm the P-I was for sale. If no buyer could be found within 60 days, the P-I would likely become an Internet-only news source with a far smaller staff. "In no case will Hearst continue to publish the P-I in printed form," the official statement said. "Regrettably, we have come to the end of the line."

Swartz, who looked a decade younger than 46, shed his suit coat before he was handed a microphone to address the newsroom. Some wept quietly; others, being reporters, were undeterred by his statement that "at this point" he couldn't answer questions. "What do you think the odds are of finding a buyer?" someone said. Swartz smiled thinly and emitted a nervous chuckle.

"You know, I started as a reporter myself, as an intern at the Wall Street Journal, and if I were you I would keep asking questions until I leave the building... but, as I said, I'm not going to be able to take questions ..."

"Why not?" someone barked.

"What triggered it now?"

"What about severance and taking care of employees?"

Swartz handed the microphone to Roger Oglesby. The publisher cleared his throat heavily and said he'd be happy to talk with groups of them later, "off the record."

Two things were immediately clear to anyone who understood the current state of the newspaper industry: No one—not even a homegrown white knight like Paul Allen or Bill Gates—was going to buy the P-I. Its circulation had plummeted by 74,000 since 2000 when The Times became a morning paper. Hearst's accountants calculated the eight straight years of hemorrhaging in Seattle at $44 million—$14 million of that in 2008, the worst year to date. Hearst was no longer even interested in buying The Seattle Times. If the P-I had a future, it was online. The upwardly mobile Swartz and Lincoln Millstein, Hearst's bow-tied digital media maven, were the architects of an industry alliance with Yahoo! "New media" was their thing. They liked what the P-I was doing with its website.

February found Washington publishers lobbying the state Legislature to grant newspapers a 40 percent break on the business and occupation tax through 2015. "Some of us, like The Seattle Times, are literally holding on by our fingertips today," Blethen told the lawmakers. There was no denying that was at least figuratively so. He had opened his books once again to impress upon the Newspaper Guild the urgency of being allowed to freeze accruals to pension funds. Blethen was also considering Chapter 11 bankruptcy, a course the Campbell family, owners of The Columbian at Vancouver, Washington, took three months later. "It's not a bailout, because it's not enough money," said House Majority Leader Lynn Kessler, the Grays Harbor Democrat who sponsored the tax cut. "But it is our way of saying to the newspapers that we do believe you're incredibly important to our state and our democracy."

By the time the tax break took effect that summer, the Post-Intelligencer's print edition was history.

On the morning of March 16, it looked like business as usual in the newsroom at the Seattle Post-Intelligencer. Outside the picture windows, ferries plied a chilly gray Elliott Bay. Keyboards were clicking, phones ringing. The tension had been building for weeks. They'd been working on a 20-page commemorative edition celebrating the paper's 146 years. "Working hard day to day was like dodging the executioner," Larry Lange, a reporter who'd been at the P-I for 29 years and nine months, remembers. Between fragments of conversation came the news there would be a staff meeting at 10 a.m. with their editor and publisher—ominous because staff meetings were almost always in mid-afternoon when the daytime and evening shifts overlapped and more people were in the office.

Roger Oglesby stepped to a microphone at the assignment desk and said, "Tonight we'll be putting the paper to bed for the last time. But the bloodline will live on." Just with a lot fewer corpuscles. Only 30 people would be needed to transform seattlepi.com into "the leading news and information portal in the region," as Hearst CEO Frank Bennack Jr. put it in a news release. He didn't mention that the survivors would be paid about 30 percent less—and that the Guild would be gone. Everyone else would get a handshake and about two weeks' pay for every year of service.

"I think we'll outsell you tomorrow," McCumber told a reporter from The Times. As the paper shredders and moving boxes were brought in, the breaking news editor, Candace Heckman, broke out three bottles of booze she had stashed away for a working wake. At 65, Lange took the news straight—worried more about his younger colleagues than himself, although he didn't feel close to being ready to retire. He finished the story he'd been working on.

The staff received a classy, heartfelt note from David Boardman. "Whatever future there is for a daily newspaper in Seattle will be built upon the legacy of courageous, competitive journalism we've built together with you over the decades," The Times' executive editor wrote.

To Carol Smith, a reporter and writing coach with a poet's soul, fell the melancholy honor of writing her newspaper's obituary. She nailed it:

> The Seattle Post-Intelligencer, the region's pioneer newspaper and the city's oldest continually operating business, a newspaper that both shaped and was shaped by the community it covered, prints its last edition Tuesday—nearly a century and a half after its forebear first rolled off a hand-cranked Ramage

press promising to be "the best and cheapest promulgator of all sorts of useful information."

The print P-I was irreverent and unpredictable, a long-shot survivor from the start. It persisted through 11 moves, and more than 17 owners. It didn't miss an edition when its building burned to the ground along with its press in the Great Seattle Fire of 1889. It outlived some 20 scrappy competitors before the turn of the 20th century, an era described by Clarence Bagley, one of its 19th century owners, as a time when newspapers "lived hard and died easy."

But it couldn't endure the firestorm of the Internet. And in the end, it wouldn't outlast its long headlock with The Seattle Times. ...

The news of the end, when it finally came, was swift and surgical. Cause of death—a fatal economic spiral compounded by dwindling subscription rates, an exodus of advertisers and an explosion of online information. News will live on. This newspaper will not. Suddenly, the obituarist's cliché seems apropos: We went down doing what we loved. ...

The P-I has been a common denominator not just in our lives, but in hundreds of thousands of others for more than a century.

Print is what we posted on refrigerator doors, and hung on walls—tangible documents of our rites and passages, of what entertains, informs or outrages us. Clippings of births and deaths— and the deeds and misdeeds in between—fill thousands of family scrapbooks. ...

The print newspaper is going away and with it, its varied afterlife. You can't sop up your basement with your computer, or wrap a fish. And what is the paper mache—that miracle sculpting media that must have launched a million budding elementary school artists—without newspaper?

Jon Hahn, a retired P-I columnist, wrote, "It's NOT just the economy, stupid. The paper is closing in no small way because of those of us who'd rather get our 'news' online, on our cell phones, on our car radios and other electronic media. ... So when the P-I's three-story landmark globe-and-revolving equator sign stops spinning... we all have to share some of the blame. Sorta like that line from the old Pogo Possum comic strip: *We have met the enemy, and he is us!*"

The rejoinder from an anonymous commenter was more blunt:

> I'll state what seems obvious to anyone without an emotional attachment to ink on dead trees: We are not the enemy for accepting a new delivery mechanism for news. The enemies are the complacent newspaper managements that failed to adapt to a changing industry—and they and their employees are suffering the consequences. The printed newspaper will die, and that's a good thing. Because the transition to online news wasn't managed well by incompetent newspaper managers, many good journalists will lose jobs, and that's a bad thing. But in the long run, news will survive, and be better for not having to pay for physical print production and distribution. Accept it, and be part of the change.

The joint operating agreement probably prolonged the Post-Intelligencer's life by at least 15 years. Frank Blethen, unquestionably, hated the deal from day one. With every ounce of his competitive juices he wanted to win in a head-to-head battle. Yet for all his craftiness—real, alleged and imagined—Blethen didn't kill the P-I. From the post-war era through the 1960s—and some say almost to the end—Hearst seemed to view Seattle almost as a remote colony or outpost. A P-I manager attending a company meeting in San Antonio in 2008 heard a Hearst executive dismiss the Post-Intelligencer as the "Northwest bureau of the San Francisco Chronicle." If that was supposed to be a joke it also revealed a kernel of truth: Hearst was the absentee owner of a marginal property. When the P-I was still reasonably profitable, thanks to its morning niche and marquee names like Royal Brougham and Emmett Watson, Hearst's attitude could have passed for benign neglect. But by failing to match the hometown Times' investments in machinery and people during the 1970s, Hearst squandered what should have been a growing advantage in the a.m. marketplace. Then in 1983, it surrendered Sundays and independent distribution as part of the JOA. The Times' revenues soared and Jerry Pennington gave the newsroom its million-dollar "margin of excellence." Finally, to get the handcuffs off its website and extract a larger share of the profits, Hearst allowed The Times to go morning. The brutal economy and the Internet finished off the P-I's print edition and pushed the Blethens to the brink of bankruptcy. David Brewster believes the best chance of saving the P-I slipped away in 1981 when People Opposed to a 1-Newspaper Town couldn't make its case that there were potential buyers. If the U.S. Ninth Circuit Court of Appeals had sustained the District Court's ruling that the JOA couldn't go forward until potential buyers were explored, Brewster believes one might have emerged. "The real missed opportunity was by us as a community," he says, "not Hearst by neglect."

There was no celebrating at Fairview and John, not even in the executive office. Hal Bernton, a Times reporter who worked at the P-I in the 1980s, organized a thank-you rally outside the P-I offices. Danny Westneat, Bruce Ramsey and a number of other Times journalists joined their soon-to-be-jobless colleagues in a little park. They stood in the rain, swapping commiserations and black-humor quips that at the rate things were going they'd all be unemployed.

Blethen issued a statement: "Though The Seattle Times and the Seattle P-I have been fiercely competitive, we find no joy in the loss of any journalistic voice." He was still worried The Times could survive. For that matter, he was worried that the industry could survive.

The person without an ounce of emotional attachment to ink on dead trees was right to suggest that too many newspaper owners were complacent or incompetent. Some were also so stupid they thought the forest would last forever. Molly Ivins, dying of breast cancer in Austin, watched them cut their newsrooms to the marrow to prop up their profits. "What really pisses me off," she said, is "this most remarkable business plan: Newspaper owners look at one another and say, 'Our rate of return is slipping a bit; let's solve that problem by making our product smaller and less helpful and less interesting." And why, Ivins asked, should the reader really care if "everything" was going to be "free" on the Internet? Because many great—not just good—journalists were losing their jobs in Seattle, Wenatchee, Wichita and Wilmington; in practically every city and town. And all the wild-hair blogs, not to mention Wikipedia, couldn't replace what Seattle lost when the P-I died. Under McCumber and Boardman, both papers "were spinning gold on a shoestring," Joel Connelly remembers—investigating the sheriff's office, the health department and football heroes who thought they were above the law.

24 | The Brand Evolves

On a quiet Sunday morning three days after Thanksgiving, a surly-looking black man in a hoodie and dark coat stood silently at the counter of Forza Coffee Company, a popular spot on the outskirts of Tacoma. A barista asked what he'd like. He produced a pistol, turned and without a word of warning opened fire on three police officers sitting together checking their laptops. A fourth Lakewood officer, waiting at the counter for his drink, wounded the shooter as he wrestled him toward the entryway. In the desperate struggle, the killer snatched the officer's handgun, shot him dead too and fled. As scanners crackled and police cars sped to the scene from every direction, the most intense manhunt in Northwest history began. It was shortly after 8:15 a.m. on November 29, 2009.

Journalism's most coveted awards are those for breaking news where enterprise and accuracy are of the essence. Over the next 42 hours, the newsroom of The Seattle Times—still regrouping after three rounds of buyouts and layoffs—did extraordinary work. A hundred and fifty staffers contributed to the coverage, from intern Cliff DesPeaux to Executive Editor David Boardman. Managing editors Suki Dardarian and Kathy Best, assistant managing editor Jim Simon and Boardman sifted every important detail for the next 42 hours. The Times' coverage demonstrated how tweets, old-fashioned beat work, online publishing and in-depth print reportage can be combined to give readers all they expect and more. In this case, the readers were also reporters—a nimble, fully engaged social media network.

Jennifer Sullivan, one of the newsroom's savviest courts and cops reporters, was home with the flu. "When her BlackBerry buzzed, she was tempted to ignore it," she told James

Ross Gardner of *Seattle Metropolitan* magazine. "Doubled over at the kitchen table, she phoned her network of sources, people inside Pierce County law enforcement, relationships cultivated over 10 years of talking to cops. She kept asking: 'What do you know?' Very little, as it turned out. But they did have a name. Sullivan speed-dialed her editor." The suspect was Maurice Clemmons, a 37-year-old ex-convict.

Eight hours passed before Times editors and reporters, furiously working the phones and knocking on doors, nailed down a second source to confirm Sullivan's tip. Dardarian and Best gave the order to put it online. "The story went live at 5:29 Sunday evening with the headline, 'Police Identify Ex-Con Wanted for Questioning.' The paper had scooped every other media outlet," Gardner wrote in a riveting anatomy of how The Times stayed out front from start to finish. In the downsizing, web producers had been moved closer to reporters and editors at the metro desk—a very good thing. Cory Haik, the assistant managing editor for digital, was on top of everything new, including platforms for real-time online collaboration. "By now," Gardner wrote ...

> all walls between old and new media—and infighting over which camp truly owned the news—had fallen. The web team set up a Google Wave account, on which it posted links to police scanner audio and communicated in real time with as many as 500 users, many feeding The Times tips about the manhunt. The newspaper's web traffic soared to 3.3 million page views, the most single-day hits in the site's history.

Dozens of people were tweeting—reporters, editors, web producers. Boardman especially was in his element, tweeting for almost 15 hours during the first day of the manhunt. "Dave's use of Twitter broke down some of the final barriers to its acceptance as a legitimate news tool," Kathy Best says. "He also demonstrated the value of using Twitter to vet and correct misinformation."

The Times soon learned that back in Arkansas where he grew up Clemmons had been a 16-year-old hell bent on trouble. His seven-month felony spree nevertheless didn't warrant the 108-year sentence he received. The Times broke the story that then-Governor Mike Huckabee, a presidential hopeful, had set Clemmons free in 2000 after 11 years in prison. Given his state's track record of throwing the book at poor black men, Huckabee said he did the right thing at the time; he didn't have a crystal ball.

Clemmons was paroled to Puget Sound in 2004 after doing more time for a home invasion robbery. When he walked into the coffee shop with a head full of demons and two loaded handguns, he was out on bail on charges of child rape and assaulting a sheriff's deputy. Sometimes he called himself "the beast"; sometimes he was "The Lord Jesus Christ." To family and friends gathered for Thanksgiving dinner, he announced he planned to kill cops and school children—in fact "as many people as he could at an intersection."

Reports pouring in that someone resembling Clemmons had been sighted were tracked by The Times with an interactive timeline map and Twitter updates. Ten staffers were tweeting literally around the clock, Kathy Best remembers.

In the early-morning hours of December 1, a Seattle patrolman encountered Clemmons on a dark street while checking out a car reported stolen two hours earlier. In the confrontation that followed, he shot him dead. Four months later, the news staff of The Seattle Times was awarded the Pulitzer Prize for its coverage of the Lakewood Police officer murders. The Stranger, which seldom misses a chance to needle The Times, wrote that the coverage "was fast, relentless, thorough and available in just about every medium in real time. It's also notable for the fact that as recently as February, the paper was still trying to convince people that it would survive. Winning an award like this is always impressive, but it's even more impressive given those circumstances." Writing in Crosscut, Chuck Taylor agreed: "This was a huge, brand-enhancing moment for The

Times. An ink-on-paper dinosaur has evolved."*

Perhaps in the nick of time.

"There would be no champagne uncorked the morning the award was announced," Gardner wrote. "There were cheers and hugs—then tears. Four innocent people had been killed. The Times just told the story."

The paper's longstanding willingness to pursue controversial stories, never mind the consequences, was acknowledged in 2009. To borrow a phrase from the UW fight song, The Times once again refused to bow down to Washington. Times reporters Ken Armstrong and Nick Perry received two prestigious national awards for "Victory and Ruins," a four-part series that documented the unsavory extracurricular activities of two-dozen members of the UW's victorious 2000 Rose Bowl team. "What price glory?" might have been a better title. Using documents unavailable at the time, the series charged that the coach, Rick Neuheisel, and athletic director, Barbara Hedges, did little to discipline players for offenses ranging from hooliganism to alleged sexual assault. Police, prosecutors, judges and the media also looked the other way. The Times displayed "the commitment to truth that will alienate readers, risk advertising accounts, and jeopardize a newspaper's standing during already precarious times," one panel of judges said. Thousands of diehard Husky fans and some advertisers were indeed livid, saying the newspaper was dredging up old news to embarrass the program. Neuheisel, who had departed Seattle in a cloud of controversy in 2003, said the series was part of an ongoing vendetta against him. Don James, the most revered of Neuheisel's coaching predecessors, was still seething over the 1992 Times exposé and Pac-10 conference sanctions that prompted him to quit. "I live in this community and I watch them beat up everybody, not just the football program," James said of The Times.

---

* Taylor was among the many who also noted that The News Tribune, Tacoma's daily, did a solid job of covering the tragedy in its back yard. "And seattlepi.com did amazingly well considering how outnumbered that post-ink staff is. But The Times had them all out-gunned, on the Web and in print."

"I've watched them beat up on Boeing and Nordstrom and all the great industries in this community. Maybe that happens everywhere. But I have lived in a lot of places and I haven't seen it elsewhere."

In 2011, The Seattle Times demonstrated that even with a hundred fewer journalists its resurgence as a great investigative newspaper was no flash in the pan. Armstrong and Michael J. Berens were awarded the Selden Ring Award and the 2012 Pulitzer Prize—the newspaper's ninth—for investigative reporting. Their series, "Methadone and the Politics of Pain," unquestionably has saved many lives. It revealed that in Washington State since 2003 more than 2,100 people on Medicaid or workers' compensation had died after accidentally overdosing on the state's "preferred" painkiller. Despite warnings that methadone was dangerous—doctors told Berens it was the "silent death"—the state was intent on saving money. Morphine was more expensive. The former Chicago Tribune reporters used high-tech tools and shoe leather to document the death toll. They analyzed hospital and death-certificate databases; parsed Drug Enforcement Administration reports and used mapping software to overlay census tracts. Armstrong and Berens also interviewed more than a hundred people. Confronted by The Times' evidence that dollar-a-dose painkillers were killing poor people, the state issued an emergency advisory. Then, a month after the last installment of the series, it told health-care professionals that methadone should be used only as a drug of last resort.

A common thread in The Times' award-winning investigative journalism over the past decade is James Neff, whom Boardman recruited from the Midwest in 2001. As investigations editor, "Jim didn't just maintain the program I'd built, he took it to the next level," Boardman says. Ron Judd is one of many Times reporters who marvel at Neff's instincts and attention to detail: "He's almost pathologically thorough. He wants to see everything you've seen—all the documents, including your interview transcripts. The guy has public access to records *wired*, which is why The Times was able to get its hands on Maurice Clemmons' whole criminal history in the span of one day."

From left, Suki Dardarian, Michael J. Berens, David Boardman, Ken Armstrong and Kathy Best outside the Columbia University Library after Berens and Armstrong received the 2012 Pulitzer Prize for investigative journalism for their series "Methadone and the politics of pain." *Seattle Times photo*

"It's where I have always wanted to end up," 36-year-old Ryan Blethen said in 2009 when he succeeded Jim Vesely as editorial page editor. He remembers his four years as Vesely's understudy as a blend of boot camp and grad school. "After I turned in my first editorial, Jim popped his head in the door and in a gentlemanly but emphatic way said, 'This is a great feature story, Ryan, but it's not an editorial.' I learned a lot from Jim—and from Joni Balter, Bruce Ramsey and Lance Dickie. You could throw anything at Lance and he could turn it into something really good."

The problem with Seattle Times editorials, critics say, is that they often seem like garnish for the publisher's cause du jour. One constant, however, is repeal of the estate tax, which the Blethens regard as confiscatory and "the No. 1 killer of family-owned business in America." Ryan also enthusiastically joins his father in warning against the concentration of media ownership. "Newspapers should be accountable to the communities they serve and not to Wall Street or corporations thousands of miles away," he says. Some wring their hands over the Internet's impact on journalism. Not Ryan. "An industry-transforming recession has exposed the decay of decades of corporate and profit-driven newspaper ownership. In the detritus comes real opportunity," he wrote in 2009. As for editorial accountability, Ryan believes newspapers have a civic duty to offer opinions and not toe any party line. He remembers something Vesely wrote to explain a mixed bag of endorsements pundits were sure to see as cognitive dissonance: "Like most Washington voters, we take our candidates one at a time."

When Vesely retired, the new Blethen on the block was instantly caught in the liberal/conservative crossfire. Ryan and his more experienced deputy, Kate Riley, oversaw editorials and columns with an ambitious "reset" theme. They explored priority-setting at every level of government in the face of the recession's huge budget shortfalls. Though it was a team effort, Ryan was the lightning rod. A swarm of bloggers diagrammed his sentences, pronounced them muddled and searched in vain "for coherence." The Times kept saying education was the state's paramount duty, but if Ryan really wanted the Legislature to find "a way to properly funnel money" to the state's hard-pressed universities, a progressive newsletter declared, "then why did his family twice endorse unconstitutional Tim Eyman initiatives to make raising revenue more difficult?" The Stranger stuck his byline on a make-believe "Public Editor" guest column. He won the alternative paper's grudging respect, albeit temporarily, when The Times editorialized that marijuana should be legalized, regulated and taxed. Nor was he intimidated by the national drug czar's suggestion that the editorial board was one toke over the line.

For Blethenologists, The Times' consistent inconsistencies are a source of endless scathing wonder. Seattle's powerful liberal bloc likes it when the editorial board backs Democrats but suspects ulterior motives. ("Frank likes Patty Murray because she opposes the estate tax and helped end the strike.") All hell breaks loose from the left when the paper anoints Republicans seen to be masquerading as moderates. Suburban conservatives, conversely, view The Times as fundamentally liberal, kowtowing to Seattle. In 2000, the paper backed George W. Bush for president and Maria Cantwell, a dot-com millionaire Democrat, for the U.S. Senate over incumbent Slade Gorton. Cantwell won in a photo-finish. When she ran for re-election, The Times endorsed Gorton's protégé and former campaign manager, Mike McGavick. In 2004, The Times backed Republican Dino Rossi for governor but abandoned Bush for John Kerry "because of an ill-conceived war and its aftermath, undisciplined spending, a shrinkage of constitutional rights and an intrusive social agenda." The Times twice backed Barack Obama for president, supported Obamacare and was foursquare for marriage equality. Yet in 2012 it endorsed Republican Rob McKenna for governor, despite the fact that he opposed same-sex marriage and had asked the U.S. Supreme Court to overturn Obamacare while serving as Washington's attorney general.

McKenna got more than an endorsement. In October 2012, after three months of intense internal debate, Frank decided The Seattle Times Company would boost McKenna's campaign with an "independent expenditure"—newspaper ads valued at a total of nearly $78,000. The Times would donate a like amount to backers of a statewide referendum legalizing gay marriage, a cause the newspaper had long supported. Frank said he hoped the "experiment" would demonstrate the power of print advertising to candidates and their consultants, who spend most of their money on TV spots and direct mail. "What we didn't say was that I was willing to try practically anything because I still didn't know if we were going to be able to survive." Ryan, by now associate publisher of The Times, told his dad he was making a big mistake. Jill Mackie, the vice president for public relations, felt the same way. "I came to work every day with my stomach in knots for three months," she remembers. "I absolutely understood Frank's motivation, but I told him it would be a disaster from the PR perspective. ... In choosing a candidate on the 'R' side and an issue that leaned left the idea was that they would balance each other out. But of course that is not how it was interpreted."

Boardman, who was usually in Frank's inner circle on major decisions, wasn't told about the plan until the afternoon before the first McKenna ad ran. By then, the decision had already been made by Frank, with the support of Alan

Fisco, the director of sales and new products. "Frank said he didn't tell me because he knew I'd be vehemently against the idea," Boardman recalls. "He was certainly right about that." Blethen says there was another reason Boardman wasn't in the loop: "I wanted him to be able to honestly say he had no idea this was coming."

When Seattle Times editors, reporters, photographers and artists opened their copies of the paper on the morning of Wednesday, October 17, 2012, they saw a dramatic full-page ad. It featured a close-up of hands engaged in a tight tug of war, with someone wielding a pair of scissors and poised to "Cut Partisan Gridlock." That was "Rob McKenna's New Direction for Washington." At the bottom it said: "Paid for by The Seattle Times Company."

The controversial McKenna ad.

The newsroom was shocked and angry. Boardman, his eyes welling with emotion, found himself in the difficult position of defending his boss in the wake of a decision he detested. He reminded the newsroom that their publisher was one of America's foremost champions of independent journalism. From his first day as publisher in 1985, Blethen had made it clear there'd be hell to pay if the advertising and circulation departments ever attempted to tell reporters what, or what not, to write. And never "is there even a whispered suggestion" that the newsroom should give the editorial board's chosen candidates better coverage, Boardman would tell readers in a column the following Sunday. "I offer this solemn promise: In these two races, as in everything else we do, we will strive to be fair, accurate and thorough. We will continue to ask probing questions of both sides. We will continue to fulfill our mission to serve this community through strong, independent journalism that makes a difference. ... On behalf of the people who proudly call themselves Seattle Times journalists, we look forward to reinforcing the thing we hold most precious: our relationship with you."

The newsroom knew Boardman was as good as his word—and probably also as good as gone. It still needed to make a statement of its own. It drafted a letter to the publisher. More than a hundred staff members signed it, including photographer Courtney Blethen Riffkin, Buster Blethen's daughter. The decision to publish the ads was "so disappointing," they wrote, because:

> It threatens the two things we value the most, the traits that made The Seattle Times a strong brand: Our independence and credibility. We know you value those things, too. ... But consider [the decision's] possible effect on The Seattle Times' core mission, journalism.
>
> We strive to remain independent from the institutions we cover. We shine a light on the process from the outside. We are not part of the process. ... By sponsoring an ad for one gubernatorial candidate, The Seattle Times—the entire company—has become one of the top contributors in support of that candidate's campaign. We are now part of a campaign's machinery, creating a perception that we are not an independent watchdog. ...
>
> The ads undermine the work we do and threaten to muddy that perception with the readers who rely on us.

Few readers or political insiders seemed to buy Frank's explanation that this was an "experiment." They, like much of the Times newsroom, believed he had tried to swing the election and in so doing had put at risk his newspaper's journalistic credibility—an asset he had always tried to protect.

Dwight Pelz, chairman of the State Democratic Party, fumed. The ads set a "horrifying precedent" that crossed "a sacred line in journalism," he said. "If CBS News announced on a national level that they were going to donate hundreds of millions of dollars in advertising for Mitt Romney to run an experiment to see whether it would elect him President of the United States, I think everybody would be horrified by that." Joby Shimomura, the campaign manager for Jay Inslee, McKenna's opponent, said, "Not even FOX News has ever done anything like this before." McKenna called the criticism "a cynical ploy."

In the weeks to come—as Boardman dusted off his resume for the first time in 30 years—the newsroom's "Truth Needle" column closely examined The Times' ads for McKenna, as well as his TV spots. It pointed out half-truths and outright errors, as well as factual assertions.

The ads precipitated a national debate. Jill Mackie acknowledged to National Public Radio that a "significant number of subscribers" had canceled their subscriptions to protest the ads. One commenter on a national journalism Website called it "a truly sad day for journalism." Another wondered, "If this had been 2008 and the ad being bought supported Barack Obama—at a time when some elevated him to deity status—would there have been the outrage?"

Same-sex marriage won handily, but McKenna lost to Inslee. Did the controversy over the donated ads cost him the election, as The Stranger's David "Goldy" Goldstein suggested? Highly unlikely, says Seattle pollster Stuart Elway, whose last sampling had McKenna ahead by a whisker. "In close elections, everything gets to be the deciding factor," Elway says, "but practically every newspaper in the state endorsed McKenna." A 40 percent share of King County is what Republicans now need to have a fighting chance in statewide races. McKenna, a former King County councilman, lost the county, 62–38. "It's a Seattle problem," McKenna says. He received less than 25 percent of the vote in the state's very liberal largest city. "The Seattle Times had nothing to do with this, aside from spurring debate within the Fourth Estate," says seattlepi.com's Joel Connelly.

"No regrets," says Frank. "We desperately needed to grow revenue and underscore our importance as an advertising vehicle. Eighty percent of our readers are voters. Alan Fisco and I had been talking for a year about all sorts of different and creative ways to sell advertising, so when 2012 rolled around we wanted to make a case that our ads are far cheaper and more impactful than TV and radio. Our belief is that if one political consultant or major candidate breaks the mold and makes a significant buy in newspaper advertising, we'll start getting more. One of the problems is media consolidation. Most of the people who own large newspapers also own TV stations, so they have never paid any serious attention to political advertising. They say, 'We're going to get this revenue one way or the other, so what does it matter?' It's been a pretty lonely effort by a few independents like us that have been trying to figure out how to crack the code. We picked up some dollars from our experiment and I believe we demonstrated the power of Seattle Times political advertising. McKenna lost a very close race because his campaign failed to follow through with an aggressive campaign in Seattle to complement our ads. We're not going to do anything controversial next time [in 2016], but we're working on ways to emphasize the effectiveness of print plus online political advertising. It's interesting that we got all sorts of criticism for the McKenna ads, but we got no criticism for giving space to the 'I Do' marriage equality campaign."

"We did," his son interjects. "And that was different."

"I never heard it."

"I did. And there *is* a difference between an issue and a political candidate," Ryan adds. "It does cross a wider line with a candidate. I wouldn't have done either, though. It just wasn't worth it to cross that line. I think it hurt our brand and our image. And you don't get that back."

When the decision was being made, did father and son have a candid talk? Did Ryan say, "Dad, this is a big mistake"?

"Yep," says Ryan.

"He said it louder than that!" Frank laughs.

"And I still cringe, thinking about it," Ryan says, shaking his head.

Blethen seems proud of his son's gumption. "We have a real newsman as our associate publisher," he says. "But I've told news people who expect me to apologize, 'I'm doing everything I can to make sure we can maintain your jobs. I'm not going to apologize for being open and transparent about something I did when I was trying to tap into one of those rare pots of money to help pay for some of your jobs in the middle of a horrendous recession.'"

Eight months after the election, Boardman received the Society of Professional Journalists' Ethics in Journalism Award for his staff's coverage of the controversial ads. His "courageous actions" dampened damage to the newspaper's credibility, a leading media ethicist said. Two weeks earlier, Boardman had been named dean of the School of Media and Communication at Temple University in Philadelphia.

Frank hugs his departing executive editor. *Seattle Times photo*

25 | Here to Stay?

When Seattle awoke on March 18, 2009, it was a one-newspaper town. Thousands of the Post-Intelligencer's 90,000 subscribers were surprised to receive The Seattle Times in its place. Many, in fact, were mad as hell. They'd keep getting The Times unless they canceled or their force-fed subscriptions expired. The Times had automatically absorbed its deceased rival's home-delivery circulation. Another 27,500 copies of the P-I were purchased from stores and newsracks; 10,000 people subscribed to both papers. That means 107,500 P-I fans were wooable.

A year later, The Times' circulation was up 30 percent to 263,468. The good news was that it had peddled 60,000 more papers; the bad news was that it had failed to win over some 47,500 potential converts. The Internet and the recession had something to do with that. Considering the perilous state of the industry, The Times had done well. The daily circulation of the 25 largest newspapers had declined by an average of 8.7 percent in the previous six months. The Times' Sunday circulation had fallen 5.2 percent. An 11 percent bump in home-delivery rates and a 25-cent increase in single-copy prices contributed to the decline. Still not good, but notably better than the industry average for metropolitan newspapers. In Dallas, the circulation of the Sunday Morning News had declined 21.4 percent. The audience was leaving for new theaters featuring free snacks; so were the advertisers. Newspapers were going bankrupt; slashing their newsrooms; cutting back on home delivery. The McClatchy Company, the Blethens' new minority partner, saw its stock drop like a 900-pound roll of newsprint tumbling off a pressroom forklift. McClatchy wrote down the value of its share of The Times to zero. That was mostly for tax purposes but sobering nevertheless, though Blethen says he won't hold his breath waiting for McClatchy to surrender its 49.5 percent for next to nothing. "Black and White and Dead All Over," a documentary, focused on the beleaguered industry. Family-owned metropolitan newspapers are an endangered species. Between 2010 and 2012, The Seattle Times would lose nearly 16 percent of its daily circulation and 3.6 percent of its Sunday circulation. Intensive efforts to boost online readership appear to have stopped the slide. It's hard to tell. Internet-age circulation audits are a maze of categories.

February 5, 2010, was a good Friday at The Seattle Times. A full page ad signed by Frank, Bob, Will and John Blethen told readers: "We have good news to share with you. ... A year ago, rumors suggested that our days were numbered. While we continue to navigate through a slow recovery, we felt it important to put these rumors to rest by sharing our good news. The Seattle Times is here to stay." The rumors were well founded. The Blethens were prepared to file for Chapter 11 bankruptcy protection to stretch out their bank debt. "All the paperwork was ready when the New York banks blinked and allowed us to renegotiate our debt," Frank says. The Times pledged two more parcels of real estate in the booming South Lake Union neighborhood as collateral to secure nearly $72 million in bank debt. In all, the company owed $127 million, plus a $56 million unfunded liability for its pension plan. Critics observed sourly that the pension fund's assets must have been "horribly mismanaged" to be in such a fix. That's silly. The pension plan was overfunded prior to the recession. Defined benefit pension plans, the old standby, were clobbered when the stock market plummeted in 2008.* On top of wage freezes and furloughs, Times employees agreed to extend a pension contribution freeze, saving the company $14 million. "If there was any lingering bitterness from the strike, it was rapidly dissipating, given the reality of the situ-

---

* Boeing's pension fund shortfall was estimated at $10.5 billion in 2014. At this writing, the unfunded public pension liabilities in the U.S. amount to nearly $1 trillion.

ation we were all in," Blethen remembers.

A continent away a few months earlier, Blethen had a lump in his throat when he stood in the offices of the family's battered flagship paper in Portland, Maine, and swallowed a bitter pill: The sale of the Maine newspapers to a regional consortium of buyers had been completed. "In 2007 when the economy was starting to go south, every rational thought I had said, 'Sell them or you'll be sorry,'" he recalls. "The emotional connection was so strong that I held off." If he hadn't dithered, the company likely would have recouped roughly half the estimated $213 million it borrowed in 1998 to buy them. Now it received only around $30 million. Frank was grateful to get that, even though he had to agree to add the Maine pension-fund liability to his sack of rocks; otherwise no deal. Somewhere in sunny California, Tony Ridder was shaking his head.

Darren Gygi/courtesy Seattle Business magazine

"I know what Tony thinks," Blethen says, eyes narrowing, "because he tells anyone who asks that Maine was 'Frank's Folly.' But by mid-2000's, if not for the strike and the Hearst litigation, we would have been debt-free, thanks to the cash-flow from the Maine and Yakima newspapers. Essentially $50 million that would have gone to pay down the debt to keep us on track was lost due to the strike. Then we found ourselves paying some $10 million in legal fees. Without Maine and Yakima we wouldn't have made it through one of the most turbulent decades in American history. Tony maintains we paid too much for Yakima, paid way too much for Maine and bought up too much land. I believe the three best things I ever did to ensure our future were buying land around South Lake Union, buying Yakima and buying the Maine newspapers."

Carolyn Kelly retired as president and chief operating officer at the end of 2010 after 33 years with The Times. Early in her career she helped make the joint operating agreement operational. Toward the end, she was instrumental in the settlement that sealed its fate. Kelly was there when the money was rolling in and they were buying and building. And she was there when the floor collapsed and she and Frank jacked it up by selling assets.

Kelly's eventual successor—there was a two-year hiatus while Blethen saved on salaries and mulled—was a stylish, self-assured MBA named Alayne Fardella. Before joining The Times in the 1990s, Fardella had been a manager with Intel and National Semiconductor. At The Times, she quickly advanced to vice president for human resources and labor, then to vice president for business operations. The Californian became the newspaper's chief operating officer in 2012 and president two years later. Compared to Sizemore and Kelly, who were more visible in the community, Fardella seemed to have slipped in under the radar. Some still don't know what to make of her, except that she works well with Frank. Blethen says she is uncommonly bright and a quick study—someone who reads people extremely well. "Alayne has earned her salary 10 times over in the past two years," he says.

Kelly believes the women who raised Blethen deserve some credit for his track record as an industry leader in hiring and promoting women and minorities. She was The Times' first female chief operating officer and president; Fardella is the second. Blethen also appointed The Times' first female opinion page editor, Mindy Cameron; Kate Riley is the second. Sharon Prill, publisher of the company's Yakima Herald-Republic, is a Filipino-American. As role models go, Blethen's father was an utter flop. His mother, favorite aunt and earthy maternal grandmother were wise and nurturing. "I always thought that being raised by a single mom set Frank apart from the other white guys in the industry," Kelly says.

In 2014 Blethen received the Leadership in Diversity Award from the Asian American Journalists Association.

When 56-year-old David Boardman departed for Philadelphia in the fall of 2013, he left a legacy of world-class investigative journalism and a piece of his heart. He had directed four Pulitzer Prize-winning projects and seven finalists. On his watch as executive editor during the worst of the paper's financial travails, The Times won two more Pulitzers. Many cited guiding the newsroom though the McKenna ad controversy as Boardman's finest hour. City Council member Jean Godden, a former columnist for both Seattle dailies, called him a journalist's journalist. "He was the heart and soul of this place," said Ryan Blethen. "If Dave hadn't saved the journalism, we wouldn't be here today," his father said. "I don't wanna get too purple about all this, but losing Boardman is a loss for the whole town," The Stranger's Dominic Holden wrote. An anonymous commenter quipped that if Boardman had strangled Blethen "he really would deserve all this canonization." Maybe "quipped" is the wrong word.

Frank now faced a tough choice. His Pulitzer Prize-winning managing editors, Kathy Best and Suki Dardarian, were both highly qualified to succeed Boardman. They were versatile, experienced newswomen with great instincts. Competitive as hell, they nevertheless liked and respected one another. Both had worked for the competition before joining The Times—Dardarian at the News Tribune in Tacoma, Best at the Post-Intelligencer. Dardarian had been at The Times for 13 years, Best six. Both were married to equally accomplished journalists. Dardarian, with inquisitive brown eyes and understated charisma, interned at The Times after graduating from the University of Washington. She worked at The Daily Herald in Everett north of Seattle before joining the News Tribune, where she was a Pulitzer Prize finalist in 1992. Best's roots were a world apart from Puget Sound. With her dimpled chin and friendly voice, it's easy to envision her as a teenager working at her family's county-seat weekly in Sullivan, Illinois, population 4,000. It was a long way from there to Washington, D.C., where Best covered the capital for the St. Louis Post Dispatch before rising to metro editor at the P-I. After a stint as an assistant managing editor at The Sun in Baltimore, she joined The Times in 2007 and oversaw its growing digital presence.

Blethen thought things over for two months before deciding to give the top job to Best. Dardarian was named to a newly created position: director of audience development and innovation, reporting directly to him. Frank charged her with finding new ways to build readership and revenue, "whatever works." Best and Dardarian set out to "reimagine" the newsroom. Jim Simon was promoted to deputy managing editor and Ryan Blethen to assistant managing editor/digital. "All of us in this room need to stay laser-focused on our mission: producing useful, meaningful, kick-ass journalism that readers can't get anywhere else," Best told the news staff. The priggish old copy editors who ordered animals' genitals airbrushed out of county-fair photos and blanched at "damn" must have rolled over in their graves to hear the editor—a woman no less—talking about kicking ass. Joel Connelly, holding the fort at pi.com, was the only observer who seemed to grasp the irony that the first female editor-in-chief in the 117-year history of The Seattle Times was an alumna of its late rival. If they were looking for an enterprising leader, they had chosen well, he wrote. During the 2001 Nisqually earthquake, reporters in the P-I's waterfront offices ducked and covered. When the shaking stopped and they emerged from under their desks, Best "was calmly completing a detailed list of earthquake assignments on the staff assignment board."

Dardarian very much wanted to be editor. Her disappointment, which she worked hard to conceal, had nothing to do with Best. "Kathy is a very talented editor," she emphasizes. "We were good friends and supporters and still are."

Dardarian quickly pulled together a team that capitalized on Seahawks fever. The Times' sports section—one of the nation's best—chronicled every stirring victory leading to a Super Bowl championship. The Times sent 16 staffers to New Jersey to cover the big game. The fanatical "12th Man" fan base gobbled up every souvenir the newspaper cranked out—posters, plaques, commemorative books and T-shirts. Advertisers snapped up special promotions to salute the Seahawks. Suki's team scored big. Still, her friends and supporters could tell she felt deadended and disconnected from the mainstream of newsroom management, her passion for a decade. Few were surprised come March when Dardarian was named senior managing editor and vice president of the Minneapolis Star Tribune, with a mandate to focus on public-service journalism and help develop digital strategies.* When the announcement was made to the newsroom, Best fought back tears. "Suki had every reason to hate me," she said. "Instead she did everything she could to help me."

The innovation fostered by Boardman, Best and Dardarian brought The Seattle Times its first Edward R. Murrow Award. Steve Ringman, Danny Gawlowski and Michael Berens were cited for their online video "Glamour Beasts," part of a series on the plight of zoo elephants. Ringman and Craig Welch teamed up for an eye-opening series on ocean acidification. Editorials by Bruce Ramsey and Jonathan Martin on the implementation of marijuana legalization in Washington State won a national award. In 2014, The Times' coverage of the Oso landslide in Snohomish County was the national breaking-news winner in online journalism. Lynda Mapes' coverage of the removal of the fish-killing dams on the Elwha River featured time-lapse photography and blog-posts. Geoff Baker explored dysfunction in the Seattle Mariners' front office. From mistreatment of the mentally ill to lead poisoning at shooting ranges, The Times is staking its survival on high-quality journalism and miscellaneous random things people want to know right now—from sports scores to stock reports. It's a blend of classic, long-form digging and apps and pixels. Some readers will be genuinely worried to learn that starfish are "melting." And they ought to be. Some just want to know if the Seahawks' top running back has a herniated disc. The trick is getting people to pay for quality information when they think it's supposed to be free. There's another trick: getting people to care about quality information.

---

* Dardarian's departure cost the Tacoma News Tribune its star columnist of 29 years, Suki's husband, Peter Callaghan.

In *The Death and Life of American Journalism*, a disquieting book published in 2010, Robert W. McChesney and John Nichols wrote:

> A world without journalism is not a world without political information. Instead it is a world where what passes for news is largely spin and self-interested propaganda—some astonishingly sophisticated and some bellicose, but the lion's share of dubious value. It is an environment that spawns cynicism, ignorance, demoralization, and apathy. The only "winners" are those that benefit from a quiescent and malleable people who will "be governed," rather than govern themselves."

Frank Blethen turned 70 in 2015. Pink-cheeked, trim and natty, he looks a minimum of 10 years younger. His smile is mischievous, his chuckle willful. He's not quite ready to step down.

By 2015, having sold the last of its South Lake Union holdings, including the landmark Times Building at Fairview and John, the company's mountain of bank debt had been reduced to a relative molehill. All that remains at this writing is a low-interest, long-term $20 million mortgage on the North Creek printing plant. Unfortunately, there's another more daunting mountain: the pension fund liability. Since so many companies are in the same boat, Congress passed measures that temporarily lower minimum annual contributions. It's near-term relief that increases long-term liability. Unless interest rates rise to reduce the liability—even a modest increase would help considerably—the bill for the next 10 years could top $100 million. The Times paid $30 million between 2012 and 2014 to shore up the pension plans.

The Times was cash-flow positive during the worst of the recession. "We're inching close to a net profit," Blethen says, "but those pension plan payments—$10 million a year—are brutal for us. We've seen some solid appreciation on our assets, but the liabilities went up because the interest rates are down. It's Catch 22. We need higher interest rates. But all things considered, our recovery from where we were in 2009 is remarkable. Our family has sold $170 million worth of property over the past decade and invested it all in the survival of this newspaper. My cousins don't get enough credit for staying the course."

In 2011, when the company sold the eight-story Denny Building adjacent to The Times Building, it leased back about half the space for a new headquarters and moved in a year later. What the new home lacks in gravitas and ghosts it more than makes up for in utility and comfort. The offices are sleekly handsome and functional. The newsroom's workspaces, all on one floor, are designed to integrate print and online reporting. The area is far brighter than the old newsroom. It also exudes more energy. In February of 2015, The Times launched a new website "optimized for tablets, phones and all other devices," after investing $4 million in a massive digital overhaul.

The Times is on the brow of Amazonia. The crisp highrise buildings that comprise the headquarters of Jeff Bezos' empire add up to one of the world's largest urban office spaces. With his spare change, Bezos in 2013 bought an iconic newspaper, The Washington Post, at a bargain-basement price, $250 million. In the months since, The Post has been busy with buyouts and benefit reductions. At the same time, however, it has aggressively recruited people who know how to build digital audiences. Visits to the Post's website grew 38 percent in 2014. "Even though I didn't know anything about the newspaper business, I did know something about the Internet," Bezos says, "so that, combined with the financial runway I can provide, is the reason I bought the company, and I'm glad I did." The Post's new newsroom is leading the way. "You can't just change it from the business side," Bezos says. "It's gotta be everything. ...The world is completely changed, and advertisers have tons of options ... ." His plan is to re-brand the Post as a national publication, like The New York Times, by cultivating the "fast-growing mobile readership."

Frank and Ryan Blethen smiled when they read that quote in Bloomberg.com. The Post's executive producer for digital news is Cory Haik, the innovative young editor who played a key role in The Times' coverage of the Lakewood police officer murders.

Rob Blethen in downtown Walla Walla in 2014. *Greg Lehman/Walla Walla U-B*

"When Bezos bought the Post, I was sad that we'd lost another family-owned paper," Frank says. "The Graham family had gone public and that was the slippery slope. We've been critical of some of Bezos' business practices—pointing out that in 2011 Amazon.com's contribution to civic life and philanthropy in Seattle was virtually non-existent—but there's no denying the guy is brilliant. What he's trying to do at the Post is what we're doing here in one of the world's most wired cities."

What if Bezos wanted to buy The Seattle Times? "After everything we've been through, it's not for sale. I've told family members and our board that I'm committed to working full time until at least 2020. When we get there, someone's going to write a case study and say, 'Here's a family-owned metropolitan newspaper that figured it out.' Then it will be up to Ryan and Rob to do their part to ensure that 30 years from now when they're ready to retire, The Seattle Times is still a viable company, committed to public-service journalism. Ryan has three kids; his brother James has three; Rob has four. I hope they'll want to carry it on. As the saying goes, 'To those who are given much, much is expected.' Realistically, however, what someone will expect is higher profits and want to cash out. I hope the family will still say, 'If you're not passionately committed to the mission, this is the wrong place for you. We'll try to accommodate you and carry on.' "

As associate publisher, Ryan Blethen seems on track to suc-

Frank and Ryan Blethen in 2015. *Erika Schultz/The Seattle Times*

ceed his father. Does he want the job? An emphatic "Oh yeah." Blethenologists wonder whether McClatchy, the Blethens' minority partner, will have anything to say about it. Highly unlikely. The Blethens have the votes to name whom they choose if they stick together. Ryan's commitment to journalism—notably his objection to the McKenna ads—and nice-guy personality are winning over some doubters. "He seems unfazed by all the nepotism crap he takes for being Frank's son," one insider says. Rob Blethen, a polished manager, doesn't have that baggage. After his stint in Maine and five years as publisher at Walla Walla, he was named general manager for advertising and circulation at the Yakima Herald-Republic in the summer of 2014. His brother David is a district circulation manager there. Frank's younger son, James, is the ad production manager in Walla Walla. Courtney Blethen Riffkin, one of Buster's daughters, is now a photo editor at The Times. Her sister, Kerry Blethen Quinn, and John Blethen's oldest daughter, Jessica, have seats on the Blethen board.

There was one more thing the writer wanted to know:
    "Everyone asks me if I've seen your famous tattoo of The Seattle Times eagle logo."
    "Do you want to see my tattoo?" Frank says, laughing.

"I do."

"Ryan and James went with me when I got it, along with my best friend. It was right after our centennial in 1996. We had revived the classic Times flag with the eagle's outstretched wings."

"He offered to pay for ours," Ryan says.

Frank pulls up his left pants leg to reveal a tattoo on his calf.

The writer squints. "You could probably get a lot better one today if you did the other calf. It's kind of blurry."

"Well, it was supposed to be very small."

"They couldn't get all the detail," Ryan notes.

"There was a rumor for years that you had it on your left butt cheek."

"I'd never deface my butt!"

"Ryan, have you ever been tempted to get a tattoo of The Seattle Times logo on any part of your anatomy?"

"I've never been tempted to get a tattoo of anything anywhere."

Frank laughs. "I've been telling people for years that I'm the only dad in Seattle who tries to talk his sons into *getting* a tattoo instead of not getting one."

Part Two: The Wenatchee World

> *"A river flows through time and space. We think of the Amazon—broad and placid, rolling easily through a chirping jungle; of the Thames—more a lane than a river; of the Mississippi, the old man. Nobody has ever called the Columbia 'old man river.'"*
> —Murray Morgan, Northwest historian

1 | Community

Wilfred Woods, the dean of Northwest newspaper owners, wore a red crown jauntily as he greeted friends and admirers at the impressive Performing Arts Center he helped build in downtown Wenatchee. The guests at his 94th birthday party were handed hats fashioned from folded pages of The Wenatchee World. Wilf's son and successor, Rufus, wore his sideways. He looked like John Paul Jones in a sport shirt. Wilf's daughters—Gretchen on violin, Kara on cello—offered selections from Haydn. In lieu of gifts, Wilf asked the crowd to donate to an endowment to ensure the center's success. "So my party has a plan, and it's not about me; it's about our community." The mayor called him a treasure.

Wilf's wife, Kathy, vetoed another big party when he turned 95 on September 30, 2014. They'd have a few friends over to the house. About 80 showed up. There was vintage Columbia Valley wine, music and laughter. "There's no magic in numbers," Wilf wrote in his front-page column, "but 95 isn't bad." A few days later, he came down with pneumonia. Thousands of people in North Central Washington held their breath and prayed. Rufus posted a photo of his dad in the intensive care unit reading the newspaper. Soon, Wilf was out of danger, home again and on the mend. And now he's 96.

Rufus and Wilfred Woods with their KBA Comet press. *Mike Bonnicksen/The Wenatchee World*

In Wenatchee the Woodses are an institution. They own and operate a daily newspaper that's steeped in history and a sense of place, yet also thoroughly modern. It's still delivered to doorsteps five days a week, but liked a lot on Facebook. Compared to the Blethens, "we're boring," Rufus claims. Less complicated, yes. Boring, no. Perhaps even more than The Seattle Times, The Wenatchee World survives as the antithesis of absentee-owner publishing. "Rather burn it down than sell it," says Rufus.

"How old would you be if you didn't know how old you were?" Satchel Paige once observed. When he reads that line, Wilfred Woods will grin, nod and offer his trademark "ha-ha!" He is the youngest 95-year-old you've ever met. There's spring in his step and mirth in his throaty voice. It was only four years ago that he stopped skiing at Mission Ridge, which he helped develop. In fact, of the good things in North Central Washington there's not much that Wilf hasn't nurtured since 1950 when he succeeded his inimitable father, the first Rufus Woods, as publisher. Rufus whistled when he was frustrated or nervous. Wilf whistles when he's content, which is almost all the time. His is a life punctuated with memorable moments, major achievements and few regrets.

Wilf is now the sage—chairman emeritus of The Wenatchee World. The resident "old fart," as he puts it. His column, a quick and folksy read, remains one of the paper's most popular features. Briskly, shoulders first, he often walks about a mile from the newspaper office to its production facility to get one of the first papers off the $4 million press his son went out on a limb to buy in 1999. Although borrowing the money "scared the living daylights" out of him, the press has proved to be a shrewd investment.

A great river flows through his time and space, and the ancient landscape he knows so well tells amazing stories. From boyhood, those rocks grew more fascinating the more he learned. He saw the Grand Coulee—"North America's most splendid runoff ditch," as one historian puts it—for the first time in 1930 when he was 11. That summer, he'd been given his first job in the family business—swatting flies in the sweaty newsroom at The Wenatchee Daily World. Now it was time for a road trip with his dad. The original Rufus by then was well on his way to becoming a legend in his own time and far beyond Wenatchee. He was "that dam (or damn) editor!" depending upon your inflection. FDR called out, "Hey, Rufus!" when he came to see the dam. Undaunted by a postwar newsprint shortage, Rufus bought a tract of timber, culled a cutting crew from his staff and led them into the woods to cut six carloads of logs. The effort yielded 40 tons of sorely needed paper for his press. A photo of the publisher and his wife wielding a crosscut saw was reprinted nationwide.

In an era when most newspapers had slogans—the Chicago Tribune styled itself as the "World's Greatest Newspaper," and The Atlanta Journal boasted it covered "Dixie like the Dew"—Rufus Woods had a bushel. Early on, the front-page "ear" opposite the weather forecast declared: "Printed in the World's Greatest Fruit Section. Where Dollars Grow on Trees." That one gave way to the "Greatest Daily in the World for Cities Under 10,000." Then, on August 26, 1925, a new slogan appeared beneath the newspaper's nameplate: "Published in the Apple Capital of the World and the Buckle of the Power Belt of the Great Northwest." It's still there. At the time, the first hydropower dam on the Columbia River was still six years from fruition, and Washington State wouldn't become the nation's top apple producer until the 1960s, so one historian observes that Rufus Woods was "either a visionary or a master of spin." Clearly he was both—"a man of parts," as they used to say— a bulky, balding force of nature. He had penetrating eyes, a twinkly smile and a persistent itch to travel. His suit pockets were stuffed with notes to himself and candy for the kids who followed him down the street. He loved history, poetry, politics, automobiles, his bright, even-tempered wife and inquisitive children. "Imagine having a father like that," Wilf says.

Around 1910, to boost circulation, Rufus began bouncing along the rutted rural roads of North Central Washington. A Model T Ford equipped with a typewriter, a camera and dictating machine became the newspaper's "Traveling Office." From Twisp to Ephrata, Leavenworth to Mansfield, when Woods pulled into town someone would call out, "Why, hello Rufus!" He'd collect news, gossip and a glass of lemonade wherever there was a cluster of potential customers. He wooed advertisers and subscribers with special editions spotlighting their towns. "What do you need around here?" he'd ask. "You need a library? We'll get one for you!" In Ephrata, pop. 628, the seat of bone-dry Grant County, he often stopped to see Billy Clapp, the town's leading lawyer. Together, they had hatched a scheme that at first drew little except derision. But now, in 1930 when Wilf— "Boy-Boy" to his dad—came along for the ride, they had reason to believe their audacious idea could become a reality. They wanted to build a dam across the Columbia, fill the Grand Coulee with irrigation water and pump the Columbia Basin's shrub land into a million-acre agricultural oasis. It would be "The greatest development project in the world!" Rufus wrote.

Rufus, among many other things, was an early champion of the Good Roads movement that transformed American mobility after Henry Ford put the country on wheels. To his satisfaction, Highway 10, up Pine Canyon to Waterville, then across the plateau to dusty Coulee City, was now paved. Their six-cylinder Chandler—Rufus had traded up—was one of the few cars on the road. "Abandoned cabins and derelict wind-

The Wenatchee Daily World's "traveling office," a 1917 Ford equipped with a typewriter, dictating machine and camera. Rufus Woods is inside, ready to roll. Charles Stohl, the paper's business manager, minded the ledgers. *Wenatchee World Archives*

mills stood as sad monuments to failed dreams and broken homesteaders. ... Even in the best seasons, when a few inches of precipitation fell upon thirsty crops, yields averaged only six bushels of wheat to the acre."

Wilf Woods has made the trip along the rim of the Grand Coulee hundreds of times over the past 80 years. He could pretty much drive it in his sleep, yet it never gets old: "When you come down the plateau, *there it is*. That Coulee is an awesome sight." With shelves full of books and studies, Wilf knows the geology of North Central Washington better than many well-schooled geologists. Brandishing maps, he loves to tell the story of how it happened:

Once upon a time, a long, long time ago—12,500 to 15,500 years ago, to be more precise—the Columbia River was choked out of its channel by a massive glacier. Then, as the last ice age thawed, cataclysmic floods swept across the channeled scablands of Eastern Washington. The Columbia "grew to contain ten times the flow of all the rivers in the world today." It carved vast channels through the volcanic terrain created eons earlier when the earth belched lava from hissing fissures.

When the flood waters receded northeast of Ephrata, the river's old channel was high and dry—a 50-mile trench, one to six miles wide, with towering basalt walls. The slack-jawed first white visitors called the big gulch the "Grand Coulee." A U.S. Cavalry lieutenant, who traversed the region in the 1880s, wrote that its walls formed "a vista like some grand old ruined roofless hall, down which we traveled hour after hour."

Near the coulee's north entrance looms a gigantic boat-shaped basalt butte. The settlers named it Steamboat Rock. It's a remnant of a once great waterfall—greater even than the awesome Dry Falls some 25 miles south. Indian legend has it that the Columbia poured over the falls "until Coyote, rejected in marriage, changed its course out of spite." White fur traders and some of the Native peoples used the coulee as an overland route between the upper Columbia and the mouth of the Snake River, according to William D. Layman, a Columbia River historian. Other Indians shunned the area because they believed it was "the abode of evil spirits"—a place of thunder and lightning "and a rumbling in the earth."

A Nebraska farm boy with a congenital sense of adventure and a law degree that never lit his wick, 26-year-old Rufus Woods saw the coulee for the first time not long after he arrived in Wenatchee in 1904. "Unmet and unnoticed," he had "twenty borrowed dollars in his pocket." Though surrounded by beautiful brown sculpted foothills formed by the ancient glaciers and tremendous floods, the Wenatchee Rufus surveyed as he stepped off the train from Seattle was nothing to write home about. There, along the banks of the Columbia, he saw a "rag-tag and bobtailed" fly-infested collection of shacks and wood-frame storefronts. He also grasped its potential. The railroad ran right through town, and the cold, clear Wenatchee rambled down from the hills to join the big river in the valley. Thanks to a new 16-mile canal, the town was poised to bloom and boom. The flume irrigated 9,000 acres of rich volcanic soil in a climate "ideally suited to fruit cultivation." In his insightful biography of Rufus Woods, Robert E. Ficken writes:

Although tinged with boosterism, the local slogan "Home of the Big Red Apple" conveyed a signal truth about Wenatchee. Over 100,000 trees, mostly Winesaps and Jonathans, were planted in the decade prior to 1907. As these trees came into bearing five to seven years after planting, production expanded at a rapid rate. The original 1902 shipment of apples for market filled two Great Northern freight cars. Exports thereafter mounted from 116 carloads in 1903 to 2,197 in 1910 and 6,893 in 1914. By the latter year, the Wenatchee district grew one-eighth of the apples sold in the United States.

But Wenatchee's economy was in one basket. And the rest of North Central Washington would remain magnificently desolate unless it acquired irrigation.

Rufus took over the struggling Wenatchee Daily World in 1907 after stints with a local weekly and the chamber of commerce. What The World stood for, Rufus declared, was "a Greater Wenatchee, for a moral and intelligent citizenship, for an ideal place in which to live." The four-page paper had 465 subscribers. His identical twin, Ralph, was an important silent partner. Ralph liked being a lawyer, and he was good at it. He was also good for a loan when Rufus was being dunned by newsprint vendors. Rufus dreamed of transforming North Central Washington into an inland empire to rival Spokane.

First he had to fend off the rival Wenatchee Republic, the house organ of the valley's conservative Republicans. In its pages Rufus was vilified as a politically suspect interloper. Since boyhood, Woods had idolized fellow Nebraskan William Jennings Bryan, the silver-tongued populist. The county's old guard Republicans charged that Rufus was "a Bryan Democrat at heart." By 1912, in their eyes he had become something far worse: an out and out traitor.

Woods also hugely admired Theodore Roosevelt's good-government reform agenda that targeted monopolies and embraced conservation. "Big eastern capitalists" now controlled vast stands of Western timber, as well as water and mineral rights, Woods wrote. Sooner or later, they would be able to "charge the public what the traffic will bear." That was already happening with the Great Northern Railway, he declared. Wenatchee's freight lifeline was "the poorest excuse for a railroad in the country." Roosevelt had targeted the cartels from the earliest days of his administration. One of T.R.'s most visionary decisions, Woods wrote, was his appointment of Gifford Pinchot as chief of the Forest Service. Roosevelt's goal was "not to preserve forests because they are beautiful—though that is a good in itself—not to preserve them because they are refuges for wild creatures of the wilderness—though that too is a good in itself," but rather to conserve them in order to guarantee "a steady and continuous supply of timber, grass, and above all, water" that would foster the growth of prosperous communities. "In speech after speech," Doris Kearns Goodwin writes in *The Bully Pulpit*, "Roosevelt lauded the passage of the 1902 Reclamation Act, which for the first time, made substantial federal funds available to construct dams, reservoirs, and other irrigation projects in the West." Above all, the president said, "We do not ever want to let our land policy be shaped so as to create a big class of proprietors who rent to others." To Rufus Woods this was holy writ.

When Roosevelt broke with his hand-picked successor, William Howard Taft, and bolted the party to run as a "Bull Moose" Progressive in 1912, Rufus Woods defected too. Roosevelt carried Washington and five others states, but the bitter schism in the GOP handed the presidency to Woodrow Wilson. Woods commiserated with his friend Werner Rupp, publisher of The Aberdeen Daily World and chairman of the State Republican Committee, when Rupp's efforts at party reconciliation proved daunting in 1914.*

---

* A scathing letter to Rupp from his own brother, Otto, a prominent Seattle attorney, italicized the bitterness. When Rupp was quoted in the Seattle papers as saying T.R. ought to be welcomed back to the fold if he renounced portions of his platform, Otto Rupp wrote: "Anyone ... who now expresses a willingness to consent that Colonel Roosevelt shall be the future nominee of the Party he so traitorously deserted, evidences nothing as much as he does a total want of self respect."

Heartbreak beyond words was added to the stress of Woods' fight for survival as a publisher. One thing Rufus and Mary Woods never spoke of in the years to come was the loss of their first two children. Wilma, 2½, and Walter, 1½, died in the space of five days in the summer of 1913 after drinking tainted milk from a Wenatchee dairy. Two other children died, and two-dozen residents in all fell ill. Daily front-page bulletins tracked the "brave and persistent fight" to save the children. Wracked by guilt, "the despairing parents departed for weeks of aimless travel."

Willa Lou, Wilfred and Kathryn—"Kay" to family and friends—were born over the next eight years. "We had a joyful upbringing," Kathryn Woods Haley recalls. In fact, their parents were very relaxed around the children and encouraged them to be adventurous. But, deep down, the sadness never went away, Wilf says. "Mother, who was passionate about music, quit playing the piano about that time."

Rufus plunged into his work and deeper in debt, borrowing heavily to buy a new typesetter and better press. He was in a desperate struggle with the Republic. William H. Cowles, the powerful Spokane publisher who shared Woods' Progressive Republican bent, loaned him $5,000.

In 1914, the competition finally folded, and Rufus set out to make The World the voice of North Central Washington—and North Central Washington an important part of the world. From the beginning, he fought for "the freeing of the Pacific Northwest from domination by outside corporate and governmental forces." And 40 years later, still insisted, "All too long have we been a colony of the East."

"A paper should stand for something," Rufus wrote, and "unite the constructive forces of the community it endeavors to serve." To Rufus, "community" was Chelan, Douglas, Grant and Okanogan counties, "the last and best part of Uncle Sam's West." Woods' Daily World wasn't just a Wenatchee paper. He had a news "stringer," paid by the published inch, in every town. If seven Peshastin Camp Fire Girls were awarded the coveted rank of Torchbearer, they got their picture in the paper. When a hundred 4-H Club members from four counties boarded a train for summer camp at the state college in Pullman, it was

A crowd gathers outside The Wenatchee World Building in 1910 for the latest updates from Seattle, where Wenatchee High School's football team was playing the Illinois state champion. *Wenatchee World Archives*

front-page news. Bowling scores were reported weekly. So was the "Moth Catch." In 1910, when Wenatchee High School's stellar football team played the Illinois state champion, Oak Park High of Chicago, hundreds gathered outside the World Building to hear play-by-play reports phoned from Denny Field in Seattle. Growers sent over carloads of their "matchless big red apples" to advertise Wenatchee's claim to fame. When the ushers began tossing them into the crowd, scrambles broke out. Mischievous fans, many fortified with alcohol to ward off the December chill, began lobbing apple cores. Rowdy youth poured onto the field. With Oak Park ahead 22-0, officials ended the game with eight minutes remaining to quell a near riot. The World's story spun the event as a win because headlines all over America would declare that "Wenatchee apples were so good they caused a riot."

It was the golden age of American newspapers. Early on, The Wenatchee Daily World became the smallest paper in the U.S. with its own photo-engraving shop. By 1916, the majority of the paper's 4,600 subscribers lived beyond Wenatchee.

Rufus subscribed to the Associated Press "A" wire, as well as United Press. He was known to reject last-minute advertising if that meant a correspondent's report would have to wait a day. By refusing liquor advertising he cost the company thousands. "I'd rather use the space to give my readers the news," he told a fellow publisher who marveled at his idealism. "The booze habit," Woods warned, "leads ...to the wrecking of business, the wrecking of families, the canceling of friendships, the loss of faith in one's self." No prude, Woods nevertheless was the sworn enemy of prostitution, gambling, drunkenness and political cronyism: "WENATCHEE—WHICH ROAD?" he asked before a municipal election.

Woods decried the dumping of garbage in the Columbia River, championed conservation and denounced exploiters and extractors of natural resources. He crusaded for equitable rail rates and was an early supporter of direct election of U.S. senators and the initiative and referendum. The World's editorial page was replete with letters to the editor. Those that castigated the publisher's views received prominent play. Rufus called the column the "Safety Valve." It's still called that today.

"Play it big! Play it like a circus!" Rufus admonished his editors. And when he found the biggest story of his life, he did just that.

2 | Two Million Wild Horses

IN THE dog days of the summer of 1918, Rufus Woods rolled into Ephrata and learned Billy Clapp had "a big idea that might make a story." It was a very big idea: "If ice could dam the Columbia and fill the coulee with water," Clapp said, "why couldn't we do the same?" The notion that irrigation water could be pumped from a giant reservoir in the coulee had been kicking around since the 1890s. Rufus nevertheless claimed the scheme "first conceived" by the pinochle-playing country lawyer was the greatest water-power innovation since the dawn of the grist mill—nothing less than "the newest, the most ambitious idea in the way of reclamation and ... water power ever formulated." Given "the complete lack of technical evidence for this breathtaking assertion, the dimensions of the project were necessarily vague," observes Woods' biographer, Robert E. Ficken.

The rest is history. But it took 20 years, the Great Depression and a president desperate to generate jobs to make Billy's daydream come true. Along the way, Rufus wore out the exclamation point on more than one Underwood. Imagine "TWO MILLION WILD HORSES!" he told his readers. "Energy that today is wasting itself away day by day as it flows down the Columbia River, the wildest big steam in the civilized world." When Rufus was really on a roll, he'd give the Shift Lock key an emphatic poke and remind his readers that a high dam at the Grand Coulee "...WOULD BE THE MOST UNIQUE, THE MOST INTERESTING, AND THE MOST REMARKABLE DEVELOPMENT ... IN THE AGE OF INDUSTRIAL AND SCIENTIFIC MIRACLES!"

They said it couldn't be done. There was "Too much water!" The river was too swift. The dam would have to be at

Rufus Woods, left, with Billy Clapp, center, and Gale Matthews, fellow members of the "Dam University," around 1940. *Wenatchee World Archives*

least 550 feet high. Baron Munchausen, the fabled teller of tall tales, was a piker compared to Woods and Clapp, a local judge wrote in 1918.

In Spokane, the Grand Coulee proposal revived talk of a "gravity" alternative. Irrigation water from the Pend Oreille River at Albeni Falls north of Spokane could be diverted south to arid counties through a series of reservoirs, canals, tunnels and siphons, sponsors said. That this project, embraced by the privately-held Washington Water Power Company, could provide irrigation at affordable rates was highly doubtful, and parts of North Central Washington would remain high and dry.

The underdog Grand Coulee "pumpers" acquired a tireless compatriot in another Ephrata lawyer, James O'Sullivan. The lanky, pipe-smoking Irishman had returned to Grant County from Michigan where he successfully managed the family construction business in the wake of his father's death. "He'll never give up," Clapp said, "and he can't be bought." They called themselves the "Dam University." Reclamation was their goal, but hydropower—"as great as a number of Niagras"—would be a crucial byproduct. "The revenue from the sale of electric energy alone would surely pay all the upkeep, interest on the investment, and provide a sinking fund for the liquidation of the cost of the project itself," O'Sullivan wrote in a 1918 article for The Wenatchee Daily World.

The Columbia Basin Irrigation League, a front organization for Washington Water Power, sneered at the "Coulee communists." Woods and Clapp passed the hat at Grange Halls to fund O'Sullivan's lobbying in Washington, D.C. It was a dollar here and $5 there; sometimes just quarters. When the Stock Market crashed and banks started closing, O'Sullivan often went unpaid. "Many and many a night," Clapp recalled, "we set up to 2 o'clock plotting what to do next. Whenever they got us bottled up in one place, we broke out in another. The same with them. When we thought we had them licked, they'd come again on a new tack."

When the battle was fully joined, the "ditchers" parried with a plan to construct a dam of their own at Kettle Falls near the Canadian border. Washington Water Power saw Grand Coulee as a threat to its rate-setting hegemony. It had deep pockets and the backing of the Spokane Chamber of Commerce, the railroads and Cowles' Spokesman-Review. That public power was the slippery slope to socialism was also largely the view of the conservative citizenry. The utility "spent a lot of money, as the Federal Power Commission demonstrated later, keeping the people of Spokane thinking right on this issue."

Eastern congressmen predicted the only customers for a dam at the Grand Coulee would be "sage brush and jackrabbits." The president of the American Society of Civil Engineers branded Grand Coulee "a grandiose project of no more usefulness than the pyramids of Egypt." *Outlook* magazine described it as the impulsive scheme of "a country lawyer and a country editor," with "an able propagandist ...imported from the middle-west." The members of the Dam University had graduated to the national stage.

Deft maneuvering by U.S. Senator Wesley L. Jones, the Republican whip and Appropriations Committee chairman, cleared the way for an unbiased feasibility report by the Army Corps of Engineers. The plain-talking lawyer from Yakima was "not possessed by ideology." What mattered was the economic development of his state. He'd been promoting federal assistance for irrigation since his arrival on Capitol Hill before the turn of the century.

The 2,000-page report, completed in 1931, concluded that the Pend Oreille gravity plan would cost a prohibitive $400 per acre. A dam at the Grand Coulee would provide irrigation at about $150 per acre. But the revenue from power sales from Grand Coulee and seven other dams the Corps endorsed along the Columbia and its tributaries would cut the cost of irrigation to only about $85 per acre. Engineering work got under way.

As the Depression deepened, Woods met with President Herbert Hoover, emphasizing that the project would generate thousands of jobs, not to mention votes. Ray Wilbur, Hoover's Interior secretary and good friend, came west to inspect the dam site. Rufus was his usual animated self as they sped down a gravel road. The country roads ran on section lines, "which meant that all turns were right angles," wrote Carl Cleveland, a Wenatchee Daily World reporter who accompanied them. "As we approached one of these turns, I saw with consternation that Rufus was not slowing down. Rather, with sweeping gestures, he was pointing out features of the landscape to the secretary." When the road took a sharp left turn, "Rufus kept straight ahead, plowing sagebrush and sand in a great cloud. Without interrupting his dissertation, Rufus swung the car in a wide circle and back on to the road, with a white-faced secretary hanging on for dear life."

Hoover, who had made his reputation as a globetrotting mining engineer and World War I relief coordinator before entering politics, was in no mood to turn left. The moon-faced president was cold, meticulous and supremely confident the economy would soon rebound. The fundamental issue, he insisted, was that using federal funds to promote relief through public works projects would lead to "collectivism" that would "deprive individuals of initiative."

Brushing aside Woods' reminders that he had previously endorsed the Columbia Basin Project, Hoover now asserted there was no market for the power. Moreover, "the farm surplus problem would be exacerbated and the public treasury was bare." With a wave of his hand, Hoover also dismissed political considerations, saying that in any case it would be impossible to start work on Grand Coulee Dam soon enough to boost his chances for re-election. Gutzon Borglum, the celebrated sculptor, wrote a friend: "I believe if a rose was placed in his hand it would wilt."

Come November, Senator Jones lost his seat after 33 years in Congress, and Hoover went down to humiliating defeat. Franklin D. Roosevelt carried 42 states, including Washington, home to some of his most fervent supporters. FDR had promised in a campaign stop at Portland that his administration would promote hydropower development of the Columbia Basin. Rufus Woods became a "Dam-o-crat." He and O'Sullivan had an agile ally in U.S. Senator Clarence Dill. The Democrat from Spokane had the ear of the new president, as did the newly elected Democratic governor, Clarence Martin of Cheney. Martin, declaring that the dam must be expedited, named Woods to a new five-member Columbia Basin Commission.

With U.S. unemployment topping 25 percent, Roosevelt authorized massive public-works projects, including a 290-foot hydro dam at Grand Coulee. The pumpers were disappointed. A "low dam" wouldn't fill the coulee. However, after visiting the Grand Coulee in 1934 and meeting with Rufus and O'Sullivan, FDR endorsed the "high dam" they wanted. At 550 feet, it could fulfill their dream of irrigation for North Central Washington. The final hurdle was Congress. Rep. Sam B. Hill, a veteran Democrat from Waterville, did do-or-die work, rescuing the project not once but twice. Dill and National Grange Master Albert Goss gave Hill strong support. The project was approved with the Rivers and Harbors Bill of 1935. Critics were appalled. "The proposition of the Grand Coulee in my judgment is the most colossal fraud in the history of America," Congressman Francis D. Culkin, a New York Republican with a colossal prescience deficit, declared. Likewise The Bellingham

Herald, which marveled at "the magnitude of this folly! There is no call for hydroelectric power. Enterprises are already equipped to supply all of the energy this state would be able to consume in a generation." *The Farm Journal* wrote, "Who wants it? Nobody. Well, perhaps not quite nobody, but nobody whose wishes need have the slightest weight with Congress and the nation."

"The Growing Giant," a cartoon by Dave McKay in the Seattle Post-Intelligencer, October 2, 1937. *Washington State Archives*

In 1936, Rufus hedged his election bets. He endorsed the reelection of Governor Martin and was transparently for FDR while giving lip-service to Kansas Governor Alf Landon, Roosevelt's challenger. The Chelan County Republican Central Committee took out a half-page ad excoriating Woods. The publisher had swapped his scruples for a "seat in the sun" on the power commission, the conservatives said. Woods deposited the check for the ad and "did not deign to reply." Rufus would come to rue the downside of federalization: Loss of local control.

When Governor Martin donned overalls to make the ceremonial first pour of concrete, an enterprising rookie reporter named Hu Blonk—The World's future managing editor—was there. And as the workforce climbed toward 7,000, each day's edition featured his reports in a special "Grand Coulee World" section: "All That's News From The Busiest Place In The West" from a newspaper that for 13 years "stood alone among the dailies of the state" in advocating the project.

Blonk rounded up "construction stiffs" to give the paper first-person accounts of the massive undertaking. The Bureau of Reclamation mimeographed a steady stream of eye-popping statistics: The dam would contain 10 million cubic yards of concrete, enough to build a 16-foot-wide highway from Seattle to Boston and back to Los Angeles. "Four battleships the size of the *U.S.S. Missouri* could be placed bow to stern and not reach across Grand Coulee's crest," nor could the Empire State Building if it was laid it on its side.

Rufus basked in it all as the archetype of the influential country editor. He corresponded with William Allen White, the Pulitzer Prize-winning sage of Emporia, Kansas. Governors, senators, congressmen and presidents returned his calls. Ernie Pyle, a Charles Kuralt-style roving reporter before his days as a war correspondent, made two trips to watch the big dam taking shape and was fascinated by the "perambulating publisher." In his nationally syndicated column, Pyle wrote:

> Rufus Woods is a big frog in a small puddle. They told me at Grand Coulee that I ought to stop in Wenatchee and see him. So I did. And I found him the oddest combination of opposite instincts I have ever seen. He's a typical small-city civic leader, and he's also a nervous searcher of the world. In appearance and action, he's the booster, glad-to-see everybody, great-little-old town-we've-got-here type of citizen. He is a little heavy and wears a gold watch chain. He has a wife and three children, a house and a car and owns a newspaper. He's a Republican because his father was. He likes to speak at luncheons, and has ten "calls," as he says, on his desk right now. But on the other hand, he is a fiend for wandering. He knows people all over the world and enough odd bits of history to make a book. Last winter he said to his wife, "I think I'll go to Russia this afternoon." He did. And when he had been back just 10 days he hopped a boat for Alaska. ...

> The children love to make auto trips with their Dad because so many exciting things happen. Mr. Woods teaches his children they must learn how to do everything—ride and cook and ski and set type and swim and speak foreign languages. ...If they all turn out to be as curious and enthusiastic as their father, they'll drive the world crazy.

Wilf Woods recalls his father astride a horse in the mountains, declaiming in stentorian tones from *The Legend of William Tell*, "Ye crags and peaks, I am with you once again!" And whenever Uncle Ralph was in town, mischief was afoot. The mirror-image twins delighted in befuddling people. One of their favorite stunts, Pyle learned, "is for one to go into a restaurant, eat his meal and then slip out. The other brother quickly slips in, says the food was no good and demands another meal. The poor waitress is always so balled up that she brings it." Then, to her astonishment, the other brother would appear. They'd laugh, settle up and leave two tips.

Besides their kinetic father, wise and diplomatic mother and Uncle Ralph, the Woods children also had the example of their mother's redoubtable sister, Eva Greenslit Anderson. Aunt Eva was an educator with a Ph.D. and an author and historian. She was the second woman ever appointed to the University of Washington Board of Regents and became an influential state legislator.

The elders encouraged independence. When Wilf was in high school, he and his siblings spent six weeks in Greenwich Village while father was traveling in Europe and mother was at a Methodist conference. They headed out each day to explore their many interests—museums, symphony concerts, operas, Broadway plays and all manner of political talks.

One of Teddy Roosevelt's friends, observing him roughhousing with his children, once declared, "You must always remember that the president is about six." So too Rufus Woods. In 1937, with work on the big dam under way, the 59-year-old publisher fulfilled his boyhood heart's desire: When the circus came to town he was there every day. And when it pulled up stakes, he went with it. "Made up in grease paint, with putty nose, shaggy wig ... and flapping shoes," he tootled a clarinet and tossed Tootsie Rolls to the children for the next two weeks. Rufus pretended to be irked that *Time, Life* and The New York Times found this novel. His wife and children certainly didn't. "We put on home circuses all the time," Wilf recalls, grinning at the memory. Father was friends with the local Game Department agent, who supplied bear cubs and fawns. The neighborhood kids brought their dogs and cats. One year, admission was charged, with all proceeds ($27) donated to Mississippi River flood victims. Rufus delighted in it all. His whimsy was a stress reliever but also part of his nature.

From early childhood, his children grasped that their father was someone special, and that owning a newspaper was a public trust. Rufus also inured them that they were bound to encounter people who disliked him or something the paper had printed. "Once when Dad and I sat on counter stools at a Mission Street café, the man next to him was quite gruff," recalls Kathryn Woods Haley. The man left abruptly. "What's the problem, Dad?" "Oh, just after World War I he and some Cashmere chaps circulated some untrue things about me. The others eventually apologized, but he never was man enough. Now he can't look me in the eye." Rufus looked everyone in the eye, his children recalled. And he always said they should too.

Rufus steeped his children in the newspaper business, anxious that at least one would carry on what he had worked so hard to achieve. Whenever The World published an "Extra" for election results, a heavyweight championship bout or a World Series game, the kids would be on Wenatchee's sidewalks at 5 a.m., hawking the headlines. They made 2½ cents a paper. Kathryn began working at the paper's switchboard at 14. She accompanied her father on a train trip to Washington, D.C., serving as his secretary as they made the rounds of politicians and lobbyists. Her sister Willa, seven years older, was already in the newsroom. Bob Woods, the son of their father's cousin, World treasurer Warren Woods, was entrusted with editing the newspaper's 60 correspondents a few weeks after graduating from the University of Washington in 1937. And young Wilf was no longer swatting flies.

The news staff of The Wenatchee Daily World in the summer of 1937. Back row, from left: E.H. McPherson, Dick Bell, Kirby Billingsley, Ben Bothun, Rufus Woods, Bob Woods; front row, from left: Willa Woods, Kathryn Woods and Lynn Leonard. *Wenatchee World Archives*

3 | "What a heritage!"

AT FAMILY-OWNED newspapers, tradition holds that the kids learn the ropes by working in every department. Wilfred Woods may be the only one who ever prompted a back-shop strike during college break.

"Let's face it: Father was old school," Wilf says. Father believed unions had accomplished some commendable reforms, but the tail was now wagging the dog. The Wenatchee Daily World was family, "a place where managers and employees worked together in 'good fellowship' for mutual advancement," Rufus insisted.

In the 1920s, Rufus rebuffed printers' union demands for higher wages, maintaining that The World was paying

Young Wilf Woods and his father huddle over a page of type in 1940. *Wenatchee World Archives*

as well or better than papers of comparable size. The issue simmered on a back burner until the Depression, which hit Wenatchee later than elsewhere. Construction of Puget Sound Power & Light's Rock Island Dam, the first to harness the Columbia, generated 2,400 jobs. By the winter of 1933, however, as dispirited, jobless men peddled apples on street corners in America's cities, the price per bushel reached an all-time low of 49 cents. When Rufus imposed a 20 percent across-the-board pay cut, the printers protested. He told them the paper's profits had declined precipitously; they should be grateful they still had jobs. Unimpressed, the printers went on strike. Rufus cobbled together a crew from other departments. Reinforcements sent by sympathetic publishers soon arrived. "The striking printers created a giveaway paper, trying to pull advertisers and subscribers from The World," Wilf recalls. "They called Dad a 'troglodyte with an itching palm.' But it didn't work. People stayed with The World." The paper maintained its open shop.

In 1940, the economy was on the rebound, locally and nationally, from soaring apple prices, work on Grand Coulee

Dam, other public-works projects and federal defense spending. When Wilf, 20, arrived home in June from his studies at the College of Puget Sound in Tacoma, his dad put him to work in the stereotyping department, producing printing plates for the press. "I wasn't taking anyone's job. But relations with them weren't the best, and Dad thought I ought to learn stereotyping. So I went in and they walked out. We recruited another kid from the mail room and the two of us learned stereotyping from scratch." Rufus put on work clothes and joined them for the first day. An uneasy truce ensued after Rufus removed Wilf in a cooling-off gesture. But when he sent the kid back into the back shop, another strike broke out. Rufus fired the lot of them. The union appealed, and the National Labor Relations Board conducted tedious hearings. Rufus had found the New Deal increasingly suspect. This was the last straw. That lackadaisical Americans with little regard for the Constitution had come to think of Uncle Sam as "some sort of magnificent Santa Claus" disgusted him. The calls and letters ran heavily in Rufus's favor. "Some contain too strong of language to be used in this column," the publisher wrote in his front-page column. "One of them advises the use of a baseball bat. ..." Future congressman Walt Horan, one of the valley's leading fruit growers, wrote:

> At a time when personal ownership, individual operation and privately planned enterprises are too much invaded for the public profit, you must be informed, Rufus, that I was one who rejoiced in your protest to foreign control of your mechanical plant. ...We have leaned so long on Washington, D.C., and Seattle and other points of remote control that we have lost the wisdom and the strength of our own convictions, springing from the soil where we toil.
>
> One thing is certain. Wenatchee and her people will not perish so long as we are of service and continue to produce a product that benefits mankind. ...
>
> And in that work there is a place for The Daily World and for Rufus Woods.

When Grand Coulee Dam began operating in 1941, it was dubbed the "Eighth Wonder of the World." Woody Guthrie, the Oakie troubadour, was awarded a month-long federal job to celebrate it in song, giving the Bonneville Power Administration's agitprop a folkie spin. For its 266 dollars and 66 cents, the BPA got two dozen songs, including "Roll on Columbia" and "Grand Coulee Dam," a blend of Tom Joad and Walt Whitman:

> *Well, the world has seven wonders that*
> *the trav'lers always tell,*
> *Some gardens and some towers,*
> *I guess you know them well,*
> *But now the greatest wonder*
> *is in Uncle Sam's fair land,*
> *It's that king Columbia River*
> *and the big Grand Coulee Dam!*
>
> *In the misty crystal glitter of that wild*
> *and windward spray,*
> *Men have fought the pounding waters*
> *and met a watery grave,*
> *Well, she tore their boats to splinters,*
> *but she gave men dreams to dream*
> *Of the day the Coulee Dam would cross*
> *that wild and wasted stream.**

To celebrate success after three decades of noisy perseverance, Rufus published a commemorative booklet. It featured facsimiles of The World's articles at defining moments along the way. He told how the opponents had used "POLITICS, INTRIGUE, MISINFORMATION, THREATS, DECEIT, BIG MONEY, RIDICULE and INTIMIDATION to obstruct the World's Greatest Power and Irrigation Project—and HOW THEY ALL FAILED!"

All that had the added advantage of being true. How-

---

* © 1964 (renewed) and 1992 (renewed) by Woody Guthrie Publications, Inc. & TRO-Ludlow Music, Inc. (BMI)

ever, as things turned out, Rufus felt he too had failed, for now at least. The electricity came before the irrigation and most of it was wired downriver. "Grand Coulee had been built, but most of the benefits had been lost to faraway urban areas and industry. Decisions were made, not by local people, but by the Bureau of Reclamation and by the Bonneville Power Administration." The dam was still a "miracle," Woods wrote, his chagrin tempered by optimism. Work on the irrigation system was set to begin in 1948. When the Spokane Chamber of Commerce published brochures hailing Spokane as "the Gateway to Grand Coulee Dam," Rufus said he didn't know whether to laugh or cry.

The Columbia was "an oil well that will never run dry," the Bonneville Power Administration declared in a breathless documentary called "Hydro!" Post-war press agents hyped the big dam's role in defeating fascism. There's no discounting that its turbines provided power to alloy aluminum for Boeing B-17s, build Liberty ships at Kaiser's yards at Portland and produce plutonium at Hanford. The dams generated the low-cost, post-war power that transformed the Pacific Northwest. *The Farm Journal*, unrepentantly antediluvian, had once editorialized: "No power company would risk a cent in plants to manufacture power for a non-existent market." Today, Grand Coulee Dam is the largest hydropower producer in the United States, and the ancient coulee holds the reservoir that irrigates much of Central Washington. "Let us never forget," Rufus wrote, "the importance of water water water." Thanks to Billy Clapp's "harebrained" idea, 600,000 acres of desert now yield apples, peaches and cherries; potatoes, sweet corn, alfalfa and wheat; barley, beans and beets, as well as world-class wine grapes. Power power power also landed Wenatchee a new aluminum plant and a thousand family-wage jobs in 1952.

Taking stock of what Rufus helped build, it's easy to make a case that Pulitzer and Hearst were pikers compared to the "Columbia Basin's Human Dynamo." What had they built other than circulation, with wars and rumors of wars, and hilltop castles with private zoos?

In 1949, Rufus was named to the Bureau of Reclama-

Wilfred Woods took this photo of his parents, Rufus and Mary, at Grand Coulee Dam in 1950 when President Truman formally dedicated the dam. Rufus died a few months later. *Wenatchee World Archives*

tion's Hall of Fame. When Chief Joseph Dam, 50 miles downriver from the Grand Coulee, was completed in 1955, its reservoir was christened Rufus Woods Lake. Billy Clapp got a lake of his own. And the big one behind Grand Coulee Dam is Lake Roosevelt. It stretches 150 miles to the Canadian border. Potholes Dam south of Ephrata was renamed to honor the indefatigable Jim O'Sullivan. He joked that many in Spokane would have preferred "Damn O'Sullivan."

In a 2012 column previewing a PBS documentary on Grand Coulee Dam and its legacy, Rufus Woods' namesake grandson ended with a quote from Blaine Harden, an award-winning writer whose father was a construction worker at the dam: "Grand Coulee Dam is the most wonderfully mixed metaphor that you can imagine. It was a club to defeat the Japanese, an elixir for the Great Depression. It made the desert into a garden, and it was a bit of cultural savager for the Indians affected and environmental butchery for the salmon." The second Rufus, who brings to the paper a strong environmental conscience, concluded: "It's important to look at it with an open mind about the great benefits and the corresponding downside effects." His grandfather would agree. Rufus had many friends among the Indians and was saddened that the federal dams wiped out fishing grounds like Celilo Falls that had been theirs for eons. Neither Grand Coulee nor Chief Joseph Dam was constructed with fish ladders. Bonneville Dam, 300 miles downstream, was. The Bonneville Power Administration boasted it had done the salmon a favor by creating "a fish super-highway" that would be far easier to traverse than the "boiling rapids." That fish swimming upstream to spawn came under the jurisdiction of a dozen different federal agencies in 1947 struck Rufus Woods as bureaucratic nincompoopery. But progress was progress, and if man could harness those two-million wild horses, surely he would have enough ingenuity to save the fish, too.

It has taken far longer than Rufus ever imagined. In 2014, The Wenatchee World comprehensively examined four decades of efforts to help salmon and steelhead survive their perilous roundtrip. Fisheries biologists and Army engineers are working on a spiral flume to help ocean-bound small fry make it past the high dams, while "promising technology is being developed that could one day use gentle suction tubes to help upriver bound salmon scale obstacles too high for a conventional fish ladder," The World noted.

Rufus and Wilf had one last road trip together in the spring of 1950. Rufus seemed to be on the rebound from a heart attack five months earlier. "It was a delightful trip across the country," Wilf told readers. "We went to Michigan for a new car, and then drove leisurely to Toronto" where Rufus wanted to inspect Ontario's innovative public power system. He was stricken as they crossed a street near their hotel and died the next morning.

The World, as per Rufus's long-standing dictum, played it big. The front page was bordered in black. A banner headline announced his death at 72. A five-column photo featured Rufus and Mary Woods standing below the spillway at Grand Coulee Dam. Wilf had taken it a few weeks earlier when President Truman officially dedicated the dam.

A "shocked and saddened" Truman telegrammed his condolences. "No one can take his place," Billy Clapp said. "We all owe him a debt of gratitude that can never be repaid." Editors, publishers, columnists and editorial writers around the nation eulogized Woods as "a hustling, bustling, constantly curious editor" and "a tub-thumping American original" who could charm anyone, from Russian peasants to the president of the United States. "Whether 'big' or 'little' he met them all on the same terms." He had started with 465 subscribers 43 years earlier and checked out with 15,000. Thomas L. Stokes, the Pulitzer Prize-winning syndicated columnist, wrote a tribute Rufus would have cherished:

> He was a dreamer and a true pioneer of our new frontier, a man-made frontier of great dams that provide cheaper power for homes and industry and water for reclaiming arid lands to offer new opportunities for our people. He is part of the saga that has made us a great nation. ...
>
> At this very time, the private utilities are organizing a great fight to stop authorization by Congress of [additional public power projects] and to prevent the government from building its own transmission lines from existing public projects so that private companies can control distribution and rates, a fight now brewing that will break forth soon in the Senate on an important front with an effort to cripple the great Southwestern Power Project in Texas, Oklahoma, Arkansas and that area.
>
> It is a good time to think of Rufus Woods, his idealism and his unselfishness, and his unflagging persistence.

If the "High Priest and Prophet of the Columbia" was a hard act to follow, the new 30-year-old publisher of The Wenatchee Daily World didn't lack for confidence. Wilf understood the business and his community. He also had his father's knack for making friends and his own serendipitous zest for adventure. Drafted into the Army in 1942, he ended up stateside, working for a general before serving with one of the first jet squadrons readying for deployment overseas. After graduating from the University of Washington in 1947, Wilf became a reporter/photographer for The World. He covered one of the biggest stories in state history—the devastating spring floods of 1948 along the Columbia. "The tributaries went crazy, too," he remembers. "The Wenatchee, the Entiat, the Stehekin. Every bridge in the Methow Valley was washed out. The Okanogan Valley was awash and we had to deliver the papers to Waterville by plane because Pine Canyon washed out. I was packing a 10-pound Speed Graphic camera." Downstream, Kennewick and Richland were inundated. Vanport, the wartime housing development at Portland's outskirts, was destroyed when a dike gave way. Fifteen people died.

G.I. Bill benefits took Wilf to a French-language institute in Paris. He wrangled credentials as a correspondent, had an audience with the pope and hopped a flight into Germany on a C-54 carrying coal during the Berlin Airlift at the dawn of the Cold War.

Wilf learned only after his father's death that Rufus had changed his will to name him majority owner of the paper. "Dad had heart trouble, so he was looking at what was going to happen to the paper. I was working there as a reporter. He must have been impressed that I was up to snuff, but he never told me what he had done." Wilf's sisters, who had married and moved away, understood their father's decision. They loved and respected their brother.

Wilf's first front-page column as publisher was one part epitaph and one part mission statement for a new World. The exclamation points and caps were an homage to Dad: "Rufus Woods belonged to one era. We are beginning another. But what a heritage he has left us! The wilderness transformed! Glorious opportunities ahead! This was his dream and his vision. He has gone. BUT THE DREAM AND THE VISION LIVE ON."

4 | Wilf's World

WHEN Henry Ford II and his "Whiz Kids" took control of the Ford Motor Company after World War II, they discovered a cluster of green-eyeshaded accountants estimating expenses by weighing invoices. Things weren't that bad at The Wenatchee Daily World when Wilfred Woods succeeded his father as publisher in 1950. But the only adding machine in the accounting department was a hand-operated relic from the '20s. His father's 82-year-old cousin, Warren Woods, who had invested $2,000 in the struggling paper in 1908, was still secretary-treasurer. "Warren was conscientious," Wilf remembers, "but the accounting, advertising and circulation systems were all antiquated."

Wilf moved tactfully. Warren was both family and part owner. It helped that Warren's son Bob, a talented journalist and heir apparent, recognized the problem. Wilf and Bob "forgot" to tell Warren that Jack Watkins, the new accountant they hired, was being groomed to succeed him. Watkins proved to be as patient and deferential as he was competent. After Warren Woods retired in 1954, Watkins was the paper's financial manager for 36 years. He was the sparkplug for a profit-sharing plan that Wilf and Bob Woods instituted in 1956.

The employees soon saw that their new publisher, though even-tempered, was decisive. Wilf fired a prickly managing editor and promoted Bob Woods. The lazy press room boss was also shown the door. "Dad never wanted to fire anybody," Wilf says, "and on the whole he wasn't a very good hirer."

The machinery wasn't very good either. Don Sampson, a fix-anything machinist whose career at The World spanned father, son and grandson, described the patriarch as a master scrounger: "Through much of Rufus's tenure, he could rarely afford new equipment. Most of our machines were bargains he had purchased from other papers." Wilf says his father bought six or seven used presses, one after the other. "The year before he died they bought a new Linotype. Other than that, we didn't have a single new piece of equipment in the whole building when I took over. ...I was also lucky to take control during good times. Dad nourished a threadbare paper through its infancy and survived the economic turmoil of the Depression. He really did most of the dirty work in establishing the paper. It was on a sound foundation when I took over."

The young publisher with a bust of his father.
Wenatchee World Archives

Hard-working Harlan Honeysett, who started out in the mail room as a high school student in 1929 and graduated to the composing room, became production manager under Wilf. Setting out to modernize the plant, they were surprised and disappointed that other papers were leery about sharing information. Wilf's affability and Honeysett's know-how opened doors. A Northwest newspaper mechanical conference was born.

"Honeysett was a genius," Wilf says. "We started a hot-metal paste-up process at a time when that was really innovative. Then in 1971 Harlan oversaw the landmark switch to 'cold type' printing with a new offset press." The back shop grew eerily quiet when the big old Linotype machines stopped clattering out type line by line. The machine that had transformed typesetting when the original model debuted in the 1880s resembled a mammoth typewriter festooned with Rube Goldberg gizmos. New, they had cost $40,000. Now they were being sold for $500. Many were simply scrapped all over America. The old crew of hot-metal craftsmen found themselves wielding X-Acto knives and "pasting up" pages. When Honeysett retired in 1978, after nearly a half-century with the paper, the technology seemed to be advancing by the hour.

Wilf's goal was clear from the beginning: He wanted to take the paper to a new level in every way. No one out-worked him, not even Honeysett. Wilf was a self-confessed "working fool"—"and a good paper needs working fools." There isn't a duplicitous bone in his body, the old-timers say.

"Wilfred is the one who really made a family of The World," Don Sampson said in 2005 when the paper celebrated its centennial. Bud Preston, the longtime pressroom foreman, agreed: "Wilfred made the paper a place that once you were hired you didn't want to leave."

Wilf's marriage in 1951 to Kathy Kingman, whose parents were Chelan area pioneers, gave him a supportive, perceptive partner. She shares his sense of whimsy and passion for the arts. They sang for many years with the Chelan Bach Fest Chorus and the Community Chorus. With the addition of three children, the Woods home was filled with music and mischief. Rufus, who arrived in 1956, was "the pickle in the middle," between Kara and Gretchen, Wilf jokes. For 10 years, they drove the kids to Seattle for music lessons every Saturday. Kara played cello; Rufus and Gretchen, violin. When Governor Dan Evans appointed Wilf to the state Parks and Recreation Commission in the 1960s, they packed the kids and two cats into a motor home and visited parks around the state. One year, the family went to Alaska in a Volkswagen Microbus. Gallivanting seems to be in the Woods gene pool.

Delivery of The World was expedited by platoons of new carriers. The number of mail subscribers receiving day-old news was greatly reduced. The World became the definitive news source for the region in the days when TV was three channels, if that, off a rabbit-ear antenna. Radio news was little more than the county extension agent's crop report. "We wanted to own Chelan, Douglas, Okanogan and Grant counties—a region equal in size to the entire state of Vermont—and we worked hard to improve our news coverage in these areas," Wilf remembers.

There was lots of news to cover in 1952. Alcoa's new Wenatchee aluminum smelter opened, drawn to the valley by low-cost electricity. Public power gained momentum and irrigation finally came to the Columbia Basin. Hundreds of volunteers produced a "Farm-in-a-Day" for a World War II combat veteran. He won the 115-acre spread near Moses Lake in a national contest sponsored by the Veterans of Foreign Wars. While shortsighted landowners on the east side of the irrigation project rejected their chance to participate, relying instead on well water that began to run dry in the 21st century, 437,000 acres had been reclaimed by 1960. By 2014, the total topped 650,000 acres.

The tree fruit industry endured two big freezes, as well as picking, packing and marketing challenges and changes in the 1950s. Cartons and bins replaced boxes. By decade's end, the introduction of controlled-atmosphere storage transformed the apple industry. Wenatchee was changing too. Retail marched steadily north; new housing encroached on orchards. Lumber mills closed. Across the river, East Wenatchee began its climb toward the ridgeline.

Woods had a dynamic economic-development mentor in Kirby Billingsley. The visionary Chelan County Public Utility District commissioner had been Rufus's managing editor during the campaign to build the high dam at the Grand Coulee. Billingsley left the paper in the 1940s to oversee the Columbia Basin Commission. In 1950, Wilf hired him to write editorials promoting the Wenatchee Valley as a prime location for an aluminum smelter. Aluminum was in high demand with the outbreak of the Korean War in 1950. The powerhouse at Puget Sound Power & Light's Rock Island Dam, 12 miles south of Wenatchee, was only partially developed. "Billingsley got the Alcoa, Puget and Bonneville people together and they worked out a lease arrangement for the unfinished powerhouse," Wilf remembers, still marveling at Billingsley's moxie. The PUD financed six new generators. Alcoa began operations just two years later. "Building of that plant and the hiring of hundreds of workers had a drastic effect upon the city, with shortages of housing bringing new subdivisions and retail trade showing great increases." Diversification was crucial to Wenatchee's future, Wilf wrote at the time. He worried, however, that progress could pave paradise and put up parking lots and cookie-cutter housing on the ancient hillsides.

Alcoa proved to be a good neighbor. When some growers downwind noted deformities in their peaches, they wondered if new orchard chemicals were to blame. "But tests showed that the same results could be produced if peaches were touched by fluoride gasses in the almost invisible exhaust from the stack of the aluminum plant. It wasn't established conclusively as a cause, but Alcoa moved decisively." The company bought out the orchardists, set up test plots and installed expensive emissions control equipment. Alcoa later donated 1,700 acres of orchard land to Washington State University.

While Wilf was writing impassioned front-page editorials supporting public power, his aunt, State Rep. Eva Anderson, was successfully promoting legislation allowing PUDs to sell power beyond their counties. The Chelan County Republican Woman's Club saw this as conduct unbecoming a Republican woman. It wrote a letter to the editor calling the PUD socialistic, and urged readers not to listen to "the Grange, The Wenatchee World and the Chamber of Commerce."

A lot of people weren't listening in Stevens County north of Spokane. Ratepayers there voted two-to-one to sell their public utility district's lines to Washington Water Power, Rufus's old nemesis. "The fullest explanation of the public-power program was never more sorely needed," Wilf told the Northwest Public Power Association. The Spokane utility had deployed "an army of paid help for door-to-door solicitation," he said, while public-power supporters came in too late and with too little to tell their story.

The Chelan County PUD, in contrast, was on a roll as a state and national poster child for public power. In 1956, three years after Kirby Billingsley became general manager, the PUD purchased Rock Island Dam from Puget Power and started construction of Rocky Reach Dam, seven miles upstream from Wenatchee. On Billingsley's watch over the next 20 years, the district also built 14 parks worth $67 million. The 1976 law making federal dam licenses conditional on the construction of parks was the handiwork of Billingsley and U.S. Senator Henry M. Jackson. "Kirby had a vision for the Columbia River that paralleled my father's," Wilf says of his friend, who died in 1993 at the age of 89. "In fact it was probably broader because Kirby also championed parks and recreation in addition to the expansion of public power. He was 'Mr. Columbia River,' and a national leader as president of the American Public Power Association."

Hu Blonk, who covered the construction of Grand Coulee Dam for The Wenatchee World, played an important role in the paper's steady growth under Wilfred Woods. Blonk had parlayed his work at the newspaper into a job as a public information officer for the U.S. Bureau of Reclamation. After 12 years, however, he'd had enough. So had his superiors. Blonk was blunt and fiercely dedicated to telling the truth. "No comment" was not in his vocabulary. In 1953, his position was eliminated. He wrote to Woods looking for something to tide him over until he found another job. Wilf said he should hightail it to Wenatchee and write some features. "Within a week, Wilf offered me a job, but I told him I had better stick to public relations; newspapering didn't pay enough." "Maybe it will," Wilf said. Bob Woods moved up to executive editor and Blonk took his slot overseeing the newsroom. Getting fired was a great career move, Blonk recalled. Only three months after his return to the family, he was managing editor "of a fearless, high-principled newspaper."

Printing the news without fear or favor was Wilf's credo. He didn't blink when a leading businessman canceled $5,000 in advertising after Blonk refused to suppress the man's driving-while-intoxicated arrest. Nor would Woods ask for or expect special treatment from political candidates he favored.

Blonk became a state and national leader in the push

for freedom-of-information laws. From Pullman to Port Angeles, the first call any new city editor invariably received was from Hu. "Congratulations," he'd say. And in the next breath, "The Bench-Bar-Press committee needs you." The coalition of judges, attorneys and news people was one of his passions.

Wilfred Woods, Hu Blonk and Bob Woods, who in 1961 became the paper's hard-hitting yet even-handed editorial writer, elevated The Wenatchee World to a national award-winning newspaper. One of the enterprising young reporters of their era was Richard W. Larsen, who arrived in Wenatchee in 1953, hot out of the University of Washington. Larsen's coverage of the 1963 libel case against the John Birchers who branded Okanogan legislator John Goldmark and his wife Sally tools of "a monstrous Communist conspiracy" was spotlighted nationally by the Associated Press. Larsen spent 12 eventful years in Wenatchee before joining the staff of Tom Foley, a freshman congressman from Spokane. Larsen went on to become chief political writer for The Seattle Times.

Although bigger papers paid far better, reporters' wages at The World were higher than most papers its size. The profit-sharing plan was another incentive. The bottom line for a number of talented newspaper people who remained at Wenatchee for years was being part of the expectation of excellence. The World fielded more reporters and photographers than many larger-circulation papers.

The profit-sharing plan didn't amount to much for the first decade—usually about three percent of a vested employee's salary. "But in 1967, the paper contributed 20 percent to the fund, and throughout the 1970s we contributed 15 percent," Wilf recalls. "Those are significant numbers that gave a generation of employees a comfortable retirement and the paper a generation of good labor relations. Of course it would be insincere to maintain that profit-sharing was purely philanthropic. As the highest-paid employee of the paper I benefited too. The company also benefited. When we went into offset printing we borrowed money from the fund—something we wouldn't be allowed to do today. And the profit-sharing allowed us to take care of our employees' pension needs without saddling the paper with the mandatory fixed costs of most pension funds. It gave us flexibility to contribute more in good times, less in lean times."

Wilfred Woods' management philosophy would fit in a fortune cookie: "Hire great people, then stay out of their way." In managing by walking around, however, not much escaped him. The staff marveled at his energy. His first priority was always the paper. But how could he also be everywhere else at the same time? In that respect, Wilf was Rufus reincarnated. One day he'd be in Olympia; the next in Washington, D.C., having lunch with President Kennedy. Then he'd be off to Seattle or Canada.

Wilfred Woods in the 1960s.
Wenatchee World Archives

Wilf and seven friends once set out on a boat trip from the mouth of the Columbia at Astoria to its source at Arrow Lake in British Columbia, 1,400 miles upriver.

As columnist and activist, the quotable young publisher quickly acquired a statewide reputation as someone with something to say and someone who got things done. Governor Al Rosellini in 1957 named Woods to his Citizens' Advisory Committee to the state's fledgling Department of Commerce & Economic Development. The Legislature gave the agency a broad mandate to promote new industry, including tourism. Woods insisted that preserving, and improving, the environment had to be part of the equation. An avid hiker and skier, he was appalled by the growing amount of litter along highways, even in remote areas. Puget Sound, flanked by crags and peaks, was awash in sewage. The heavy fines enacted in California might be the "stiff medicine" that could make a difference, Woods wrote.

When 39-year-old Dan Evans, a progressive Republican who loved the outdoors, became governor in 1965, he enlisted Woods to join state and national good-government advocates, urban planners and environmentalists in designing a "blueprint" for orderly growth. The Wenatchee World had already hosted the first of three major conservation conferences. Interior Secretary Stewart Udall was the keynoter in 1964, with Senators Magnuson and Jackson and Woods among the speakers. "In those sessions, and in lobby talk, resource engineers and industrial developers had their first personal encounter with preservationists and ecologists," The Seattle Times noted. The World sponsored a series of trips through Canada and Alaska to study energy resources and organized regional resource meetings. "Water was an especially volatile topic in the late 1960s and early 1970s," Woods recalls. "There were high-level discussions of taking water from the upper Snake or the lower Columbia and diverting it to the Southwest or California. We headed that off."

As chairman of the Parks and Recreation Commission, Woods outflanked Bert Cole, the imperious head of the Department of Natural Resources. Cole had traded part of Lake Wenatchee State Park without notifying the commission. Woods was livid. Two dozen other state parks on trust lands were "subject to the same threat of unilateral action," Woods warned. Cole backed down.

At a conference in 1969, Woods recalled how Wenatchee businessmen had hoped to land a pulp mill when the valley's lumber industry hit a slump in the 1950s. "Today," he said, "nobody would stand for a pulp mill in this area." He was also worried about "shoot-from-the-hip" environmental zealots who wanted to yank out the dams. They thought power just came from an outlet in the wall, Wilf said. Sometimes he was progressive; sometimes he was conservative. When the voters expanded public-disclosure laws to require office-holders and appointees to reveal their private finances, he resigned from the Parks and Recreation Commission. "Somehow," he said, "this disclosure business has gone wild." In all this, he was his own man, yet also his father's son.

In his spare time, Woods issued a call for a constitutional convention; championed a new Court of Appeals to clear the logjam of cases awaiting action by the state Supreme Court;

campaigned for the North Cascades Highway; served on the State Centennial Commission; was a trustee of the State Historical Society; spent a decade on the board of the American Forestry Association; worked with the county and Forest Service to create the Mission Ridge ski area; boosted the growth of Wenatchee Community College; created a music conservatory in the old Woods family home and headed a committee that thwarted a move to legalize gambling in Washington state. The assertion that the plan would keep out professional gamblers was a classic "big lie," Woods said in speeches statewide. Expanding gambling offended every ounce of his Methodist aversion to bad habits. Wilfred Woods, The Seattle Times concluded, could be found in the middle of practically any movement that resisted double-talk or represented progress for "our remarkable corner of the world."

What counted as a rare failure was the paper's campaign to develop water transportation from the Tri-Cities to Wenatchee. "We lost the war," Wilf says, "but the effort gave birth to our port districts in Chelan, Douglas and Grant counties. So even though we don't have ports, we helped create these entities working to enhance the economic development of our region."

On Wilf's watch, The World's circulation nearly doubled—from 15,000 to 29,000 weekdays, and to a peak of 33,000 on Sundays.

His son had not one but two tough acts to follow.

5 | The Second Rufus

In Wenatchee, the apple never falls far from the tree. The apprenticeship of Rufus Woods' namesake grandson began with time-honored tasks. Young Rufus, a skinny 13-year-old with a bushy head of hair, became a "printer's devil" in 1969. He did the flunky work of "killing out" pages after the paper hit the street. He'd put the headline fonts back in their cases; save the photo-engravings of notables and consign to the "hellbox" any type that couldn't be recycled. From there it would be melted down and recast. Some days, he would arrive at the paper before school to sort through the thicket of perforated tape the AP and United Press teletype machines had clacked out overnight.

Just two years later, The Wenatchee World, like many American newspapers, installed a new Goss Urbanite press and switched to offset printing. Rufus learned how to wax phototype and paste up pages. As he moved through his teenage years, he worked in the pressroom, "stuffed" circulars into the paper, handled a motor route for the circulation department and pitched in on proofreading. On busy nights in the sports department, when coaches called in details of games, he'd be manning the phones. During college, he sold ads and wrote news stories.

Rufus Woods, who turned 58 in 2014 and looks more like his father as his mustache grays, is one of the few publishers today with that kind of diverse, hands-on experience. However, unlike Wilf, who says, "I never knew anything else but to go down to The Daily World," Rufus was conflicted. He attended the University of Puget Sound in Tacoma. And, like his father before him, sang with the school's nationally-known Adelphian Choir. "But I just wasn't sure what I wanted to do. I dropped out of college; came back home; worked at the pa-

Rufus Woods as managing editor.
Wenatchee World Archives

per, then kind of stalled out." Wilf, a wise father, recalled his own energizing break from college during World War II and subsequent globe-trotting. He conspired with the UPS professor who managed a study-abroad program that focused on the burgeoning Pacific Rim. "I was 'invited' to join that group," Rufus says with a wink to his dad. He spent a year in Southeast Asia—Japan, Korea, China, Indonesia, Thailand, Sri Lanka, India and Nepal. His columns on his travels demonstrated his growth as a writer. "The experience got me all fired up to go back to school and get interested in things." He ended up serving as co-director of the program after receiving a bachelor's degree in Asian Studies in 1980.

Woods next worked as a reporter for the Associated Press in Seattle and Olympia. In 1984, he received a master's degree in business administration from Dartmouth College. Many journalists maintain that editors with MBAs have sapped newsrooms of their creativity. Mike Fancher of The Seattle Times was featured in a stinging book on the topic. "MBA is short for 'Mediocre But Arrogant,' " Woods jokes. "But for me it's been a great exercise in learning and problem-solving—in appreciating what your own limitations are and searching for solutions."

Woods came home to stay in 1986. After stints in circulation and accounting, he became managing editor in 1992. Neither he nor his father had any inkling that the next 22 years would be so tumultuous for Wenatchee and its newspaper of record. During the '90s, the town was buffeted by acts of God, man and Mother Nature.

In 1992, the apple industry was rebounding from a controversial *60 Minutes* report on Alar, a chemical orchardists sprayed on apples to regulate growth, boost color and extend shelf life. The CBS show, with 40 million Sunday-night viewers, opened its February 26, 1989, lead-off segment with a skull and crossbones superimposed on an iconic Red Delicious apple. Alar, reporter Ed Bradley said, was "the most potent cancer-causing agent in our food supply." The national reaction seemed instantaneous. Apples were removed from many school cafeterias; supermarket chains pulled them from their produce departments. Sales tanked. Growers said it was "a hoax based on junk science" perpetrated by rabid environmentalists. "When used in the regulated, approved manner," Alar posed no health risks, said C. Everett Koop, the U.S. surgeon general. "In laboratory tests," one former earth-sciences professor noted, "the amount fed to mice before any effect was noted was equivalent to an average adult eating 28,000 pounds of Alar-treated apples each year for 70 years, or a 10-pound infant eating 1,750 pounds per year." Before the year was out, however, the EPA moved to ban Alar. The manufacturer voluntarily halted domestic sales. Federal courts dismissed the class-action libel suit Washington apple growers filed against CBS and anti-Alar groups. One investigative reporter concluded: "There was indeed an overreaction to the *60 Minutes* report, as viewers confused a long-term cumulative threat with imminent danger. But Alar is a potent carcinogen, and its risks far outweigh its benefits." You can still start an argument in a Wenatchee coffee shop just by saying "60 Minutes."

Wenatchee, otherwise, was largely unaffected by the early '90s national recession. The population of the two-county area increased 5.2 percent in the space of two years. Tourism was booming. Many of the newcomers to Chelan and Douglas Counties came from California, including a steadily increasing number of Latinos. The World launched a Spanish-language weekly, El Mundo.

The end result of all that growth? "Local retail sales going through the roof during the past three years," The World reported in 1992. "And more businesses picking up the Wenatchee area's scent." Home equity was increasing at 1½ percent per month. "Welcome to Boom Town, Pardner!" one headline said. The downside was that employment growth was mainly in the lower-paying service and retail sectors. Manufacturing was eroding. Alcoa laid off smelter workers when the Bonneville Power Administration couldn't meet residential and commercial demands, foreshadowing the energy crisis that hit the West eight years later. Sawmills closed. Family-owned orchards, struggling under the weight of huge loans and the global economy, were disappearing on the outskirts of the Apple Capital of the World. Retail pushed north from old downtown and across the river in blue-collar East Wenatchee. Kmart encroached on the home-owned Sav-Mart. Sofa World was worried, too. The California expatriates building handsome houses in the foothills complained about drift from pesticide spraying. Many of the town's conservative old-timers found it all disquieting, as did the growing number of liberal newcomers. The longtime mayor who backed a rezone to pave the way for Walmart was defeated in his bid for re-election.

Wenatchee found itself gallingly back in the international news in 1993 as the "Prozac capital of the world" when a local psychologist told Oprah Winfrey he had recommended the antidepressant for most of his some 700 patients. "Freud really is dead," he said. "But it's very hard for the people who run this business to understand that. If you've got a treatment for the common cold of mental illness, use it." Whatever Prozac's efficacy, Wenatchee became fodder for David Letterman's monologue and was portrayed in *Psychology Today* "as a town of unnaturally tranquil rubes." When the magazine chased down the sales statistics for a follow-up story, it turned out that Wenatchee's per capita consumption of Prozac was below the national average.

A year later, a lightning storm at the apex of a long hot summer ignited a hundred fires in Chelan County. On Tyee Ridge in the Entiat Valley northwest of Wenatchee, the worst wildfire anyone could remember "chewed through miles of dense, dry national forest land" at upwards of 500 acres per hour. An army of 9,000 firefighters mustered from all over the nation fought the fires. In all, from Lake Wenatchee to Lake Chelan, Leavenworth to Cashmere, 187,000 acres and 40 homes went up in smoke that summer.

Layoffs at Alcoa's aluminum smelter, which for 40 years had leveled out Wenatchee's agricultural mood swings and given upward mobility to the work-force, hit hard in 1993 and 1994.

What happened next changed the city and impacted the way the paper perceived itself, says Andy Dappen, the freelance writer who in 2005 compiled a warts-and-all history of The Wenatchee World's first 100 years.

In the spring of 1995 after a Pentecostal church in East Wenatchee was alleged to be a coven of perverts, the national media arrived en masse to chronicle the epidemic of awfulness in the valley. Major American newspapers and magazines had long since elevated the "Trouble in River City" genre to an art form. Now they outdid themselves as they analyzed what ailed Wenatchee, a seemingly idyllic town ruing "a loss of innocence." The Chicago Tribune's headline was "Norman Rockwell meets hell." It was more like Ann Rule meets Stephen King. The Los Angeles Times called its story "Little Town of Horrors":

> Nobody can say for sure when this sweet town, a place of apple orchards, cafe counters with fresh cherry pie and a slow-moving river, once named the fourth-best little city in the country, lost its innocence.
>
> Maybe it was when two 12-year-old boys, playing on the banks of the Columbia last August, got a rock thrown at them by a migrant farm worker, then leveled their rifles and pumped 18 rounds into his body.
>
> Or was it in March, when the pastor of the Pentecostal Church of God House of Prayer was accused—in a case linked to charges against about two dozen adults—of hosting child sex orgies, some in the church basement?

Or maybe the morning in April when Mandy Huffman, a popular junior high school student, and her mother were found fatally stabbed, bludgeoned and sexually mutilated in their East Wenatchee home. ...

To say there is trouble in paradise doesn't even come close when you're talking about this town of 20,000, the geographical center of Washington state and still, to most appearances, the kind of place people think of when they talk about escaping the ills of urban America.

The Wenatchee World's own headline summed it up like a front-page parental guidance warning: "Bad news beyond imagination"

The "sex ring" story was too bad to be all true. "There's something not quite right about this," Joann Byrd, the veteran journalist who oversaw the opinion pages at the Seattle Post-Intelligencer, told Kathy Best, the P-I's metro editor.

Steve Maher, The World staff writer who covered the damage suits that evolved from the case, recalled a decade later that the initial charges were consigned to three paragraphs in the back pages. "No one at the paper was connecting the dots, even though many people were being arrested on the basis of outrageous allegations."

"Child witnesses told investigators of sex parties in which they were passed around like party favors," Jim Kershner, a Spokane reporter with a reputation for even-handedness, wrote in *American Journalism Review*. The pastor and his wife "were charged with first-degree rape and molestation of children on the church altar while the entire congregation watched and sometimes joined in. Police had several child witnesses and victims but, by far, the majority of the accusations came from one 11-year-old girl who, according to news reports, named over 80 different molesters. ...But one fact explains why this case raised such powerful questions of police propriety: The 11-year-old girl is the foster daughter of Robert Perez, the lead detective in the investigation."

Reporters and editors at The World nevertheless believed Perez' superiors when they said his objectivity hadn't been compromised.

Tom Grant, a reporter for KREM-TV in Spokane, was one of the first to raise the specter of a witch hunt. The Wall Street Journal's Dorothy Rabinowitz scathingly characterized the sex-ring case as "patently nonsensical," with charges filed on the basis of "spurious evidence and extorted confessions." She called The Wenatchee World's coverage "blindly credulous and extraordinarily unfair."

In the newspaper business, nothing feels worse than being branded a lapdog by out-of-town media. The community, likewise, resented the implication that Wenatchee was home to the original cast of *Deliverance*. Or, as the Chelan County prosecutor put it, "Those East Coast reporters can make you look like a complete goober."

Steve Lachowicz, The World's assistant managing editor at the time, was appalled by the "shameless pretensions at journalism" by "so many national journalists (and I am forced to use the term loosely)" who failed "to get so many of their facts straight, ignoring credible evidence of abuse presented in numerous trials." Lachowicz told Kershner the out-of-town reporters "came in and did their big splash," while The World printed more than 200 stories exploring all facets of the case. "We did it bit by bit, day by day, following the trends and the developments in the whole thing. And we trusted in the end that all of the material we reported on both sides would somehow lead to some conclusions."

In the beginning, however, they had trusted too many of their sources. As new facts emerged, the newsroom was conflicted by hindsight and pride. Rufus Woods, an introspective man, was drawing some conclusions. While he took offense at the journalistic "heroics" of Grant and Rabinowitz—to him they seemed sanctimoniously blind to shades of gray—it was becoming increasingly clear that police and prosecutors had been playing fast and loose. Woods was angry with them, too—and with himself. It was a galling wakeup call.

Innocence Project Northwest volunteers—law school students and attorneys—discovered information that Maher and his editors found "simply amazing," including the revelation that many of the confessions were concocted.

Tracy Warner, a seasoned reporter, had been elevated from The World's copy desk to editorial page editor just as the sex-ring story was breaking. Twenty years on, he still finds it difficult to sum up "the intensity of the experience, because it felt as if we were under siege. It was shocking to me how many of the reporters who came here had already decided what the story was. Some just wrote their stores based on other reporters' stories. I counted 17 factual errors in one column by a national writer. I got really defensive because there was this assumption that we were all corrupt—*the entire community*—or in denial. Many of us also realized there were a lot of screwy things going on—things we hadn't covered that well. We ran stories that weren't as objective as they should have been. It was just a nightmare. I started waking up at 4 a.m."

Warner interviewed jurors and one of the children who claimed to have been molested. Her story was horrific. He was still leery of Detective Perez, regarded as a bully by police beat reporters. As the sex-ring story became a national sensation, Warner inspected some of the confessions Perez had elicited. Rabinowitz had charged they were much too literate to have come from the defendants, mostly poor people with not much education. Warner surmised their statements had been paraphrased by Perez, then signed by the suspects. "But when I interviewed Perez, he told me the confessions were word-for-word transcriptions. I realized that was a lie. I was incensed and hugely conflicted. I still thought children had been molested, but I also thought there was a possibility innocent people had been convicted and that every case was spewed with reasonable doubt. Editorially, I had been defending the authorities against the onslaughts of the national media. After my interview with Perez, we wrote an editorial demanding that the police chief resign."

As convictions were overturned right and left, some readers complained bitterly that the newspaper had switched sides and was being unfair to the police and prosecutors. "Now both sides couldn't stand me," Warner remembers.

Rufus Woods says that once he and most of the newsroom got over their chagrin at being portrayed as too close to their sources—the truth hurt—they resolved to become "a lot better watchdogs."

The best thing about small towns, Garrison Keillor observes, is that people are so close. And the worst thing about small towns is that people are so close. Rabinowitz asserted that in the "tight little island" of a rural community, local reporters are "really immune from other pressures" and feel as if they can do no wrong. Warner says the exact opposite is true. At Wenatchee, Walla Walla, Aberdeen and Anacortes, reporters routinely encounter the people they're writing about—at the pool, the post office, the supermarket and soccer game. "If you come in to cover a story with a point of view, and you're from out of town, you can listen to one side of the story, whatever side you want, and you can go home and write whatever you want, and nothing ever happens," Warner says. "But if you live in the town where it's happening, everything's different."

Woods says the tightrope of "community journalism" is finding a way to remain an integral part of a community while maintaining a crucial degree of detachment—the commitment to question authority. Or as Mr. Dooley, the fabled Irish bartender, put it, "...to comfort the afflicted and afflict the comfortable."

Woods believes some of the initial child-abuse arrests and convictions were solid; then the investigation became, as Steve Maher put it, "a runaway train." Woods says, "The investigation was so fatally flawed and irresponsible that the truth never came out. It tainted everything. That was the worst experience of my life. In many ways, we failed the community. We weren't very skeptical as an institution. It was a humbling experience and an important lesson for all of us."

6 | "Now what the hell?"

Wilfred Woods had an epiphany not long before his 78th birthday in 1997: "I just decided, 'Hey, it's time to kick loose and put him in charge.'" He was confident his son was ready. Certainly readier, in any case, than he'd been when his father died unexpectedly and he became publisher at the age of 30. Rufus, who was 41, understood every aspect of the operation. Wilf also recognized that the challenges confronting the family business were more difficult—transformational, in fact—than any he had faced. "I decided it was time for fresh ideas." He strolled into Rufus's office, whistling of course, and said, "You're the new publisher."

"That was it," Rufus remembers. "And I was sort of like, 'Now what the hell?'" Happily, Wilf would be still around as chairman of the board, always ready to listen and offer advice, yet never meddlesome.

Rufus Woods became publisher of The Wenatchee World at the beginning of the Internet age. The newspaper industry's century-old business model faced an array of structural challenges. Nationally, newspaper readership had been on a steady decline for two decades, slip sliding away at 2 to 3 percent per year. No amount of carrier pizza parties and new subscriber discounts could stop the bleeding.

The World, benefitting from Wenatchee's status as a regional retail and health-care hub and county seat, was faring better than most. In 1997, 60 percent of the households in the newspaper's prime market still subscribed—even after a mixed-blessing year when a record apple harvest produced poor prices. Such are the vagaries of agriculture. Wilf and Rufus were content with profit margins—6 to 7 percent—that would have been intolerable to the chains. Nor were they interested in selling.

Newspaper families, some fractured by third-generation, cousin-vs.-cousin feuds, sold their birthrights for irresistible sums as the consolidation of newspaper ownership accelerated in the 1970s. For the chains, the warning signs should have been there beyond their short-term, bottom-line mentality. Afternoon papers were increasingly hard-pressed by competition from television news. Clogged freeways presented major delivery problems for metropolitan dailies. Congress approved the Newspaper Preservation Act in the hope that joint operating agreements—expedient marriages between rivals—would halt the decline of two-newspaper towns. Seattle, for a while at least, proved they could work.

In the 1980s, the Cable News Network began beaming breaking news live to offices, airports and living rooms—from the explosion of space shuttle *Challenger* to ground zero at the beginning of the first Gulf War. Comcast and other cable providers launched commercial production services in their communities. Every hometown Ford dealer wanted to see himself on TV. Department store managers, meantime, increasingly had little say in media buys; it was all corporate, and corporate didn't know beans about Wenatchee or Walla Walla. Walmart, which did minimal newspaper advertising, was on its own inexorable march out of Arkansas, decimating main street businesses.

Then came the rise of the Internet. Craigslist clobbered classifieds. Data aggregators and freelance poachers stole newspapers' stories and wooed their customers. Retailers who hadn't a clue about the difference between a "hit" and a "unique visitor" boasted that they had launched their own Web sites.

Undaunted, Rufus Woods set out to make The Wenatchee World "the best paper of its size in the country." Getting there, he fully grasped in the wake of the sex-ring fiasco, meant harder-nosed reporting, "asking tough questions and seeking the truth." Peerless print quality, customer service and a diversified business plan were also essential.

To replace himself, he hired an outsider as managing editor. Gary Jasinek, a news team leader at the News Tribune in Tacoma, was a habitually skeptical 46-year-old newsman with wide-ranging experience and a fighter pilot's mustache. At Wenatchee, Jasinek quickly began recruiting top-flight reporters and editors from around the nation. He also won over most of the newsroom veterans with his integrity and appetite for investigative reporting. A series that exposed local government's indifference to Affirmative Action—particularly for Latinos, whose numbers had tripled to 20 percent of the area's population in less than a decade—won a national Public Service Award from the Associated Press Managing Editors' Association. When bureaucrats attempted to stonewall requests for public documents, The World fired back with Freedom of Information Act requests, protests to the Public Disclosure Commission and lawsuits, if that's what it took.

Wilf and Rufus in 2000 when they were honored by their alma mater, The University of Puget Sound. *Ross Mulhausen/UPS Arches magazine.*

Jasinek's Socratic attitude also helped the newsroom parse what went wrong during the sex-ring debacle. He was a strong advocate of reader interaction, writing columns that explained how a good newspaper is the eyes, ears and conscience of the community. Still, when the paper scrutinized the management of the Chelan Public Utility District and found it wanting, some longtime readers said they missed "the old Wenatchee World," which "didn't go out of its way to make people look bad," as one put it. Woods and Jasinek took that as evidence of progress. They also forged a partnership with the Yakima Herald-Republic to share stories the Seattle-centric Associated Press bureau was missing and team up for investigative projects. The story-sharing arrangement eventually expanded to 10 other Northwest newspapers. Jasinek and Sarah Jenkins, the Herald-Republic's innovative editor, were kindred souls. Their papers sent a reporter-photographer team to China for 17 days for a series spotlighting the threat to U.S. growers from China's fast-emerging apple industry. It won three national awards.

In other departments, too, Woods brought in outsiders, some of them from other industries. "We were a bit insular and inbred. Fresh thinking and outside experience were critical to help us meet the challenges we were facing." Some saw this as a sign that The World was no longer family—and that Rufus was overreacting; thinking like an MBA; passing over people who had paid their dues and deserved to be promoted. They worried that some of his "trendy" ideas to build readership blurred the distinction between news and advertising.

Rufus believed that without course corrections there'd be no Wenatchee World.

An investment that "scared the living daylights" out of his father addressed the other major challenge the paper faced in 1997—print quality. Rufus, his production director and press manager were of one mind: Renovating their old press was a stop-gap solution at best and good money after bad.

Not since the Woods family purchased the paper in 1907 had The World ever borrowed a substantial amount of money from a commercial bank. But in 1999 the company borrowed $4 million to buy a German KBA Comet, the pressroom equivalent of a Porsche 911 Turbo. Rufus secured another $3 million to convert a former fruit warehouse into a 30,000-square-foot, high-tech production facility that would be named in honor of his father.

"Most papers would have stuck with the old Urbanite and wrung higher profit margins from an adequate press," Bob Koenig, the pressroom manager, said when the newspaper installed the first Comet in America. The reality of the marketplace was that anything not printed with uncompromising quality was suspect. It was a hi-def world. The vintage

1970 presses couldn't produce the razor-sharp, full-color-on-every page product readers expected and commercial customers demanded. In terms of speed, low newsprint wastage and quality control, the Comet is a shooting star. Everything goes from computer to printing plate. The World can print color on 32 consecutive broadsheet pages. A press run takes less than 30 minutes. The commercial printing business, however, has been the godsend. The company's commercial-printing footprint—weekly newspapers, niche publications, tourism brochures and fliers—extends 165 miles east to Spokane, 160 miles west to Port Townsend and 340 miles south to Bend, Ore.

Nationally, 75 percent of print classified revenue has been lost since 2000, though the rate of decline is slowing. The Comet has limited The Wenatchee World's losses there as well. Classified advertising on Fridays routinely runs to eight or 10 pages, with crisp color photos of all manner of things for sale: homes, cars, guitars, boats and beagles—even hay and horse manure. Despite being postage-stamp size, every photo is legible. The classified display ads for auto dealers pop off the page.

In print quality, The World delivers an unsurpassed daily product to readers and advertisers. That most of them take for granted all that vibrant color—and no inky fingers—demonstrates the daunting realities of publishing a daily newspaper today. When Wenatchee placed its order for the Comet, some doubted the return on Rufus's investment penciled out.

"I spent more in the first year than he had in his entire career," Rufus says, with a laugh and a nod toward his father. "We had to do something to position ourselves for the future in terms of print quality, so it wasn't a hard decision. One example I learned from Dad was to hire really talented people and try to stay the heck out of the way. Steve Schroeder, our production manager at the time, had a great business sense. Bob Koenig was outstanding, too. They did due diligence on which new press we should buy. Everything was focused on one goal: Have we maximized our commercial print operation? Our annual revenues have increased 10-fold. We've succeeded because of the capabilities of the press and the attention to detail by our commercial print team and the press crew. We deliver better quality than any other web press commercial print operation. Of all the things we've done that was the one that really I'm quite proud of."

"You should be," Wilf says. "I'm proud of you."

"We wouldn't be here today if Rufus hadn't bought that press," says Rufus's sister Gretchen, the newspaper's Human Resources manager. "He's extraordinarily bright. A leader. The guy you want out front. TV. The Internet. Craigslist. On-line retailers. Direct mail. These are all the people who are eating a piece of our lunch. It's either drastically change or call it a day."

After some retrenching, The Wenatchee World celebrated its centennial in 2005 on an introspective, upbeat note by publishing a book that looked back and ahead. A new slogan was added to the editorial page: "The Fiercely Independent Voice of North Central Washington."

Three years later, the onset of the brutal recession exacerbated every problem newspapers faced. Newspaper chains that had routinely extracted profits of 25 percent, and pushed for more, laid off reporters, photographers and editors in across-the-board, company-wide cuts. Newsrooms were hit hardest. Between 2000 and 2010, 77 Gannett Company daily newspapers lost, on average, nearly 32 percent of their circulation, including a 12.4 percent decline in 2009. Advertising revenues—print and online—fell nearly 52 percent nationally between 2003 and 2012. As consumer confidence plunged, local news content shrank and the erosion of ad revenues, circulation and credibility accelerated. Print publication days were reduced; printing farmed out. The phrase "paper cuts" took on a whole new meaning.

The Wenatchee World jettisoned some 4,500 marginally profitable subscribers in outlying areas. The original Rufus, who put his heart and soul into winning those far-flung readers, may have rolled over in his grave.

In 2009, as the recession intensified, The World laid off workers for the first time in its 104-year history—five from the newsroom, four from advertising and three from circulation. Many papers had cut much earlier and far deeper. While

Jasinek understood the economics of survival, the prospect of dismantling what he'd worked so hard to build was unpalatable. In his 13 years at Wenatchee, The World's reportage and design had become among the very best. At year's end, he bowed out gracefully.

"We did a lot to cut expenses, but we just couldn't quite get there," Rufus says. "We hung on as long as we could. Ultimately, you get to a point where you have to remain viable."

In 2009 when the state's publishers lobbied the Legislature for a reduction in the business tax, Rufus said he didn't think it was enough to make a difference. Besides, the state had its own financial troubles. "I don't think it's up to the government to make us survive," he said. "We need to figure out how to make that happen. We're like any other business. We need to find new ways to do things."

Though Woods views Jeff Bezos as the poster child for "unfettered predatory capitalism," the Amazon mogul's advice to those who lament the loss of their old business models— "Complaining is not a strategy"—speaks to the challenge the newspaper industry is facing. Woods believes the industry has done a poor job of making the case that rumors of its death are greatly exaggerated.

In 2013, Bezos bought The Washington Post. In the previous two years, Warren Buffett's Berkshire Hathaway Inc. had acquired 28 smaller newspapers for $344 million. Asked why, given the conventional wisdom that the industry was dying, Buffett said: "Newspapers continue to reign supreme in the delivery of local news. If you want to know what's going on in your town—whether the news is about the mayor or taxes or high school football—there is no substitute for a local newspaper that is doing its job. A reader's eyes may glaze over after they take in a couple of paragraphs about Canadian tariffs or political developments in Pakistan; a story about the reader himself or his neighbors will be read to the end. Wherever there is a pervasive sense of community, a paper that serves the special informational needs of that community will remain indispensable to a significant portion of its residents."

When The Seattle Times closed down its zoned edition

for the east side of Lake Washington in 2008 as the recession set in, its popular Eastside columnist, Sherry Grindeland, was laid off. She wrote:

> I've enjoyed covering the Eastside but have long been frustrated by how little respect community journalism garners in the world. The stories that win Pulitzer prizes are the big exposés and mega-investigative reports. For every high quality story like that, there are thousands of smaller stories about our friends, our neighbors and people on the other side of town that should be told. When I talk to high school students, I often say there are two kinds of stories. There are the big ones that win prizes. And there are the stories that people clip out of the newspaper and put in scrapbooks or send to relatives back east. I do the clip-and-save kind. I still believe there is a place for community journalism.

Rufus Woods was doing a lot of thinking about clip-and-save journalism. Had The Wenatchee World, in its determination to never again grow too close to its sources, strayed too far from community journalism?

7 | Community Glue

In 2005, a book Wilf and Rufus commissioned to chronicle The Wenatchee World's first century featured a chapter by an employee-turned competitor. Mike Cassidy's advice about indispensability rang true.

Cassidy, who had published the monthly Wenatchee Valley Business Journal for 14 years, credited his success to copying the "homespun" formula Rufus's grandfather used to make The World the neighbor you were always glad to see on your doorstep. "The World featured your friends, neighbors and community figures. It brought local news and colorful characters to life. ...It knitted the region together into an extended community." All he did, Cassidy wrote, was to apply that "community glue" philosophy to "a different niche." Lately, though, Cassidy perceived that The World's shift "toward a more professional, detached, journalism-by-the numbers style of reporting" was eroding its influence:

> [T]he editors and reporters used to be encouraged to get involved in the community. Being on the board of the YMCA or the president of Rotary was a good thing. The editorial staff now takes a hands-off approach so that they are less attached and more objective. ... There's no right or wrong approach, but I think there's much to be said about reporters loving their community and working hard to improve it. ...
>
> To me the genius of the old Daily World was that it found the right formula to build community—while still being objective. That's what

made it so successful as the primary news source of North Central Washington and (as surprisingly often) a beloved community institution.

Being simultaneously detached and involved is a tall order. Rufus Woods believes the litmus test of a good newspaper is whether it finds ways to have it both ways: "Mike Cassidy is a master at walking the line, and his words were prescient. When we were preparing to celebrate the newspaper's centennial, I was coming to the same conclusion—that we had probably gone too far in one direction with our reporting and lost some of our community glue. We needed to find new ways to engage our readers because our readers—and thousands more we'd lost or never had—were finding new ways to engage themselves in the digital era."

By 2008, Facebook had engaged 100 million users. Five years later 67 percent of U.S. Internet users were members. The phenomenon was becoming multi-generational. Facebook growth among 45 to 54-year-olds was up 46 percent in the space of a year. Nationally, 30 percent of adults on Facebook in 2013 cited it as a key news source. YouTube—gobbled up by Google 18 months after its birth—is hugely popular with the 18-to-34 demographic. A billion unique visitors were watching six billion hours of video per month at the beginning of 2014. And the tweet goes on.

When he was managing editor of The Columbian at Vancouver, Wash., in the 1980s, Denny Dible developed a national reputation as a wild-hare newspaper futurist. His "Just say yes!" philosophy left listeners somewhere between bemused and incredulous when he proselytized at editors' meetings. "If the high school cheerleaders, pompoms and all, bop into the newsroom and ask your city editor to run a squib promoting their weekend car wash, he's going to say no, isn't he, because you have 'standards' at your newspaper?" Practically everyone would nod. "And you're not going to run a photo of a ribbon-cutting at a new hair salon, are you, because you have 'standards' at your newspaper?" More nods. "And the 'Pet of the Week' is a silly idea, too, because you have 'standards' at your newspaper." More nods; more emphatic now. "I'm telling you you're all wrong," Dible would declare. "Your standards are outmoded. The sooner you 'Just say yes!' the better your readers will feel about your newspaper as essential to their lives."

On the rebound from the recession, The Wenatchee World says yes a lot. There's a Pet of the Week featuring Humane Society animals that need good homes. Atop a features page there's a standing invitation to "Get in the picture"—"Send us your group's photo and we'll run it in this space." There's a Reader Scrapbook, photo contests and a front-page Neighbors Care fund drive. It's not just ephemera or touchy-feely "good stuff." (Overdosed on breakfast-time TV, a writer for the *New Yorker* asked himself, "I wonder if they could pay me enough money to fake feeling that good in the morning.")

The World's reader-generated content is highlighted by "Community Connections," a feature that spotlights columns by a stable of 30 contributors. A classroom teacher shares how each reading of *To Kill a Mockingbird* is a new lesson for her and her students; a Native American storyteller shares highlights of a symposium on the work of a Colville tribal member who in the 1920s became the first American Indian woman novelist; the president of Wenatchee Valley College writes about the school's efforts to help military veterans adapt to college life. Other writers have focused on the arts, organic agriculture, conservation, poverty and homelessness.

The World does a particularly good job of engaging young people in ways that build bridges and bring history to life. To mark Veterans Day in 2013 it teamed up with Okanogan High School, veterans groups and the United Way to publish "In Their Honor," a 40-page supplement. It featured student interviews with veterans of all ages, from Iwo Jima to Iraq. The students earned points toward varsity letters in volunteering, and the newspaper made financial contributions to United Way and Vets Serving Vets.

Wilf's homespun "Talking it Over" column is a throwback to an era when many publishers had front-page columns. Names make the news, and Wilf knows thousands. He weaves in the lore from nearly a century of living in the valley—FDR's visit to the Grand Coulee; the big floods in '48; toe-strap skiing in the 1930s, when he'd look for a hillside wheat field without a fence at the bottom. "No turns, just go!"

Tracy Warner, the editorial page editor, steps out from behind the editorial "we" to write a personal perspective twice a week. After 36 years in Wenatchee, he knows his community.

"The Safety Valve" column of letters to the editor is still a must read. The World prints more letters than many metropolitan newspapers.

Rufus's "Common Ground" column and video interviews with community leaders concentrate on solutions. "There's so many situations where people who are natural enemies have produced breakthroughs—Bill Clinton and Newt Gingrich, for instance, on welfare reform," Woods says. "We can get something done if we ask 'What's the goal?' and ignore the polarized positions. To me that is the essence of how things have always gotten done. With all the polarization at the time, it's a wonder that Grand Coulee Dam got built. Some of that was my grandfather's perseverance as a crusading editor; but a lot of it was timing, with the Depression and the New Deal. That a conservative area like North Central Washington benefitted hugely from liberal Democrat activism is both ironic and instructive about keeping an open mind. When the settlers came across, it didn't matter what political persuasion they were. When there was work to be done and things had to happen to help a neighbor, they helped. We had a responsibility as a community. We just have to rekindle it. Civility. That's the civics lesson. We have to start to rebuild community by calling people to a higher level of leadership and promoting dialogue. And you can't keep readers with canned news and wire-service stories."

At 58, Rufus Woods is a medium-size, athletic man in khakis, with close-cropped graying hair, inquisitive brown eyes and a friendly face. He's fluent in MBA-speak—"monetizing platforms"—but an even more passionate newspaperman than he was as a young reporter and editor. He's strong-willed, yet straightforward and given to wry self-deprecation: "I may be stubborn but I'm not stupid."

"In many cases, journalism has become an end in itself," Woods says, leaning back in his desk chair. "News organizations over the years have become to a great extent hidebound in tradition. I'm fortunate to have had a grandfather and father who were steeped in history—*made* history—but they were always concerned about the future.

"The World, like most papers, created huge walls between advertising and news for not just public-service journalism but for all information that was produced. So we treated, for ethical reasons, a story about a Little League team the same as a scandal at a public agency. News organizations like ours became vehicles for sitting in an ivory tower and passing judgment on everyone around us. We were disconnected from our community. Journalism had become a lot of rules and procedures that made it easy for us to produce the paper and feel smug in our standards."

All "good" newspapers concentrated on what was wrong in their communities, Woods says. And most still do. "Even though we had a lot of constructive community information in our paper, we lacked balance. We didn't focus enough on where things were succeeding. We had forgotten about the core of what a news organization should be about—building stronger, more resilient communities. Journalism is a means to that end, not an end in itself. Traditional media invest so much time in dwelling on problems. No wonder people have turned away from newspapers and television news. Newspapers that follow the traditional model end up de-motivating people. How does that help the community? To me, the key balance is in spending at least as much energy focusing on what works as what doesn't work."

In 2009, as revenues plummeted and layoffs could be forestalled no longer, Woods shared his epiphany with the newsroom. The skepticism was polite but palpable. "They had a fear that we were going to focus only on syrupy 'happy news,' " Woods recalls. "That was not what I wanted. I wanted us to highlight meaningful stories about ordinary people doing extraordinary things that build a great sense of community. I adopted a new title for my column—'Common Ground'—to put my energy where my mouth was. The focus was on finding stories where people were succeeding, particularly when people had dropped their old fighting stance and looked for a solution that everybody could live with. Rather than make a big deal out of it and trying to impose some sort of new standards, I just started living this new reality. Today it seems to me that our news report is pretty balanced. We're committed to covering community problems, which is a bedrock role of a good newspaper, but we're also telling stories about solutions. To me, that's equally important.

"When I ask reporters about the stories they are most proud of in their careers, they invariably point to ones where human beings have come together and succeeded in the face of overwhelming odds. That tells me all we need to do is unleash them to write the stories they are passionate about. We have great writers, editors and photographers. The World has always been great at features and human interest stories, going back to the work of the late Hu Blonk. As a young reporter covering the construction of Grand Coulee Dam, Blonk sought out the working stiffs and discovered great stories other writers overlooked. My grandfather knew that human stories sold papers. It's even truer today.

"One thing won't change: We will preserve the checks and balances. Some lines will never be crossed. But that's a fraction of what we do. The future for us is co-creating the content of the newspaper with our readers. As one strategic thinker told me, 'Quit thinking about your readers as people you sell things to and instead consider them contributing members of your community.' We're building networks of contributors. We connect people with each other and ideas," Woods continues. "We are the central point of discussion about important topics. I envision us not only delivering relevant, timely, compelling content through digital and print, but also bringing people together face-to-face to chart our course as a community. We'll do less production of news and more curation, facilitation and aggregation. Gone are the days where we manage the process from stem to stern. Our future will be different but the role has never been more vital. Failure is not an option."

"Failure is not an option" also sums up a crisis that pushed the City of Wenatchee to the brink of bankruptcy and prompted the newspaper to reflect on how community spirit had comprised its skepticism. Before the crisis was over, the Toyota dealer who bought the naming rights to the city's new 4,300-seat Town Center must have wondered whether he had leased an Edsel.

They built it and it was undeniably swell—a beautiful $53 million multipurpose arena for ice hockey and soccer, high-school hoops, concerts, conventions and Cirque du Soleil. But not enough people came. It was in the black—barely—in terms of operating expenses, but the debt load was staggering.

The Greater Wenatchee Regional Events Center was conceived in 2004 when real estate was sizzling in Chelan and Douglas counties. Global Entertainment Corporation of Tempe, Arizona, had developed similar arenas in other midsize cities, with professional ice hockey as the major attraction. The mayor was gung ho to cement Wenatchee's status as the recreational hub of North Central Washington. So was the Chamber of Commerce. "A lot of us said to ourselves, 'This doesn't make sense,' but we didn't really say anything," Rufus Woods says with a rueful sigh. "From the outset, our reporters were more skeptical than our editorial board, questioning Global's track record in other markets. So at least they had learned something from the sex-ring case. We supported it as a newspaper because it seemed like it could be really good for our community long-term." Listening intently as Rufus tells the story, Wilf shakes his head: "It was really oversold, and we were too."

The Legislature in 2006 authorized Wenatchee and the other municipalities in the two-county area to siphon off a portion of local sales tax receipts and create a regional Public Facilities District to own and operate the arena. Global would be the contractor, promoter and facility manager. "This is beyond my wildest dreams," the mayor declared at the ribbon-cutting. How wild would be revealed in due course.

If timing is everything, Town Toyota Center's debut in October of 2008 was inauspicious, coming as it did in the throes of a liquidity crisis that precipitated the worst downturn since the Great Depression. The business plan, regardless, was flawed from the outset. The builder, naturally, still expected to be paid. Desperate, the Public Facilities District issued nearly $42 million in short-term bond anticipation notes, with the city as de facto underwriter. Things got much worse before they got better. "We could see they weren't making the numbers they needed," Rufus recalls. "In a litany of editorials, we begged, pleaded, cajoled and hammered to try to get the council and mayor to deal with the looming crisis. We were basically ignored by the powers that be."

With revenues falling far short of projections, the Public Facilities District was unable to secure long-term financing. It defaulted on its debt in December of 2011. The city was also revealed to be in way over its head. Its general-obligation bonds were downgraded to "junk" by Moody's Investors Service. The state treasurer warned that a permanent default on the loans might impact bond issues statewide. As mea culpas go, an editorial The Wenatchee World ran at the time is remarkable for its candor:

> If only someone with sense and financial acuity could have dug through the wishful thinking and pipe dreams and told us it wasn't going to work. Maybe a quick dose of sobriety might have saved us. We would not be saddled with a $42 million debt and no means to pay it. We could not be blamed for financial contagion or embarrassed by our foolishness, lack of foresight, empty due diligence, poor judgment and pending insolvency. Maybe we would not be waiting for the lawyers of the world to scour us clean to satisfy part of our horrid debt. If only ...

The Securities and Exchange Commission's investigation into the debacle concluded that the Public Facilities District, the city's Executive Services director, Global's CEO and the mayor—since departed—had withheld facts and misled investors. Global's initial estimate that the arena would produce $1.2 million a year was revised to $370,000 just before the arena opened. Nevertheless, in a conference call among the principals, the mayor "made an impassioned argument that Global's projections had not been sufficiently optimistic, that they knew the local citizens better than Global, and those citizens would ultimately support the regional center," the SEC said. Based on the mayor's "verbal assertions," Global revised its projections. The official statement to would-be investors featured the hyped estimates. Moreover, "hidden" in an appendix was a tell-tale paragraph noting that the city's debt capacity was only $19.3 million—less than half the amount of the loan. Nor were investors told "that an independent analyst had twice questioned the revenue projections...."

The Public Facilities District became the first municipal bond issuer ever fined by the Securities and Exchange Commission. By then, having been collectively gifted with hindsight, the news was not shocking, just "shameful," The World editorialized.

It's the rest of the story, the Woodses say, that tells you something important about the citizens of North Central Washington: They would not stiff their creditors.

The Legislature balked at a bailout but allowed the City of Wenatchee to impose a two-tenths of a percent sales tax increase. Another tenth of a percent increase was set for a regional vote in the spring of 2012. The World painstakingly detailed the implications of default in its news columns and editorials. A task force of community leaders was assembled to plan a campaign. "At the first meeting, I said, 'Who should lead this?' And they said, 'You should.' " Rufus gulped, then accepted. He ended up donating advertising space as well. Woods has no regrets. "I put our credibility on the line for something I felt was absolutely essential. A default would have economically devastated the region. People were signing up to help from all walks of life, all over the political spectrum, from the most conservative to the most liberal. Our new mayor, Frank Kuntz, has a finance background and ice water for veins. The attitude was 'We're going to solve this thing ourselves.' I also said publicly and in print that we had failed the community in not doing due diligence on the arena plan." When you make a mistake, Woods says, contrition helps, "but you also need to get smarter."

Sixty-five percent of the voters approved the new tax. "That vote was nothing short of a miracle," the third-generation publisher says, "a defining moment because it showed this community is a special place."

Town Toyota Center at this writing appears to be on solid footing.

8 | Connecting

Rufus Woods' vision for the future of the franchise is to make The Wenatchee World "the most community connected newspaper in the country."

The late Andy Rooney once delivered a grumpy commentary for *60 Minutes* on "All the stuff in newspapers that really isn't news—horoscopes, comic strips, crossword puzzles, 'Dear Abby' and the such. I guess publishers think they have to be all things to all people, but I just want to know what's going on in the world." With that, he unceremoniously dumped into the wastebasket all the sections he wasn't the least bit interested in reading. That was in the 1970s. Flash forward to the second decade of the 21st century. People are doing Sudoku on their iPads, googling March Madness brackets and tweeting the wind chill factor.

"The last five or six years have served to kill off the view that has persisted in our industry for decades—that we have to do everything from soup to nuts," Rufus says. "The next iteration for us is *Wenatchee World 3.0*. What we have to do is some important things really well. We have to treat this like a production line and come up with ideas for great local stories. Then we have to write those stories, edit them, design them and deliver them as something special and essential. The real opportunity is to meaningfully and thoughtfully engage the community in telling more of the story, because we can only tell a small slice of it. There are so many stories that are really important. There's so much talent and wisdom and knowledge in the community. And it's not just getting people to write things for us as news stories, it's getting them to share the community's experience and share the journey of the community. The core of connectivity is still a newsroom filled with

Rufus Woods talks over a news story with veteran reporters Dee Riggs and Rick Steigmeyer. *John Hughes/ The Legacy Project*

writers, editors and photographers who understand their community because they are a part of it, not just passing through."

At this writing, in the winter of 2015, there are 22 people in The World's newsroom. That's about eight fewer than a decade ago, yet a creditable number for a paper of its size and twice as many, for instance, as in the newsroom at The Olympian, a capital city newspaper.

The company also publishes a sophisticated magazine, *Foothills*, every other month; *Business World* and *Home Finders* every month and *Lake Chelan This Week* during the tourist season. Every aspect of the newspaper's design, in print and on line—"presentation" in the parlance of today's journalism—is bright and easy to navigate. Thanks to Marco Martinez, the newspaper's features editor, and Rufus's relentless efforts at outreach, there's no boilerplate in the features section. High school sports and outdoor recreation matter in North Central Washington—and to The World. In stories, columns and photos, the newspaper's sports coverage is remarkable for the size of the staff.

Multi-tasking has always been the norm at smaller newspapers. More so today, given cutbacks in the industry. Everyone at The World seems especially adept at juggling jobs. Cal FitzSimmons, the managing editor, also edits *Business World,* writes the interview feature for *Foothills* and serves on the Editorial Board. Joe Pitt, the gregarious general manager, doubles as the advertising director. He's been in the newspaper business for 35 years, leaving the East Coast in 2012 because he wanted to work for a family-owned newspaper in the Northwest where he grew up. Wyatt Gardiner, the bright young circulation manager, also oversees production. Every editor is also a reporter. So is the publisher, whose home phone number, by the way, is listed. The photographers can write and the writers can take pictures. Rick Steigmeyer, one of The World's most versatile reporters, maintains a "Winemaker's Journal" blog. He's been with the paper for 22 years. Dee Riggs, a writer who radiates empathy, is now in her 36th year. Martinez has been with the paper for 14 years. They could have gravitated to big-city papers years ago.

To FitzSimmons, Wenatchee is big enough to be endlessly intriguing and small enough to feel like home. A Spokane native, he came to Wenatchee in 2010 from the Pulitzer Prize-winning Daily News in Longview. Earlier stops were at Missoula, Pendleton and the Tri-Cities. Like Gary Jasinek, his predecessor, FitzSimmons is a resolute newsman with deeply-held views about professional ethics. Sometimes he seems gruff, yet his email "blasts"—thumbnails of the day's headlines—reveal a tongue-in-cheek streak. He enjoys give-and-take with readers, defusing ire with even-tempered explanations of why the newspaper does what it does and how mistakes happen. He is especially keen on treating difficult stories with sensitivity. Reflecting on a rash of tragic and unexpected deaths, he wrote a thoughtful column about the emotional tightrope reporters and editors face as they weigh whether a story contains too much information. Those who believe "what sells papers" is the rule have never seen a reporter staring at her computer screen after interviewing the family of a teenager who died in a drunken-driving collision. There are no perfect answers, FitzSimmons wrote; no one-size-fits-all solutions in the stylebook of life. "Experience can help you make better decisions, but there's always times where there is no good decision. Finally, we are members of the community. Most of us have experienced tragedies of our own and felt the pain the people we are writing about are feeling. Perhaps those are the best lessons. What would we expect for news coverage if someone we loved died tragically?"

Given the ferocity and speed of what became the largest wildfire in state history, it's remarkable no one died in the summer of 2014 when the Carlton Complex fires destroyed 300 homes and incinerated 250,000 acres. "I swear, it was like 24 hours of terror and a week of hell," the Okanogan County sheriff told Wenatchee World reporter K.C. Mehaffey. The newspaper's coverage of the tragedy featured all-hands-on-deck enterprise, empathy for the victims and analysis of what went wrong. It was a newspaper that felt the pain.

The Wenatchee World's print circulation in 2014 was 15,600 weekdays and 17,500 Sundays, some 42 percent below its all-time highs in the 1970s. As mentioned earlier, however, 4,500 of that was lost by design. Paid print-product penetration of its prime market is still about 44 percent. Aggressive efforts to win online readers have produced bankable dividends. In addition to a Web page with breaking news, photo galleries, polls, blogs and videos, The World offers online-only subscriptions, a facsimile "E-Paper" and e-mail newsletters. After experimenting with a metered approach—10 or 20 free "views" before making nonsubscribers pay for access to the Web page—the newspaper has reverted to a "paywall." The Seattle Times made the same decision in 2013. The Woodses say A.L. "Butch" Alford, the charismatic longtime editor and publisher of the Morning Tribune at Lewiston, Idaho, "had it right all along." From the beginning of the Web page era, Alford flatly refused to give away his paper's content. "We could double our unique visitors and page views and not bring in any great amount of dollars if we gave it all away," Rufus says. "Quality newsgathering costs money." The World has also cultivated its Facebook "likes"—30,250 in the fall of 2014, only some 2,500 fewer than the Spokesman-Review and easily twice as many as The Walla Walla Union-Bulletin, the exceptional small daily owned by The Seattle Times.

In parsing newspaper circulation data and Web site traffic, the old warning about "lies, damn lies and statistics" has never been truer. A debate rages within the newspaper industry—and among ad buyers—over how to count special "branded" editions, PDF "replica" editions and what constitutes a bona fide print subscriber, not to mention how to calculate online readers. Some newspapers have stopped paying for independently audited circulation reports. The World's rate card still features audited data.*

When print circulation is combined with online readership, The World has more readers than ever–30,400 weekdays and 34,750 on Sunday. "Online we have 100,000 unique visitors every month and 1.5 million page views," Rufus says. "Our audience is enormous—much bigger than it ever was in our print-only days. We need to continue to build our audience on multiple platforms."

A significant challenge for The Wenatchee World is how to win the allegiance of a Latino community that has quadrupled to 30,000 in Chelan and Douglas counties since 1990. Latinos are 28 percent of the area's population. Newspapers throughout the West have struggled to create successful Spanish-language offshoots. The Woodses sold their first attempt, El Mundo, to its editor in the 1990s. They launched another publication, Informa Hispano, a few years later but pulled the plug in 2011. El Mundo, meantime, has survived with franchises statewide. Many retailers catering to the Spanish-speaking market believe their niche clientele will gravitate their way without traditional newspaper advertising. "It's a hard sell, and we're not alone," Rufus says. He believes the best strategy is to be "genuinely inclusive" in news coverage of the Latino community. "They're a vibrant part of the community. That's the way to cover their news."

In 2013, The Oregonian, founded in 1850 and the longest continuously published newspaper in the Northwest, reduced home delivery to four days a week and moved to emphasize its online presence. The Chronicle at Centralia and The Daily World in Aberdeen, meantime, abandoned three days of print

---

* Nationally, newspaper online advertising growth is hard-won: 3.7 percent in 2012, and still only about 15 percent of total ad revenues. In 2012, newspapers lost about 15 print dollars for every digital dollar they gained.

publication in favor of larger papers on Tuesdays, Thursdays and Saturdays and an expanded Web presence. The Wenatchee World discontinued its Monday edition in 2011 and switched its big weekend edition to Sunday mornings. Reader resistance was minimal and there was no loss of advertising. Rufus has no plans to drop another day of publication any time soon. "But you never say 'never.' "

Ryan Blethen, associate publisher of The Seattle Times, candidly admits that if he succeeds his father as publisher he is not the least bit wedded to the notion that the litmus test of a "real" daily newspaper is whether it is printed seven days a week. "I'm with Ryan," says Rufus. "It's just a number. The trick is what are you doing to be embedded in your community? If you aren't making that connection, then you're in a commodity business and you're dead meat. The expense for producing a paper—the fixed-cost printing expense—is dramatic. The key is what value you bring to your audience and how strong your advertising can be. So if you can deliver a compelling product [with fewer days of print publication]—take the national weekly edition of The Christian Science Monitor or The Wall Street Journal—you bring the issue into perspective. If that's what people want, give it to them. In some cases, they're so time-constrained that fewer print days is really going to work best for them.

"People are going to see right through any of your marketing if all you are about is extracting money. And that's what a lot of newspapers are today—they're money extraction. There's no soul. There's no heart. They don't care. They're not invested. They're not interested, and everybody knows it."

9 | A Few Nuggets

Wilfred Woods has been "so ubiquitous at cultural events around the Wenatchee Valley, it feels like a prankster is dragging cardboard cutouts of the man around town," wrote Andy Dappen, who produced the newspaper's centennial history. Wilf lately has developed a crowd-pleasing talk where he channels his father. He dons a fedora, grasps his lapels and jabs the air to describe doing battle with the enemies of public power. The "High Priest and Prophet of the Columbia" is alive again, exclamation points and all.

The Department of Geological Sciences at Central Washington University taps Wilf's expertise on the Ice Age floods. He has led tours at the Wenatchee Valley Museum and Cultural Center and narrated a video for the campaign by the Chelan-Douglas Land Trust to raise $8 million to protect 364 acres of the Wenatchee Foothills from development. His son was co-chairman of the successful campaign. Savoring the gravitas in Wilf's gravelly voice, one viewer said the video "convinced some of us to donate money and some of us to genuflect." In 2009, together with Bill Gates Sr., Woods received the Medal of Merit, the state's highest award for public service, during a special legislative ceremony at the state Capitol.

It's a tonic to encounter a 95-year-old with a mind as agile as a cricket. In 2013 when Wilf was one of the speakers at the opening of the Secretary of State's new state Capitol exhibit, "Grand Coulee to Grunge: Eight stories that changed the world," he struck up a lively conversation with Krist Novoselic, the bassist for Nirvana.

Wilfred and Kathy Woods, with their lifelong passion for music, inspired Harriet Bullitt, the ebullient Seattle philanthropist, to found a music center at her Sleeping Lady Resort at

Kathy and Wilfred Woods at the Performing Arts Center of Wenatchee in 2014 when they received a lifetime achievement award for their support of the arts.
Don Seabrook/Wenatchee World

Leavenworth. It has morphed into the Icicle Creek Center for the Arts, with the Woods Family Music & Arts Fund as a major supporter. The fund also matched the $30,000 recently raised by the Wenatchee Valley College Foundation to purchase a Steinway Concert Grand Piano for the school's recital hall. The state-of-the-art Performing Arts Center the family championed in downtown Wenatchee is a source of great satisfaction. Wilf and Kathy also helped found the Community Foundation of North Central Washington. They've been stalwarts of United Way and the Wenatchee YMCA.

Inspired by the example of their grandparents and parents, Rufus and his sisters volunteer widely. Gretchen Woods and Kara Woods Hunnicutt, accomplished classical musicians, teach, perform and volunteer. Rufus is as ubiquitous as his father. The Land Trust campaign is one of his passions. He also headed the United Way campaign, serves on the YMCA board and is active with the Youth and Government high-school legislature. His wife Mary is active in several non-profit groups. In 2012, the

Woodses were saluted by the Association of Fundraising Professionals as the state's Outstanding Philanthropic Family.

"The arc of intergenerational commitment to one's place matters greatly," says William D. Layman, the award-winning Columbia River historian. "For those of us who live in Wenatchee, the Woods family and their enterprise go beyond being a trustworthy keeper and provider of our collective story. Together, family and newspaper have been our conscience... a bulwark for community self-determination and a sturdy vehicle to realize a healthier future."

Gary Jasinek, The World's former managing editor, worked for some of the best chain-owned and family newspapers during his career. A key difference is that chains "cannot have a family newspaper's intimate connection and obligation to the communities their papers serve. At The World, operating decisions favor the good of the paper, the community, employees, and the owners/family. Usually in something like that order," Jasinek says. "There's no obstructionist vetting at the corporate level, no shareholders to appease, no financial imperative that overrides doing the right thing. It's working without a net, but it's also liberating, and has allowed the Woods family to be a force for good in North Central Washington for more than a century."

If Rufus Woods has inherited his father's remarkable longevity, his retirement as publisher is at least 20 years off. ("Sadly Dad's memory seems to have skipped a generation," Rufus quips, marveling at Wilf's ability to unerringly recall names and dates.) Rufus has no children, but his sister Gretchen's 11-year-old daughter, Alyssa, just started her first paper route. His cousins' offspring are also possible successors. One of them—Kelli Scott—joined The World's digital-edition staff at the beginning of 2014. She worked at the paper as a reporter in 2003 after graduating from Oregon State University with a degree in communications, then spent several years as an aide to Congressman Norm Dicks, the powerful Democrat from Bremerton.

Thinking about the future and the past, Rufus reflects on public-service journalism and his father's legacy: "We've killed innovation in this profession by turning it into a corporate enterprise rather than a profession with a purpose. That's what I want to bring back—what my grandfather had here, a purpose-driven enterprise. Why are people going to want to pick up this paper? First of all, it is a business. We have to show retailers that the advertising works. But the second piece is for readers: We must create something of substance. It's the serendipity of picking up the paper and saying, 'I didn't know that. I've learned something.' "

Rufus and Wilf celebrate Wilf's 95th birthday in 2014 with cupcakes and merlot. John Hughes/ The Legacy Project

One thing they had both long since learned is that adaptation is crucial to survival. After almost 108 years of afternoon delivery, The Wenatchee World switched to morning delivery in April of 2015. And on Sundays it added a 24-page section produced by The Washington Post to beef up its national news report. Wilf was excited at the changes.

"Wilfred Woods really is an incredible human being," Rufus says. "The influence he's had on my career and on the people around here is nothing short of profound. It's what he has accomplished and the tone he's created; the positive sense of what can be done with a daily newspaper is really a model for our industry. What many don't know is how he's treated people in this plant over the years. When people were short of money and trying to buy a house, he'd co-sign loans. When you talk to some folks who worked here when times weren't as flush, they'll tell you he was a boss's boss. There's the example of my dad instituting a profit-sharing plan, sharing the wealth. This has never been an enterprise about making a lot of money. We could have always made more money. We could have had condos in Maui, I suppose, if we wanted. The main purpose of this newspaper has been public service. That's something I've always admired about him. The guy is my hero in terms of what he's accomplished, and how he's accomplished it. He never has anything ill to say of anyone. He's not been successful by boosting himself up and dragging others down. Even when he's disagreed with people it's never been disagreeable. He's just not nasty. The man doesn't have an enemy in the world. And he's also a visionary in terms of 'What do we need and where are we going next?' He's never had the rearview mirror," Rufus says.

"A lot of people in their careers get to a point where all they want to do is talk about the good old days. Wilfred Woods is an historian and knowledgeable amateur geologist, among many other things, but for Dad it's always, 'What's next?' When he was 88, he and I ran slalom gates at Mission Ridge—dual slalom. He tried to learn to skate-ski when he was in his 80s. He doesn't see limitations. He sees opportunities. I think that's extraordinary. His front-page column and his whole demeanor have always been about that.

"He was a really good manager, and a people person. That had some aspects that weren't so good. I think later in years he trusted people more than he should have. But that was the point where it was my turn to step in.

"I really want to get on the record what he has meant to my career. The wisdom for him to step back and let me make my own mistakes—and I've made them! He's been such a huge support, and to so many families for so long. He's been a model for how you do it right. It's the most amazing gift, to grow up with him, work for him and now to work with him for the last 18 years. I still can't keep up his social schedule! I really can't. I've got a lot of irons in the fire and projects, but I mean at 95 he's in more stuff than I am at 58. It's just unbelievable. I want to savor these days with him."

On March 1, 1907, when the original Rufus Woods took control of The Wenatchee Daily World, he wrote a statement of his principles under the headline "Our Salute to the Public."

> In the great game of life, the moves on the checkerboard of Time have been such that fate hath decreed that we re-enter the newspaper field. At least we are here. Why it should have happened—like the great mystery of life itself—we hardly know.
> But being here, we hope to some day reach the kingrow and have our efforts crowned by the approval of our fellowmen.
> In the newspaper field there is lots of fun, lots of work, and lots of money—so it is hoped.
> Concerning the first, we desire our share. Concerning the second, it may be of some interest to know that we expect to be wedded—to our work. And concerning the third, we will pray to the gods who guard the exchequer that they may open the treasury bags as they go by and drop a few nuggets our way.
> "With malice toward none, and charity for all," the work begins. The views advanced in this paper will not always coincide with those of all our readers. It may make enemies—we hope not.
> Along these lines the poet has expressed himself:
>
> *By thine own soul's law learn to live;*
> *And if men thwart thee, have no heed,*
> *And if men hate thee, have no care;*
> *Sing thou thy song and do thy deed,*
> *Hope thou thy hope and pray thy prayer.*
>
> This shall be our motto.

"What was true then remains so today," Rufus Woods' grandson wrote a hundred years later. "The philosophy describes why we continue publishing an independent daily newspaper. The day the stockholders vote that higher returns come before serving the community or producing quality journalism is the day I look for another job."

Did they ever think of selling the paper?

"Never for a moment," says Rufus.

"Exactly," says Wilf.

"Rather burn it down than sell it," says Rufus. "There are people here who have gone through four years without a salary increase—people paying more for health insurance. Yet they just pour their heart and soul into their work. I could just never sell it out from under them. How could you do anything but push ahead?"

"He's doing a great job!" Wilf says, standing to grab his coat. It was almost press time.

"You get older and realize time is marching on and you may not last forever. Hahahaha! But here I am, still going! Just another old fart!"

Wilf whistled through the office, out the door and down the street to get one of the first papers off the Comet. He knew everyone along the way. Well, almost.

Source Citations

Part One: The Seattle Times
Abbreviations: The Seattle Times: **Times**; Seattle Post-Intelligencer: **P-I**; Seattle Star: **Star**; Seattle Argus: **Argus**; the Weekly and Seattle Weekly: **Weekly**; Associated Press: **AP**; United Press International: **UPI**; Wall Street Journal: **WSJ**; Spokesman-Review: **S-R**; Spokane Chronicle: **Chronicle**; Los Angeles Times: **LAT**; New York Times: **NYT**; Columbia Journalism Review: **CJR**; American Journalism Review, **AJR**; Pacific Northwest Quarterly: **PNQ**; Editor & Publisher: **E&P**; Puget Sound Business Journal: **PSBJ**

Quotations from Frank Blethen, unless otherwise attributed, are from Legacy Project oral history interviews.

Chapter One: A Complicated Legacy
"The road to success," quoted in *Raise Hell*, p. 138
"Old newspapermen say," Morgan, *Skid Road*, p. 185
"Times signals to flash," Times, 11-5-1928, p. 1
"Congratulations on your part," quoted in *Raise Hell*, p. vii
"the last of the buckaroo publishers," quoted in Sue Lockett John, *Myth and Newspaper Competition,* http://citation.allacademic.com/meta/p_mla_apa_research_citation/0/1/4/4/0/pages14406/p14406-1.php
"That exposé" and **"brave, idealistic, outspoken,"** David Boardman, ASNE Editorial Leadership Award letter of nomination, 2011, Legacy Project files, Washington State Library
"legend in his own mind," Knute Berger, *Chain Gangs*, Weekly, 10-9-2006
"In the glory years," Ibid.
"The rise of the Internet," Todd S. Purdum, *Prancing on a Volcano*, Vanity Fair, February 2013, p. 78
"We are all inundated," Susan Cheever, *e.e. cummings, a life*, p. xii
"a mobile-first and cloud-first world," Satya Nadella, memo to

Microsoft employees, *Bold Ambition & Our Core*, 7-10-2014
"profound shift from fiber to cyber," David Boardman, Poynter Institute essay, *Hey, Publishers: Stop Fooling us, and yourselves*, 7-16-2014
"Now Purchased by Kidnappers," *The Onion*, 10-26-09

Chapter Two: The Colonel
"When he bought into The Times," and "During the two decades," *Raise Hell*, p. viii
"never had any original ideas," quoted in *Seattle Times Centennial—the Blethen Legacy*, Times, 12-31-95
"You frizzle-headed old bastard," *Counsel for the Damned*, p. 126
"homesick, hungry and out of luck," *Raise Hell*, p. 6
"Against tremendous odds," Ibid., p. 10
"What more do you want?" quoted in Ibid., p. 78
"a pale evening imitation," Ibid., p. 95
"captive organ," quoted in Ibid., p. 97, 100
"had not preempted that role," Berner, *Seattle 1900-1920*, p. 6
"FAIRY TALE OF THE FABULOUS WEALTH," *The day Seattle's ship came in*, Times' Pacific Magazine, 7-13-97; *Fairy Tale*, Times 7-16-1897, p. 1
"fact or fancy," Ibid.
"an even more fabulous cargo," Ibid.
"GOLD! GOLD!" *Latest news from the Klondike*, P-I, 7-17-1897, p. 1
"When the first miner," Gray, *Gold Diggers*, pp. 119-121; *1890, The rush is on*, P-I, 3-17-2009
Mass exodus, Newell, *Totem Tales*, p. 89
"we will pound the life out of those whelps," Speidel, *Sons of the Profits*, pp. 313-315
"Up came stacks of merchandise," Ibid., p. 323
"a virtual monopoly of the northern trade," *Seattle 1900-1920*, p 22
"pampered and protected," *Raise Hell*, p. 76
"The city grew so fast," Nelson, *Seattle*, p. 52
Hearst appointed C.B. Blethen, *Blethen appointed*, Idaho Statesman, 5-2-1903
"political guttersnipe" and "debauched, half-insane," Blethen, P-I, 11-6-1904
'the vilest attack," quoted in *Raise Hell*, p. 145
"splash, color [and] action," Ficken, *Rufus Woods*, p. 18
"a journalistic prostitute," Ibid.
Taxpayers "skinned" by Thomson, Wilson, *Shaper of Seattle*, pp. 154-155
"the moral yeast," Berner, *Seattle 1900-1920*, pp. 9-10

"more ink and less sincerity," *Raise Hell*, p. 112
"a somewhat disreputable walrus," quoted in *Skid Road*, p. 171
"Practically at the very moment," Times, 7-18-1913; quoted
Seattle Past to Present, p. 110
"The irony of Blethen's paper," *Skid Road*, p. 192
"Few Seattle citizens," *Skid Road*, p. 181
"tranquility was not for him," *A Unique Figure*, P-I, 7-14-1915
"softening with age," Ibid.
"Col. Alden J. Blethen is dead," quoted in *Raise Hell*, p. 236

Chapter Three: Seeds of Discontent
"turmoil was his lot and portion," *A unique figure*, P-I, 7-14-1915
The Times T-Mat Honor Medal, Thomas, *Bylines and Bygones*, p. 65
Ticketed for parking, Star, 7-2-1907
Blethen-Kingsley marriage, *Clarence Blethen Will Wed*, Star, 8-7-1909; King County Marriage Certificate 26659, 8-10-1909, Washington State Digital Archives
"Mrs. Clarance Blethen Dies," Bellingham Herald, 7-6-1908
"averaging 15,000 calls per day," *Silver Jubilee of Seattle Times*, Fourth Estate, 7-29-1922, p. 17
Francis runs away, *Son of Editor Goes in Search of Adventure*, Times, p. 1, 11-16-1916; *Francis Blethen Found*, Ibid., 11-17-1916
"General Blethen reporting for duty," quoted in Scott, *Governors of Washington*, p. 57
"the most despised man in the state," quoted in Clark, *The Dry Years*, p. 200
"bend its knee to no one," quoted in *More Lives Than a Cat: A Chronological History of the Seattle Post Intelligencer*, by Mike Barber
"we found ourselves fighting," quoted in *Raise Hell*, p. 251
"100-percent-American" and circulation claims, Printers Ink, p. 22, 7-15-1920
"misrepresentations" and "garbled figures," Ibid., 8-5-1920, p. 13
"the economic ebullience," and "office and store building," Berner, *Seattle 1921-1940*, p. 181
"brave patriots," *Legion Pushes Campaign*, Olympia Daily Recorder, 1-19-1922
Anything "alien," Berner, *Seattle, 1921-1940*, p. 36.
"Council Clique," quoted in Ibid., p. 80
"communistic and confiscatory," Ibid., pp. 142-143
"There will be no real depression," *Wall Street Crash to Cause No Depression*, Times, 10-27-1929, p. 1
"particularly enthusiastic," *Annual Business Review*, Times, 1-5-1930
"We Need the Money!" advertisement, Times, 10-1-1931

"disregarded expense," Davis and Quinn, *The Blethen Family and the Seattle Times Company*, Harvard Business School, 2001, p. 8
"the toast of the Yacht Club," Philbrook's Boatyard restoration of the motor yacht *Canim*, web page
"one of the few people in the United States," Speidel, *Through the Eye of the Needle*, p. 108; Classic Yacht Association, *Classic Motoryacht Designers: Ted Geary*, web page; also Sailboatdata.com

Chapter Four: Shared Burdens
"for a period of five years," Ridder Bros. v. Blethen, 142 F.2d 395 (Ninth Circuit Court of Appeals) 4-29-1944
"to create contention and distrust," Blethen Family Study, Harvard Business School, p. 8
"first major newspaper financing," *Banks to offer $2,000,000 bond issue*," Times, 1-7-1930
"If there is anything clear," 24 Wn.2d 552, Herman H. Ridder et al., Appellants, v. Rae Kingsley Blethen et al, Respondents, No. 29756, Department Two, Washington Supreme Court, 2-28-1946
Young Blethen's "considerable aptitude" and "great promise," *Alden J. Blethen is killed*, Times, 9-13-1930; *Death, Blind Tyrant*, P-I, 9-17-1930
"by 15 percent in 1930," quoted in Nasaw, *The Chief*, p. 426
"Foolish fears," *Blame THIS on Hoover!*, Times, 10-9-1931, p. 1
"truly independent newspaper," Editorial, Times, 11-9-1932, p.1
"I Don't Read Hearst," Seldes, *Lords of the Press*, p. 230
"sympathy and encouragement," quoted in Nasaw, *The Chief*, p. 494
"constant enemy" and "chief exponent of Fascism," Ibid., p. 232
"tilling the soil," *Text of Al Smith's attack*, Times, 11-1-1936, p. 19
"47 states and the Soviet of Washington," quoted in O'Connor, *Revolution in Seattle*, p. 1
"You had to be a hustler," McCallum, *Dave Beck*, pp. 48-49
"unprotected by union contracts," Ames, Simpson, *Unionism or Hearst*, p. 1
"If the Communists want to relieve me," NYT, 8-21-1936
"found themselves being elbowed aside," *Unionism or Hearst*, p. 61
"The enemies of the Guild," Ibid., p. 62
"swarms of pickets," Ibid, p. 64
"How do like the look of Dave Beck's gun?" Editorial, Times, 8-14-1936, p. 1
"slobbered all over," quoted in Nasaw, *The Chief*, p. 528
"Seven years of depression," Ibid., p. 529

"arrived triumphantly," Ames, Simpson, *Unionism or Hearst,* p. 131
"make it the best paper," NYT, 11-27-1936
$126,000,000 in debt, Swanberg, *Citizen Hearst,* p. 484
Boettiger's salary, Ibid., p. 479
"My Day" was a fixture, *First Lady 'Drops In',* Times, 5-1-1937, p. 1
"he boosts the salaries," *The Stroller,* Argus, 6-19-1937
Painful cuts, Swanberg, *Citizen Hearst,* p. 500
"Conservation Committee," Ibid., pp. 484-485
Citing "irreconcilable differences," Scates, *Magnuson,* p. 144

Chapter Five: The General Surrenders
C.B. Blethen II's prison record, McNeil Island Penitentiary Register 13758, Ancestry.com
Prominently bylined "By Clarance B. Blethen 2d," David Brewster, *The Real Seattle Times,* Seattle magazine, November 1969, p. 35
"AX SLAYER FOUND INSANE!" Times, 9-4-1936, p. 1
"clean-editing policy," *The Real Seattle Times,* p. 35
"broken chunks of concrete," Karolevitz, *Kemper Freeman Sr.,* p. 65
"a new great wonder of the world," *I Go For a Ride,* Times, 6-30-1940
"utterly amazing," Ibid.
"two reasons for eating crow," Ibid.
"one of only a few publishers," *Gen. Blethen Dies,* Times, 10-31-1941, p. 1
"just another Ridder suit," *Will Attacked in 2ⁿᵈ Ridder Suit,* Times, 11-11-1942, p. 5
"C.B. Jr. had assigned to one of the Ridders," *Ridders' suit is dismissed,* Times, 9-13-1946, p. 2
"had good and sufficient reason," 24 Wn.2d 552, Herman H. Ridder et al., Appellants, v. Rae Kingsley Blethen et al, Respondents, No. 29756, Department Two, Washington Supreme Court, 2-28-1946
http://courts.mrsc.org/mc/courts/zsupreme/024wn2d/024wn2d0552.htm
War contracts per capita, Warren, *The War Years,* p. XVI
The "flying fortress," Bill Yenne, *Hap Arnold,* Regnery History, 2013, p. 64
"fiercely pro-internment," Brian Thornton, *Heroic editors in short supply,* Newspaper Research Journal, Vol. 23, Spring/Summer 2002
"The average tame Jap," quoted in Ibid.
An analysis of wartime editorials, Ibid.

"able-bodied Japanese men," quoted in Jennifer Speidel, *After internment*, Seattle Civil Rights & Labor History Project, http://depts.washington.edu/civilr/after_internment.htm
Became more strident, Rochelle Krona, *World War II and Japanese internment in the Seattle Star*, Seattle Civil Rights & Labor History Project, http://depts.washington.edu/civilr/news_seattle_star.htm
On Bainbridge Island, Luke Colasurdo, *The internment of Japanese Americans as reported by Seattle area weekly newspapers*, Seattle Civil Rights & Labor History Project, http://depts.washington.edu/civilr/news_colasurdo.htm
"Hearst astounded observers," Procter, *William Randolph Hearst*, pp. 236-237
Allen asked Beck for help, Berner, *Seattle Transformed*, p. 220
"Seattle Times Buys Out Star," P-I, 8-14-1947, p. 1; Star, 8-13-1947, p. 1; Times, 8-13-1947, p. 1
"Come on over" and "He ruled with an iron hand," Watson, *My Life in Print*, p. 15
"There's only one sky," *The Real Seattle Times*, p. 37
"one of the best city editors in the country," Watson, *Digressions of a Native Son*, p. 19
Ray Collins' explanation of how newsrooms work, quoted in Rick Anderson, *Paper Tiger*, Weekly, 11-30-2000
Smaller newspapers were hit hardest, Davies, *The Postwar Decline of American Newspapers*, p. 7

Chapter Six: Pulitzer Pride
"Have you no sense of decency, sir?" Army-McCarthy Hearings transcript, 6-9-1954; http://www.youtube.com/watch?v=fqQD4dzVkwk
Dies' blunderbuss attacks, Harris, *Five Came Back*, p. 62
"Not less" than 150 professors, quoted in Berner, *Seattle Transformed*, p. 228
"outstanding men," and "We had a very amenable," Canwell Oral History, p. 144, 159
"a five-buck raise," *A man of influence, modesty steps down*, Times, 1-2-1977, p. A-14
"a point of considerable conflict," Canwell Oral History, p. 160
"Somewhere along the line," Ibid.
"Well, we think he's a commie," Ibid.
"great newsman," Ibid., p. 253
"ACLUer," Ibid., p. 216, 253
"cream" anyone, Ibid., p. 158
"a deep personal revulsion," Brokaw, *The Greatest Generation*, p. 378

"[W]hat they didn't realize," Un-American Activities, Second Report, p. 23
A "phony" story, quoted in *When the "Red Scare' came to Seattle*, Times, 1-23-1998
"This is wrong," quoted in McConaghy, *The Seattle Times's Cold War Pulitzer Prize*, PNQ, p. 26
"It's obvious the committee isn't," quoted in *When the "Red Scare' came to Seattle*
"I asked if I could see the register," Ibid.
"There it is—Rader—1938," quoted in *The Seattle Times's Cold War Pulitzer Prize*, PNQ, p. 27
"cooking up this phony Rader cause celebre," Canwell Oral History, p. 201
"Raymond Allen ... was out of town," *The Seattle Times's Cold War Pulitzer Prize*, pp. 27-28
"a tense four hours," Ibid., p. 28
"the perilous climate, Ibid., p. 29
"guilty of giving protection," Scates, *Magnuson*, p. 151
"always referred to at our house," MacLeod to author, 5-23-2014
"if East Coast editors had had half the courage," Ibid.
"Innocent people were terrified," *Ed Guthman dies*, Times, 9-2-2008, p. 1
"Despite all of their disdain," quoted in *Magnuson*, p. 160

Chapter Seven: The Third Edition
"War's end will mark," *Dawn of the Pacific Era*, 1944 magazine advertisement, Washington State Archives
"mid-century Seattle was white," *On Common Ground*, Times, 12-29-1996
Strikes between 1951 and 1961, *Labor's Monkey Wrench*, Canadian Journal of Communication, Vol. 31, No. 3, 2006
"Hey, John, still on strike?" Duncan to author, 6-5-2014
"a substantial number," *Seattle Times Strike*, E&P, 7-25-1953
"Now it was the P-I's turn," *It's been awhile, but this is old hat*, The Newspaper Guild bulletin, 12-15-2000
"the biggest bonanza of comics," *Back Comics Begin Today*, Times, 10-19-1953, p. 1
"a touch of cap-tipping courtesy," *The Real Seattle Times*, p. 33
"You're sure getting a lot of bylines," Duncan to author, 5-23-2014
"All The News That Fits We Print," Ibid., 6-5-2014
 "I got tired of seeing," Ibid.
"I don't think we should have anything," *Barrel Roll In a 707?*, Times, 2-28-1990

"The press just dropped the ball," Ibid.
"It was either pressure on the publishers," Duncan to author, 5-28-2014
"They never figured out," Susan Gilmore, *Bob Twiss, master of Boeing beat*, Times, 9-3-2001; Sterling, *Legend & Legacy*, p. 193
"impregnable in his office," *The Real Seattle Times*, p. 33
"the biggest sacred cow," Mark Worth, *Boeing, the Media's Sacred Cow*, The Washington Free Press, April 1993, http://wafreepress.org/01/Boeing4.html

Chapter Eight: Changing Times
civic "sluggishness," Sale, *Seattle, Past to Present*, p. 202
"that with a quick call or two," Corr, *KING*, p. 110
"he headed straight to Olympia," David Brewster, *What's the bee in Frank Blethen's bonnet*, Crosscut.com, 10-29-2012
"our country is losing," quoted in *The Future Remembered*, p. 21
"talked him out of stopping," Murray, *Century 21*, p. 96
"When the Space Needle passed," *The Future Remembered*, p. 49
Times overtakes the Post-Intelligencer, Audit Bureau of Circulations report for the six-month period ending March 31, 1960
"**Several developments**," Morton, *40 Years of Death in the Afternoon*, AJR, November 1991
"At 380 pages," Duncan, *Meet Me at the Center*, p. 48
"**Fabulous Fair in Seattle**," Life magazine, 2-9-1962, cover
God would "rule the world," Lane Smith, *Graham Draws Record Crowd To Fair*, Times, 7-9-1962, p. 2
Elvis "blazed a glittering path," Dick Moody, *Girls Swoon, Go Cross-Eyed Over Presley*, Times, 9-8-1962
one could "safely assume" and "widespread belief," *How 'Open' an 'Open Town'?*, Times, 3-1-1964
Carroll, was keeping The Mob out, Corr, *KING*, pp. 158-159
"If you cleaned this city up," Chambliss, *On the Take*, p. 47, 59
"Exceeded a hundred million dollars," Ibid., p. 54
"was carried for over a year," *The Real Seattle Times*, p. 32
"too damn long," Duncan to author, 7-3-2014
"the vast news-gathering resources," Announcement, P-I, 4-1-1960, p. 1
"some shenanigans," MacLeod to author, 5-27-2014
an astute "student," Rosellini oral history, p. 197-198
"the advertising and circulation departments," *The Real Seattle Times*, p. 37
"**Mr. McGrath to see Mr. MacLeod**," Duncan to author, 7-3-2014

Chapter Nine: Growing Pains
"A short, bald man," Duncan to author, 7-3-2014
"dangerous extremist," *The John Birch Society*, Times, 4-3-1961
"faint, knowing smile," Corr, *KING*, p. 110
"timed big announcements," Ibid., pp. 157-158
"no overriding consensus," *Times rating of nominees*, Times, 11-1-1964, p. 1
"mandate for moderation," *Mandate for Moderation*, Times, 11-4-1964
"After John Kennedy's funeral," Crowley, *Rites of Passage*, p. 32
"not worse than the disease," *The Open Housing Measure*, P-I, 2-28-1964
"to sell, rent or lease," Taylor, *The Forging of a Black Community*, p. 204; *Seattle Municipal Election*, Times, 3-8-1964.
"to what extent pre-Civil War," *Indians—With Allies—on the Warpath*, Times, 3-3-1964
"World's Fair zip," Walt Woodward, *United Plan for Seattle*, Times, 11-3-1965, p. 1
"the stupidest 'no' vote," quoted in Hughes, *John Spellman, Politics Never Broke His Heart*, p. 68
"plodding" provincialism, Bunzel, *Why My Sunday Mornings are Such a Drag*, Seattle magazine, November 1969, p. 58
"called in well," Robbins, *Tibetan Peach Pie*, pp. 205-206
"mountain climbers and bird watchers," quoted in Joel Connelly, *The Wilderness Act*, Seattle pi.com, 9-3-2014
"so-called 'friends' " and "the blight," *Facing facts on Pike Plaza*, Times, 10-1-1971
"to stay just far enough ahead," Brewster, *V-T Day*, Weekly, 1-21/27-1981, p. 15; Crowley, *Rites of Passage*, p. 40
"The Times carried 3.4 million inches," *The Real Seattle Times*, p. 34
"He eventually kicked me out," Sizemore to author, 7-8-2014
"not rushing into things," *The Real Seattle Times*, p. 37
"convinced him to stay," Ibid.
"the size of a beach umbrella," Elizabeth Rhodes, *Longtime Times editor dies*, Times, 4-3-2000
"the brother most interested," *The Real Seattle Times*, p. 41
"only a few close friends," Ibid., p. 35
"didn't flinch," MacLeod to author, 5-27-2014
"debt free and grossing $30 million," *The Real Seattle Times*, p. 32
"Voting shares could only be held," Blethen Family Study, Harvard Business School, p. 9
"The 1956 agreement," Ibid.
"The Blethen Corporation and Knight-Ridder," Ibid., p. 4

"broadly experienced" and "dedicated to," Ibid., p. 5
"the most literarily gifted," Mike Lewis, *A cast of characters*, P-I Commemorative Section, 3-17-2009
"unseemly female exposure," *The Real Seattle Times*, p. 34
"country's largest weekly," Ibid.
"A touch of peevishness," Ibid., p. 41
"the whole newspaper industry," Ibid., p. 40
"cozy with a shadowy figure," P-I, 8-21-1968, p. C-5
"Had brow-beat," Ibid.
"no ordinary business," Seattle Times Newsroom Policies and Guidelines, ASNE Web page: http://asne.org/content.asp?pl=236&sl=19&contentid=326
"so we walked it around," Hamer to author, 8-26-2014
"The fact that the staff was unionized," Fancher to author, 8-26-2014
"just a small part of moving," MacLeod to author, 8-26-2014

Chapter 10: An Irrational Decision
barely averted bankruptcy, T.M. Sell, *Wings of Power*, p. 26
"press releases that were always favorable," Frank Blethen interview by Lorraine McConaghy, Museum of History and Industry, 11-12-2010
"I hope when I get to Seattle," Ibid.

Chapter 11: Bylaws and Bygones
Satiric characterizations of The Times and P-I: Frank Wetzel, *The Times' Corporate Character*, quoted in Times, 4-19-1987, p. A-14
"whored and sold his soul," Scates, *War & Politics By Other Means*, pp. 84-87; *Surrender Is Bizarre*, AP in Spokane Daily Chronicle, 5-5-1979
denounced as "rapacious," Knute Berger, *Chain Gangs*, Weekly, 10-9-2006
"argued that the merger gave," *Editor labels merger unfair*, AP in Ellensburg Daily Record, 4-30-1981
"a mild yelp of indignation," *The Times' Corporate Character*, quoted in Times, 4-19-1987, p. A-14
"so unfailingly polite," and "kick butt," Ibid.
"if Knight-Ridder hadn't gone to bat," Ridder to author, 10-6-2014
"a strong advocate" and "lived life," Susan Gilmore, *Alden Blethen lived a full life*, Times, 2-3-2006
"his family's history," Blethen Family Study, Harvard Business School, p. 13

"The new checks and balances," Ibid.

Chapter 12: The Golden Carrot of Togetherness
"Don't worry," Charles Dunsire, *Mr. Press*, pp. 165-166
"Suddenly, the air," Connelly to author, 7-23-2014
Nalder kicked a file cabinet, David Brewster and Cynthia Wilson, *V-T Day*, Weekly, 1-21/27-1981
"more than a miracle," *Seattle Times, P-I go head to head*, Times, 3-5-2000; *Mr. Press*, p. 166
"a kind of lockdown," *V-T Day*, Weekly, 1-21/27-1981
"The war's over," recalled to author by Casey Corr, 10-16-2014
"V-T Day," Ibid.
Its circulation had grown, *Seattle Times, P-I go head to head*, Times, 3-5-2000
"It felt like we'd been sold down," MacLeod to author, 7-23-2014
"Bullshit," Ibid.
"I don't have a paper now," *V-T Day*, Weekly, 1-21/27-1981
"the golden carrot," quoted in *Monopoly Games—Where Failures Win Big*, Stephen R. Barnett, CJR, May-June 1980, p. 47
"surprisingly fascinating," *Mr. Press*, p. 170
Bennack told Hearst's board, Ibid., p. 171
"many of us thought JOAs," MacLeod to author, 7-23-2014
Guild "was useless," Connelly to author, 7-23-2014
"bourgeoisie, suburban, prudish" and "we needed them both," Brewster to author, 2-25-2013
"whether Hearst deliberately" and "ill-suited," *V-T Day*, Weekly, 1-21/27-1981, p. 15
"My contention is," *Editor labels merger unfair*, UPI in Ellensburg Daily Record, 4-30-1981
illegal price-fixing, John P. Patkus, *The Newspaper Preservation Act: Why it fails to preserve newspapers*, Akron Law Review, Vol. 17:3, Winter 1984, p. 435
Nixon's change of heart, quoted in Wikipedia from: Bagdikian, *The New Media Monopoly*, Boston: Beacon Press. pp. 204-217; Woodward and Redmond, *The Publishers' Six Big Lies: A Federal Trial Shows How SF's Daily Newspapers Have Misled the Public for Decades*, San Francisco Bay Guardian, 5-10-2000
"a gunnysack full of graduates," Watson, *Digressions of a Native Son*, p. 141
"Dwyer just shredded," quoted in *Slade Gorton*, p. 137
"Our situation is so serious," Connelly to author, 7-23-2014
"Our argument," Brewster to author, 2-25-2013
"maybe to somebody good," Ibid.

"but they wouldn't break ranks," Ibid.
"the absence of willing purchasers," *The Newspaper Preservation Act: Why it fails to preserve newspapers*, Akron Law Review, Vol. 17:3, Winter 1984, pp. 444-445
"without exploring the alternative," quoted in Ibid., p. 445
"met its burden," Ibid., p. 445
Guzzo and Asbury comments, *Mr. Press*, pp. 180-181
"We would look at that," quoted in Ibid., p. 174
"Murdock had never made," Ibid.
"vaporous," Ibid.
"a commercial appendage," quoted in Ibid., p. 186
"We almost won," Brewster to author, 2-25-2013
"we would be a morning paper," *The Battle for Seattle*, AJR, May 2000

Chapter 13: The Margin of Excellence and a Shocking Loss

"Twelve pages of funnies," *Every Sunday is SuperSunday*, house ad, Times, 5-29-1983
"no increase in present base rates," Eric Scigliano, *The P-I's still the P-I*, Weekly, 5-25/31-1983
The Times' ad rates for Sunday, Ibid.
Projected circulation gains, Dunphy, *Increases in circulation, revenue projected*, Times, 4-19-1981
"critical watchdog," Dick Clever, *Pulp Fiction*, Weekly, 10-9-2006
Watson's return, Jack Broom, Watson obituary, Times, 5-12-2001
It felt like "full circle," Watson, *My Life in Print*, p. 61
"a bunch of bright kids," Duncan to author, 8-12-2014
Terry McDermott lead writing, Fancher column, *New Times Columnist*, Times, 9-3-1995
"a watershed event," Blethen Family Study, Harvard Business School, p. 10
Net profit estimates, Dunsire, *Mr. Press*, p. 170
"Any idiot can manage," quoted in Herb Robinson, *Time to Pack Up Memories*, Times, 12-6-1991
"all that amazing energy," King to author, 1983 Allied Daily Newspapers convention
"Daddy Warbucks," MacLeod to author, 5-23-2014
"good to his word," Ibid.
Pennington's death: *Seattle Times publisher drowns*, Whidbey News-Times, 3-20-1985, p. 3; *W.J. Pennington, publisher, dies*, Times, 3-15-1985; Duncan, *Death of Jerry Pennington stuns civic leaders*, Times, 3-16-1985; Island County Coroner Death Investigation Report 85-23 and autopsy, 0-62-3-85

"this couldn't be Jerry," MacLeod to author, 8-16-2014
Mrs. Pennington's story related to author by Susan Pennington Merry, 8-27-2014
Frank Blethen becomes publisher, *Frank Blethen, Times publisher; Sizemore is president,* Times, 3-19-1985, p. 1

Chapter 14: Core Values
"an idea guy," Jack Broom, King obituary, Times, 10-18-2012;
"A newspaper editor," King to author, Allied Daily Newspapers Convention, 1983
"like any other striving young man," and "a large and pervasive bureaucracy," Underwood, *When MBAs Rule the Newsroom,* p. xvii, p. xxi
"he gave me room to be myself," MacLeod to author, August 2014
"a transformative figure," Ibid.
"Fancher sees things I do not see," quoted in Carol M. Ostrom, *"Zen Master" of Times newsroom retires,* Times, 5-4-2008
"MacLeod may be an asshole," quoted in J. Kingston Pierce, *The Times Tough Guy,* Weekly, 6-3/9-1987
"He's real good at saying no," etc., Ibid.
"a better accounting of reporters' time," Ibid.
Catcalls endured by Cathy Henkel, Mike Fancher, *Grand slam of honors for sports editor,* Times, 3-13-2005
"It was like the world came to an end," Ibid.
"kick-ass" job, *Cathy Henkel leaving Seattle Times,* comment string, SportsJournalists.com, 11-7-2008
"Cash flow, not net income," *Momentum, The Seattle Times: A Decade of Accomplishment,* p. 23
The Times' opinions grew more liberal, James Bush, *Times change,* Weekly, 10-9-2006
"Herb had assembled a diverse," Hamer to author, 8-25-2014
"Don't ever cross him," Ibid.
"destiny at stake," W.R. Hearst Jr., *Voters should feel safer with Bush,* P-I, 11-6-1988
"When Frank took over," Hamer to author, 8-25-2014
Blethen on Dukakis, UPI, *Times endorses Dukakis,* Ellensburg Daily Record, 10-4-1988
"That Frank went left for Dukakis," Vesely to author, 8-24-2014
"It was a deep and sincere belief," Ibid.
"Frank believed KVI's format," Carlson to author, 9-15-2014
Cameron abortion column, *An intensely personal, private decision,* Times, 7-5-1992
"There was groundbreaking aspect," Vesely to author, 9-10-2014

"we either agreed or Frank had it his way," Cameron to author, 8-20-2014
"Ask practically anyone," Vesely to author, 8-25-2014
"soft-spoken, maybe even shy," J. Kingston Pierce, *Frank Blethen, the new man at the top of The Times*, Weekly, 1-23-1985
"not likely to ever compete," Ibid.

Chapter 15: Fiduciary Duties

"the young prince of politics," quoted in Hughes, *Slade Gorton*, p. 207
Adams case details, *8 more women accuse Adams*, Times, 3-1-1992
"created out of whole cloth," "worst kind of journalism," "saddest day of my life," Ibid.; Cheryl Reid, *Anonymous Sources Bring Down a Senator*, AJR, April 1992; Tim Klass, *Accused senator won't run*, AP, 3-1-1992
"An open license," Lee Moriwaki and Mark Matassa, *Media critics attack, defend*, Times, 3-2-1992
"that were above reproach," Susan Gilmore, *DeVore obituary*, Times, 10-27-2008; *DeVore dies*, NYT, 10-31-2008
"The choice we faced," *Anonymous Sources Bring Down a Senator*, AJR, April 1992
"I told Frank," Fancher to author, 9-4-2014
"How could we know this," Boardman to author, 9-2-2014
"meticulous, convincing journalism," quoted in *Anonymous Sources Bring Down a Senator*, AJR, April 1992
"You may ask how we can afford," and other quotes about Yakima purchase, O. Casey Corr and Polly Lane, *Seattle Times Co. to Buy Yakima Herald-Republic*, Times, 12-17-1991
"they paid way too much," and "That's the easiest money," Ridder to author, 10-6-2014
"That was the lifeblood," Ibid.
"So are handguns," *The Media Business*, NYT, 7-5-1993
"These ads were designed to kill," *Smokeless in Seattle*, AJR, October 1993
The ban wasn't mandatory, *Media & Marketing*, LAT, 11-15-1995
"If you're making less," Related to author by Robert Merry, 8-27-2014
Blethen's earnings, Terry McDermott, *JOA: 10 years later*, Times, 5-23-1993
"fiduciary responsibility," Susan Paterno, *Independent's Day*, AJR, October 1996
"The Seattle Times always underperformed," Ridder to author, 10-6-2014

"untold disasters" and other analysis of JOA 10 years later, *JOA: 10 years later*, Times, 5-23-1993
"ordinariness" and "The editorials almost worship," quoted in Ibid.
"Newspapers are the dinosaurs," quoted in Ibid.
"We're not publishing to make money," *Momentum, The Seattle Times: A Decade of Accomplishment*, pp. 18-19
"I felt like they were just trying to acquire," Ridder to author, 10-6-2014
"He exaggerates," Ibid.

Chapter 16: The Stare-Down
"The Wall Street Journal of Silicon Valley," http://encyclopedia.jrank.org/articles/pages/6345/Ridder-Tony.html#ixzz3DhCY6s99
"and one of its best," and "second only to the New York Times," Susan Paterno, *Whither Knight-Ridder*, AJR, January/February 1996
"Darth Ridder," quoted in http://encyclopedia.jrank.org/articles/pages/6345/Ridder-Tony.html#ixzz3DhCY6s99
"a Faustian bargain," *Whither Knight-Ridder*
"like being in the presence of a machine," Davis Merritt to author, 9-23-2014
"mired in mediocrity," quoted in Susan Paterno, *Independent's Day*, AJR, October 1996
"You sell your soul," quoted in Susan Paterno, *The Battle for Seattle*, AJR, May 2000
"a decent return," "Don't stare him down," and "You won't win," quoted in *Independent's Day*
"Ultimately, economics will control," and "Dangle enough money," quoted in Ibid.
"I thought $25 million was insulting," Ridder to author, 10-6-2014
"neighbors from hell," "Doggate," Mariana Parks and John Hamer, *A doggone case*, Eastsideweek, 8-14-1996, and *Behind Doggate*, Eastsideweek, 8-21-1996; Steve Christilaw, *Seeing Red*, Mercer Island Reporter, 8-21-1996; Rick Anderson, *Man bites court*, Eastsideweek, 11-13-1996.
"We'll shoot this dog," Goldy, *We'll Shoot This Dog*, horsesass.org, 11-7-2006
"If not for human error," Eric Nalder and Duff Wilson, *The Pang Fire*, Times, 6-11-1995
"riddled with fraud," and "sleeping in dilapidated cars," *Tribal Housing, From deregulation to disgrace*, Times, 12-1/5-1996
"I watched him take like 60 inches," Taylor to author, 2-18-2014
"horrible—the worst in the nation," AP, *Nordstrom pulls ads from Seattle papers*, Pullman Daily News, 3-28-1990

"**Many of us were bitter,**" Bruscas to author, 10-14-2014
Lightbulb joke, quoted in comments to Ted Van Dyk, *Journeymen journalists out to pasture,* Crosscut, 4-8-2008
"**a little bit of enamel,**" quoted in Deborah Wang, *Cross-Town Rivalry,* KUOW News, 3-11-2009
"**puffy**" and "**defiantly middlebrow,**" Brewster to author, 9-5-2014

Chapter 17: Roots and Branches

"**I couldn't believe what I was seeing,**" quoted in Fancher, *Photo of Death Showed Grim Reality,* Times, 4-17-1994
A freshman at Swarthmore, Walter Isaacson, *The Great Connectors,* Vanity Fair, October 2014, p. 190
rarely showed dead bodies, *Photo of Death,* Times, 4-17-1994
Internet statistics, Internet World Stats, http://www.internetlivestats.com/internet-users/
Debut of "WebEdition/Education," Mike Fancher, *Times takes small step,* Times, 8-27-1995
"**Electronic classified,**" quoted in Merritt, *Knightfall*
"**Classified ads are the bedrock,**" Marshall McLuhan, *Understanding Media: The Extension of Man,* p. 207
Basil lent a hand, Fancher, *Blethen Family Makes Visit to Roots,* Times, 10-19-1997
"**The country was high, wild and empty**" and "**It was so evocative,**" Boswell and McConaghy to author, 9-26-2014
A photo they'd never seen, Fancher, *Journalism and History Come Together,* Times, 8-4-1996
They piled into a van, Fancher, *Blethen Family Makes Visit to Roots,* Times, 10-19-1997
"**I told my dad,**" Ryan Blethen to author, 10-8-2014
"**of all the companies,**" quoted in Steve Wilmsen, *Seattle Times Co. Buys Maine Newspapers,* Boston Globe, 9-2-1998, p. D1
"**driven by cold financial calculations,**" John Morton, *Blood Ties Drive A Deal,* AJR, November 1998
"**The Blethens ended up bidding,**" quoted in Bill Richards, *The Blethens and The Times,* Seattle Business magazine, May 2009
"**As Frank Blethen said,**" *Blood Ties Drive A Deal*
"**It gives my generation ... a touchstone,**" *Blethen Family Makes Visit to Roots*
"**people under 30 are far more comfortable,**" *The nation isn't ready,* Times, 5-21-1996
"**It all comes down to a simple idea,**" Mindy Cameron, *A time to celebrate family,* Times, 11-24-1996
"**I was very proud,**" "**And the next generation shall,**" quoted in Kate

Riley, *Getting to "I do" took patience*, Times, 9-15-2012

Chapter 18: The Battle for Seattle
"truly a historic day," and "within two years," Stephen H. Dunphy & James V. Grimaldi, *Times Going to Morning*, Times, 2-2-1999, p. 1
"I knew it would piss them off," MacLeod to author 10-6-2014
"When they discover news," Steve Miletich, *P-I, Times face off in battle for mornings*, P-I, 2-3-1999, p. 1; James Bush, *Suicide Pact*, Weekly, 2-11-1999
"It's almost as good as sex!" quoted in Susan Paterno, *The Battle for Seattle*, AJR, May 2000
"After four frustrating years," Rozen to author, 10-9-2014
"we did not have an online presence," James Wallace to author, 10-16-2014
"A bonehead decision," Ibid.
"loss notice clause," section 3.5, *Newspaper Cessation Date*, p. 9, and section 7.1.4, *Loss Operations*, pp.20-21, Amended JOA, Washington State Archives
"as expeditiously as possible," Ibid., p. 21
"Up until [this announcement]," quoted in James Bush, *Suicide Pact*, Weekly, 2-11-1999
$150 for second production facility, *Times Going to Morning*, Times, 2-2-1999, p. 1
"a fake war," quoted in Jeffrey Leib, *Duel at dawn*, Denver Post, 7-23-2000
"I maintain that both," quoted in James Bush, *Suicide Pact*, Weekly, 2-11-1999
"My guess is," quoted in Ibid.
Circulation details, Ibid.
"Good MORRRRNing Seattle!" Jean Godden, *It's great to be back*, Times, 3-6-2000, p. B-1
"Perhaps most conspicuous," *The Battle for Seattle*, AJR, May 2000
"There is an art," quoted in Ibid.
"a headline service," quoted in James Bush, *Going to War*, Seattle Weekly, 3-14-2000
"all the blather," *The Battle for Seattle*, AJR, May 2000
"Ken always had your back," Connelly to author, 10-18-2014
"This demonstration of Hearst's deep pockets," quoted in *Suicide Pact*
"Why would Hearst spend that kind of money" and "there's a lot of suspicion," quoted in *The Battle for Seattle*
"No one in newspapers can say," Ibid.

Chapter 19: Momentum Meltdown

"unprecedented in our 104-year history," Momentum, *The Seattle Times: A Decade of Accomplishment*, p. 1

"That accomplishment was particularly meaningful," Blethen Family Study, p. 2

"the ever-increasing rewards," *Momentum*, p. 55

"By sharpening our skills," and "the best is yet to come," Ibid., p. 20, 55

"Yeah, wow, let's do this," Matthew Rose and Patricia Callahan, *Publisher fights to keep paper in family*, WSJ, 2-18-2001

"It feels like a death in the family," quoted in Mike Fancher, *Inside the Times*, 11-26-2000

"When I had my children," Nina Shapiro, *Striking divisions*, Weekly, 12-7-2000

"We had somewhat awkward moments," Joel Connelly to author, 10-18-2014

"Several of us were mystified," Ibid.

"It all started in 1987," Nina Shapiro, *Striking Spin*, Weekly, 12-14-2000

"We were beaten," *Newspaper unions settle in Seattle*, AP, 3-30-1987

"This time we didn't flinch," *Striking Spin*

"We had almost a half-century," Jim Simon and Barbara A. Serrano, *Times strike ends*, 1-9-2001

"Fuck you to death," quoted in Nina Shapiro, *Frank the Flamer*, Weekly, 12-21-2000

"I'd occasionally want to kick a door," Matthew Rose and Patricia Callahan, *Publisher fights to keep paper in family*, WSJ, 2-18-2001

"by the union's refusal," *Striking divisions*

"crucial leverage," Ibid.

"I didn't think the two-tier salary scale," Ith to author 10-14-2014

"The circulation and advertising people," Judd to author, 10-30-2014

"I thought I had won the lottery," Taylor to author, 2-18-2014

"Hungry kids a home" and "same leaking boat," Judd to author, 10-30-2014

"wussyness" and the "real problem," Josh Feit and Dan Savage, *The Real Strike Paper*, Stranger, 12-14/20-2000

"Seattle isn't Detroit," Judd to author, 10-30-2014

"Irish affinity" and "a lot more than the Hearsts," Casey Corr to author, 10-21-2014

Detroit strike costs, *Striking similarities*, CJR, January/February 2001, and John Morton, *Seattle strikes out*, AJR, March 2001

"We're going to find a way," James Bush, *Each side accuses the other*, Weekly, 12-21-2000

"An incredibly cynical ploy," Ibid.
"an assault on the newspapers," Ibid.
"The strike was necessary," James Bush, *Back to work*, Weekly, 1-4-2001
"We're still here, Frank!" Ernest Mailhot, *Seattle Times workers vote to reject*, The Militant, 1-15-2001
"spinning out of control," quoted in *Newspaper workers feel new strength*, Workers World, 1-25-2001, http://www.workers.org/ww/2001/seattle0125.php
"This is the first contract ...that we haven't," quoted in *Newspaper workers feel new strength*, Workers World, 1-25-2001, http://www.workers.org/ww/2001/seattle0125.php
"What none of us realized," Eli Sanders, *The State of Our Unions*, The Stranger, 4-16-2009
"sentiment within the Guild," John Morton, *Seattle strikes out*, AJR, March 2001

Chapter 20: Joint Operating Angst
"Some long and candid," "trying to come to grips," "things had changed," Judd to author, 10-24-2014; *Family issue*, WSJ, 2-14-2001
"entitlement mentality," Ibid. and Bill Richards, *Blethen's Choice*, Seattle Business, June 2009
"It never occurred to us," "almost pathologically incapable," quoted in *Paper Cuts*, PSBJ, 1-26-2001
Details of spring board meeting, Bill Richards, *Blethen's Choice*, Seattle Business, Jun 2009
"Nothing will ever have the impact," quoted in *Boeing Airplane's former CEO*, Steve Wilhelm, PSBJ, 10-15-2014
"I'll never work in journalism again," Kevin Fullerton, *-30-*, Weekly, 5-8-2002
"ultraliberal, pro-labor stance," *Times to city: Ease up or we'll walk*, E&P, 6-11-2001
Kelly on outlying circulation, *Seattle papers cut delivery area*, E&P, 1-21-2002
a "textbook case," Gene Johnson, *Seattle Times responds to criticism*, Associated Press, 3-22-2002; Pat Kearney, *The Race is On*, The Stranger, 3-28/4-3 2002
Third consecutive year of losses, *Losses arm Times with license to kill*, E&P, 1-13-2003
"If the P-I doesn't invoke it, we will," *Seattle: A good (bad) year*, CJR, March-April 2003
"creative and gutsy," quoted in Ibid.
"It sets up an adversarial relationship," quoted in Ibid.

"not going to be chased out of Seattle," quoted in *RIP for the JOA?* E&P, 1-27-2003
"inexcusable," quoted in Bill Richards, *Times spending*, Times, 5-2-2003
"stonewalling," *Conflicted disinterest*, Weekly, 10-9-2006
MacLeod retires, Mike Fancher, *Alex MacLeod closing chapter*, Times, 2-9-2003
"an upfront inducement," Bill Richards, *Hearst threatened*, Times, 9-8-2004
"yield substantial losses," *Newspaper in Seattle sues rival*, NYT, 4-29-2003
"It's hard to understand," *Snit in Seattle*, WSJ, 5-1-2003
"force majeure," other details, Ibid.
"18-month clock," *6 scenarios of separation*, E&P, 5-26-2003
"Simply stated," *P-I: We'd die without the JOA*, E&P, 5-12-2003
"The reality is," Bill Richards, *Times' finances*, Times, 9-10-03
1993 Hearst memo, *Ruling on Thursday*, E&P, 9-22-2003
"crucial to the future of the P-I," Bill Richards, *Judge hears arguments*, Times, 9-13-2003
"trying to force a square peg," Ibid.
"In all those issues," Ibid.
"an anomaly," *Who knows where Times goes?*, E&P, 9-29-2003
"of paramount importance," quoted in *Q&A, What's next*, Times, 9-28-2003
"A sad moment," *Appeals court backs Times*, KOMO News, 3-22-2004, http://www.komonews.com/news/archive/4120631.html
"The price will be so high," *The struggles continue*, PSBJ, 4-30-2004
 "new-world melting pot," http://www.vulcan.com/

Chapter 21: A Surprising Call
Ridder version of Blethen's call, Ridder to author, 10-6-2014
Insufficient evidence of "improper conduct," *Justice Dept. drops antitrust investigation*, Times, 5-14-2005
"By the plain terms," *State Supreme Court rules*, AP, 6-30-2005
"A chance to be profitable again," Ibid.
"This case is far from over," *Ruling may end a 2-paper era*, LAT, 7-1-2005
"We're going to closely examine," *State Supreme Court rules*, AP, 6-30-2005
Stephen Sparks' claims and **"ruse,"** Bill Richards, *An ex-exec claims*, Crosscut, 4-1-2007, http://crosscut.com/2007/04/01/seattle-newspapers/1288/An-exexec-claims-iSeattle-Timesi-secretly-undermin/

Sparks not on witness list, Eric Pryne, *New Hearst, Times JOA*, Times, 4-18-2007
"It's downright cockeyed," Chuck Taylor, *Chronicling The Times and P-I*, Crosscut, 4-1-2007, http://crosscut.com/2007/04/01/seattle-newspapers/1292/Chronicling-iTimesi-iPIi-as-they-fight-death/

Chapter 22: A Brief Reprieve
"It was all green to go," Jordan to author, 11-18-2014
"Hopefully our work is done" and **"We will rise again if we have to,"** quoted in Eric Pryne, *Committee ends court fight*, Times, 6-21-2007
"Hearst is the one that blinked," quoted in Eric Pryne, *Seattle Times, P-I reach agreement*, Times, 4-17-2007
"I don't know if newspapers will survive," quoted in Eric Pryne, *Agreement reached*, Times, 4-16-2007
"The damned JOA," quoted in Knute Berger, *The Seattle Times' suburban retreat*, Crosscut, 4-8-2008
"terribly flawed" business plan, Ibid.
"I'm just happy to be happy," quoted in *Seattle P-I and Times settle legal dispute*, P-I, 4-16-2007
"a lot of very direct and skeptical questions," quoted in *Seattle newspapers settle legal dispute*, Cassandra Tate, HistoryLink.org Essay 8181
"No one is more determined," quoted in Heidi Dietrich, *All in the family*, PSBJ, 10-3-2004
"Adapt or die" year-end message, *Blethen paints bleak financial picture*, Times, 12-27-2007
"to grow value again," Ibid.
"I respectfully declined," Ryan Blethen to author, 10-8-2014
"nepotism personified," quoted in Philip Dawdy, *Putting on Heirs*, Weekly, 4-14-2004
"shake things up a bit," *2000 Bush story haunts reporter?* E&P, June 2004
"central banks around the world," Eric Petroff, *Who is to blame for the subprime crisis?*, http://www.investopedia.com/articles/07/subprime-blame.asp

Chapter 23: Swift, Surgical & Sad
"a bunch of rumor," quoted in *KING-TV: Seattle P-I for sale*, Times, 1-8-2009
"In no case" and **"Regrettably, we have come to the end of the line,"** quoted in *Seattle Post-Intelligencer faces closure*, WSJ, 1-12-2009
"At this point" and dialogue with Swartz, transcribed from *The end of the Seattle P-I*, http://www.youtube.com/

watch?v=TWuWRMzngTM
"holding on by our fingertips," quoted in *Newspaper publishers seek tax cut*, AP, 2-18-2009
"It's not a bailout," quoted in *Newspapers in WA get tax break*, AP, 7-2-2009
"like dodging the executioner," Lange to author, 11-25-2014
"Tonight we'll be putting the paper to bed," *Seattle P-I to publish last edition*, Seattlepi.com, 3-16-2009
"the leading news and information portal in the region," Ibid.
"I think we'll outsell you tomorrow," quoted in Eric Pryne, *Last edition of print P-I*, Times, 3-16-2009
"Whatever future there is," quoted in Carol Smith, *The pioneering P-I slips into the past*, seattlepi.com, 3-16-2009, http://www.seattlepi.com/local/article/The-pioneering-P-I-slips-into-the-past-1302639.php
Carol Smith's obituary for the P-I, Ibid.
"It's NOT just the economy," Jon Hahn, *Reflections of a Newsosaur*, 3-16-2009, http://newsosaur.blogspot.com/2009/03/bright-light-in-seattle-about-to-go-out.html
"I'll state what seems obvious," Ibid., comment string
"Northwest bureau of the San Francisco Chronicle," Rozen to author, 9-5-2014
"The real missed opportunity," Brewster to author, 11-27-2014
"What really pisses me off," quoted in *The Death and Life of American Journalism*, p. 37
"spinning gold on a shoestring," Connelly to author, 12-1-2014

Chapter 24: The Brand Evolves
"When her BlackBerry buzzed," James Ross Gardner, *Fairview Fanny and the Angel of Death*, SeattleMet, 6-17-2010, http://www.seattlemet.com/news-and-profiles/articles/the-seattle-times-pulitzer-prize-maurice-clemmons-0710/1
"The velocity" and ensuing quoted passage, Ibid.
"the beast" and **"The Lord Jesus Christ,"** *A path to murder*, Times, 12-6-2009
"The Times' coverage was fast," Eli Sanders, *The Seattle Times wins a Pulitzer*, The Stranger, 4-12-2010.
"This was a huge, brand-enhancing moment," Chuck Taylor, *As bullets fly*, Crosscut, 12-3-2009
"seattlepi.com did amazingly well," Ibid.
"The Times just told the story," *Fairview Fanny and the Angel of Death*
"the commitment to truth," *Seattle Times reporters honored*, Times,

4-19-2009

"**I watch them beat up everybody,**" quoted in Derek Johnson's DAWGS of WAR Blog, 7-21-2008, http://derekjohnsonbooks.wordpress.com/2008/07/21/the-2000-washington-huskies-respond-to-the-seattle-times/

The "silent death," *Seattle Times wins 2012 Selden Ring Award*, USC Anneberg News, 2-27-2012, http://annenberg.usc.edu/News%20and%20Events/News/120227SeldenRing.aspx

"**Mapping software,**" Michael J. Berens, *How we linked methadone deaths to poverty*, Times, 12-10-2011

"**It's where I have always wanted to end up,**" Linda Mapes, *Ryan Blethen named editorial-page editor*, 5-20-2009

"**This is a great feature story,**" Ryan Blethen to author, 10-8-2014

"**Newspapers should be accountable,**" quoted in *The Death and Life of American Journalism*, p. 158

"**An industry-transforming recession,**" Ryan Blethen, *Recession could fuel new era*, Times, 6-12-2009

"**Like most Washington voters,**" quoted in *Seattle Times goes off the deep end*, Daily Kos, 10-22-2006

"**for coherence**" and "**a way to properly funnel money,**" *The search for a long-term answer for coherence*, The Cascadia Advocate, 4-17-2011, http://www.nwprogressive.org/weblog/2011/04/the-search-for-a-long-term-answer-for-coherence-in-ryan-blethens-columns.html

"**because of an ill-conceived war,**" *Kerry for president*, Times, 9-9-2004

"**I absolutely understood,**" Mackie to author, 12-11-2014

"**I think you'll hurt our brand,**" Ryan Blethen to author, 12-29-2012

"**I offer this solemn promise,**" David Boardman, *A vow to continue impartial reporting*, Times, 10-20-2012

News staff protest letter, quoted in and reproduced in *Times news staffers protest its political ads*, Times, 10-18-2012, http://seattletimes.com/html/localnews/2019468650_adcampaign19m.html

"**horrifying precedent**" and "**a sacred line in journalism,**" quoted in *Candidates for governor weigh in*, The Capitol Record, 10-18-2012

"**If CBS News announced,**" quoted in *Times news staffers protest its political ads*, Times, 10-18-2012, http://seattletimes.com/html/localnews/2019468650_adcampaign19m.html

"**Not even FOX News,**" quoted in *Seattle Times political ad*, Jimromensko.com, 10-18-2012, *http://jimromenesko.com/2012/10/18/seattle-times-political-ad-campaign-absolutely-takes-the-cake/*

"**a cynical ploy,**" quoted in *Candidates for governor weigh in*, The Capitol Record, 10-18-2012

"A significant number of subscribers," quoted in Goldy, *Did the Seattle Times cost Rob McKenna the election?*, Stranger, 11-14-2012
"A truly sad day" and "would there have been the outrage?" Poynter.org MediaWire, 10-19-2012, http://www.poynter.org/news/mediawire/192191/seattle-times-staffers-protest-free-political-ads-in-letter-to-publisher/
Did The Times cost McKenna the election?, *Did the Seattle Times cost Rob McKenna the election?*, Stranger, 11-14-2012
"In close elections, everything," Elway to author, 12-2-2014
"It's a Seattle problem," quoted in Goldy, *Rob McKenna blames me*, Stranger, 1-25-2013, http://slog.thestranger.com/slog/archives/2013/01/25/rob-mckenna-blames-me-for-single-handedly-costing-him-the-election
"The Seattle Times had nothing to do with this," Connelly to author, 12-2-2014
"Courageous actions," *Times editor wins national ethics award*, Times Today File blog, 7-25-2013

Chapter 25: Here to stay?
P-I circulation data, ABC audits, 3-31-2009 and 3-31-2010
Times circulation data, Ibid.
Decline of 25 largest papers, Bill Richards, *circulation figures mixed at Seattle Times*, Crosscut, 4-26-201
"Here to stay," house ad, Times, 2-5-2010
Bank debt and pension fund figures, Linda Mapes, *Seattle Times restructures debt*, Times, 2-5-2010; Bill Richards, *Circulation figures mixed at Times*, Crosscut, 4-26-2010
"horribly mismanaged," Goldy, *Taking financial advice from the Blethens*, Stranger, 3-16-2012
"Sell them or you'll be sorry," quoted in *3-Minute Briefing: Frank Blethen*, Harvard Business School Alumni Bulletin, 3-1-2014, https://www.alumni.hbs.edu/stories/Pages/story-bulletin.aspx?num=3253
$1 trillion public pension liability, *How do we pay*, bizjournals.com/Denver, 2-24-2014
"I always thought that being raised," Kelly to author, 12-9-2014
"a journalist's journalist," Jean Godden, *Loss at The Times*, Crosscut, 7-11-2013
"the heart and soul of this place," and "If Dave hadn't saved," quoted in Linda Mapes, *Top Editor leaving*, Times, 7-10-2013
"I don't wanna get too purple," Dominic Holden, *David Boardman leaving*, Stranger, 7-10-2013
"kick-ass journalism," quoted in *Kathy Best named new editor*,

Times, 9-30-2013
"calmly completing a detailed list," Joel Connelly, *Kathy Best is new editor*, pi.com, 9-30-2013, http://blog.seattlepi.com/seattlepolitics/2013/09/30/kathy-best-is-new-editor-of-seattle-times/
"We're good friends," Dardarian to author, 12-9-2014
"Suki had every reason to hate me," quoted in *Star Tribune's managing editor settles in*, Minnpost, 5-23-2014, http://www.minnpost.com/business/2014/05/star-tribunes-pulitzer-winning-managing-editor-settles-after-seattle-loss; confirmed by Best to author, 12-3-2014
"A world without journalism," *The Death and Life of American Journalism*, p. x
"Even though I didn't know anything," quoted in *Bezos on 'the thing we're changing,'* Capital Playbok, 12-2-2014, http://www.capitalnewyork.com/article/media/2014/12/8557644/bezos-thing-were-changing-emthe-washington-postem
"The world is completely changed," quoted in *Amazon's Jeff Bezos explains*, BITs, http://bits.blogs.nytimes.com/2014/12/02/amazons-bezos-explains-why-he-bought-the-washington-post/?_r=0
"fast-growing mobile readership," quoted in Bloomberg Businesswek, *Jeff Bezos' new plan*, 10-6-2014, http://bits.blogs.nytimes.com/2014/12/02/amazons-bezos-explains-why-he-bought-the-washington-post/?_r=0

Part Two: The Wenatchee World

Abbreviations: The Wenatchee Daily World and Wenatchee World: **WW**; *Buckle of the Power Belt*: **Dappen**; *Rufus Woods, The Columbia River & The Building of Modern Washington*: **Ficken**; *Hail Columbia*: **Sundborg**; *A River Lost*: **Harden**; Seattle Post-Intelligencer: **P-I**; Seattle Times: **Times**; New York Times: **NYT**; Associated Press: **AP**; United Press International: **UPI**; *Wall Street Journal*: **WSJ**; Spokesman-Review: **S-R**; Spokane Chronicle: **Chronicle**; Los Angeles Times: **LAT**; Puget Sound Business Journal, **PSBJ**; Columbia Journalism Review: **CJR**; American Journalism Review: **AJR**

Quotations from Wilfred and Rufus Woods, unless otherwise attributed, are from Legacy Project oral history interviews.

Chapter One: Community

"A river flows," Morgan, *The Columbia*, p. 10
"There's no magic in numbers," Wilfred R. Woods, *On the big 9-5*, WW, 9-30-2014, p. 1
"Splendid runoff ditch," Harden, p. 94
"A master of spin," Dappen, p. 335
"Why, hello Rufus!" Kathryn Woods Haley, *Rufus Woods, Recollections*, p. 3
"You need a library?" Dappen, p.57
"The greatest development project," WW, 7-18-1925, p.1
"Abandoned cabins," Ficken, p. 60
"Ten times the flow," *Cataclysms on the Columbia*, p. 3
"When the flood waters receded," Harden, p. 94
"Grand old ruined roofless hall," quoted in *Cataclysms on the Columbia*, p. 114
"Coyote, rejected in marriage," *Cataclysms on the Columbia*, p. 23
"The abode of evil spirits," quoted in Harden, p. 94
"Unmet and unnoticed," Ficken, pp. 7-9
"Rag-tag and bobtailed," Ibid., p. 9
"Ideally suited to fruit cultivation," Ibid., pp. 11-12
"Tinged with boosterism," Ibid, p. 12
"A Greater Wenatchee," quoted in Ibid., p. 18
"a Bryan Democrat at heart," Ibid., p. 33
"Big eastern capitalists," Ibid., p. 32
"the poorest excuse," Ibid., p. 30
"not to preserve forests," quoted in Goodwin, *The Bully Pulpit*, p. 352
"We do not ever want," Ibid.
"The despairing parents," Ficken, p. 40
"Brave and persistent fight," WW, 7-30-1913, p.1
"he so traitorously deserted," Otto B. Rupp and W.T. Dovell to W.A. Rupp, 5-19-1914, Rupp Personal Correspondence File, Hughes Collection
"The freeing of the Pacific Northwest," Ficken, p. xi
"Colony of the East," WW, 1-26-48
"Should stand for something," Dappen, p. 18
"The last and best part," Ibid.
"A spirit of jealousy," WW, 12-27-10, p. 1
"I'd rather use the space," Kathryn Woods Haley, *Rufus Woods, Recollections*, p. 7
"The booze habit," Dappen, p. 40
"WENATCHEE—WHICH ROAD?" Ibid., p. 81
"Play it big!" quoted in Ficken, p. 17

Chapter Two: Two Million Wild Horses

"A big idea," Sundborg, p. 20
"If ice could dam," Johnson, *Rufus Woods* reprinted in *The Washingtonians*, p. 450
"Necessarily vague," Ficken, p. 61
"The wildest big steam," Woods, *Battle for Grand Coulee Dam*, p. 57, WW, 1944
"THE MOST UNIQUE," WW, 6-7-20; 12-16-1920
"High and dry," Sundborg, P. 24
"He'll never give up," Ibid., P. 39
"A number of Niagras," Sundborg, p. 31
"Revenue from the sale," WW, 1918; quoted in Northwest Power and Conservation Council Columbia River History
"On a new tack," Sundborg, p. 39
"Spent a lot of money," Ibid., p. 28
"Sage brush and jackrabbits," *Grand Coulee Dam: History and Purpose*, Northwest Power and Conservation Council web site
"A grandiose project," Quoted in *Grand Coulee Dam changed face of history*, Times, 8-18-1991
"A country lawyer," Sundborg, P. 225
"Not possessed by ideology," Schwarz, *The New Dealers*, p. 48
"About $85 per acre," Ibid., p. 187
"Plowing sagebrush," quoted in WW, 3-5-13, p. 1
"Deprive individuals of initiative," Schwarz, *The New Dealers*, p. 47
"Farm surplus problem," Ficken, p. 114
"if a rose was placed in his hand," Quoted in James Tobin, *The Man he Became*, p. 297
"The most colossal fraud," Sundborg, p. 225
"The magnitude of its folly!" quoted in Sundborg, p. 225
"Who wants it?" Ibid.
"Seat in the sun," and "did not deign to reply" Quoted in *Rufus Woods: a compassionate crusader*, Times magazine, 10-21-73
"Four battleships," Morgan, *The Columbia*, p. 146
"A big frog," *Rambling Reporter*, Pittsburgh Press, 10-22-1936
"The children love," *Rambling Reporter*, Pittsburgh Press, 9-25-1939
"The poor waitress," Ibid.
"You must always remember," Morris, *The Rise of Theodore Roosevelt*, p. 356
"Made up in grease paint," Ficken, pp. 167-168
"Can't look me in the eye," Kathryn Woods Haley, *Rufus Woods, Recollections*, p. 3

Chapter Three: "What a heritage!"
"Good fellowship," Ficken, p. 89
"An all-time low," Ibid., p. 141
"A troglodyte," Dappen, p. 141
"Magnificent Santa Claus," Ficken, p. 146
"Foreign control," WW, 8-7-40, p. 1
"THEY ALL FAILED!" Woods, *Battle for Grand Coulee Dam*, cover, WW, 1944
"Lost to faraway areas," Ficken, p. xiii
"Would risk a cent," quoted in Dappen, p. 73
"Water water water," quoted in Ficken, p. xiv
"Hall of Fame," NYT, *Rufus Woods Again Honored*, 12-2-1949
"Damn O'Sullivan," Sundborg, p. 434
"Cultural savager," quoted in Rufus Woods column, WW, 3-20-2012
"with an open mind," Ibid.
"Promising technology," Christine Pratt, *Over great heights*, WW, 10-9-2014, p. 1
"Drove leisurely to Toronto," WW, 6-6-1950, p. 1
"On the same terms," WW, 6-6-50, pp. 4-10
"He was a dreamer," *His Idealism and His Unflagging Persistence*, Times, 6-1-1950
"THE DREAM AND THE VISION LIVE ON," WW, 6-6-1950, p.1

Chapter Four: Wilf's World
"Forgot" to tell," Dappen, p. 170
"Rarely afford new equipment," Ibid., p. 107
"Did most of the dirty work," Ibid., p. 142
"Made a family of the world," Ibid., p. 140-142
"We wanted to own," Ibid., p. 143
"Farm-in-a-Day," *Man returns after winning farm 50 years ago*, WW, 5-28-2002
"437,000 acres," *1950s, a decade to remember*, WW, 6-20-2012
"Building of that plant," *1950s, a decade to remember: Korean War results in quick completion of Alcoa Plant*, WW, 6-19-2012
"Tests showed," *Dilemma: Growth while still saving the environment*, Times, 12-28-1969
"Calling the PUD socialistic," *1950s, a decade to remember: Korean War results in quick completion of Alcoa Plant*, WW, 6-19-2012
"A army of paid help," *PUD aims need publicity*, Times, 4-13-1956
"A fearless, high-principled newspaper," Dappen, p. 175
"The profit-sharing plan," Ibid., p. 143
"Stiff medicine," *As a state editor sees it*, Times, 7-2-1958
"In those sessions," *Dilemma: Growth while still saving the*

environment, Times, 12-28-1969
"Water was an especially volatile," Dappen, p. 144
"Subject to the same threat," *State agencies clash,* Times, 3-19-1969
"Nobody would stand for a pulp mill," *Dilemma: Growth while still saving the environment,* Times, 12-28-1969
"Shoot-from-the-hip zealots," Ibid.
"This disclosure business," *Publisher resigns,* Times, 12-30-1976
"A classic big lie," Times, 10-15-1964
"Could be found in the middle," Times, 11-5-1967, p. 11
"We lost the war," Dappen, p. 144
"On Wilf's watch," Ibid., p. 146

Chapter Five: The Second Rufus
"A hoax based on junk science," *The True Alar Story,* OnEarth Magazine, 3-22-2011
"Regulated, approved manner," quoted in H. Aaron Cohl, *Are We Scaring Ourselves to Death?*
"In laboratory tests," *Alar: The Great Apple Scare,* Heartland magazine, 3-1-2007
"Local retail sales," *Wenatchee Shines in Economic Gloom,* WW, 10-22-1992
"Welcome to Boom Town!" WW, 1-12-1992. p. 1
"But Alar is a potent carcinogen," *The Alar 'Scare' Was for Real,* CJR, September/October 1996
"Unnaturally tranquil rubes," *Prozacville, USA,* Psychology Today, 1-1-1995
"Chewed through miles," *The fires of 1994,* Columbian, 8-2-2004
"A loss of innocence," *Norman Rockwell meets hell,* Chicago Tribune, 8-20-1995
"Norman Rockwell meets hell," Ibid.
"Little Town of Horrors," *Little Town of Horrors,* LAT, 7-25-1995
"Bad news beyond imagination," 5-5-1995, WW, p. 1
"There's something not quite right," quoted in *Practicing Journalism,* p. 3
"Connecting the dots," Dappen, pp. 264
"Passed around like party favors," *Witch Hunt in Wenatchee?,* AJR, June 1996
"Patently nonsensical" and "blindly credulous," quoted in Ibid.
"like a complete goober," quoted in Ibid.
"Shameless pretensions," quoted in Ibid.
"Simply amazing," Dappen, p. 266
"The intensity of the experience," Warner to author, 11-19-2013
"I realized that was a lie," Ibid., 11-20-13

"Tight little island" and "Everything's different," quoted in *Witch Hunt in Wenatchee?*, AJR, June 1996
"A runaway train," Dappen, p. 268

Chapter Six: "Now what the hell?"
"The best paper of its size," Dappen, p. 313
"Asking tough questions," Ibid., p. 276
"Most papers would have stuck," Ibid., p. 285
"75 percent of print classified revenue," Pew Research Center, http://stateofthemedia.org/2013/newspapers-stabilizing-but-still-threatened/newspapers-by-the-numbers/
"77 Gannett Company daily newspapers," http://gannettblog.blogspot.com/2011/09/heres-2000-2010-circ-for-nearly-all.html
"We hung on," *Wenatchee World layoffs*, WW, 2-1-2009
"I don't think it's up to the government," quoted in *Newspapers in WA get tax break during bad times*, AP, 7-2-2009
"unfettered predatory capitalism," *The sorry values of Amazon*, WW, 4-11-2012
"Complaining is not a strategy," Bezos on *60 minutes*, 12-1-2013
"Newspapers continue to reign," quoted in *When it comes to billionaires buying newspapers*, Forbes, 8-11-2013
"I've enjoyed covering the Eastside," quoted in Knute Berger, *The Seattle Times's suburban retreat*, Crosscut, 4-8-2008, http://crosscut.com/2008/04/08/mossback/13238/iThe-Seattle-Timesi-suburban-retreat/

Chapter Seven: Community Glue
"a different niche," Dappen, p. 282
"the genius of the old Daily World," Ibid., p. 283
Facebook statistics: Business Insider, *7 Statistics About Facebook Users*, 11-16-13; Pew Research Journalism Project, 11-4-13, http://www.journalism.org/
"A billion unique visitors," Ken Auletta, *Outside the Box*, p. 56, New Yorker, 2-3-2014
"Beyond my wildest dreams," quoted in *Company left a trail of trouble*, WW, 5-5-2011
"If only," *Someone should have stopped us*, WW, 12-10-2011
"an impassioned argument," *SEC document outlines deceit*, WW, 11-9-2013
"shameful," Ibid.

Chapter Eight: Connecting
Interviews with Joe Pitt, Cal FitzSimmons, Frank and Ryan Blethen
"I swear, it was like 24 hours of terror," quoted in *Remembering the nightmare*, WW, 8-31-2014, p. 1
"Rate card data," Pew Research Center's Project for Excellence in Journalism, *The State of the News Media 2013*, http://stateofthemedia.org/2013/newspapers-stabilizing-but-still-threatened/newspapers-by-the-numbers/

Chapter Nine: A few nuggets
"it feels like a prankster," Dappen, p. 140
"some of us to genuflect," *New video*, WW, 3-7-2013
"The arc of intergenerational," Layman to author, 12-23-2013
"There's no obstructionist vetting," Jasinek to author, 12-17-2013
"In the game of life," *Our Salute to the Public*, WW, 3-1-2007
"What was true then," *In celebration of our first 100 years*, WW, 1-2-2005
"The day the stockholders," quoted in Dappen, p. 257

Afterthoughts & Acknowledgements
Elway interview, Danny Westneat, *Voters in a funk*, Times, 10-19-2014, B-1
Obama quote, Michael O'Brien, *Obama Open to Newspaper Bailout Bill*, The Hill, 9-20-2009; http://thehill.com/blogs/blog-briefing-room/news/59523-obama-open-to-newspaper-bailout-bill

Bibliography

Allen, John Eliot, and Burns, Marjorie, with Sargent, Sam C., *Cataclysms on the Columbia*, Timber Press, Portland, 1986
Ames, William E., and Simpson, Roger A., *Unionism or Hearst*, Pacific Northwest Labor History Association, Seattle, 1978
Atkins, Gary L., *Gay Seattle, Stories of Exile and Belonging*, University of Washington Press, Seattle, 2013
Barber, Mike, *More Lives Than a Cat: A Chronological History of the Seattle Post-Intelligencer*, unpublished manuscript, copyright 1996/2009
Bauer, Eugene E., *Boeing, The First Century & Beyond*, Second Edition, TABA Publishing Inc., Issaquah, WA, 2006
Becker, Paula, Stein Alan J. and the HistoryLink staff, *The Future Remembered, The 1962 Seattle World's Fair and Its Legacy*, Seattle Center Foundation in association with HistoryInk/HistoryLink.org, Seattle, 2011
Berger, Knute, *Space Needle, The Spirit of Seattle*, Documentary Media LLC, Seattle, 2012
Berner, Richard C., *Seattle 1900-1920*, Charles Press, Seattle, 1991;
    Seattle 1921-1940, Charles Press, Seattle, 1992
    Seattle Transformed, Thomson-Shore Inc., 1999
Billington, Ken, *People, Politics & Public Power*, Washington Public Utility Districts' Association, Seattle, WA, 1988
Boswell, Sharon A., and McConaghy, Lorraine, *Raise Hell and Sell Newspapers, Alden J. Blethen & The Seattle Times*, WSU Press, Pullman, 1996
    100 Years of a Newspaper and its Region, The Seattle Times, 1997
Bottenberg, Ray, *Grand Coulee Dam, Images of America*, Arcadia Publishing, 2008
Brewster, David, *The Real Seattle Times*, Seattle magazine,

November 1969
Brewster, David, and Buerge, David M. (editors), *Washingtonians, A Biographical Portrait of the State*, Sasquatch Books, Seattle, 1988
Brokaw, Tom, *The Greatest Generation*, Random House, New York, 1998
Chambliss, William J., *On the Take*, Second Edition, Indiana University Press, Bloomington, 1988
Clark, Norman H., *The Dry Years*, University of Washington Press, Seattle, 1988
Corr, O. Casey, *KING, The Bullitts of Seattle and Their Communications Empire*, University of Washington Press, Seattle, 1996
Crowley, Walt, *Rites of Passage*, University of Washington Press, Seattle, 1995
Dappen, Andy, *Buckle of the Power Belt, Recollections of The Wenatchee World's First 100 Years*, The Wenatchee World, Wenatchee, WA, 2005
Davies, David R., *The Postwar Decline of American Newspapers, 1945-1965*, Praeger Publishers, Westport, CT., 2006
Davis, John, and **Quinn, Cathy**, *The Blethen Family and the Seattle Times Company*, Harvard Business School, 2001
Dorpat, Paul, and McCoy, Genevieve, *Building Washington, A History of Washington State Public Works*, Tartu Publications, Seattle, 1998
Duncan, Don, *Washington, The First One Hundred Years*, The Seattle Times, 1989
 Meet Me at the Center, Seattle Center Foundation, 1992
Dunne, Peter Finley, *Observations by Mr. Dooley*, Harper & Brothers Publishers, New York, 1902
Dunsire, Charles, *Mr. Press*, Writer's Showcase, Lincoln, Neb., 2000
Dwyer, William L., *Ipse Dixit, How the World Looks to a Federal Judge*, University of Washington Press, Seattle, 2007
Dyar, Ralph E., *News For An Empire*, The Caxton Printers Ltd., Caldwell, Idaho, 1952
Ficken, Robert E., *Rufus Woods, The Columbia River & The Building of Modern Washington*, WSU Press, Pullman, WA, 1995
Frederick, Timothy, *Albert F. Canwell, An Oral History*,

Washington State Oral History Program, Office of the Secretary of State, Olympia, 1997
Goodwin, Doris Kearns, *The Bully Pulpit*, Simon & Schuster, New York, 2013
Gray, Charlotte, *Gold Diggers*, Counterpoint, Berkeley, Calif., 2010
Haley, Kathryn Woods, *Rufus Woods, Recollections of Kathryn Woods Haley*, Tacoma, 2011
Harden, Blaine, *A River Lost, The Life and Death of The Columbia*, W.W. Norton & Company, New York, 2012
Harris, Mark, *Five Came Back*, The Penguin Press, New York, 2014
Hirt, Paul W., *The Wired Northwest, The History of Electric Power, 1870s-1970s*, University Press of Kansas, Lawrence, 2012
Hobsbawm, Eric, *Fractured Times, Culture and Society in the 20th Century*, The New Press, New York, 2013
Holbrook, Stewart H., *The Age of Moguls*, Doubleday & Company Inc., Garden City, N.Y., 1953
Hughes, John C., *Slade Gorton, A Half Century in Politics*, Thomson-Shore, 2011
   John Spellman, Politics Never Broke His Heart, Thomson-Shore, 2013
Johnson, Jalmar, *Builders of the Northwest*, Dodd, Mead & Co., New York, 1963
Kaiser, David, *No End Save Victory*, Basic Books, New York, 2014
Karolevitz, Robert F., *Kemper Freeman Sr. and the Bellevue Story*, The Homestead Publishers, Mission Hill, S.D., 1984
Kershner, Jim, *Albert F. Canwell*, HistoryLink.org Essay 9887, 2011
Layman, William D., *Native River, The Columbia Remembered, Priest Rapids to the International Boundary*, WSU Press, Pullman, 2002
McCallum, John D., *Dave Beck*, The Writing Works Inc., Mercer Island, WA, 1978
McChesney, Robert W., and Nichols, John, *The Death and Life of American Journalism*, Nation Books, 2011
McConaghy, Lorraine, *The Seattle Times's Cold War Pulitzer Prize*, Pacific Northwest Quarterly, 89:1, Winter 1997/98, pp.

21-32
McCool, Daniel, *River Republic, The Fall and Rise of America's Rivers*, Columbia University Press, N.Y., 2012
McCormmach, Russell, *Power Lines, Giant Hydroelectric Power in the Pacific Northwest, An Era and a Career*, Third Edition, Palimpsest Books, Eugene, Ore., 2012
Mencken, H.L., *A Gang of Pecksniffs*, Arlington House Publishers, New Rochelle, N.Y., 1975
Merritt, Davis, *Knightfall: Knight Ridder and How the Erosion of Newspaper Journalism Is Putting Democracy at Risk*, AMACOM, New York, N.Y., 2005
Morgan, Murray, *The Columbia*, Superior Publishing Co., Seattle, 1949
    Skid Road, The Viking Press, New York, 1951
    The Dam, The Viking Press, New York, 1954
    Century 21, The Story of the Seattle World's Fair, Acme Press Inc., Seattle, 1963
Nasaw, David, *The Chief, the Life of William Randolph Hearst*, Houghton Mifflin Company, New York, 2000
Nelson, Gerald B., *Seattle, The Life and Times of an American City*, Alfred A. Knopf, New York, 1997
Neuberger, Richard, *Our Promised Land*, reprint edition, University of Idaho Press, Moscow, 1989
Newell, Gordon, *Rogues, Buffoons & Statesmen*, Superior Publishing Co., Seattle, 1975
    Totem Tales of Old Seattle, Superior Publishing Co., Seattle, 1956
Pettegree. Andrew, *The Invention of News*, Yale University Press, New Haven, 2014
Pitzer, Paul C., *Grand Coulee, Harnessing a Dream*, WSU Press, Pullman, 1994
Potts, Ralph Bushnell, *Seattle Heritage*, Seattle Printing Co., 1955
Procter, Ben, *William Randolph Hearst, The Later Years, 1911-1951*, Oxford University Press, 2007
Rader, Chris, and Behler, Mark, *Wenatchee*, Images of America, Arcadia Publishing, Charleston, S.C., 2012
Rader, Melvin, *False Witness*, University of Washington Press, Seattle, 1969
Rieder, Ross, *Seattle Post-Intelligencer/Newspaper Guild Strike*

1936, HistoryLink.org File 2495, 2009

Roberge, Earl, *Columbia, Great River of the West*, Chronicle Books, San Francisco, 1985

Robbins, Tom, *Tibetan Peach Pie*, Ecco, an imprint of Harper Collins Publishers, New York, 2014

Rosellini, Albert D., *Legislative Oral History Project*, Washington State Archives, Olympia, 1987

Sale, Roger, *Seattle Past to Present*, University of Washington Press, Seattle, 1976

Scates, Shelby, *Warren G. Magnuson and the Shaping of Twentieth-Century America*, University of Washington Press, Seattle, 1997

War & Politics By Other Means, University of Washington Press, Seattle, 2000

Scott, George W., *Governors of Washington*, Civitas Press, Seattle, 2012

Seldes, George, *Lords of the Press*, Julian Messner Inc., New York, 1938

Sell, T.M., *Wings of Power, Boeing and the Politics of Growth in the Northwest*, University of Washington Press, Seattle, 2001

Schwarz, Jordan A., *The New Dealers*, Alfred A. Knopf, New York, 1993

Smith, Payton, *Rosellini, Immigrants' Son and Progressive Governor*, University of Washington Press, Seattle, 1997

Speidel, William C., *Sons of the Profits*, Nettle Creek Publishing Co., Seattle, 1967

Steinle, Paul, and **Brown, Sara**, *Practicing Journalism*, Marion Street Press, Portland, 2014

Sterling, Robert J., *Legend & Legacy, The Story of Boeing and its People*, St. Martin's Press, New York, 1992

Sundborg, George, *Hail Columbia*, The MacMillan Co., New York, 1954

Swanberg, W.A., *Citizen Hearst*, Charles Scribner's Sons, New York, 1961

Tate, Cassandra, *Seattle Post-Intelligencer (1863-2009)*, HistoryLink.org File 8956, 2009

Taylor, Quintard, *The Forging of a Black Community*, University of Washington Press, Seattle, 1994

Thomas, Christy, *Bylines and Bygones*, Exposition Press, New York, 1964

Tobin, James, *The Man he Became*, Simon & Schuster, New York, 2013
Tollefson, Gene, *BPA & The Struggle for Power at Cost*, Bonneville Power Administration, Portland, Ore., 1987
Un-American Activities in Washington State 1948, Second Report, Washington State Printer, Olympia, 1948
Underwood, Doug, *When MBAs Rule the Newsroom*, Columbia University Press, New York, 1995
Van Dyk, Ted, *Heroes, Hacks & Fools, Memoirs from the Political Inside*, University of Washington Press, Seattle, 2007
Warren, James R., *The War Years, A Chronicle of Washington State in World War II*, History Ink/University of Washington Press, Seattle, 2000
Watson, Emmett, *Digressions of a Native Son*, The Pacific Institute, Seattle, 1982
Once Upon a Time In Seattle, Lesser Seattle Publishing, Seattle, 1992
My Life In Print, Lesser Seattle Publishing, 1993
Wicker, Tom, *On Press*, The Viking Press, N.Y., 1978
Williams, Hill, *The Restless Northwest, A Geological Story*, WSU Press, Pullman, 2002
Wilson, William H., *Shaper of Seattle, Regional Heber Thomson's Pacific Northwest*, WSU Press, Pullman, 2009

"...as I look back over a misspent life, I find myself more and more convinced that I had more fun doing news reporting than in any other enterprise. It is really the life of kings." —H.L. Mencken

Afterthoughts & Acknowledgements

You were supposed to be 10 before you could get a paper route at The Aberdeen Daily World, but my mom knew the circulation manager. I was barely 9 in the fall of 1952 when I set out on my new Schwinn to deliver The World along Simpson Avenue in Aberdeen's mud-puddled west end. Pretty soon, the kid who delivered the Seattle Post-Intelligencer in the morning along the same route quit. For the next two years I was in the clover with two jobs, earning about $40 a month. The tips at Christmas time were terrific. One oldtimer always gave me a dollar, and a Finnish lady greeted me one drizzly December morning with a sack of homemade chocolate-frosted donuts. What got me down was the Sunday P-I. It was too fat to wrap with a rubber band and lob. I broke a window the first time I tried it.

When I was 14, by happenstance, we moved next door to the people who owned The World, Pete and Primrose Foelkner. I was washing one of their Buicks one afternoon when Mrs. Foelkner, the Society editor, asked me what I wanted to be when I grew up. "A newspaper reporter!" I declared. Before long I was filling paste pots in the newsroom and raising hell as editor of the Aberdeen High School Ocean

Breeze. At the University of Puget Sound, I met historian Murray Morgan, who regaled me with his experiences as city editor of the Grays Harbor Washingtonian, Hoquiam's morning daily, in the 1940s. I told him I was torn between becoming a history teacher or a newspaperman. "You'll have a lot more fun as a newspaperman," he said.

  I spent 42 years at The Daily World and had the time of my life. There were times when I seriously considered taking a job with a bigger paper. It always came down to a sense of place. Gritty old Grays Harbor, awash in history, was home. I hugely admired Jim King, the avuncular editor of The Seattle Times. But my dream was to make The Daily World as good a paper as The Wenatchee World, for early on I came to see Wilfred Woods and his editors as the gold standard of community journalism. I never succeeded, but it wasn't for a lack of trying. I worked with some of the best people in the business and was proud when they cited me as a mentor.

Since I already knew so many of the people who play key roles in this book, I thought it would be "a snap," as I foolishly boasted to my teammates 14 months ago. The more I dug, the harder it got—especially concerning The Seattle Times and the endlessly fascinating Blethens. Here are some things I now know for sure:

  It's a lot easier to be the publisher's son in Wenatchee than in Seattle.

  It's ironic that so many newspaper people are nervous about being interviewed, which italicizes my gratitude to those who generously offered their help and spoke so candidly—Frank Blethen and Rufus Woods in particular.

Some people are going to be disappointed by things I included and things I left out. Others won't believe certain facts. I look forward to reading their books.

For now at least, this one ends without an end. It's more like "to be continued." Can two exceptional family-owned newspapers, one big, one small, survive in a digitized world? Or as The Times put it in a recent Sunday feature, "So little time, so many apps."

As the 2014 general election drew near, Seattle Times columnist Danny Westneat interviewed my old friend, pollster Stuart Elway. A childhood steeped in grass-roots politics—his father was mayor of Hoquiam, a state legislator and candidate for Congress—led Elway to a Ph.D. in communications. In the 1990s he conducted a series of Front Porch Forums for The Times as the newspaper reached out to an increasingly fragmented readership. Elway has been gauging Northwest voter sentiment for four decades. "In all that time," Westneat wrote, Elway says "we are in the biggest funk" he's ever seen. "People are very dissatisfied with what's going on, but the really unusual thing is there's no anger or energy for change going along with that. ...This has become the 'to hell with it' election." Westneat read the results as "an indictment of the political leaders in this state. It's not that people are disgusted with lawmakers for doing the wrong things—because that would suggest action of some sort. Voters are completely ...bored. Uninspired. Tuned out."

I agree, but we're also suffering from the ennui of information overload and intellectual laziness.

President Obama, whose landmark 2008 victory owed much to social media, observed a year later that good journalism is "critical to the health of our democracy," adding: "I am concerned that if the direction of the news is all blogosphere, all opinions, with no serious fact-checking, no serious attempts to put stories in context, that what you will end up getting is people shouting at each other across the void but not a lot of mutual understanding."

Here are some of the people who care passionately about mutual understanding and helped me tell this story:

Afterthoughts & Acknowledgements

Special thanks to Sharon A. Boswell and Lorraine McConaghy, who literally wrote the book on Colonel Alden J. Blethen; to Robert E. Ficken, for his painstakingly researched—as usual—biography of Rufus Woods; to George Sundborg and Murray Morgan, for the best books about the Grand Coulee Dam and the Columbia, and to Andy Dappen for his invaluable collection of stories chronicling The Wenatchee World's first hundred years.

I am also indebted to: Gerry Alexander, David Ammons, N. Christian Anderson, Rick Anderson, Doug Barker, Knute Berger, Hal Bernton, Kathy Best, Rob Blethen, Ryan Blethen, David Boardman, David Brewster, Mark Brown, Angelo Bruscas, Jeff Burlingame, James Bush, Peter Callaghan, Mindy Cameron, John Carlson, Joel Connelly, Casey Corr, Kelly Corr, Suki Dardarian, Lance Dickie, John Dodge, William Downing, Rick Doyle, Don Duncan, Charles and Judy Dunsire, Stuart Elway, Dan Evans, Steve Excell, Mike Fancher, Alan Fisco, Cal FitzSimmons, James Ross Gardner, Wyatt Gardiner, Tommi Halvorsen Gatlin, Dave Gauger, Mary Ann Gwinn, Ken Hatch, Walter Hatch, John Hamer, David Horsey, Curtis Huber, Tom Ikeda, Ian Ith, Peter Jackson, Peter Jansen, Gary Jasinek, Larry Jordan, Ron Judd, Carolyn Kelly, Larry Lange, Sean Lanksbury, William D. Layman, Greg Lehman, Alex MacLeod, Jill Mackie, Marco Martinez, Rob McKenna, W. Davis "Buzz" Merritt Jr., Bob and Sue Pennington Merry, Carl Molesworth, Ralph Munro, Scott North, Susan Paterno, Joe Pitt, David Postman, Eric Pryne, Ken Raske, Sam Reed, Bill Richards, Tony Ridder, Dee Riggs, Kate Riley, Douglas Ross, Cliff Rowe, Lee and Sydney Rozen, Eli Sanders, Erika Schultz, Darryl Sclater, Nina Shapiro, Mason Sizemore, Shirley Stone, Chuck Taylor, Terry Tazioli, Rowland Thompson, Jonathan Tolton, Robert F. Utter, Jim Vesely, Tracy Warner, Frank Wetzel, Steven Wood and Gretchen Woods. Also, endless thanks to my teammates: Trova Heffernan, Lori Larson, Laura Mott, Carleen Jackson, Holly Harris, the amazing staff of the Washington State Library and Secretary of State Kim Wyman.

John C. Hughes, Olympia, October 1, 2015

Index

4-H Club 245
60 Minutes 278, 302, 344
707 jetliner 62, 321
737 jetliner 4, 144
747 jetliner 99
9/11 attacks 5, 144, 183, 188, 193, 203
13 Coins restaurant 35

Aberdeen Daily World, The 244, 352, 353
Aberdeen, Wash. 74, 111, 244, 284, 306, 352
ACLU 51, 320
Acohido, Byron 144, 145
Adams, Brock 130, 131, 148, 328
Adelphian Choir 276
AdWeek 139,
Aeronautical Mechanics Union 45
Akron Law Review 108, 325, 326
Alar 278, 343
Alaska 13, 45, 123, 254, 268, 274
Alaska-Yukon-Pacific Exposition 64
Albany, Oregon 86
Albeni Falls 249
Alcoa 269, 270, 279, 280, 342
Alexander, J.D. 147, 160, 167
Alford, A.L. "Butch" 305
Alger, Horatio 9
Alice in Wonderland 42
Al-Jazeera 181
Allen, Paul 94, 122, 151, 192, 200, 206
Allen, Raymond 52, 53, 320, 321
Allen, William 46, 62
Allied Daily Newspapers 173, 326, 327
Almquist, June Anderson 75, 76, 121
al-Qaeda 183
Amazon.com 152, 165, 233, 234, 339, 344
American Journalism Review 65, 139, 165, 168, 281

American League 106
American Newspaper Guild 35, 37, 59
American Public Power Association 271,
American Society of Civil Engineers 250
American Weekly 25
Ames, William E. 35, 318, 319, 346
Anacortes, Wash. 284
Anderson, Eva Greenslit 255, 270
Anderson, Lenny 60, 61
Anderson, N. Christian III "Chris" 6, 86-88, 355
Anderson, Rick 47, 90, 320, 329
Anderson, Ross 80, 119, 123, 170
Andreessen, Marc 151
Angelos, Constantine "Gus" 60, 61, 74
AOL 151
Argus, The 12, 17, 20, 38, 104
Argyros, George 112
Arizona 43, 83, 146, 299
Arizona State University 82
Armistice Day 27
Armstrong, Ken 215-217
Army Corps of Engineers 251
Arrow Lake 273
Asbury, Bill 98, 100, 108
Associated Press Managing Editors' Association 287
Associated Press, The 30, 87, 89, 247, 272, 277, 287, 288
Association of Fundraising Professionals 310
Astoria 273
AT&T 152
Atlanta Journal, The 239
Auburn, Wash. 45
Audit Bureau of Circulations 322

Index

B-17 "Flying Fortress" 44, 261
Bagley, Clarence 208
Bainbridge Island 45
Baker, Geoff 231
Balch, Dick 85
Balter, Joni 217
Barnes, Andrew 132
Barnes, C. Richard 178, 179
Baron Munchausen 249
Batten, James K. 141
Bean, Lamont 107
Bean, Judge Roy 10
Beck, Dave 34-39, 45, 46
Belafonte, Harry 58
Bellevue American 42
Bellevue Journal-American 5, 89, 104, 105, 112
Bellingham Herald, The 252, 253
Bench-Bar-Press Committee 272
Bend, Ore. 289
Bennack, Frank A. Jr. 101-103, 108, 163, 164, 198, 207
Berens, Michael J. 216, 217, 231
Berger, Knute 4, 5, 346
Berlin, Germany 48
Berlin Airlift 265
Berlin, Richard E. 106
Berner, Richard C. 19, 26, 27, 346
Best, Kathy 167, 212-214, 217, 229, 230, 231, 281, 355
Bezos, Jeff 152, 233, 234, 291
Billingsley, Kirby 257, 269-271
bin Laden, Osama 181
Black Press 6
Blethen Corporation 43, 77, 78, 88, 93, 95-97, 117, 141, 168, 194
Blethen v. Hearst 186
Blethen, Colonel Alden J. 1-3, 8-22, 64, 67, 165, 203
Blethen, Alden J. Jr. "Joe" 16, 18, 21, 24, 25
Blethen, Alden J. III "Buster" 22, 31, 32, 84
Blethen, Alden J. IV "Buster" 84, 86, 91-97, 117, 135, 140, 170, 200
Blethen, Barbara "Bobbi" 135
Blethen, Basil 153, 155
Blethen, Cal 158
Blethen, Charlene 155
Blethen, Christine (Farrey) 135, 155, 158

Blethen, General Clarance B. "C.B." 3, 16, 18, 21, 22, 24, 25, 27-34, 36, 38, 40, 41, 44
Blethen, Clarance B. II "Judge" 22, 32, 40-44
Blethen, Courtney (Rifkin) 135, 221, 235
Blethen, David 135, 235
Blethen, Debbie 170
Blethen, Diane 43, 83
Blethen, Florence 16, 24
Blethen, Francis A. Sr. "Frank" 22, 23, 32, 40-42, 50, 56, 64, 76, 77, 82
Blethen, Francis A. Jr. "Frank": "last of buckaroo publishers," 3; resists advertiser pressure, 3, 4, 146; "it's a legacy," 4; "legend in his own mind," 4; tattoo, 236; ADD, 83; scathing portrayal of father's stepmother, 23; goal to build family harmony, 24; admiration for Elmer Todd, 31; birth 1945, 43; parents divorce, 43; 1950 Pulitzer "set the standard," 55; relationship with father, 82, 83; balks at working for Times, 82; characterizes mother, 83; Pennington as "father figure" mentor, 83; comes to work at Times, 83; first year "miserable," 84; falling out with Uncle Jack, 85; named associate publisher, then publisher at Walla Walla, 86; returns to Seattle, 91; uncle and Pennington in dispute over bylaws, 91-94; cousins discuss legacy, 94, 95; revised bylaws, 96; attends Harvard, 97; objects to JOA, 101, 102, 109; embarrassed by WPPSS disclosures, 111; Pennington's death, 115, 116; "like a father to me," 117; becomes publisher, 117; recruits new blood, cites "core values," 121, 122; boosts newsroom, 122, 123; backs Dukakis, liberalizes edit page, 124-126; opposes estate taxes, 127; "no model of political consistency," 129; backs Adams expose, 131; buys Yakima daily, 132; squabbles with Tony Ridder, 132-134; bans tobacco ads, 133; battle with Ridders heats up, 137-139; goes nose to nose with Tony, 139-141; offers to buy out Ridder, 141, 142; "Doggate," 142-144; visits Maine, buys papers, 153-156; changes position on gay marriage, 159; Times goes morning, 160-165; growth and accomplishments, 168, 169; rejects $750 million buyout offer,

169, 170; costly strike, 170-181; "fuck you" e-mail, 173, Sizemore leaves, 183, 184; battle over stop-loss provision, 186-192; sells real estate, 192; invites Ridder to make offer, 193, 194; JOA settlement reached, 197-199; promotes Boardman, 199; struggle to survive, 200-202; Ryan and Rob sent to Maine, 202; Ryan returns, 203; Maine papers for sale, 203; reaction to death of P-I, 210; Lakewood shooting Pulitzer, 212-215; investigative excellence, 216, 217; Ryan named edit page editor, 217; McKenna ad decision, 217-223; Boardman departs, 224; bank debt refinanced, 226; Maine papers sold, 227; promotes Best, 229; recession weathered, 232, 233
Blethen, James 135, 235, 236
Blethen, Jessica 135, 235
Blethen, John A. "Jack" 22, 32, 41, 42, 44, 56, 64, 69, 71, 76, 79, 85, 86, 88, 91, 92, 93-95, 101, 114, 117, 136, 140
Blethen, John P. 84, 92, 94, 96, 135
Blethen, Kathleen Ryan 42, 43, 83
Blethen, Kerry (Quinn) 158, 135, 235
Blethen, Marion 16, 24
Blethen, Rachael Kingsley "Rae" 22, 24
Blethen, Robert C. "Bob" 84, 93, 95, 96, 117, 128, 135, 153, 155, 165, 200
Blethen, Robert C. Jr. "Rob" 135, 157, 158, 202, 203, 234, 235, 355
Blethen, Rose Ann (Mrs. Alden J. Sr.) 16, 32
Blethen, Ryan 7, 31, 135, 157, 158, 202, 230, 233, 234, 236, 307
Blethen, Sue 135, 155
Blethen, Trace 135, 158
Blethen, William K. Sr. "Bill" 22, 32, 41, 42, 50, 56, 64, 69, 76, 84, 94
Blethen, William K. Jr. "Will" 84, 93-96, 117, 128, 135, 153, 155, 165, 200
Blonk, Hu 253, 254, 271, 272, 298
Boardman, David 4, 7, 113, 125, 130, 131, 145, 146, 188, 199, 207, 211-213, 216, 217, 219-222, 224, 229, 231
Boeing Co., the 3, 31, 44-46, 58, 62, 63, 65, 85, 98, 115, 144, 146, 154, 161, 165, 171, 180, 183, 216, 226, 261
Boettiger, John 38, 39

Bolsheviks 27
Bone, Scott 20
Bonneville Power Administration 260, 261, 263, 279
Boren, Virginia 58
Borglum, Gutzon 252
Boswell, Sharon A. 8, 10, 19, 153, 154, 346, 355
Bothell, Wash. 132
Bradley, Ed 278
Brainerd, Erastus 16, 17
Brando, Marlon 72
Brazier, Carl E. Sr. 40, 58
Brazier, Carl E. Jr. 58
Brazier, Dorothy Brant 58
Bremner, Anne 190, 198
Brewster, David 78, 79, 99, 104, 105, 107-109, 135, 136, 143, 148, 185, 187, 192, 195, 198, 210, 355
Bridges, Harry 35, 39, 45, 48
British Columbia 90, 273
Brougham, Royal 26, 57, 60, 169, 210
Brown, Beriah Jr. 14
Brown, Bob 136
Brune, Tom 145
Bruscas, Angelo 146, 147, 355
Bryan, William Jennings 12, 124, 243
Bryant, Arlene 124
Bryant, Hilda 104
Bulletin, The 4, 25
Bullitt, Harriet 308
Bunting, Ken 147, 166
Bunzel, Peter 73
Bureau of Reclamation 254, 261, 271
Bush, George H.W. 125, 126
Bush, George W. 127, 132, 176, 191, 202, 203, 218, 219
Bush, James 166
Business World 303
Byrd, Joann 148, 281

Cable News Network 286
Caen, Herb 47
Cahill, Harry 32, 41
California 33, 72, 227, 273, 274, 278, 279
Callaghan, Peter 231, 355
Cameron, Mindy 114, 121, 128, 129, 157-159, 176, 184, 228, 355

Index

Canim yacht 28
Canova, Greg 190, 191, 198
Cantwell, Maria 127, 218, 219
Canwell, Albert F. 48-54, 106
Canyon Creek Lodge 52
Carlson, Edward E. "Eddie" 65
Carlson, John 128, 355
Carroll, Charles O. "Chuck" 67, 80
Cashmere, Wash. 256, 280
Cassidy, Mike 293, 294
Central Area 71
Central Washington University 308
Centralia, Wash. 27, 306
Century 21 64, 66, 80
Chadwick, Harry 17, 20
Chamber of Commerce, Seattle 14, 21, 50, 58
Chamber of Commerce, Spokane 250, 261
Chamber of Commerce, Wenatchee 299
Chambers, Tom 195
Chandler automobile 240
Charlotte Observer 97
Cheever, Susan 6
Chelan 245, 268
Chelan Bach Fest 268
Chelan County 269, 275, 278, 279, 282, 299, 306
Chelan County Republican Central Committee 253
Chelan County Republican Woman's Club 270
Chelan County Public Utility District 269, 270, 287
Chelan-Douglas Land Trust 308
Cheverton, Dick 111
Chicago Tribune, The 38, 216, 239, 280
Chief Joseph Dam 262, 263
Children's Orthopedic Hospital 58, 114
Chin, Brian 161
China 48, 277, 288
Christian Science Monitor 307
Chronicle, The (Centralia, Wash.) 306
Chronicle, San Francisco 102, 166, 209
Church Council of Greater Seattle 177
Cichy, Ben 80
CIO 34
Clapp, Mrs. Norton 76
Clapp, William "Billy" 240, 248-250, 261, 262, 264
Clark, Jim 151
Clemmons, Maurice 213, 214, 216
Cleveland, Carl 251
Clinton, Bill 127, 133, 157, 178, 296
Clinton, Gordon S. 67
CNN 2
Coast Artillery 24, 42
Coastal Journal 155
Cobain, Kurt 150
Cochrane, Chuck 86, 88, 157, 202
Cold War 46, 53, 54, 64, 265
Cole, Bert 274
College of Puget Sound (now university) 259, 276, 287
College of William and Mary 75
Collins, Ray 47
Columbia Basin Commission 252, 269
Columbia Basin Irrigation League 250
Columbia Basin Project 252, 261, 269
Columbia River 240-242, 247, 248, 260, 271, 310
Columbian, The (Vancouver, Wash.) 113, 206, 294
Colville Tribe 295
Committee for a Free Press 104
Committee for a Two-Newspaper Town 190, 191, 198
Communist Party 34, 36, 48, 50-52, 54, 60, 272,
Community Foundation of North Central Washington 309
Congressional Quarterly 80
Connelly, Joel 90, 99, 100, 103, 104, 107, 108, 111, 147, 148, 160, 167, 170, 171, 211, 223, 230, 355
Corr, Casey O. 128, 146-148, 177, 184, 355
Corr, Kelly 190, 195, 197, 355
Corsaletti, Lou 90
Costco 152
Cotterill, George F. 20
Coughlin, Dan 104
Coulee City 240
Court of Appeals, U.S. Ninth Circuit 44, 108, 210
Court of Appeals, Washington State 191, 274
Cowles, William H. 245, 250

Craigslist 152, 153, 181, 193, 286, 290
Crosscut 5, 195, 214
Crowley, Walt 71
Culkin, Francis D. 252
Cunningham, Jack 108
Cunningham, Ross 49, 50, 65, 67-71, 79, 80, 124
Czechoslovakia 48

Daily Herald, The (Everett, Wash.) 6, 112, 175, 229
Daily News, The (Longview, Wash.) 123, 304
Daily World, The (Aberdeen, Wash.) 111, 244, 306, 352, 353
Dappen, Andy 280, 308, 355
Dardarian, Suki 212, 213, 217, 229, 230, 231, 355
Dartmouth College 41, 277
Davis Wright Tremaine 141, 197
Death and Life of American Journalism 232
Defense of Marriage Act 157
Democrat-Herald, The (Albany, Ore.) 86
Democratic Party 16, 17, 33, 124, 127, 130, 222, 252
Denny Building 233
Denny Field 246
Denny Hill 18
Department of Commerce & Economic Development, Washington State 273
DesPeaux, Cliff 212
Detroit 63, 104, 177
DeVore, P. Cameron "Cam" 131
Dible, Denny 294, 295
Dickie, Lance 127, 128, 217, 355
Dicks, Norm 310
Dies, Martin 48
Dietrich, Bill 113, 123, 125
Dill, Clarence 252
Dodd, Rick 94, 95
Dodge, John 111, 355
Donohoe, Ed 57
Donworth, Todd & Higgins 31
Dore, John "Irish Johnny" 38
Doughty, Jack 90
Douglas County 245, 269, 275, 278, 299, 306, 308

Dry Falls 242
Dukakis, Michael 124-127, 129
Duncan, Don 60-63, 68-71, 79, 113, 115, 144, 355
Dunsire, Charles 98, 102, 104, 108
Dunsire, Judy 355
Dwyer, William L. 106-109

East Wenatchee 269, 279, 280, 281
Eastside Journal, The 164, 173
Eastsideweek 143
Eastvold, Don 70,
eBay 152
Editor & Publisher 59, 166, 189
Edward R. Murrow Award 231
Egan, Tim 90, 99
Eisenhower, Dwight D. 39
El Mundo 278, 306
Ellington, Anne L. 191
Elliott Bay 3, 13, 206
Ellis, Jim 67, 72
Elway, H. Stuart 222, 354, 355
Elwha River 231
Empire State Building 254
Emporia, Kansas 254
Entiat River 265
Entiat Valley 279
Environmental Protection Agency 278
Ephrata, Wash. 240, 242, 248, 249, 262
Europe 14, 22, 33, 36, 41, 204, 255
Evans, Dan 71, 268, 273, 355
Everett, Wash. 6, 23, 65, 112, 175, 229
Excelsior 13
Exxon Valdez 123, 125
Eyman, Tim 165, 218

Facebook 7, 150, 238, 294, 305
Fairview Avenue 32, 56, 210, 232
Fancher, Elaine 155
Fancher, Michael Reilly 80, 81, 91, 100, 111, 113-115, 118-121, 123, 124, 126, 131, 146, 150, 151, 155, 157, 166, 169, 176, 196, 199, 277, 355
Fardella, Alayne 228
"Fairview Fanny" 57, 79, 90, 113, 126, 148, 162
Farley, James A. 34
Farm Journal, The 253, 261

Fassio, Virgil 98, 99, 112, 116
FBI 58, 67
Federal Mediation and Conciliation Service 59
Federal Power Commission 250
Feit, Josh 176
Ficken, Robert E. 242, 248
First Seattle Dexter Horton Securities Company 30
Fisco, Alan 219, 220, 223, 355
Fishback, Charles 12
Fisher, Patricia 125
FitzSimmons, Cal 303, 304, 355
Fobes, Natalie 123
Foley, Linda 178
Foley, Tom 75, 272
Foote, Patricia 121
Foothills magazine 303
Ford Model T 240, 241
Ford, Henry 240
Ford, Henry II 266
Forest Service, U.S. 244, 275
Forward Thrust 72, 73, 80
Forza Coffee Company 212
FOX News 128
Fred Hutchinson Cancer Research Center 122, 146, 185, 186
Frederick & Nelson 28
Freedom of Information Act 287
Freeman, Kemper 41
Freeman, Miller 41
Fuhrman, Harold 114, 123

G.I. Bill 265
Gallup Poll 158
Gannett Company 102, 127, 155, 177, 201, 290
Ganzi, Victor 188, 189
Garden State Newspapers 132
Gardiner, Wyatt 304, 355
Gardner, Ross 213, 215, 355
Gates, Bill Sr. 94, 308
Gates, Bill III (aka "Jr."), 94, 122, 151, 206
Gawlowski, Danny 231
Gay, Jerry 76
Gazette, The 4
Gilmore, Susan 130
Gingrich, Newt 296

Glenn, John 66
Global Entertainment Corporation 299, 300, 301
Godden, Jean 165, 229
Gold Rush 14, 15, 56, 154
Goldmark, John 106, 272
Goldsmith Prize for Investigative Reporting 131
Goldsmith, Steven 147, 160
Goldstein, David "Goldy" 143, 222
Goldwater, Barry 71, 124
Gonzaga University 184
Goodwill Industries 114
Goodwin, Doris Kearns 244, 348
Google 22, 152, 181, 213, 294
Gorton, Slade 73, 106, 126, 127, 219
Goss, Albert 252
Goss Urbanite press 276
Graham, Billy 66
Graham family (Washington Post) 234
Grand Coulee 239-242, 248, 250, 251
Grand Coulee Dam 248, 250-252, 254, 258, 260-263, 269, 271, 295, 296, 298, 355
Granite Falls, Wash. 51-53
Grant County 240, 245, 249, 269, 275
Grant, Lou 70
Grant, Tom 282
Great Depression 27, 32, 33, 36, 38, 46, 91, 140, 203, 248, 251, 258, 262, 267, 296, 299
Great Northern Railway 13, 243, 244
Greater Wenatchee Regional Events Center 299
Greeley, Horace 10
Greenwich Village 255
Gregoire, Chris 127
Grindeland, Sherry 292
Grove, The 90
Guillen, Tomas 123
Gutenberg 6
Guthman, Ed 47-55
Guthrie, Woody 260
Guy Gannett Communications 155, 156
Guzzo, Louis 65, 74, 108
Gwinn, Mary Ann 123, 125, 170, 355

Hadley, Jane 147

Haik, Cory 213, 233
Hamer, John 80, 81, 125, 126, 143, 146, 355
Hanford 261
Hannula, Don 74, 79, 125, 128
Harden, Blaine 262, 348
Harlem Globetrotters 60
Hartley, Roland H. 24
Harvard Business School 30, 77, 97, 113, 168
Harvard University 94, 97, 106, 122
Hawaii 31
Hearst Corporation 4, 5, 25-27, 30, 32-39, 57, 59, 60, 65, 90, 94, 98-108, 136, 147, 149, 160-164, 166, 167, 172-174, 176-178, 186-193, 195-198, 205-210, 227, 261
Hearst, William Randolph 1, 16, 17, 25, 33, 35, 36, 38, 45, 65, 105, 149
Hearst, William Randolph Jr. 125
Heath, David 185
Heckman, Candace 207
Hedges, Barbara 215
Henderson, Paul 111, 115
Henkel, Cathy 121
Herald-Republic, Yakima 88, 132, 157, 168, 228, 235, 287, 288
Herbert, Frank 79
Hill, James J. 13
Hill, Sam B. 252
Hills, Lee 93
Holden, Ashley 48
Holden, Dominic 229
Home Finders magazine 303
Honeysett, Harlan 267, 268
Hoover, Herbert 2, 33, 251
Hoovervilles 34
Horan, Walt 259
Horsey, David 90, 110, 148, 162, 355
Horvitz, Peter 163, 164, 173, 188, 199, 200
House Un-American Activities Committee 48, 50
Houston, Darrell Bob 79
Huckabee, Mike 214
Huffman, Mandy 281
Huntington's disease 76, 96, 97, 114, 136, 170, 200

Icicle Creek Center for the Arts 309
Iglitzin, Dmitri 190, 191
Imus, Don 16
Industrial Workers of the World 19
Informa Hispano 306
Innocence Project Northwest 282
Inslee, Jay 222
Intel 181, 228
International District 72
International News Service 25
International Newspaper Guild 178
International Typographical Union 59
iPhone 3
Iritani, Evelyn 110, 147
Ith, Ian 174, 355
Ivins, Molly 211

Jackson, Henry M. 64, 65, 271, 274, 355
Jackson, Michael 150
Jackson, Phil 118
James, Don 131, 215
Jarvis, Jack 66
Jasinek, Gary 286-288, 291, 304, 310, 355
Jenkins, Sarah 288
Joad, Tom 260
John Birch Society 70
Johnston, Alvin "Tex" 62, 63
Joint Fact-Finding Committee on Un-American Activities 50
Joint Operating Agreement (JOA) 5, 99-114, 121, 131, 134, 135, 146-148, 160-163, 168, 173, 186-191, 194, 195-197, 199, 209, 210, 228
Jones, Wesley L. 250
Jordan, Larry A. 196
Judd, Ron 171, 175-177 179, 182, 216, 355

Kansas City Journal, The 10
Kansas City Star 361
Kansas City, Mo. 10, 20, 153
KBA Comet press 238
Keaton, Buster 28
Kelley, Steve 113
Kelly, Carolyn 121, 141, 184, 185, 196, 228, 355
Kennebec Journal, The 155
Kennebunkport 202, 203
Kennedy, John F. 273
Kennedy, Robert F. 39
Kennewick, Wash. 265

Kent, Wash. 5, 133
Kerouac, Jack 79
Kerry, John 135, 158, 219, 235
Kershner, Jim 281, 282
Kessler, Lynn 206
Kettle Falls, Wash. 250
KING Broadcasting 73, 80, 124, 205
King County 5, 62, 67, 68, 80, 105, 106, 127, 135, 165, 174, 188, 199, 222
King County Journal 5, 188, 189
King County Superior Court 44, 189, 196
King Features 25, 99
King, Jim 73, 75, 76, 81, 88, 90, 100, 105, 112, 114, 118, 119, 123, 353
King, Martin Luther Jr. 72
King, Stephen 280
Kingdome 104, 106
Klondike 14, 15, 64
Kmart 279
Knight Newspapers Inc. 78, 94, 139
Knightfall 140
Knight-Ridder 78, 93, 94, 102, 117, 132, 133, 136-140, 142, 152
Knox, Maine 1
Koch, Anne 175
Kodachrome 7
Koenig, Bob 188, 289
KOMO-TV 74
Koop, C. Everett 278
Koufax, Sandy 79
KREM-TV 282
Kuralt, Charles 254
KVI radio 128

Lachowicz, Steve 282
Lacitis, Erik 111
Lake Chelan This Week 303
Lake Roosevelt 262
Lake Union 83, 137, 192
Lake Washington 24, 41, 62, 67, 72, 89, 150, 153 292
Lake Wenatchee State Park 274
Lakeside School, The 94
Lakewood Police 214, 233
Lakewood, Wash. 212, 214, 233
Landes, Bertha K. 26
Landon, Alf 253
Lange, Larry 206, 207, 355

Langlie, Arthur B. 49
Larsen, Richard W. 75, 79, 125, 128, 272
Layman, William D. 242, 310, 355
Layton, Mike 90
Leavenworth, Wash. 240, 280, 309
LeClercq, Dave 83
LeClercq, Sheila 83
Levesque, John 178
Lewinsky, Monica 127
Lewis, Mike 79
Life magazine 66
Limbaugh, Rush 16
Lincoln, Howard 151
Lindeman, Charles B. "Charlie" 39
Linotype machine 151, 267
Lippy, Tom 13
Los Angeles Times, The 55, 121, 167, 280
Lowry, Mike 126, 190

Mackie, Jill 219, 292, 355
MacLeod, Alex 80, 81, 91, 112, 118-120, 145, 160, 166, 169, 170, 182, 188, 355
MacLeod, Henry 47, 49, 55, 57, 62, 68, 72, 73, 75, 84, 88, 105, 119, 166
Magnuson, Warren G. 54, 57, 65, 274
Maher, Steve 281, 282, 284
Maine 1, 9, 10, 153-155, 157, 168, 170, 182, 189, 195, 202-204, 227, 228, 235
Maine Sunday Telegram 155
Malkin, Michelle 128
Mansfield, Wash. 240
Mapes, Lynda 231
Marine Corps 41
Mariners, Seattle 106, 112, 151, 154, 231
Marlboro Man 133
Martin, Clarence 252
Martin, Jonathan 231
Martinez, Marco 303, 304, 355
Massi, Frank 94
Mayo, Phyllis 121
McCann-Erickson 136
McCarthy, Joseph 48
McChesney, Robert W. 232
McClatchy Company 5, 175, 201, 225, 226, 235
McClure's Magazine 19
McConaghy, Lorraine 8, 10, 53, 54, 153, 154, 355

McCoy, John 146, 147
McCumber, David 166
McDermott, Jim 190
McDermott, Terry 113, 134
McDonald, Sally 174
McGavick, Mike 127, 219
McGovern, George 106
McGrath, Russell 46, 47, 49, 50, 52, 53, 55, 68, 69, 72, 106
McKenna, Rob 127, 219, 220, 222, 223, 229, 235, 355
McKinstry, Steve 113
McLuhan, Marshall 151, 152
McNeil Island Penitentiary 40
Meagher, Cynthia 121
Medal of Merit, Washington State 308
Medina 24
Mehaffey, K.C. 305
Mercer Island 42, 142
Merritt, Davis "Buzz" 139, 140, 355
Merry, Robert 94
Merry, Sue 116
Methow Valley 165
Metro 67, 72, 80, 148,
Meyers, Georg 60
Miami 141, 142
Microsoft 122, 151, 154, 181
Miller 41
Millstein, Lincoln 206
Minneapolis, Minn. 8, 11, 13, 20, 153, 231
Mission Ridge 238, 275, 312
Mississippi River 237, 256
Missoula, Mont. 304
Missouri 10, 75, 124, 254
Model T Ford 240
Momentum, A Decade of Accomplishment 169
Monorail 66, 191
Moody, Dick 66
Moody's Investors Service 300
Morgan, Murray 2, 20, 65, 237, 353, 355
Morning Sentinel 155
Morning Tribune, The (Lewiston, Idaho) 11, 114, 305
Morton, John 65, 156, 177, 180
Moses Lake, Wash. 269
Mount St. Helens 123
Moyers, Bill 108

Mr. Dooley 284
Municipal League 27, 80
Murdoch, Rupert 108
Murray, Emmett 171
Murray, Patty 178, 218

Nash, Cyndi 124
Nalder, Eric 90, 99, 100, 112, 113, 123, 125, 130, 144-146, 184
NASA 38, 65
Nasaw, David 38
National Basketball Association 67
National Guard 16, 24, 41
National Labor Relations Act 34, 176, 184, 259
National Labor Relations Board 176, 184, 259
National Lampoon 144
National Public Radio (NPR) 222
Natt, Ted 123
Nebraska 242, 243
Neff, James 216
Nelson, Deborah 28, 144, 145
Netscape Navigator 151
Neuheisel, Rick 215
New Deal 33, 34, 42, 259, 296
New Jersey 78, 230
New York 10, 22, 29, 33, 51-53, 68, 74, 87, 107, 115, 128, 129, 133, 139, 152, 195, 201, 205, 226, 233, 252, 256
New York Times News Service 68
New York Times, The 22, 68, 87, 107, 128, 129, 133, 139, 152, 201, 233, 256
New Yorker magazine 115, 295
Newspaper Preservation Act 5, 98, 99, 104, 105, 108, 109, 162, 191, 286
News Tribune, Tacoma 5, 112, 215, 229, 231, 286
Newsweek 187
NFL 106,
Nichols, John 232
Niendorff, Fred 49
Nikon 76
Nintendo 151
Nirvana 150, 308,
Nixon, Richard 55, 73, 106
Nordstrom 3, 146, 216,
North Africa 47

INDEX 365

North Cascades Highway 274
North Creek 132, 165, 168, 232
Norton, Dee 90
Novoselic, Krist 308
Nuremberg 66

O'Boyle, Robert 124
O'Hagan, Maureen 186
O'Sullivan, James 250, 252
Oak Park High School, Chicago 246
Obama, Barack 127, 219, 222, 354
Obamacare 219
Ocean Shores, Wash. 70
Oglesby, Roger 167, 173, 178, 182, 199, 205, 207
Okanogan County 245, 269, 272, 305
Okanogan High School 295
Okanogan Valley 265
Olmstead Brothers 64
Olympian, The 303
Olympic Hotel 24, 63
Onion, The 7
Oregon State University 121
Oregonian, The 6, 306
Oso landslide 231
Outlook magazine 251
Owen, John 111

PACCAR Inc. 114
Pacific Northwest Newspaper Guild 170
Pacific Rim 26, 64, 110, 277
Pacific-10 131
Paige, Satchel 238
Paris, France 265
Parks and Recreation Commission, Washington State 268, 274
Paterno, Susan 165, 355
Patkus, John P. 108
Pay'n Save Corporation 107
Pearl Harbor 45
Pelz, Dwight 222
Penhale, Ed 147
Pend Oreille River 249, 251
Pendleton, Ore. 304
Penney-Missouri Award 124
Pennington, Dorothy 116
Pennington, Weldon J. "Jerry" 58, 74, 76, 77, 81, 83-86, 88, 91-95, 97, 101-103, 113-117, 136, 137, 194, 200, 210
Penny Press, The 11, 16
Pentecostal Church of God House of Prayer 280
People Opposed to a 1-Newspaper Town (PO1NT) 104, 210
Perez, Robert 281, 283
Perry, Bob 90
Perry, John H. 25
Perry, Nick 215
Peshastin Camp Fire Girls 245
Petroff, Eric 204
Philpott, Jeffrey 187
Phoenix, The 202
pi.com 5, 230
Pierce, J. Kingston 120
Pike Place Public Market 74
Pinchot, Gifford 244
Pine Canyon 240, 265
Pioneer Square 34, 105
Popular Front 34, 51
Porsche 84, 288
Port Angeles, Wash. 14, 272
Port of Seattle 58
Port Townsend, Wash. 289
Portland Press Herald 155, 202
Portland, Ore. 6, 195, 203, 227, 252, 261
Postman, David 200, 355
Potholes Dam 262
Poynter Institute 187
Presley, Elvis 66
Press Herald, The 155, 202, 203
Prill, Sharon 228
Prochnau, William 73
Progressive "Bull Moose" Party 244
Prozac 279
Pryne, Eric 130, 148
Psychology Today 279
Public Disclosure Commission 287
Public Facilities District 299-301
Public Utility Districts 27
Publicola 5
Puget Sound 12, 20 26, 32, 34, 44, 97, 113, 114, 116, 146, 163, 182, 183, 214, 229, 273
Puget Sound Business Journal 182
Puget Sound Power & Light 258, 269
Pulitzer Prize 4, 54, 70, 76, 111, 115, 123, 125, 131, 139, 148, 170, 180, 186, 214, 216,

217, 229, 254, 264, 304
Pulitzer, Joseph 1
Pullman, Wash. 245, 272
Purdum, Todd S. 6
Puyallup River 72
Pyle, Ernie 254, 255

Quan, Millie 121
Queen Anne Hill 22, 154

Rabinowitz, Dorothy 282-284
Rader, Melvin 51-55
Rainier Bank 114
Rainier Club 19, 43, 92
Raise Hell and Sell Newspapers 8, 154
Ramsey, Bruce 128, 160, 177, 210, 217, 231
Ray, Dixy Lee 74
Raymond, Steve 115
Reagan, Ronald 98, 126
Reddin, "Round John" 59
Reese, Tom 150
Republican Party 11, 12
Requiem Mass 31
Richards, Bill 187, 195, 355
Richland, Wash. 265
Ridder Brothers 29
Ridder Publications Inc. 77, 139
Ridder, Bernard H. Jr. "Bernie" 93, 94, 136, 137
Ridder, Tony 132, 134, 138, 140, 152, 156, 169, 176, 187, 193, 201, 227, 355
Riffkin, Courtney Blethen 135, 221, 235
Riggs, Dee 303, 304, 355
Riley, Kate 128, 218, 228, 355
Rinearson, Peter M. 115
Ringman, Steve 231
Rivers and Harbors Bill of 1935 252
Robbins, Tom 74, 78
Robinson, Herb 71, 74, 76, 124-126, 128
Rocky Reach Dam 271
Roe v. Wade 128
Romney, Mitt 222
Rooney, Andy 302
Roosevelt, Anna 38
Roosevelt, Eleanor 39
Roosevelt, Franklin D. 33, 252
Roosevelt, Theodore 243
Rose Bowl 215

Rosellini, Albert D. 60, 69, 71, 273
Ross, Doug 197, 198
Ross, J.D. 27
Rossi, Dino 127, 219
Rothschild, Mary 100, 170
Rothstein, Barbara 108
Rozen, Lee 160, 161, 355
Rudman, Steve 147
Rule, Ann 280
Runyon, Damon 9
Rupp, Otto 244
Rupp, Werner A. 244
Russia 66, 254

S.S. Portland 14
Safeco Insurance 114
Sale, Roger 19
Salem, Ore. 127
Sampson, Don 266, 268
San Antonio 189, 209
San Diego 48, 181
San Francisco 13, 14, 25, 33, 47, 152, 166, 189
San Francisco Chronicle 102, 209
San Francisco Examiner 102
San Jose Mercury News 139, 184
San Simeon, Calif. 33, 38
Sandburg, Carl 10
Sanders, Eli 179, 355
Santa Monica, Calif. 33
Savage, Dan 17, 176
Sav-Mart 279
Sayre, Mel 57, 70
Scates, Shelby 54, 80, 90, 104, 147
Schafer, Jim 121, 136, 172, 174
Schell, Paul 184
Schneider, Andrew 147, 160
Schroeder, Steve 289
Schwabacher's Wharf 14
Scott, Kelli 310
Scripps Newspapers 25, 46
Seahawks, Seattle 4, 106, 230, 231
Seattle Central Labor Council 36
Seattle City Hall 184
Seattle Fire Department 144
Seattle General Strike 25
Seattle magazine 73, 79, 80, 104
Seattle Metropolitan magazine 213

INDEX 367

Seattle Press-Times 1
Seattle Rotary Club 72
Seattle Star, The 4, 16, 36, 40, 45, 46
Seattle Sun 4
Seattle Symphony Orchestra 67
Seattle Times Building 1, 2, 18, 20, 43, 137, 143, 178, 199, 232, 233
Seattle University 187
Seattle University Chieftains 60
Seattle Weekly 5, 6, 163, 166, 171, 175, 184
Seattle Yacht Club 28
Seattle YMCA 13
Seattle-King County Bar Association 105
SeattleMet 5
Securities and Exchange Commission 301
Selden Ring Award 216
Shimomura, Joby 222
Shults, Alex 46
Silver Star 47
Simon, Jim 212, 230
Simpson, Roger A. 35
Singleton, Bob 140
Singleton, William Dean 132
Sizemore, H. Mason 75, 91, 114, 117, 119, 121, 132, 133, 141, 144, 151, 155-157, 172, 174, 178, 179, 183, 184, 188, 195, 196, 228, 355
Skadden, Arps 141
Skid Road book 2
Skid Road 9, 15
Smith, Carlton 123
Smith, Carol 147, 207
Smith, Lane 73
Smith, William French 108
Snake River 242
Snohomish County 4, 65, 231
Society of Professional Journalists 187, 224
Sofa World 279
South County Journal 164
South Dakota 139
South Lake Union 137, 192, 204, 226, 228, 232
Soviet Union 64
Space Needle 56, 65
Sparks, Stephen 195, 196
Spokane Chamber of Commerce 250, 261
Spokane, Wash. 13, 48, 75, 202, 243, 245, 249, 250, 252, 261, 262, 270, 272, 281, 282, 289, 304

Spokesman-Review, The 49, 202, 250, 305
Sputnik 64
Squire, Watson 12-13
St. Paul, Minn. 13, 29
Starr, Dan 74
State Grange 27
Statesman Journal, The 127
Steamboat Rock 242
Stehekin River 265
Steigmeyer, Rick 303, 304
Stevens County 270
Stiffler, Lisa 199
Stokes, Thomas L. 264
Stranger, The 5, 176, 180, 203, 214, 218
Sullivan, Jennifer 212, 213, 229
Sulzberger, Arthur Ochs Jr. 152
Super Bowl 4, 230
SuperSonics, Seattle 67, 106
Swartz, Steven R. 205, 206

Tacoma, Wash. 5, 14, 23, 113, 212, 229, 259, 276, 287
Taft, William Howard 244
Talmadge, Phil 190
Tang, Terry 128
Taylor, Chuck 145, 175, 184, 195, 214, 355
Tazioli, Terry 76, 124, 355
Teamsters 34, 36, 37, 39, 55, 57, 172, 175
Tempe, Arizona 299
Temple University 7, 36, 48, 224
Temple, Shirley 48
The Caine Mutiny 103
The Legend of William Tell 255
The Panic of 1893 11
Thiel, Art 111, 146, 147, 166, 171, 174
Thomas, J. Parnell 48
Thompson, Rowland 173, 355
Thomson, Reginald Heber 18
Time magazine 39, 131
Tizon, Alex 144, 145
Todd, Elmer Ely 6, 25, 30-33, 42-44, 48, 50, 52-55, 58, 77, 91, 97
Tokyo 45
Torvik, Solveig 147
Touche, Ross & Company 58
Town Toyota Center 299, 301
Tri-Cities 275, 304
Truman, Harry S. 54, 262, 264

Tucson, Ariz. 106
Twisp, Wash. 240
Twiss, Bob 57, 63, 81
Twitter 213, 214
Tyee Ridge 279

U.S. Bureau of Reclamation 254, 261, 271
U.S. Census Bureau 5
U.S. Department of Justice 101, 162, 187, 189
U.S. District Court 44, 108
U.S. Navy 19, 42, 104
U.S. Ninth Circuit Court of Appeals 44, 108, 210
U.S. Postal Service 152
U.S. Supreme Court 105, 109, 176, 219
Udall, Stewart 274
Underwood, Doug 118, 119, 163, 164, 248
Union National Bank 31
Union Record, The 25, 173, 176
Unionism or Hearst 35
United Press International 70
United Way 168, 295, 309
University of Kansas 202
University of Minnesota 16
University of Missouri 75
University of North Carolina 31
University of Washington 21, 35, 41, 47, 48, 60, 64, 78, 92, 106, 114, 131, 203, 229, 256, 265, 272
University of Washington Board of Regents 39, 255
Upper Skagit River 27
U.S.S. Missouri 254

Valley Daily News 5
Vancouver, Wash. 113, 206, 294
Vanderveer, George F. 9, 15
Vanity Fair 6
Vanport, Wash. 265
Vermont 269
Vertrees, Orman 80
Vesely, Jim 104, 127-129, 158, 184, 203, 217, 218
Victoria, B.C. 14
Victrola phonograph 26
Vietnam 70, 73
Vindicator, The 180

Virginia 31, 58, 75, 91
Volkswagen 84, 268
Vulcan Inc. 200

Wall Street 28, 139, 140, 174, 181, 217
Wall Street Journal, The 107, 129, 139, 174, 186, 187, 205, 282, 307
Walla Walla Union-Bulletin, The 85, 87, 132, 184, 305
Walla Walla, Wash. 6, 51, 86-88, 91, 92, 117, 157, 200, 234, 235, 284, 286
Wallace, James 146, 147, 161
Walmart 279, 286
Walton, Sam 152
Wappenstein, Charles W. "Wappy" 9, 19
Warner, Tracy 283, 284, 355
Washington Athletic Club 58
Washington Mutual 204
Washington Post Company 6
Washington Post, The 6, 148, 233, 299, 311
Washington Public Power Supply System (WPPSS) 111
Washington State Pavilion 67
Washington State University 155, 202, 270
Washington Supreme Court 31, 44, 190, 191
Washington Water Power Company 249, 250, 270
Washington, D.C. 18, 111, 148, 179, 229, 250, 256, 259, 273
Watergate 55, 106
Waterville, Wash. 155, 240, 252
Watkins, Jack 266
Watson, Emmett 46, 47, 49, 57, 61, 62, 100, 106, 112, 210
Weiss, Ivan 171, 184
Welch, Craig 57, 231
Wenatchee Community College 275
Wenatchee Foothills 308
Wenatchee High School 246
Wenatchee Performing Arts Center 235, 309
Wenatchee Republic, The 243
Wenatchee Valley Business Journal 293
Wenatchee Valley College Foundation 309
Wenatchee Valley Museum and Cultural Center 308
Wenatchee YMCA 309
Wernher, von Braun 66

Westneat, Danny 210, 354
Wetzel, Frank 89-91, 105, 199, 355
Weyerhaeuser, Frederick 13
Whidbey Island 115
White, William Allen 254
Whitman, Walt 260
Wilbur, Ray 251
Will, George 131
Williams, Jack 152
Williams, Richard 44
Willmsen, Christine 186
Wilson, Duff 144, 145, 146, 185
Wilson, John L. 13
Wilson, Marshal 60, 70
Winfrey, Oprah 279
Wobblies 19, 27, 34, 51, 154
Woods, Alyssa 310
Woods, Gretchen 237, 268, 290, 309, 310, 355
Woods, Kara (Hunnicutt) 309
Woods, Kathryn "Kay" (Haley) 245
Woods, Kathy Kingman 235, 308, 309
Woods, Mary (Wilfred's mother) 245, 263
Woods, Ralph 243, 255
Woods, Rufus 237, 238, 262, 268, 276, 277, 283, 285-294, 296, 299-303, 305-307, 309-315, 354
Woods, Rufus G. 18, 238, 239-267, 269, 270, 273, 282, 290
Woods, Walter 245
Woods, Warren 256, 266
Woods, Wilfred 235, 237, 238-241, 245, 255-259, 262-277, 285-287, 290, 293, 295, 299, 308- 312, 314, 353
Woods, Willa Lou 245, 256, 257
Woods, Wilma 245
World Series 21, 256
World Trade Center 183
World War II 42, 51, 56, 58, 76, 183, 266, 269, 277
World's Fair Commission 65
Wright, Willard 92

Yahoo! 206
Yakima Herald-Republic, the 88, 132, 157, 168, 228, 235, 227, 287
Yakima, Wash. 57, 132, 202, 227, 228, 251
Yale 41, 56, 78

Yamauchi, Hiroshi 151
Yesler Way 15
Young, Caroline 147
Youngstown, Ohio 180
Youth and Government 309

About the author

JOHN C. HUGHES joined the Office of the Secretary of State as chief oral historian in 2008 after a 42-year career in journalism, retiring as editor and publisher of The Daily World at Aberdeen. He is a former trustee of the Washington State Historical Society, past president of Allied Daily Newspapers of Washington and an award-winning investigative reporter, columnist and historian. Hughes is the author of seven other books: *On the Harbor, From Black Friday to Nirvana*, with Ryan Teague Beckwith; *Booth Who?*, a biography of Booth Gardner; *Nancy Evans, First-rate First Lady; Lillian Walker, Washington State Civil Rights Pioneer; The Inimitable Adele Ferguson; Slade Gorton, A Half Century in Politics,* and *John Spellman: Politics Never Broke His Heart*